Business and Management

Course Companion

Paul Clark
Peter Golden
Mark O'Dea
John Weiner
Phil Woolrich
with
Jorge Olmos

Great Clarendon Street, Oxford OX2 6DP

Oxford University Press is a department of the University of Oxford.
It furthers the University's objective of excellence in research,
scholarship, and education by publishing worldwide in

Oxford   New York

Auckland   Cape Town   Dar es Salaam   Hong Kong   Karachi
Kuala Lumpur   Madrid   Melbourne   Mexico City   Nairobi
New Delhi   Shanghai   Taipei   Toronto

With offices in

Argentina   Austria   Brazil   Chile   Czech Republic   France   Greece
Guatemala   Hungary   Italy   Japan   Poland   Portugal   Singapore
South Korea   Switzerland   Thailand   Turkey   Ukraine   Vietnam

Oxford is a registered trade mark of Oxford University Press
in the UK and in certain other countries

British Library Cataloguing in Publication Data

Data available

ISBN 978-0-19-915225-4

10 9 8 7 6 5 4

Printed in Great Britain by Bell and Bain Ltd., Glasgow

Acknowledgements

We are grateful to the following to reproduce the following copyright material.

p8: János Gehring/Shutterstock; p24: Mark Newton /Alamy; p29t: SC Johnson;
p29b: Brendan Beirne/Rex Features; p31: Registered Trademark of Tata Sons
Limited printed with permission from Tata Sons Limited; p33: Walmart; p35:
Texas Instruments; p36t: Enron; p36b: OUP; p37: OUP; p73: Huw Jones/Alamy;
p88: Swatch; p89: Helene Rogers/Alamy; p111: Steve Helber/AP/PA Photos; p112:
DPA DEUTSCHE PRESS-AGENTUR/DPA/PA Photos; p157: Josef
Muellek/Dreamstime.com; p158: Alex Segre/Alamy; p171: MCI WorldCom; p182l:
LG Electronics; p182r: Chris Ratcliffe/Rex Features; p184: Rex Features; p185:
Samuel Jones/Amnesty International; p195t: Audi of America, Inc.; p195b: Hans
Dieter Seufert/MPI/Culture-Images; p197: Dyson; p198: Dyson; p202: Google;
p204l: John Poland; p204r: Disney; p210: Seth Perlman/Associated Press; p215:
Rob Crandall/Alamy; p219: Picture Perfect/Rex Features; p220: Francis Dean/Rex
Features; p224: McDonald's India; p234: Mike Lane/Alamy; p251: Aijaz
Rahi/AP/PA Photos; p252: Catherine Karnow/Corbis; p259: Shannon Burns; p267:
Eugene Hoshiko/Associated Press; p269: I-stock; p275: Compound Security
Systems; p276: Frank van den Bergh/I-stock; p284: Rex Features; p295: General
Motors; p296t: Lenscap/Alamy; p269b: The Bridgeman Art Library; p308:
dasilva/Shutterstock; p309t: Beth A. Keiser/Associated Press; p309l:
NetPics/Alamy; p312: Alex Segre/Rex Features; p314: Andre Csillag/Rex Features;
p315t: Ryan McNutt/mcnutt.wordpress.com; p315m: Vint Falken/Flickr; p315r:
Virtual Worlds Forum; p316: Shawn Shahani/shawnshahani.wordpress.com;
p317: Nielsen; p318: Tibor Illyes/Associated Press; p323: Holger
Mette/Shutterstock; p328: Corbis/Bettmann; p329: Henry Mintzberg Ltd.
Collection; p341: Ene/Dreamstime.com; p343: Shutterstock/8781118005; p347t:
Sean Gladwell/Shutterstock; p347b: The Hay Group Management Limited; p348:
AOL; p349: cloki/Shutterstock; p352: Andres Peiro Palmer/I-stock; p356:
Volkswagen Group; p357: Bentley Motors Limited, Lamborghini, Audi AG,
Volkswagen, Seat, Skoda; p359t: Mint Photography/Alamy; p359m:
Reuters/Corbis; p359b: KPA/Zuma/Rex Features.

We have tried to trace and contact all copyright holders before publication. If
notified the publishers will be pleased to rectify any errors or omissions at the
earliest opportunity.

Paper used in the production of this book is a natural, recyclable product made
from wood grown in sustainable forests. The manufacturing process conforms to
the environmental regulations of the country of origin.

Course Companion definition

The IB Diploma Programme Course Companions are resource materials designed to provide students with extra support through their two-year course of study. These books will help students gain an understanding of what is expected from the study of an IB Diploma Programme subject.

The Course Companions reflect the philosophy and approach of the IB Diploma Programme and present content in a way that illustrates the purpose and aims of the IB. They encourage a deep understanding of each subject by making connections to wider issues and providing opportunities for critical thinking.

These Course Companions, therefore, may or may not contain all of the curriculum content required in each IB Diploma Programme subject, and so are not designed to be complete and prescriptive textbooks. Each book will try to ensure that areas of curriculum that are unique to the IB or to a new course revision are thoroughly covered. These books mirror the IB philosophy of viewing the curriculum in terms of a whole-course approach; the use of a wide range of resources; international-mindedness; the IB learner profile and the IB Diploma Programme core requirements; theory of knowledge; the extended essay; and creativity, action, service (CAS).

In addition, the Course Companions provide advice and guidance on the specific course assessment requirements and also on academic honesty protocol.

The Course Companions are not designed to be:

- study/revision guides or a one-stop solution for students to pass the subjects
- prescriptive or essential subject textbooks.

IB mission statement

The International Baccalaureate aims to develop inquiring, knowledgable and caring young people who help to create a better and more peaceful world through intercultural understanding and respect.

To this end the IB works with schools, governments and international organizations to develop challenging programmes of international education and rigorous assessment.

These programmes encourage students across the world to become active, compassionate, and lifelong learners who understand that other people, with their differences, can also be right.

The IB learner profile

The aim of all IB programmes is to develop internationally minded people who, recognizing their common humanity and shared guardianship of the planet, help to create a better and more peaceful world. IB learners strive to be:

Inquirers   They develop their natural curiosity. They acquire the skills necessary to conduct inquiry and research and show independence in learning. They actively enjoy learning and this love of learning will be sustained throughout their lives.

Knowledgable   They explore concepts, ideas, and issues that have local and global significance. In so doing, they acquire in-depth knowledge and develop understanding across a broad and balanced range of disciplines.

Thinkers   They exercise initiative in applying thinking skills critically and creatively to recognize and approach complex problems, and make reasoned, ethical decisions.

Communicators   They understand and express ideas and information confidently and creatively in more than one language and in a variety of modes of communication. They work effectively and willingly in collaboration with others.

Principled   They act with integrity and honesty, with a strong sense of fairness, justice, and respect for the dignity of the individual, groups, and communities. They take responsibility for their own actions and the consequences that accompany them.

Open-minded   They understand and appreciate their own cultures and personal histories, and are open to the perspectives, values, and traditions of other individuals and communities. They are accustomed to seeking and evaluating a range of points of view, and are willing to grow from the experience.

Caring   They show empathy, compassion, and respect towards the needs and feelings of others.

They have a personal commitment to service, and act to make a positive difference to the lives of others and to the environment.

Risk-takers   They approach unfamiliar situations and uncertainty with courage and forethought, and have the independence of spirit to explore new roles, ideas, and strategies. They are brave and articulate in defending their beliefs.

Balanced   They understand the importance of intellectual, physical, and emotional balance to achieve personal well-being for themselves and others.

Reflective   They give thoughtful consideration to their own learning and experience. They are able to assess and understand their strengths and limitations in order to support their learning and personal development.

A note on academic honesty

It is of vital importance to acknowledge and appropriately credit the owners of information when that information is used in your work. After all, owners of ideas (intellectual property) have property rights. To have an authentic piece of work, it must be based on your individual and original ideas with the work of others fully acknowledged. Therefore, all assignments, written or oral, completed for assessment must use your own language and expression. Where sources are used or referred to, whether in the form of direct quotation or paraphrase, such sources must be appropriately acknowledged.

How do I acknowledge the work of others?
The way that you acknowledge that you have used the ideas of other people is through the use of footnotes and bibliographies.

Footnotes   (placed at the bottom of a page) or endnotes (placed at the end of a document) are to be provided when you quote or paraphrase from another document, or closely summarize the information provided in another document. You do not need to provide a footnote for information that is part of a 'body of knowledge'. That is, definitions do not need to be footnoted as they are part of the assumed knowledge.

Bibliographies   should include a formal list of the resources that you used in your work. 'Formal' means that you should use one of the several accepted forms of presentation. This usually involves separating the resources that you use into different categories (e.g. books, magazines, newspaper articles, Internet-based resources, CDs and works of art) and providing full information as to how a reader or viewer of your work can find the same information. A bibliography is compulsory in the extended essay.

What constitutes malpractice?
Malpractice is behaviour that results in, or may result in, you or any student gaining an unfair advantage in one or more assessment component. Malpractice includes plagiarism and collusion.

Plagiarism is defined as the representation of the ideas or work of another person as your own. The following are some of the ways to avoid plagiarism:

- Words and ideas of another person used to support one's arguments must be acknowledged.

- Passages that are quoted verbatim must be enclosed within quotation marks and acknowledged.

- CD-ROMs, email messages, web sites on the Internet, and any other electronic media must be treated in the same way as books and journals.
- The sources of all photographs, maps, illustrations, computer programs, data, graphs, audio-visual, and similar material must be acknowledged if they are not your own work.
- Works of art, whether music, film, dance, theatre arts, or visual arts, and where the creative use of a part of a work takes place, must be acknowledged.

Collusion is defined as supporting malpractice by another student. This includes:

- allowing your work to be copied or submitted for assessment by another student
- duplicating work for different assessment components and/or diploma requirements.

Other forms of malpractice include any action that gives you an unfair advantage or affects the results of another student. Examples include, taking unauthorized material into an examination room, misconduct during an examination, and falsifying a CAS record.

Contents

Introduction

This book is designed as a companion to your study of IB Diploma Programme Business and Management. The aim of the authors is to communicate business and management theories in an informed, student-friendly and concise manner. However, areas that are often more difficult to comprehend first time are explained in a more detailed way and this we hope will ensure that you understand why we do something in a certain way and, for example, not just calculate the numbers through practice and rote learning. After all, if you know *why* then you will retain knowledge and develop greater understanding without recourse to mechanical methods of learning.

We also aim to encourage you to appreciate the multi-faceted and integrated nature of problem-solving in the business world. For example, business strategy cannot be tackled successfully until you have a good foundation of theory across the key department functions and also an appreciation of the business environment.

One of the important aspects of success in IB Diploma Programme Business and Management is the need to accept that there are often a variety of possible methods, strategies and solutions and that it is not the same as studying a law in physics and knowing that it will always hold firm. Business strategies reflect the environment and the specific objectives and constraints facing a particular firm, and so they cannot always be replicated or used in every business context.

This Course Companion has been designed to address your specific needs as an IB Diploma Programme student, but it also covers much of what is required for other national exams as well as being a good basic book for those new to the subject at first year undergraduate level.

Specifically we aim to:

- cover the needs of both standard and higher level IB students with a clear focus on the IB learner profile. For example, we have included research projects, devised international contexts for case studies, used a range of world currencies and employed sources from around the world. Higher level extensions recognise that higher level students are required to examine issues in further depth and to employ higher level skills; particularly those of analysis and evaluation

- profile important theorists or businesses and thereby ensure that you gain an applied and historical perspective of why individuals, theories or firms have emerged and become successful

- identify Theory of Knowledge (TOK) connections. This will ensure that you appreciate that TOK applies equally to business concepts as much as it does to any other IB subject

- provide opportunities for you to discuss ethical issues and to judge to what extent business success

and ethical approaches are linked. Perhaps ethical stances are developed as good marketing tools and are only in vogue when economic conditions are strong. This is something that you, the reader, can judge from the case studies presented and also from the real world situations you hear and read about

- include sample IB style exam questions within each chapter to support your learning

- include study workpoints to encourage you to reflect and apply new concepts

- place you, the student, in real-life situations through the inclusion of apposite case studies

- identify possible internal assessment projects and extended essay titles.

No particular background in business studies is expected or required to use this book. However, it is not expected that this Course Companion will be your only resource. For example, understanding of many of the topics included in this companion will be enhanced by further reading of newspapers and magazine articles, which will provide a current context for your study and will help develop your use and understanding of appropriate business terminology.

In line with the aims of all Diploma Programme group 3 subjects, this Course Companion sets out to encourage critical thinking and the development of your abilities to identify, analyse and evaluate business behaviours. To support these processes, business techniques and tools are introduced and applied, which will allow you to collect, describe and analyse business data. An appreciation of your own culture is encouraged, but contrasts with cultures of other societies are developed through the use of international case studies and business investigations. After studying IB Diploma Programme Business and Management, it is expected that you will appreciate that business environments are dynamic and no certainty can be guaranteed. The addition of the strategy unit ensures that you recognise that IB Business and Management is an holistic subject, rather a series of unconnected topics.

This Course Companion includes three chapters on internal and external assessment with advice from examiners on maximizing your performance in these elements. The final chapter is a glossary of key terms to support your study and revision.

The authors, who reside in different parts of the world, are grateful to all those friends and family members who read the drafts and suggested improvements; as well as to the support of the OUP editorial team whose patience and gentle pushing ensured that this international project was completed.

Paul Clark and Peter Golden
February 2009

1.1 Nature and organization of business

By the end of this chapter, you should be able to:

- identify the processes and functions of a business
- explain the nature of business activity and the reasons for setting up a business
- distinguish between different types of business organizations in the private and public sector
- evaluate the most appropriate form of ownership for a firm
- compare and contrast the objectives of non-profit organizations and other organizations.
- explain and analyse the costs and benefits of private-public partnerships

The nature of business activity

What is a business?

IB Diploma Programme Business and Management considers a diverse range of business organizations and activities, and the cultural and economic contexts in which they operate. It aims to promote understanding of both the implications of business activity in a global market, and the creation of businesses and how they act as "global citizens".

The nature of business activity inevitably varies from country to country and reflects the needs and resources of the local environment. However, organizations are increasingly being operated in a way that considers the international perspective, cultural diversity and the need for international cooperation.

Whatever the location, a business uses a combination of inputs to make the outputs, or goods and services, it then creates and sells. The inputs or "factors of production" are land, labour, capital (money and machinery), and enterprise or entrepreneurship.

- *Land.* Businesses will need space to operate from, even an Internet organization will need some office space.
- *Labour.* All businesses use varying degrees of labour. A labour-intensive business is one that has a high proportion of labour inputs. This category might include potato or pea farms, restaurants, and call centres.
- *Capital.* Capital inputs cover both money and machinery. A capital-intensive business is one that has a high proportion of its inputs as machinery. Examples might be automated car production plants and bulk chemical processing.
- *Enterprise or entrepreneurship.* This final input is the key factor of production as it is the entrepreneur or business person who harnesses the other inputs effectively to create added value for consumers and profit for the owner. If the owner or manager of the business hasn't got the drive, energy, and determination to succeed then it doesn't matter how good the other inputs are, the business will probably underperform.

The outputs of a business are dependent on the quantity and quality of the inputs and how they are combined. Outputs can be finished goods ready for movement to wholesalers and shops, or they might be component parts that other manufacturers will need to make a product. A ball bearing manufacturer will find its components are included in a diverse range of finished goods, for example washing machines, conveyor belt systems in coal mines, and consoles for aircraft. An output can also be service related, for example a meal in a restaurant or the dry cleaning of a suit.

Business functions

Businesses often have four main functional areas: finance, marketing, human resource (HR) management, and operations (production). However, all four departmental areas are interrelated and a successful business will always try to ensure that there is good team spirit and communication between each function.

- *Finance.* This is the part of an organization that monitors the movement of funds into and out of the business, produces accounts and prepares forecasts or budgets, and ensures that invoicing of customers happens and suppliers are paid. It is a vital function in providing information for other departments and decision makers.
- *Marketing* (including sales). This area covers market research and identifying what customers want through to the designing and packaging of the goods or services offered. In addition, it looks at deciding the product's price and the type of promotion used. It would also consider how it is to be distributed and sold, for example via catalogues, websites, shops, or even all three.
- *HR management.* This covers the recruitment, rewarding and motivating, and training of staff throughout the organization. It also covers the releasing or redeployment of staff when necessary.
- *Operations management* (production). This represents the engine room of the business—it is the production of goods or the delivery of a service. Those working in this area will be looking at quality and stock control, methods of production, and productive efficiency.

To be a good organization you need to have the best, well-motivated and effectively managed people in all four areas of the business. To be a successful business the challenge is making the four areas work as one.

Primary, secondary, and tertiary sectors

Business activity can be classified into three economic sectors: primary, secondary, and tertiary.

Primary sector

This covers business activity that is involved in the extraction of raw materials (for example, coal or gold) and also agriculture and fishing. Often such industries are closely monitored by governments due to the scarce nature of the materials and food sources and also the pollution effects of extraction methods.

Secondary sector

This economic sector includes industries that create a finished or useable product. These industries generally take the output of the primary sector then manufacture finished goods or components for other industries. In recent decades the secondary sector has declined in importance for many developed economies because of a loss of international competitiveness.

Tertiary sector

This area covers the provision of services to businesses and individual consumers. It includes the transportation and distribution of goods, wholesale and retail services, and adviser and consultancy-type businesses. In the developed world this sector has grown in importance. The Netherlands, for example, is one country where economic output is dominated by services.

Quaternary sector

A fourth sector may be identified which includes organizations providing information services through ICT. Some commentators believe this now applies to all other sectors, particularly the tertiary sector.

HL

Economic structure

Changes in economic structure in a country can have significant implications for individual businesses. If there is a move towards a service-based economy, those still manufacturing will no doubt be increasingly reliant on importing component parts. Their customers are also likely to be based abroad and so the business will be vulnerable to fluctuating exchange rates and also the economic cycles in the other countries involved. Equally, the quantity and quality of labour inputs in this sector may well be deteriorating. This is because school leavers will be increasingly moving into the service sector as this is the growth area, and the remaining workforce will be ageing and their productivity may decrease.

If there is a move away from primary to secondary sectors in an economy, the impact on individual businesses might include less available labour inputs as the working population is attracted towards higher-growth sectors. It's possible that businesses will need to become more capital intensive as a result and invest in automation or the latest machinery.

Student workpoint 1.1

Business investigation

1　In Western Europe the secondary sector has declined in importance and tertiary industries dominate their economies.

　a Identify, by researching your locality, which manufacturing businesses have closed down or relocated in recent years.

　b What reasons are you aware of for this happening or, if you do not know, what reasons might explain it?

2　Enterprise is a key factor of production. Find out what government policies or actions have been taken to help foster an entrepreneurial culture in your country or local area. Government websites and newspaper websites should be a good place to start your research.

Types of business organization

Public and private sector organizations

Businesses operate in the private or public sector, although recently in some countries the distinction between the two has become less clear.

The public sector covers activities that are within the control or direction of governments. These organizations do not have outside shareholders and are solely accountable to the government for their performance. Often they do not publish financial information, although in many democratic countries there are independent accountants and advisers who will monitor their efficiency. In many countries public sector organizations cover activities such as the state health, education, police, and prison services.

Private sector organizations are those that are owned by individuals and not run by the state. They generally operate with the main objective of making profit, although charities and independent schools would not.

Businesses in the private sector include "public and private" limited companies, which can sound very confusing to new business management students. Why aren't public limited companies in the public sector? Well, the word "public" here means that the shares are traded on a stock market and available to any members of the public to buy and sell. This explains why in the UK-quoted stock market companies are called "public companies". They certainly focus on profit and are not run by government.

Starting a business

Reasons for starting a business

- Talking with friends or relatives, you identified a business opportunity or gap in the market.
- You lost your job and found it easy to start your own business to provide the same service you did when employed by others.
- An inheritance appeared. A windfall of cash encourages you to have a go and run your own business—the dream you've always had now feels possible.
- Your family has always been in business and you are now ready to go your own way and do your own thing. You've learned the skills required to be successful in this or a similar industry.

There are always various reasons why someone starts up a business and, although the scenarios outlined above might explain the immediate reasons, you probably had it in you already to set up a business at some time.

Identifying a market opportunity

Market mapping is a method used to assess the current goods or services in a market and through this to identify possible gaps and opportunities. The would-be business person should consider two variables to compare existing products with, for example, products for old and young consumers and products for the affluent market and those at the cheap end of the spectrum.

A market map for cars could look like Figure 1.1.

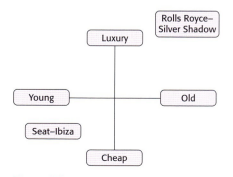

Figure 1.1

A Rolls Royce would appeal to the old and rich segment of the market. However identifying which segment a product fits isn't so easy.

Student workpoint 1.2

Be a thinker

1 Add cars from your own country into the quadrants you think they should appear. Are there any obvious gaps in this market?

2 Devise two different variables or spectrums for mapping the car market and draw your own market map.

3 Discuss your views on the new map. Did you all agree about which quadrant each car went in?

Possible problems faced by start-ups

- *Finance.* New businesses find it hard to raise capital. In the first instance, they may not be able to provide any security for loans, such as personal guarantees or property. This is often true for young people who may have little savings. Secondly, a new business obviously has no track record for a bank to assess and therefore the risks are greater for banks.

- *Location.* Anyone involved in a new start-up wants to minimize costs and so it may be desirable to work from home to begin with. This is not always ideal from an image viewpoint, but a good location may be very costly and a drain on cash flow at the very time when sales are negligible.

- *Developing a customer base, brand loyalty, and so repeat business.* It is imperative to build long-term relationships with customers so that they return time and time again, but this takes time and money. Investing in after-sales service or offering bespoke advice can be at odds with the short-term need to get money into the business almost without worrying about the quality of goods or services.

- *Poor cash flow.* Many new start-ups fail, not because their product is poor or that they can't make a profit, but because they don't manage their cash flow in the early years. It is imperative that entrepreneurs and small business owners manage cash as their first priority when establishing their businesses. This might mean chasing new customers for payment and slowing down payments to suppliers.

- *The personality of the entrepreneurs.* Have they the desire and industry to make this business work, at all costs to them—and possibly their families too?

- *HR management skills.* Are the entrepreneurs able to manage and motivate a workforce?

Student workpoint 1.3

Business investigation

Identify a new business in your locality and consider how well the entrepreneurs have started the business.

1 Have they invested in service and product quality?

2 Have they cut costs in terms of what you see?

3 Are they successful and, if so, why?

Profit-based organizations

Sole traders or sole proprietors

This is when the business is set up by an individual and where that person is the owner; the sole trader (known as a sole proprietor in some countries) is not a company in any legal sense and has no shareholders. In fact the "person is the business" and the two are the same, which explains why a sole trader may be described as, for example, Mr Vincent Vasquez trading as "Blinko".

As there is no legal distinction between the business and the person, the assets and liabilities of the two are not separated. This leads us to a very important weakness of being a sole trader: "unlimited liability". If the individual is sued, for example for giving bad advice or supplying a faulty product, there is no limit on his or her liability. This means that if the business cannot pay the debt or court fine the person's private assets can be seized to pay it off. The person's private wealth is not protected from the creditors.

There is also a positive linked point: ownership and control of the business is with the sole trader, as the firm doesn't have directors and separate shareholders.

Sole traders do not need to file financial accounts with public registrars and so competitors, customers, and suppliers cannot easily discover the sales and profits they make. Sole traders only need to submit accounts to the tax authorities. Another advantage is that they pay different tax rates from companies and have more opportunities to reduce their taxable profits through the large number of extra allowances.

Sole traders can include trades people such as plumbers and carpenters, some shopkeepers, individual accountants and lawyers, and many consultants in IT and other fields.

Partnerships

These are organizations where two or more individuals choose to work together as co-owners. These organizations are also not companies. As with sole traders, there are no shareholders and the owners all have unlimited liability. Their private wealth is at risk if the business fails.

However, there is one further disadvantage from this unlimited liability—the partners are liable for each other's debts. Let's take an example. A two-person law firm owes a customer $5 million for giving bad advice. When the business is closed down its cash reserves show that it can only pay $2 million. Partner A has private wealth of $1 million and partner B has wealth of $20 million. Now, as the partners jointly owe another $3 million to clear their debt to the client you might think that it should be divided equally and that they now owe $1.5 million each, but you would be wrong. The partners are liable for each other's debts, and as the customer knows that partner B has more wealth the customer will chase partner B for the remaining $3 million and probably ignore partner A. The moral may be, if you go into partnership with other people get a very good insurance policy to cover giving bad advice, or else you could end up paying for more than you bargained for! Most partnerships will take out extensive insurance policies to cover bad advice and faulty goods affecting customers and the public more generally, but it is still possible to come to grief.

The advantage of a partnership is that you can share the risks a little more than when a sole trader. You can also specialize in certain tasks. Many accountants and law practices are partnerships. Accountants PwC have thousands of partners around the world as does Freshfields, a large international law firm.

As with sole traders, partnerships do not need to file financial accounts with public registrars, but do file accounts for the tax authorities. Another advantage is that they pay different tax rates from companies and have more opportunities to reduce their taxable profits through the large number of extra allowances. Partnerships also make no distinction between the owners and the managers of the business—they are usually the same people.

Partnerships usually establish a rule book to avoid arguments or confusion arising later on. However, in some countries, if no partnership agreement exists it will be assumed that profits and losses are shared equally. Arguments over strategic development for the business are often a serious issue, something a sole trader would never face.

Partnerships look more substantial to potential customers than sole traders, as their letterhead will list all the partners' names, or for very large organizations it may indicate that the names can be viewed at one of the organization's offices.

Companies or corporations

Companies are very different from the first two types of business organization we've looked at. A company has shareholders and directors, and they are not always the same people. This means that there is separation in ownership and control (management of the business). The shareholders are limited in their liability to the amount of their investment. If they have invested $100,000 then that is the limit to the amount they can lose; their private wealth is untouchable and equally they can not be held liable for other shareholders' debts.

To establish a limited company the owners must complete registration documents and pay a small fee; this is no longer considered a major disadvantage. Companies also have to file annual financial information to public registrars—for details of some of these organizations see the websites listed on p. 179. This means that various external stakeholders can analyse how well the business is performing and that may impact on whether a supplier will continue giving credit, whether a customer will place an order, or whether a bank will lend more money.

It is often considered that a company presents a more solid and trusting image than a sole trader. After all, the company's letterhead will have a registration number, and most large businesses are companies.

Limited liability companies can be divided into those that are privately owned, for example within a family, and companies that are public corporations with shares that are traded on a stock market. In the UK companies are either private (Ltd) or public limited (plc) while, for example, in Germany private companies have a suffix of Gmbh and public companies have AG.

Student workpoint 1.4

Business investigation

Complete the following summary table covering the key features of the three different types of business organization.

Features	Sole trader (or proprietor)	Partnership	Limited companies; corporations
Separation of ownership and control (management)	? *No*	? *No*	Yes
Limited liability	? *unlimited*	Unlimited and liable for other partners' debts	? *Limited Liability*
Disclosure of financial information to public	? *No*	No	? *Yes*
Tax benefits	? *Yes*	? *Yes*	None
Ease of setting up	No legal documents	Partnership deed	? *legal documents*
Image	Small, but friendly service	? *medium size*	? *Large, trusted, Big name.*

1 When establishing a business, which type of organization would best suit these two scenarios? Expand your answers.

   a Two brothers were employed in a local building company that had been struggling with a downturn in demand for new houses and had decided to make staff redundant to cut costs, including the brothers. They each receive compensation of £50,000 for loss of job. They decide to set up in business together as a specialist building firm converting old houses into small flats around the site for the 2012 London Olympics. They will employ three staff to start with and will need to borrow £200,000 from a bank. They have very different private wealth but are close brothers and have always wanted to work together.

b A scientist at a Swedish university has recently discovered a drug that will stop some men losing their hair. He has patented the drug and predicts it would have worldwide sales of up to $300 million. He is considering selling the manufacturing rights to a large Swedish drug company and taking annual royalties from them. An alternative is that a private equity company has found a team of managers and is prepared to set up a new technology company with an investment of some $25 million to get the business up and running. The investors believe that if successful the company can then go on to the stock market in five years' time or be sold at a greater value to a competitor.

Final thoughts

As businesses develop and become more established the chances are that the organizational type will change—often from them being unlimited liability to limited liability companies. In addition, the need for future finance to support expansion may encourage the owners to change the status of the business, such as changing from private to public limited company. How much control they want will also dictate the type of organizational structure. For example, a number of well-known entrepreneurs have taken their companies off the stock market and have become private limited companies. In this way they are free from the media spotlight and do not need to meet short-term profit objectives, which may hinder longer-term development plans. Examples include Richard Branson with his Virgin empire and the musical composer and producer Sir Andrew Lloyd Webber with The Really Useful Group.

Organizational type therefore depends on people's changing objectives and the context of the business.

Student workpoint 1.5

Partners are "jointly and severally liable" for each other's debts; but shareholders in companies have limited liability to the amount they invested.

Discuss whether you think this is fair for all stakeholders.

Non-profit and non-government organizations (NGOs)

Non-profit organizations

Some organizations are not run for profit, for example charities and pressure groups. Charities include well-known international organizations like the Red Crescent, Médecins sans Frontières, and Oxfam; and also local fundraising groups, religious groups, and private schools. Pressure groups include political parties, trade unionists, commercial lobby groups (such as the hand gun association in the US or the pro-drinks group in the UK called the Portman Group); and local protest action groups, perhaps trying to stop a new airport or motorway from being built in a rural area.

All these non-profit organizations need to be established carefully and comply with legal requirements for charities and the like. If they don't, they might lose their charitable status and this may mean their funding or tax benefits are lost.

Charities tend to be run along business lines; they aim to minimize costs in order to maximize net revenue and therefore charitable donations. They also seek to educate or inform the public about their area of expertise or concern. This may mean highlighting poverty in inner cities or in other parts of the world or putting pressure on governments to increase resources in healthcare areas which have very low funding, for example the elderly or those in a particular part of the country.

Charities therefore focus their objectives on money raising, education, and lobbying. These objectives would also be the same for pressure groups, although their aims and objectives tend to be more targeted and money raising is a means to an end not an end in itself as with charities.

Non-government organizations (NGOs)

This covers a diverse range of organizations, but they all tend to be involved in economic development and humanitarian issues. Many charities can also be considered to be NGOs, or not for profit organizations.

NGOs plan and implement specific projects in developing countries, such as the earthquake relief in Pakistan in 2007. They also try to influence government policies on areas such as poverty and human rights. They work in the field where a disaster happens and often in places that official government aid does not reach.

The business impact of non-profit organizations and NGOs

Non-profit organizations and NGOs have both a direct and an indirect impact on business. Pressure groups trying to stop low wages or child factory workers in Africa may have an impact by persuading European consumers to stop buying cheap clothes from shops that sell these products. Charities with retail outlets (e.g. Amnesty International) may have an impact on the sales of other shops in the high street. Equally, there is opportunity for manufacturers to devise life-saving products or vaccines. For example, a UK company recently invented a special bottle that can clean the worst river or pond water and make it drinkable for humans. The likely sales of this device will no doubt make the inventors very rich indeed. Organizations can also offer sponsorship to NGOs and thereby improve their corporate image.

Student workpoint 1.6

Be a researcher

Look at the websites for two NGOs and make short notes about when they were established, their recent activities in the field, and any lobbying they have undertaken.

→

Then look up news stories from online newspapers and see if you can find out about the people running the organizations and even the organization's funding.

Compare your findings with your classmates' research for the charities they've chosen.

HL

Public and private enterprise

Organizations in the public and private sector are not mutually exclusive; they do work together at times. Sometimes they work together on one-off projects like building a new road and renting it out to motorists to use (by paying a toll). In the UK there have been two specific initiatives between the two sectors:

● public private partnerships (PPP)
● private finance initiative (PFI).

Data response exercise

Read the following case study and answer the question that follows.

Case study

What are public private partnerships?

Public private partnerships (PPP) have been at the heart of the UK government's attempts in recent years to revive Britain's public services.

What is a PPP?

Any collaboration between public bodies, such as local authorities or central government, and private companies tends to be referred to as a public private partnership (PPP).

The UK government believes that private companies are often more efficient and better run than bureaucratic public bodies. Since the early 1990s, in trying to bring the public and private sector together, the government has hoped that the management skills and financial acumen of the business community will create better value for money for taxpayers.

What is a PFI?

Governments and local authorities have always paid private contractors to build roads, schools, prisons, and hospitals out of tax money.

But in 1992, the UK government hit on a way of getting the contractors to foot the bill. Under PFI (private finance initiatives) contractors pay for the construction costs and then rent the finished project back to the public sector. This allowed the government to get new hospitals, schools, and prisons without raising taxes. PFI may still be in its early stages for hospitals and schools, but it is well established as a way of paying for new roads and prisons.

For example, in 2003 there were eight new private prisons—with more in the pipeline, and major road

schemes like the Thames crossing and the Birmingham relief road were being financed through PFI.

The complex nature of PFI contracts and the political obstacles involved in getting big, controversial schemes such as the London Underground PPP off the ground meant that progress in some areas was slow.

The National Health Service (NHS) probably saw the most new PFI activity between 1992 and 2003. Six major PFI projects were completed in the NHS, with a further 17 hospitals and other facilities under construction and a further 45 in the pipeline.

It was estimated that trade in public services could ultimately net the private sector an extra £30 billion a year. This broke down roughly into £10 billion in central government contracts, £5 billion in education, and £5 billion in local authority contracts.

If privatization represents a take-over of a publicly owned commodity, advocates say, then PPP is more like a merger, with both sides sharing the risks and, hopefully, seeing the benefits.

What are the drawbacks?

In 2003, the union said profits for the companies involved would total between £1.5 billion and £3.4 billion over the next 30 years, about £5 a year for every tax payer in the country. One big criticism of PFI is that the only way companies can turn a profit is by cutting employees' wages and benefits. Unions talk of jobs being "privatized". Their members are shifted into the private sector, where they have fewer employment rights and benefits such as pensions and childcare.

Advocates of PPP say that many hospitals and schools would not have been built at all if it was not for private finance—the public money was simply not available.

What are the advantages?

From 1992, the UK government staked its reputation on delivering better public services but it was also aware that there was a limit on how far taxes could be raised.

PFI is a fast, effective—and in the short term at least—cheap way of getting new facilities built. The biggest hospital-building programme in living memory was launched thanks to PFI.

There are some areas where public-private schemes may ultimately prove unsuitable. Some PFI projects, such as Capita's managing of the housing benefit system in Lambeth and some IT projects, have already proved disastrous.

Examination question

Evaluate what the costs and benefits of cooperation between the public and private sector might be in some of the examples above or in any that you are aware of in your country. *[10 marks]*

1 Business organizations and management

1.2 Objectives, stakeholders and the external environment

By the end of this chapter, you should be able to:

- explain the importance of objectives in managing an organization
- distinguish between objectives, strategies and tactics
- examine the importance and value of corporate social responsibility
- explain the interests of internal and external stakeholders and discuss possible areas of conflict between stakeholder
- prepare a PEST analysis and evaluate the impact of the external environment on a firm's objectives and strategy

Organizational objectives

The importance of objectives

Imagine a situation where you leave your house in the morning with no idea of where you are going, and no idea of what you are going to do when you reach somewhere. You would be adrift like a ship without a rudder and as a result end up achieving little or nothing.

Luckily, when most of us wake up, we do have an idea of where we are going and what we are going to do, although some people have a much clearer idea than others. If it is during a normal week, we are likely to be setting off for school or work and have a good idea of what we will be doing when we arrive—going to classes, or attending meetings, writing e-mails, and so on.

If we have some clear objectives, then we can plan our day and make some judgments about our level of success or failure. As a reader of this book, it is likely that your ultimate objective or purpose will be to pass your IB Diploma Programme and more specifically the business and management course. Whether or not you have the motivation or ability to do so may significantly affect your success, but at least you have an objective and can work towards this and have a measure of success when you receive your results. In essence you have set yourself a SMART objective. A SMART objective is defined as follows.

- **Specific.** The objective should state clearly what you are trying to achieve.
- **Measurable.** The objective should be able to be measured without massive resources devoted to research and evaluation.
- **Achievable.** The objective must be achievable within the available resources (financial, human, and other), and not too ambitious.
- **Relevant.** The objective must be useful to the overall process of achievement of your goal.
- **Time-constrained.** The objective must contain a time limit, otherwise it will be impossible to measure.

> **"If you don't know where you are going, you'll end up someplace else."**
> "Yogi" Berra (1925–), Major league baseball player and manager.

> **"A person who aims at nothing is sure to hit it."**
> Anon

You could make your target SMART**er**. You add the "**er**" by ensuring that you can **e**xtend the target (or make it **e**xciting) to offer more incentive and **r**ecord the results or **r**eward achievement of the objectives. The IB Diploma Programme is student centred, so teachers should encourage students to "search deeper" and challenge themselves to achieve more. Certainly the results of your examinations are recorded and getting to your desired university or gaining your dream job would definitely be a reward for your efforts.

Student workpoint 1.7

Business investigation

Here is a list of business objectives.

- A supermarket chain has set itself the objective of increasing market share from 20% to 80% within three years. — Needs to be reasonable, 20% to 40%
- An international school sets itself the objective of becoming the best in the world. — need time constraint, not specific, not very realistic
- A taxi company has the objective of increasing gross profit by 3% this year. ✓
- A football club has set itself the objective of improving its future performance. — needs to be more specific, no time constraint
- An electricity company has set itself the target of reducing consumer complaints from 8% to 6% within the next 12 months. ✓

1 Which of these objectives do you think are the most useful, and which are not very helpful? Explain your reasoning. The taxi company + electric company (✓)

2 Modify the objectives you believe are inadequate. international School + football club

3 Produce three SMARTer targets for your business and management course. E: Exciting
R: Record + Reward

Business organizations are no different from individuals or IB students—they need direction and purpose. Managers, therefore, must have clear aims and goals for the organization from which to set objectives, converted into measurable results. These results are the measures of success. Setting objectives is the fundamental starting point for any organization and provides the meaning for the organization's existence.

Organizations need objectives because they:

- identify what the business aims to achieve and a sense of direction
- provide a focus for every individual in the organization
- drive the decision-making process and the setting of strategy
- provide the means for measuring performance and success
- can be broken down to provide targets for individual parts of the organization
- motivate employees
- help the development of good teamwork.

The most common business objectives are:

- survival—to reach the point where the business breaks even and moves into profit
- profit maximization—to maximize the difference between total revenue and total cost

- market share—to develop market share by taking business away from competitors
- market growth—to increase overall sales to decrease the risk of business failure
- corporate image—to develop an approach that links certain beliefs, attitudes, and values to the business to create competitive advantage
- quality improvement—to maximize the quality of products and services to ensure long-term success, which is embodied in processes such as total quality management (TQM) (see p. 254)
- "satisficing"—to accept what is satisfactory, rather than maximizing returns. This may be because the owners are looking for an "easy, but satisfying" environment, or it may be a compromise position to satisfy conflicting objectives of shareholders.

These objectives will inevitably change over time, but the key thing about objectives is that they should drive decision making. There would be no point, for instance, if a business states its objective to be market growth, but then cuts its marketing budget way below that of its competitors.

Student workpoint 1.8
Business investigation

1 Visit the Procter & Gamble website at www.pg.com to learn more about this global giant.

2 Find out the company's locations, products, and brands.

3 Read the section on "Purpose, values and principles". You may want to save a copy of this for use later on in this unit.

4 Now investigate how Unilever compares by going to http://unilever.com

Management by objectives (MbO)

MbO is a strategic management practice used to increase performance across the organization by attempting to match individual objectives with those of the organization. The process of MbO was first outlined by Peter Drucker (1954).[1] It was the development of the stepped process of MbO that underpinned the concept of SMART objectives.

---

[1] Drucker, P. 1954. *The Practice of Management*. London, Heinemann.

MbO relies on the setting of objectives for each employee and then, through an appraisal system, measuring individuals' performance against the objectives set. The intention is that the setting of objectives will be jointly discussed and agreed between the manager and the subordinate, not imposed from above. The process involves:

- setting strategic objectives
- translating these objectives into goals and targets for each member of the organization
- designing or redesigning work practices to allow the achievement of goals and targets
- motivating the workforce to achieve their goals and targets
- measuring performance against goals and targets within a specified time frame—normally annually
- providing feedback, which can form the basis of rewards and bonuses, and becomes the starting point for the next objective-setting phase.

MbO became very fashionable in the 1980s, but was criticized for the way it was implemented in many organizations. First, the process was often "top–down" rather than negotiated and, second, the emphasis on certain objectives meant that other equally important issues were neglected. For MbO to be successful, employees must feel that they "own" the process of objective setting and that the objectives are achievable and worthwhile.

In the 1990s, Drucker defended his system, pointing out that: "It's just another tool. It is not the great cure for management efficiency." In a sense this is a lesson to be considered throughout your business course. Managers have a "toolbox" available to them to manage their organizations. One tool alone, be it ratio analysis (see p. 174), or indeed MbO, is not normally sufficient. It is the combination of tools that is likely to improve performance and reduce risks in decision making. A good business and management student is one who can select an appropriate and effective combination of business tools and techniques to analyse and evaluate a situation.

Peter Drucker (1909–2005)

Source: www.nsc.gov.tw

"Checking the results of a decision against its expectations shows executives what their strengths are, where they need to improve, and where they lack knowledge or information."

Peter F. Drucker was born in 1909 in Vienna and educated in Austria, Germany, and England, earning a doctorate in public and international law. In 1933 he emigrated to England, where he worked in banking and took part in the legendary Keynes seminars. At the age of 29 he settled in the US and in 1949 became professor of management at New York University. From 1971 until his retirement he was the professor of social science and management at Claremont University, California.

Drucker's special focus was on the organization and work of top management. He began his long consulting career with General Motors and then worked with many major corporations, including General Electric, Coca-Cola, Citicorp, IBM, and Intel. For nearly half a century, Peter Drucker inspired and educated managers and influenced the nature of business with his influential articles in *The Harvard Business Review*. He wrote a regular column in the *Wall Street Journal* for over 20 years and articles in publications including *The Economist, The Financial Times, Fortune* and *Harpers*.

Drucker's books on economics, politics, society, and management have been translated into 37 languages and are highly respected. He is credited with creating the foundations of modern management and is considered to be the "the man who invented management" (the *New York Times*).

A number of his books became classics, for example *The Practice of Management*, in which Drucker developed "management by objectives" (MbO), a management concept based on objective setting and self-supervision. This criticized the authoritarian leadership style operating in many businesses at that time. In *Managing for Results*, he focused on the economic constraints on business and identified key success factors in managing performance.

Drucker's ideas are extensive, but he is particularly noted for promoting the need for community and predicting the "end of economic man". He saw profit as a requirement for business survival, but not its sole focus. He promoted volunteering in the non-profit sector as this developed a sense of belonging and civic pride. He advised several non-profit organizations including the Salvation Army, the American Red Cross, and the Navajo Indian Tribal Council. He strongly believed that employees are assets, not liabilities, and taught that "knowledge workers" are the essential ingredients of a modern economy. He wrote that an enterprise is most effective when decentralized and when customers are considered its main responsibility.

HL

Objectives and change

Organizations need to change objectives in response to changes in the internal and external environment. The business environment is constantly changing and internal resources—labour, machines, technology, finances, and so on—also vary over time. A business does not work in a bubble. Its activities are influenced by factors outside of the business over which it has no control. These changes may mean that an excellent corporate plan set two years ago is no longer so good or "fit for purpose". Success in the past doesn't always guarantee success in the future. Therefore, an organization's objectives need to be kept constantly under review.

Negative changes in the internal environment that can provoke change include such HR problems as high staff turnover, lack of skills, reducing productivity, and low motivation. There may be financial issues too, such as poor cash flow. These problems are a threat to the business. Organizations will have to adjust their objectives to address these issues and put in place appropriate strategies to improve the situation.

Similarly, positive changes in the internal environment should lead to a review of business objectives. Particularly talented employees need to be developed, unexpected revenues invested, new product ideas investigated. All of these will have implications for strategic planning and corporate objectives.

The external environment provides both opportunities and threats. It is often the case that an organization may have to alter radically the way that it does business in response to a major change in the external environment, especially if the change undermines the competitive advantage or unique selling proposition (USP) that the organization enjoys. These required changes could result from many factors, including new competition, changing technology, or unexpected economic recession, such as the "credit crunch" that started in 2008.

The history of commerce is littered with the remains of "household names" that failed to adapt to the changing business environment, perhaps because they did not have the resources to do so or they became complacent or arrogant about their position. When change happens, it can happen very quickly and undermine the whole foundations of a business empire. The bank failures of Lehman Brothers in the US and Landsbanki in Iceland are significant examples. In 2007 these institutions seemed completely secure, but a year later they both filed for bankruptcy with huge debts.

A strategy is not for ever. It must be continuously checked and reviewed. Targets for the business and all its departments are set at the beginning of a planning cycle. The corporate plan is likely to have planning horizons—times when actual results and performance are compared to initial targets and a review of progress made. This review should form the basis of the next planning cycle and can lead to a business changing its objectives in response to progress, or lack of progress, in achieving its goals.

When asked to evaluate the need to change objectives in light of changes in the external and internal environment, there are several crucial factors to consider.

- How significant are the changes?
- Can the business continue operating in its present form?
- What are the resource costs of change, for example financial implications and costs, HR requirements, and new technologies required?
- Can the business retain its competitive advantage?
- Can the business reposition its products (goods or services) or seek new customers and/or products?
- What will be the consequences of senior management imposing new objectives on the business?
- How can the workforce be involved in the process of changing the direction of the business?

At the core of many business failures are changes in technology. These changes may remove the USP that provided competitive advantage. Businesses that survive do so by facing these changes and adapting the way that they conduct their business or produce their goods or services.

Case study

Polaroid cameras

Polaroid was started by entrepreneur Edwin Land in 1937 inspired by his young daughter's demands to see the pictures "now". He invented a system that developed the image inside the camera itself, rather than having to use the normal photographer's darkroom, and this became the company's feature. The first Polaroid camera was sold in 1948, but the popularity of the camera did not really grow until the production of the 1965 Swinger, which was voted one of the Top 50 gadgets of the last century by *PC World* magazine.

The 1980s and 1990s saw continued popularity for the Polaroid, helped by its most famous user, Andy Warhol. Polaroid peaked in popularity in 1991 when its sales of mainly instant cameras and film came close to $3 billion. When photography went digital in the late 1990s, all cameras become instant cameras and Polaroid's USP disappeared. Polaroid went bankrupt in 2001, before being taken over four years later by a Minnesota-based consumer products company.

Polaroid now focuses on other ventures, which include portable printers for mobile phone images, and digital cameras. The company's president, Tom Beaudoin, said,

"We're trying to reinvent Polaroid so it lives on for the next 30 to 40 years." However, this vision of the future was again put in jeopardy as Polaroid filed for bankruptcy in December 2008 after its parent company was investigated for alleged fraud.

Source: Adapted from: www.livemint.com

How and why was Polaroid forced to change its objectives after 2001 to respond to changes in the external environment?

Student workpoint 1.9
Business investigation

The Polaroid case study shows that the company was successful because it had exploited new technology to gain a competitive advantage. However, the best technology is not always enough to guarantee business success.

1 Research the following technology conflicts:

 a video tape formats: the battle that took place in the 1970s and early 1980s between Sony's Betamax tapes and JVC's VHS format to gain

dominance in the standard used for video tape-recording for home use

 b DVD formats: the commercial battle between Sony's Blu-ray and Toshiba's HD-DVD to become the DVD industry standard.

2 Write a 500–1,000 word report on why Sony lost the battle of the video tape format, but forced Toshiba to exit the DVD market in 2008. Identify external and internal factors that influenced the outcomes in both cases.

Changes in technology, of course, are not the only elements of the external environment that affect the operations of a business. Organizations will also have to address the other three factors in what is known as PEST analysis:

- political and legal changes
- economic changes
- social and cultural changes.

Some of these changes happen rapidly and with a significant effect on short-term strategy. For example, there may be sudden supply shocks such as increases in the price of energy. Other changes may happen over a longer period, such as alterations in social behaviour and cultural values.

PEST factors are examined in greater detail on p. 45–51.

The hierarchy of objectives

There is a distinct **hierarchy of objectives** in an organization (see Figure 1.2). At the top level, an organization will often create a "mission" setting out the purpose of the organization itself. This will be followed by a set of objectives relating to less significant, although still important, operational aspects such as market share, customer satisfaction, and employee motivation. These objectives will be broken up by function and communicated to those entrusted with achieving them.

- **Mission and vision statements** are normally written by the founders, or senior managers, of the business. They provide a "guiding hand" for all business activities and the overall principles on which the business operates.
- **Corporate objectives** are set by senior management and are the practical application of the organization's mission statement in

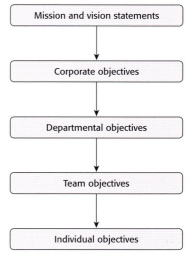

Figure 1.2 Hierarchy of objectives

that they detail specific goals for the entire enterprise and are quantifiable. One example might be: "the business will achieve a return on capital of 10% on any investments made in 2010". Corporate objectives are long term in nature. Setting these objectives is part of corporate planning, which is the process by which an organization analyses its objectives, priorities, strategies, and environment in light of its mission.

- **Departmental objectives** are corporate objectives broken down to allow each department to know what it must achieve if the corporate objectives are to be fulfilled.
- **Team and individual objectives** provide a day-to-day focus for all employees to guide their actions so that these contribute to the overall objectives of the organization.

One key tool used to examine corporate strategy and strategic planning is MOST analysis, which uses the hierarchy of objectives as a framework. This helps clarify:

- the organization's purpose and where it intends to go (**m**ission)
- key goals that will help to achieve the mission (**o**bjectives)
- the options to achieve the mission and objectives (**s**trategies)
- how these strategies will be put into action (**t**actics).

Now we'll examine these four elements of strategy and strategic planning.

Mission and vision statements

Although the terms are sometimes used interchangeably, mission statements and vision statements do two distinctly different jobs.

The mission statement

This is a concise description of what an organization currently does. It defines why the organization exists and the key measure or measures of the organization's success. It is a "practical statement" and in simple terms it can be defined as "who we are and what we do", by putting corporate aims into words. Its prime audience is the leadership team and shareholders, but every employee should be aware of the mission statement and able to express its purpose. When developed it should define the organization's business, its objectives, and its approach to reach those objectives. Over the years, the business will build on this to establish its core competence—skills that competitors cannot easily match or imitate.

Example: Singapore Airlines' mission statement is:

Singapore Airlines is a global company dedicated to providing air transportation services of the highest quality and to maximising returns for the benefit of its shareholders and employees.

The vision statement

In contrast to the mission statement, the vision statement describes the desired future position of the company. It also defines the organization's purpose, but does so in terms of the organization's values rather than specific measures, such as market share or profit targets. Values are traits or qualities that represent an individual's highest priorities and deeply held driving forces. For a business, corporate values represent its core beliefs and are set out in its vision statement. For employees, the vision statement gives direction about how they are expected to behave and it should inspire and motivate them to perform to their best. When shared with customers, it should shape their understanding of the business and its activities and outline why they should remain loyal to its goods and services. Finally, it should express how the organization values its key stakeholders: its shareholders, customers, suppliers, and the internal community.

Example: Samsung's vision statement is:

We will devote our human resources and technology to create superior products and services, thereby contributing to a better global society.

Employees of the business will be expected to uphold and promote the values of the business. This will be easier if they understand and share these values. It would seem sensible, or possibly essential, that employees and other stakeholders of the business have the opportunity to help in the preparation of these statements, if they are to represent accurately the core aims and values of the business.

Excellent mission and vision statements are brief, memorable, and practical, as well as inspiring. Aspects of the mission and vision statements are normally combined to provide a statement of the organization's purposes, goals, and values. These purposes, goals, and values, represented and supported by the actions of senior leaders, are especially important in the development of a shared corporate culture (see Chapter 2.5).

> **"A leader shapes and shares a vision, which gives point to the work of others."**
> Charles Handy, (1932–) management guru

> **"To choose a direction, an executive must have developed a mental image of the possible and desirable future state of the organization. This image, which we call a vision, may be as vague as a dream or as precise as a goal or a mission statement."**
> Warren Bennis, (1925–), writer on leadership

student workpoint 1.10
Be a thinker—discuss and explain

Look at the three examples of mission statements below. What is not said by these mission statements and does it matter?

Disney: "To make people happy."

Nike: "To bring inspiration and innovation to every athlete in the world."

Sony: "To experience the joy of advancing and applying technology for the benefit of the public."

Now compare Microsoft's mission statement with that of IBM (given below). Which style of statement do you think is most successful and why? How can you explain the different styles of the two companies?

Microsoft: "To enable people and businesses throughout the world to realize their potential."

IBM: "We strive to lead in the creation, development and manufacture of the industry's most advanced information technologies, including computer systems, software, networking systems, storage devices and microelectronics. We translate these advanced technologies into value for our customers through our professional solutions and services businesses worldwide."

The role of mission and vision statements in an organization
Mission and vision statements usually appear on all company literature, alongside logos and other images of the business, and are

generally included in documents such as business plans and staff handbooks. They are often used as part of a marketing message designed to influence public perception of the business and its activities. As a consequence, they are frequently criticized for being little more than a public relations (PR) exercise and not representing the reality of the business. They are often so vague that they have little practical application.

However, mission and vision statements can serve a very important role because they inform, and encourage the involvement of, internal and external stakeholders.

Internally these statements:

- guide management thinking on strategic issues
- provide stability during periods of significant change
- set performance standards for the whole organization
- provide employees with a focus on common goals
- inspire employees to work more productively
- guide employee decision making
- help establish a framework for ethical behaviour.

Externally these statements:

- create goodwill and attract similar-minded individuals or groups to invest in the business
- create closer links and better communication with customers, suppliers, the local community, and shareholders
- serve to promote the business and its operations to the general public
- act as a marketing tool, defining what the business represents.

In many industries, changing markets and customer preferences require organizations periodically to re-evaluate their strategic mission. This process will serve to focus employees on the highest objectives of the company.

In some cases, mission, and vision statements may be non-commercial. Non-profit organizations still need to provide a focus and collective vision. Consider the following mission and vision statements.

Example: the mission statement of the Salvation Army

The Salvation Army, an international movement, is an evangelical part of the universal Christian Church. Its message is based on the Bible. Its ministry is motivated by the love of God. Its mission is to preach the gospel of Jesus Christ and to meet human needs in His name without discrimination.

Example: the vision statement of Tennis Australia

To grow, manage, promote and showcase the sport of tennis throughout Australia, recognising the health, social, economic and entertainment benefits of sport, and tennis in particular, for people of both sexes, all ages and abilities.

Neither of these organizations is profit making, but they still require those who work for them, or with them, to understand the nature and objectives of the organization.

Case study

S. C. Johnson

Turning "philosophy" statements into action

The value of mission and vision statements is the extent to which they reflect reality and are able to be put into practice. S.C. Johnson regularly appears in lists of the most respected US companies and was a pioneer as a socially responsible company. The company was listed as No. 27 in the "100 Best Companies to Work For" list published by *Fortune* magazine in 2008. The organization is respected for its commitment to putting its values into practice.

In 1976, S. C. Johnson formally stated its guiding philosophy called "This We Believe". In this statement the company expresses its beliefs in relation to its five stakeholder groups: employees, consumers, the general public, neighbours and hosts, and the world community. Here is what the company states.

Employees: We believe our fundamental strength lies in our people.

Consumers: We believe in earning the enduring goodwill of the people who use and sell our products and services.

General public: We believe in being a responsible leader in the free market economy.

Neighbors and hosts: We believe in contributing to the well-being of the countries and communities where we conduct business.

World community: We believe in improving international understanding.

What makes this statement different from those of many other business mission statements is that S. C. Johnson breaks down its responsibilities to each group into identifiable and measurable objectives. For instance, in the employees' section, it explains its "no meeting day policy". This states that there will be no meetings on two Fridays per month, enabling employees to be more productive heading into the weekends and decreasing the need to take work home. Several publications, including *News Week* and the *Wall Street Journal*, praised this policy as an innovative approach to more productive, less stressed employees.

Student workpoint 1.11

Business investigation

Investigate S.C. Johnson's CSR philosophy at www.scjohnson.com/family/fam_com_phi.asp

Select two of the "This We Believe" statements from the company's website and describe three specific and measurable targets associated with each of these statements.

Case study

Nike

Nike has become targeted by pressure groups, because of accusations concerning human rights issues and factory working conditions in developing countries. In response, Nike has published a well-developed focus for its corporate responsibility on improving conditions in contracted factories, aiming for carbon  neutrality, and making sports available to young people across the world.

However, criticism of the company continues.

→

Business project

1 Read the CSR report on the Nike website at http://nikeresponsibility.com

2 Search for recent news stories on Nike's business activities, such as those reported by Sourcewatch, at www.sourcewatch.org/index.php?title=Nike

3 Produce a 500–1,000 word report evaluating Nike's commitment to CSR.

Steps in creating a successful mission statement

1 Identify the organization's USP (unique selling point). This is the idea or approach that differentiates the organization from its competitors, and is the reason customers buy its products and not its competitors'.

2 Identify the key measures of the organization's success.

3 Combine the organization's USP and key measures of success into a tangible and measurable goal.

4 Refine the words into a concise and precise statement expressing the USP, success measures, and desired result.

Case study

Fashion Café

Fashion Café is situated in a premium position in a desirable location in a city centre. Its USP is that the employees wear clothes supplied by independent local and national clothing outlets and on every Friday afternoon present a fashion show exhibiting all the clothes worn that week. Customers can order these clothes on forms left on each table and receive a discount on the clothes, and also on the food and drink purchased in the following week. The café promotes sustainability by using organic produce and clothes using natural fibres, and promises that a percentage of all profits will be paid to charities active in areas where products are sourced.

The mission statement of Fashion Café is:

"To offer a stylish location for people who share our passion for natural food, lovingly made fresh every day, and our fascination for fashion. Our products will sustain and be sustainable and we strive to exceed our customers' expectations in all aspects of our business by adding value to all our operations."

Steps in creating a successful vision statement

Once the mission statement is created, a vision statement is required to support the message to stakeholders. To create a vision statement, a business needs to take these steps.

1 Identify the values that underpin the business and its operations.

2 Focus on the aspects of operations that customers and stakeholders value most.

3 Prepare a statement that motivates employees and strengthens the message to other stakeholders.

The key issues underpinning the operations of Fashion Café are:

- the combination of food and fashion
- the freshly prepared food
- the organic nature and sustainability of the products
- exceeding customer expectations and adding value
- contributions to charitable organizations.

The vision statement of Fashion Café is:

We will always act responsibly and sensitively in the community where we operate, while promoting high-quality products to enhance people's lives and to bring a sense of joy and the promotion of style. We will support our suppliers to ensure our products are sustainable while sharing our rewards with those who contribute to our success.

Student workpoint 1.12

Business investigation

The mission statement

Using USP analysis, SWOT analysis (see p. 66), and core competence analysis as a starting point, produce a mission statement for:

1 your school or college

2 a multinational business known to you or one that you can investigate online.

Your mission statement should:

● address the commitment the organization has to its key stakeholders, including customers, employees, shareholders, and communities

● communicate the message in clear, simple, and precise language

● ensure that the mission can be translated into corporate objectives that are measurable, actionable, and achievable

● develop support throughout the organization.

Extension activities

1 Write SMART corporate objectives to action your mission statement.

2 Approach a local business and offer to produce a mission and vision statement for the organization. Turn these statements into practical objectives— strategic and tactical. This could be the basis of a business and management internal assessment.

The vision statement

Read the Tata vision statement below detailing its five core values and use the same style to prepare a value statement for a company you have some knowledge of, or one that you can investigate. Add more information specific to the company and its business.

If the company has a vision statement already, prepare your statement first then compare it to the existing statement and review any major differences you can identify.

● Are these differences fundamental?
● Do they surprise you and, if so, in what way?
● Do the vision statements reflect reality?

Case study

A principled business: Tata and its "five core values"

The Tata Group has always sought to be a value-driven organization. These values continue to direct the Group's growth and businesses. The five core Tata values underpinning the way we do business are:

● Integrity: We must conduct our business fairly, with honesty and transparency. Everything we do must stand the test of public scrutiny.

● Understanding: We must be caring, show respect, compassion, and humanity for our colleagues and customers around the world, and always work for the benefit of the communities we serve.

● Excellence: We must constantly strive to achieve the highest possible standards in our day-to-day work and in the quality of the goods and services we provide.

● Unity: We must work cohesively with our colleagues across the Group and with our customers and partners around the world, building strong relationships based on tolerance, understanding and mutual cooperation.

● Responsibility: We must continue to be responsible, sensitive to the countries, communities, and environments in which we work, always ensuring that what comes from the people goes back to the people many times over.

Source: http://tata.com/

Aims and objectives

In a war situation, one army is likely to target the resources of another, such as buildings or equipment, with the objective of destroying them. Hitting the target is therefore a pretty important measure of success! Generals will lay out their strategy, but this will involve both short-term and long-term objectives. Aims, objectives, and measures of success are distinctly different concepts, but can be easily explained by considering the following:

an army *aims* weapons at a target, such as enemy tanks
with the *objective* of destroying these tanks
success is measured by *achieving* the objective and destroying the tanks and contributing to winning the war—this is the *measure of success.*

Similarly a business develops its objectives by identifying its targets.

For example, let's say a clothing retailer decides to focus its marketing on a particular target segment of the population—the "tweenager" fashion market. ("Tweenager" is a currently fashionable marketing term for pre-teens, girls in particular, aged between 7 and 11, who have substantial purchasing power in many developed countries.)

The retailer then quantifies what it wants to achieve, by setting objectives for market share, growth or value. As mentioned in the last section on vision statements, the business is likely to have guidelines outlining rules about the way it achieves its objectives, especially targeting this potentially vulnerable group. These guidelines may be translated into a strict ethical code covering acceptable promotion and selling techniques. This ethical code could state, for instance, that it is inappropriate to pressurize young children to conform to an image that would be regarded as too "adult". The code will normally be published on the organization's website and in its annual report.

Once the retailer has clarified and developed its objectives, it can decide on the best way of achieving them and exactly how it will monitor and measure its success. This is greatly helped if the targets set are SMART targets. These are then incorporated into the retailer's business plan while providing a focus for the development of its business strategy. Details of this process are developed more fully in Chapter 6.

Possible SMART targets for the fashion retailer may include targets:

- to increase sales by 10% to girls aged 7 to 11, over the next two financial years
- to gain a 25% market share within 18 months
- to increase gross profit margin by 5% over the coming financial year
- to create brand loyalty in order to persuade at least 20% of present customers to purchase at least one item from the teenage fashion lines offered by the company, within three months of their twelfth birthday.

Achievement of these targets will then act as the *measures of success.*

Objectives can be **strategic** or **tactical**.

A **strategy** is a long-term plan illustrating how the business will achieve its objectives. Strategic objectives, therefore, represent significant long-term goals. For example, the objective of increasing gross profit margin by 5% for the fashion retailer might be achieved by expanding into a new overseas market. This strategic objective will require high-level decisions to be made by senior managers, because it involves significant use of resources. Decisions made in support of this proposed overseas expansion will form part of the policy of the business.

Tactics are the actual activities that a business will employ to implement its strategy on a day-to-day basis and are put into action at the individual department or employee level. They should contribute positively to the overall strategy of the business. For example, managers may contact different property agents overseas to identify the best rental properties available to locate new fashion outlets.

Strategic, long-term objectives should be realistic, challenging, and attainable statements of where the senior management wants an organization to be in three to five years' time following the direction outlined in the mission and vision statements. Long-term objectives function as starting points, to make it easier to prioritize and allocate resources and to coordinate short-term, tactical objectives.

Strategic objectives	Tactical objectives
Long-term objectives about the future direction of the whole organization	Short-term objectives to help implement the organization's strategy
High-risk objectives because of a considerable uncertainty	Lower-risk objectives because there is less uncertainty
Set by senior managers, often at board of director level	Set by employees lower in the hierarchy—usually at department level
Involve major capital investment or resource commitment	Few resource commitments
Once implemented, are difficult and potentially expensive to alter	Easy to change with little financial implication

If an organization does not achieve its strategic objectives, this can have a significant impact and may result in the ultimate failure of the entire operation. For instance, a business that enters a new overseas market may find that actual sales are far below those predicted, resulting in sales revenue not covering entry costs. The business has committed significant resources (human and financial) to the planned expansion. It may be difficult for it to pull out of the new market completely as it would have to accept these losses. However, a decision to remain in the market and commit more resources may be fatal to the business.

Did you know?

Walmart ※

Wal-Mart in Germany

Cross-border, cross-cultural business is a challenge even for the biggest companies. Companies have to be sensitive to the local cultures and tailor their offerings to the local market. In August 2006, Wal-Mart, the world's largest retailer, announced that it was exiting operations in Germany, selling all 85 of its hypermarkets to Metro, the German supermarket chain. The US-based chain said its second-quarter net profit slumped 26% to $2.08 billion, after it registered a charge of $863 million for the sale of its German stores.

Wal-Mart's biggest mistake was to ignore the local culture and buying habits and impose on its German operations a US chief executive, who did not understand Germany or its culture. Indeed, he insisted that all business operations be carried out using the English language.

The Wal-Mart example tells us that even the biggest of the companies are not immune to strategic failures. Companies need to understand the local culture in order to capitalize on the local market. The lessons learned from Wal-Mart's experience in Germany, Korea, and Japan can be applied by other retailers who are planning on expanding in India and China. Large retail chains such as Tesco, Metro, and Carrefour have to be very careful when they plan to invest in countries outside their home markets.

Ethical objectives

Ethics is the branch of philosophy concerned with rules of human behaviour. It considers what is "right" and "wrong" and examines how moral principles and values are created and evolve. Setting ethical objectives is therefore a process by which organizations apply ethical values to their targets and establish basic principles about their behaviour in achieving these targets. Ethical values cover all aspects of business conduct, from corporate strategies and treatment of employees and suppliers to sales and accounting practices. In fact, most activities of a business have some ethical features.

Ethical behaviour goes beyond legal requirements placed on a business, as it concerns discretionary decisions and behaviour; in other words, what a business chooses to do rather than what it is forced to do. Business ethics are relevant both to the conduct of an individual within an organization and to the conduct of the organization as a whole.

An organization may ask strategic questions such as these.

- Is it ethical to reduce costs by exploiting cheaper resources in less economically developed countries? For example, large Western multinational companies have been accused of using child labour in some of their overseas factories.
- Is it ethical to sell products that are legal, but known to harm those who use them, for example cigarettes and alcohol?
- Is it ethical to target children with advertising messages?
- Is it ethical to manufacture products that are used to kill? What about the arms industry, for instance?
- Is it ethical to look for loopholes in the law to avoid paying tax?

These are "big" questions that elicit strong views, but there are many smaller, tactical issues at an individual level, which still have ethical dimensions. Examples of questions about individual behaviour, which will contribute to the overall ethical approach of an organization, include: "How do I manage my team?" and "Should I 'massage the truth' or be disrespectful when selling products or services to my customers?"

In theory, business ethics are a shared set of attitudes, morals and rules of behaviour that underpin the decision-making process. But in practice not everybody agrees on what is ethical and what is not. After all, individuals in everyday life have very different moral and ethical standards, so why should we expect individuals in organizations to be any different? One reason, perhaps, is that organizations often have identified and clearly stated corporate cultures, so anyone who voluntarily joins the organization is signalling at least some agreement with the existing culture and the values attached.

We've already examined mission and vision statements, which are philosophical summaries of an organization's ethical and moral attitudes. Alongside these statements, organizations may publish detailed ethical codes of practice, ethical policies, or ethical guidelines, which guide employees in their responses to situations that potentially challenge their honesty and integrity.

● ● ● ● ● ● ● ● ● ● ● ● ● ● ● ● ● ●

"Whenever I'm caught between two evils, I take the one I have never tried."
Mae West (1893–1980)

"I believe that every right implies a responsibility; every opportunity an obligation; every possession a duty."
John D. Rockefeller, Jr. (1839–1937)

These guidelines set out general principles about the organization's beliefs on matters such as quality, treatment of staff, or the environmental effects of the organization's activities. They detail procedures to be used in specific ethical situations, such as a conflict of interest or situations where employees are offered gifts or favours.

Case study

 **TEXAS INSTRUMENTS**

The Texas Instruments ethics quick test
Is the action legal?
Does it comply with our values?
If you do it, will you feel bad?
How will it look in the newspaper?

If you know it's wrong, don't do it!
If you're not sure, ask.
Keep asking until you get an answer.

This ethics test is provided to Texas Instruments employees, produced at the size of a business card, for them to carry around with them.

Source: www.ti.com/corp/docs/company/citizen/ethics/index.shtml

---

Stages in developing an ethical policy

An organization's core ethical values and standards underpin everything it does and guide employees on their business conduct. Senior managers need to establish clear processes to move their organizations forward. These normally involve the following actions.

1 *Set explicit ethical objectives supported by appropriate policies and procedures.* The organization needs to establish detailed codes of ethics and expectations, which are explicit, clearly written, and communicated to employees and other stakeholders. It is essential that following these codes becomes part of day-to-day activities.

2 *Show the support of senior management for these ethical policies and procedures.* Senior managers should demonstrate their commitment to implementing and enforcing ethical objectives by making them central to business planning. This can be achieved by building ethical success criteria into employee appraisal and the award of bonuses for meeting specific ethical targets. A clear disciplinary process should exist to punish breaches of ethical responsibilities.

3 *Develop supporting training programmes and courses.* To support ethical goals and policies, all employees and managers should participate in training courses where the organization's ethical objectives are carefully communicated. This training must help employees recognize and make ethical decisions. The same training may be offered to other stakeholder groups such as suppliers and distributors to make sure that all those involved in the marketing and distribution of an organization's goods or services act to the highest possible standards and do not undermine the organization's image.

4 *Monitor the success of ethical programmes.* It is an essential part of the success of ethical codes of practice that they are monitored with on a day-to-day basis. Many organizations create channels for employees to report on unethical conduct and promise anonymity for "whistle blowers" who report unethical conduct.

Did you know?

Unethical business practices: the Enron scandal

Enron, a US energy company founded in 1985, was one of the world's leading energy and communications companies but became a symbol of corporate fraud and corruption.

At the end of 2001 it was revealed that Enron had lied about its profits, concealing debts and "window dressed" its accounts. When the deception was discovered, the company was forced into bankruptcy, and a criminal investigation launched with several executives charged with fraud and money laundering. (See the case study on p. 171 for more details.)

The scandal also had a political dimension because of Enron's close links with the White House, as it had provided millions of dollars to finance President Bush's 2000 election campaign.

Case study

Ethical robots

An international team of scientists and academics is working on a "code of ethics" for robots as they become more sophisticated. Scientists believe the boundaries for human-robot interaction must be set before super-intelligent robots develop beyond our control. In Japan, human-like robots such as Honda's Asimo already walk on two legs, and more advanced versions are expected to be undertaking everyday domestic tasks and helping to care for elderly people in as little as 20 years.

The European Robotics Research Network (Euron) has examined the problems likely to arise as robots become smarter, faster, and stronger. Euron has identified key ethical concerns that include human control of robots, preventing illegal use, protecting data acquired by robots, and establishing clear identification and traceability of the machines.

The question is, what authority will be delegated to robots? For example, will robots be given the ability to execute lethal force, or any force, like crowd control? Already some robots are being employed on borders between countries. The desire for a code of ethics is a sign of reality finally catching up with science fiction. Ethical problems involving machines were predicted in the 1950s by the science fiction writer Isaac Asimov in his book *I, Robot*. In the book Asimov stated several laws of robotics:

"Robot may not injure human or, through inaction, allow human to come to harm.

Robot must obey human orders, unless they conflict with first law.

Robot must protect itself if this does not conflict with other laws."

Source: Adapted from *The Sunday Times*, 18 June 2006

Discussion points: be reflective

1 "Vision the future"—as a group, brainstorm how your lives will be affected by new technologies in the home, at school, and in the workplace.

2 Discuss the ethical and social issues raised by increasing application of new technologies.

Why do organizations consider setting ethical objectives?

Ethics in the market-place and the workplace are becoming increasingly important as organizations move into a period of intense competition for public and consumer support. Organizations are under pressure to develop and maintain policies on business ethics and social responsibility to ensure that they have the support of employees and other stakeholders.

To help create competitive advantage, most organizations want to be perceived as "ethical" as this brings with it potential commercial advantages. However, being an ethical business is a relatively subjective assessment, linked to the products or services the business offers, its founding vision, goals, and values, and its reputation among its stakeholders. Unethical behaviour and the resulting bad press may have a significant effect on sales, profits, and even the survival of a business. So organizations will seek to manipulate perception through good marketing and PR. Increasingly, organizations are putting in place ethical policies to prevent ethical breaches and preparing contingency plans to react to any breaches that might damage their reputation.

Did you know?

The Australian Wheat Board (AWB)

In October 2005, Australia's monopoly wheat exporter, the AWB, was accused of paying almost $300 million in bribes to former Iraqi leader Saddam Hussein in a so-called oil-for-food scandal. Within weeks of the scandal breaking, AWB lost more than a third of its market capitalization. Analysts estimated that it might also lose up to two thirds of its value if its wheat export monopoly was removed as a consequence of the massive damage to its reputation.

This provides a high-profile example of how poor management of so-called "soft" business ethics issues can rapidly translate into hard financial outcomes for shareholders.

It is usual for organizations to apply ethical approaches to all their business functions. For instance, a business may produce ethical guidelines and policies for HR, accounting practices and financial reporting, sales and marketing methods, production, and the treatment of intellectual property. These would be published:

- internally through departmental handbooks and procedures
- externally in annual reports and on business websites.

Ethical considerations have become a particularly important element of the corporate agenda, partly in response to the success of pressure groups, such as Greenpeace, and social campaigners, like Ralph Nader in the US, and partly in response to the success of organizations that have adopted more ethical and socially responsible policies.

Theory of Knowledge

Consider these ethical issues.

- You should not reduce business costs by exploiting cheaper resources in less economically developed countries.
- You should not sell products that are legal, but known to harm those who use them.
- You should not target children with advertising messages.
- You should not manufacture products that are used to kill.
- You should not "massage the truth" to ensure a sale.
- You should not be disrespectful to customers.

1 Prepare a definition of the concept of ethical behaviour.

2 Where do you believe ethics come from?

3 Which of the statements in the bullet list above are moral statements and which are conventions?

4 What evidence do you have, or would you want to have, to support your position?

5 Why do some economists and politicians believe that it is not the role of business to be ethical or socially responsible, but just to make a profit? Can this approach be justified?

Extension questions

1 a Explain the following ethical approaches:
   ● moral relativism
   ● moral absolutism
   ● self-interest theory
   ● utilitarianism.

   b Apply these different approaches to the six ethical issues outlined.

2 Prepare a plan for one of the following "Theory of Knowledge" essays, but with a focus on the business environment.

"Moral wisdom seems to be as little connected to knowledge of ethical theory as playing good tennis is to knowledge of physics." (Emrys Westacott). To what extent should our actions be guided by our theories in ethics and elsewhere? (TOK prescribed title, 2009).

Are reason and emotion equally necessary in justifying moral decisions? (TOK prescribed title, 2008).

Do questions like "Why should I be moral?" or "Why shouldn't I be selfish?" have definitive answers as do some questions in other Areas of Knowledge? Does having a definitive answer make a question more or less important? (TOK prescribed title, 2006).

Corporate social responsibility (CSR)

CSR describes an organization's duties to its internal and external stakeholder groups, which it may or may not willingly accept. In other words, it is the way an organization behaves towards its shareholders, customers, employees, suppliers, and society in general. The last stakeholder group is very broad, and therefore being socially responsible implies that the organization operates as a good corporate citizen, both locally and globally.

CSR is an umbrella term under which the ethical rights and duties existing between companies and society are discussed. So there is a distinct crossover between ethics and CSR, since CSR is often about doing ethical things. In both cases, the business attempts to maximize its positive impacts on stakeholders and society and minimize its negative impacts. However, the distinction between ethics and social responsibility rests on the idea that ethics are the concerns of individual managers and employees, whereas CSR is a concern of the entire organization.

All organizations will need to comply with legal requirements in day-to-day operations, but CSR means going beyond these legal duties and accepting that the sole function of a business is not just making profit for its shareholders. The question is whether acting responsibly is merely a marketing tool or whether it is a genuine part of an accepted set of values that guides all that a business does. Perhaps the acid test of a organization's CSR credentials is when the economy is in recession and survival is a priority. Does the business put social responsibilities before profit then?

Whether or not managers and owners genuinely believe in CSR or not, accepting the need to be responsible does appear to make good business sense. Indeed in recent years, more businesses than ever claim to put CSR before profit.

"Conducting your business in a socially responsible way is good business. It means that you can attract better employees and that customers will know what you stand for and like you for it."
Anthony Burns, CEO Ryder Systems (1944–)

Here are some suggested reasons why businesses should act in a socially responsible manner.

- It improves the image of the business and its goods and services and can provide it with competitive advantage.
- It attracts new customers and can create customer loyalty and repeat purchase behaviour. Research has shown that consumers are more likely to choose products they perceive as being produced in a socially responsible manner.
- It attracts like-minded employees to join the business and improves the motivation of existing and new staff. As a result, staff turnover may fall and productivity may increase.
- It reduces the possibility of negative publicity and also the likelihood that pressure groups will act against the organization's interests.
- It ensures goodwill among all stakeholder groups, which may prove beneficial at times of crisis. For example, suppliers and employees may be prepared to wait for payment during a cash flow crisis, because they feel a sense of loyalty to the organization, which has treated them well.

Like many other business decisions, acting responsibly should be considered as a long-term benefit, that may have short-term costs. The question is whether the business is willing to accept these short-term costs, especially when competitors are not.

Did you know?

Survey results

Published 30 April 2008

Ninety percent of Bangkok consumers would pay more for a product if it were created in a socially responsible manner. And more than one third (36%) said that the priority for corporate social responsibility (CSR) efforts should be educational support for young people to create a better future. These findings are part of a study of consumer attitudes released today by Vero Public Relations, a corporate communications consultancy with offices in Bangkok and Ho Chi Minh City. BMRS Asia, a leading Bangkok-based marketing research company, formulated and conducted the survey.

"The results tell us that social purpose as a corporate message has strong appeal to consumers in Bangkok and can help companies build relationships with consumers and other stakeholders," said Brian Griffin, managing director (Thailand and Vietnam).

Source: www.veropr.com/Public-Relations-News/Corporate-Social-Responsibility.php

Social auditing

The purpose of a social audit is to assess the impact of an organization's operations on its stakeholders and wider society. It is a similar process to a financial audit as the organization generates a set of social "accounts" that evaluate social performance against non-financial criteria and benchmarks. However, unlike financial auditing there are no legal obligations on an organization to carry out a social audit, although it helps the business address potential problems that might later lead to legal liability. For instance, a strong emphasis on

"Social auditing is the process whereby an organization can account for its social performance, report on and improve that performance. It assesses the social impact and ethical behaviour of an organization in relation to its aims and those of its stakeholders."

The New Economics Foundation

health and safety may mean the organization avoids prosecution for any accidents caused by the negligence of the organization and its employees. Social auditing should also result in more informed planning and better management.

Social audits are usually conducted by an independent group that prepares a published report assessing the organization's wider external impact. This report helps clarify social objectives and encourages the business to come up with action plans to sort out any deficiencies that have been identified.

Practical objectives and outcomes of social auditing

Of course, a business is not socially responsible just because it carries out a social audit of its operations. What counts is that it responds to the audit and changes business practices where necessary, even if that involves financial costs. Social auditing is increasingly being considered part of quality initiatives and integrated within management approaches, such as total quality management (TQM)—see p. 254.

In response to the findings of a social audit, a business may set action plans, objectives, and specific targets relating to:

- the environment, in areas including pollution, waste disposal, and resource depletion
- HR and the treatment of employees and other individuals in the distribution chain—this could cover issues relating to recruitment, promotion, health and safety, and remuneration
- energy usage, such as business practices to improve energy efficiency
- community programmes where the business helps organize or fund community-based initiatives in education, the arts, or the environment
- product and service quality, with emphasis placed on the durability and safety of products sold and the honesty of services provided.

HL

Changes in CSR over time

There is a clear debate as to the level and extent of CSR. As society changes and evolves, so does the pressure on organizations to conform to particular norms of behaviour. After all, businesses are made up of individuals who are also consumers and citizens, so businesses are reflections of those individuals' social values. Why should we expect less from a business in terms of social behaviour than we might expect from our immediate friends or neighbours? Indeed, businesses should play a role in the "stewardship" of our environment, since they enjoy the benefits of its resources. As concerns increase about resource depletion and environmental damage from production and consumption, so do the pressures on organizations to conform to defined codes of behaviour and good practice.

However, some economists and politicians argue that it is not an organization's role to act responsibly as this costs money and therefore reduces profit to shareholders. All businesses should be doing is being productively efficient by making the most efficient use of scarce resources. These politicians and economists believe that protection of the environment and individuals in the production chain is the role of governments and the legal system, not that of commercial organizations. This narrow viewpoint dates back to the classical economists, such as Adam Smith, and runs counter to the evidence that companies most celebrated for their high ethical standards and responsible behaviour, such as the Co-operative Bank (see below), are also among the most successful in commercial terms.

Data response exercise

Read the text below and answer the questions that follow.

Case study

In 1992, the Co-operative Bank plc in the UK became the world's first bank to introduce a customer-led ethical policy. Since then thousands of people have had the opportunity to choose a bank which will not do business with unethical companies and organizations.

Among its commitments, the Co-operative Bank made one not to invest in businesses that have core activities contributing to global climate change through the extraction or production of fossil fuels. The bank has also been actively addressing the climate change impact of its operations and encouraging others to do their bit too. It has even launched a new credit card offering lower interest rates on purchases made from a designated list of ethical companies. As a further incentive for the ethical consumer, half an acre of Brazilian rainforest is automatically purchased and protected in the name of the cardholder.

While it turns many businesses away because they conflict with its ethical policy, the Co-operative Bank equally seeks to support a whole range of organizations in the third sector—offering specialist banking and finance services to charities and voluntary organizations. The bank's charities team provides banking facilities and flexible loan finance to a range of organizations from small local charities to high-profile international charities.

Sources: www.coolearth.org and www.hippyshopper.com

The Co-operative Bank's full ethical policy can be read at:

www.co-operativebank.co.uk/partnership2001/pr/ethical_policy.html

Examination questions

1   Define the term corporate social responsibility (CSR)   [2 marks]
2   With reference to the Co-operative Bank, analyse the advantages and disadvantages of being socially responsible.   [8 marks]
3   Discuss why attitudes to CSR may change over time.   [10 marks]

Websites

You may find these websites interesting.

- www.nader.org: Ralph Nader
- www.neweconomics.org/gen/: New Economics Foundation
- www.ethicalconsumer.org/: Ethical Consumer online magazine.

Some interesting additional information and extension materials on CSR and social auditing can be found at:

- www.socialenterprisemag.co.uk
- www.prwatch.org: Centre for Media and Democracy
- www.fcsr.pl/fcsr_eng_nasipartnerzy_wbj.html: Polish CSR foundation

Stakeholders

People and organizations with an interest in a business are stakeholders in it. Let's look at internal stakeholders first. They are employees, managers, and shareholders.

- *Employees* are stakeholders because their career and livelihood depends on the organization's existence and development. If the organization is successful the employees hope to share in that success. For example, as an organization grows and expands its operations overseas it might offer career development opportunities in other countries for its existing workforce. For some employees, this can be a life-changing experience and a chance to see the world. Equally, if an organization is struggling the employees should perhaps be involved in decisions about what to do (although this is not always the case).
- *Managers* include the employees who run the business—so this group includes directors. Their jobs depend on the success of the organization and they would be keen to know and be rewarded if there were plans to sell the organization or float it on a stock market.
- *Shareholders* have the ultimate stake in a company because by holding shares they own it. Sometimes students interchange stakeholders and shareholders, but remember shareholders are a sub-set or example of stakeholders, one of several other groups who have an interest in its success. Also remember that some organizations are not companies, and do not have shareholder stakeholders.

In addition to internal stakeholders there are also a number of external stakeholders. Like the internal stakeholders, these are interested parties, individuals or businesses affected by an organization's operations—suppliers, customers, and various special interest groups.

- *Suppliers* are organizations that supply goods and services to a business, so they have an interest in its success and performance. If the business is making above-average profits for the industry, it could be that the suppliers are suffering by not getting the right price for their goods and services. Suppliers and their customers need to build good two-way relationships and realize that all businesses in the supply chain need to make a profit, but not at the expense of others. Some food processing companies in the UK, for example, are worried that their customers, the large supermarkets, are not allowing them to make sufficient profit to survive in the industry in the long term. However, if a supplier's customer is struggling to stay afloat the supplier may be prepared to offer payment holidays to help the customer survive—after all, this is better than losing a customer for ever.
- *Customers* need to know that their suppliers are going to remain in business for the long term; they can not afford to lose a supplier unless they know there are plenty of other organizations willing and able to supply their vital components or materials.

- *Special interest groups* among an organization's external stakeholders include the following.
  — Bankers. Banks and other lenders have a stake in businesses they help and support. They receive interest but the terms and conditions of any loan repayments may change if they feel a particular business is struggling. They may, for example, give "repayment holidays" to help a company with cash flow problems or, conversely, they may decide to increase interest charges on any new lending because they are worried about the organization's solvency. How a lender responds to a financial crisis often depends on how strong the relationship and trust is with the borrower.
  — Environmentalists. Businesses are increasingly aware of the financial gains that can come from being seen to minimize their effect on the environment. Not all businesses can be green but doing a little more than the competition can help an organization's market share. Environmentalists will lobby and pressure businesses and politicians and often sensible compromises can be achieved through discussion with these stakeholders.
  — Community action groups. Sometimes citizens and communities become engaged in protest at the way business and politicians dictate changes. Imagine this example. Planning permission is granted for a new lorry park in a village near a motorway. The lorry park may bring noise pollution and local people feel it has been imposed on them. Consulting with people in this village and the wider local community might help alleviate people's worries and bring some modifications to the original plan (although this is not always the case).

Many organizations also support their local communities and sponsor local charities, sports teams, and schools. These actions can help reduce tensions between stakeholders.

  — Competitors. Competitors have a specific interest in other businesses in their industry. They may be keen to know another organization's plans for expansion or development and how these plans may affect them. This may result in changes to the product line—Mars introduced an ice-cream version of its popular chocolate bar, then other chocolate makers copied this approach because they were concerned about losing market share.

HL

Stakeholder conflicts and conflict resolution

Stakeholders all have varying objectives and demands and it can be very difficult to reconcile competing needs and aspirations. For example, shareholders will want to maximize profitability while employees will want to maximize their wages, which will add to costs and reduce profits. Similarly, local communities will want to minimize pollution while the directors may want to grow the size of the business—which may add to pollution—and with it their salaries (as there appears to be some correlation between organization size and directors' pay). Conflicts and pressures between stakeholders are therefore commonplace. Happiness is when we can find a compromise or solution to the conflicting objectives that satisfies everyone—see Figure 1.3.

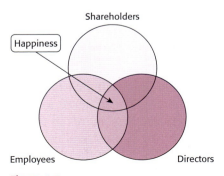

Figure 1.3

Solutions to stakeholder conflicts

Arbitration

In larger organizations, when workers and managers can not agree on changes to working practices, pay rates, or how staff are managed both sides can use the services of an arbitrator or reconciliation service. These independent and respected individuals or groups will have been asked to decide on what is fair from the evidence presented by both the company and the workforce representatives. At the start of the process or talks both sides can agree that the solution is binding on them, that is, they will accept whatever solution is recommended by the arbitrator.

Workers' councils

Sometimes it can be beneficial to set up a workers' council made up of representatives from all areas and all positions of responsibility in the organization. They meet regularly and provide a forum for discussing concerns and issues that specific groups may face. It also means that all internal stakeholders feel that they are being consulted about strategic changes that may be happening.

Stakeholder directors

These might be workers, bankers, or community group representatives. In some cases appointing a worker director can also produce similar results to a workers' council but perhaps more detailed discussions and information can be aired. Worker directors have to bear in mind that they may receive financially sensitive information about the company and must be careful how they use this knowledge to persuade the workforce that a certain compromise is the best solution they might get. Community directors can work in similar ways, perhaps gaining more local charitable donations in exchange for company expansion in a town. Bankers in some countries, such as Germany and Japan, often sit on the supervisory boards of directors. The banks may be shareholders as well as lenders. In this way, it's hoped that the interest of the company and the lenders are united and the banks are less likely to suddenly stop providing financial support.

Performance-related pay

Paying workers more if they improve their productivity can be a compromise solution to conflict, especially when a business is struggling to increase its efficiency and where workers want more money. The problems often reappear shortly after the pay rise though, as workers tend to get used to the new level of wages and then want more. Where there are cycles like this it can be because there is more underlying discontent about the management methods in the business and workers' dissatisfaction is not really because of low wages.

Share option schemes for workers

Instead of increasing costs by increasing workers' pay, shareholders and managers may agree to start a share option scheme, where workers can buy shares in the company at a discount. Assuming the value of the shares rises in the medium term, the workers' wealth will also rise when they sell their shares. Existing shareholders will see a dilution or reduction in the proportionate stakes but it is usually quite small.

Usually such schemes work in very large companies and often those listed on stock markets.

Competitors joining forces

Competitors may join forces to form distribution groups and gain negotiating power, for example with large retailers. In some industries where the power in the distribution channel is with the large retailers it pays for competitors to join together, possibly in a collusive way, and force the retailers to give them more for their produce. This has happened in food retailing, for example with milk supplied from dairy farmers to the supermarket groups in the UK.

Case study

BCW Inc.

BCW Inc. is a US engineering company based in Texas that employs 150 workers and makes specialist tools for the oil industry. The company makes profits of $18 million on sales of $250 million. Its managers want to grow the business by buying another competitor based in a town 20 miles away and bringing the two businesses together on one of the sites. The combined group would have sales of some $400 million but would only have profits of $20 million in the first year.

Several stakeholders have issues.

- Bankers are concerned about lending funds for the purchase, as the company has high debts already.

- Workers are concerned about job losses and wage cuts when the two businesses are brought together on one site.
- Shareholders are concerned that bank payments may mean less dividends (or income) for them.
- Local politicians are worried that one town will have a rise in unemployment because of the job losses.
- In the other town, people are worried about more noise pollution.

1 Evaluate possible solutions to reconcile the conflicts between stakeholders.

2 In general, do you think it is always possible or even sensible to find solutions to such conflicts?

External environment

Businesses do not operate in a "goldfish bowl"; they have to be alert to the external environment, reacting to possible threats and seizing opportunities as they arise. For example, businesses that have taken account of global warming concerns in their goods or services may have found that consumer preferences have switched in their favour. By identifying changing situations in the external environment, organizations that are flexible and responsive can plan ahead, get one step ahead of competitors who are slower to adapt, and gain market share from them.

As we have seen, the Co-operative Bank plc in the UK is an example of a bank that has re-branded itself as a greener and more caring bank; it also says that it will not invest in unethical companies wherever they are in the world. Through considering changes in society's attitudes, it devised a clever marketing strategy and is now attracting younger customers and is far removed from its previous rather old and tired image. A more general example involves organizations in Europe that planned ahead for the enlargement of the EU in 2002. The ones that set up factories in Poland were able to make substantial cost savings and still have the sales benefits of being in the new single market.

PEST analysis

A PEST analysis is a useful way to assess the impact of the external environment on an organization's future activities. This type of analysis is used in all areas of the business, so it is examined in later chapters in the context of different business activities (see p. 45–51 and 303–5). A PEST analysis considers four aspects to the external environment— political, economic, sociological, and technological factors.

Table 1.1 gives some examples.

Political issues include:	Economic issues include:
elections resulting in a new governing party	a rising exchange rate or interest rate
the country joining a trading bloc (for example, the EU)	economic growth slowing
a new law on competition being passed	unemployment rising
Sociological issues include:	**Technological issues include:**
more one-parent families	Internet security improvements for customer payments
more people interested in environmental issues	new composite materials
more people buying online	new machinery or patents developed by a competitor

Table 1.1 PEST factors

Once the analysis has been completed, the organization's decision makers need to use the information and consider what changes, if any, may need to be made to its objectives and strategies. A PEST analysis can be undertaken as a one-off event, but it should be something that is part of an ongoing process of continuous review, planning, and reaction. In international marketing (see p. 223–4) we use PEST analysis to consider the pros and cons of entering foreign markets.

The basic PEST analysis has been further extended with STEEPLE and PESTLE. The former categorizes the external environment into seven sections: social or cultural, technological, economic, environmental, political, legal, and ethical. PESTLE is similar, except it doesn't identify ethical issues as a separate area. Both of these alternative analytical tools will allow you to construct a matrix similar to the PEST method.

A business should consider what the influences are in the external environment and list them in a grid similar to Table 1.1. Don't forget that there are both threats (negatives) and opportunities (positives) when a business undertakes a PEST analysis. Indeed, there may be dozens of possible factors in each category. It can be constructed through consultation or can be undertaken by senior managers only— how it is done reflects on the organization's culture and its objectives.

Student workpoint 1.13

Be a researcher

Select a well-known company in your country and then make a list similar to the one in Table 1.1, outlining what key external issues the company faces. This activity can be more interesting if you discuss it with your friends.

We will now look in more detail at the four component areas of a PEST and see how the external environment can have an impact on businesses' objectives and strategies. Again, you will find similar sections, relating to specific areas of the business, in later chapters.

Political factors

This category can involve a range of areas, such as changes in employment, consumer, competition, and tax laws; or a new government, which may well bring new political objectives that the business world will need to evaluate, and which may also change the tax and spending system. A new government may also consider nationalizing (buying private businesses) or privatizing (selling state-run organizations). For example, the UK government buying up failing banks in 2008/9.

Employment law

This may cover changes to the role and operation of trade unions, changes to minimum redundancy payments, changes to minimum wage law—for example, in the UK the minimum wage is lower for 18-year-olds than for 22-year-olds. Discrimination laws, covering disabilities, sex, age, and race often exist.

Impact on an organization's objectives and strategies:

Changes in trade union rules about voting and strike action may make a business consider substitution of labour with capital (machinery) or even relocation from one country to one where unions are less influential. Discrimination laws and redundancy payments may add to the cost of employing labour (for example in the area of maternity rights) and in some cases make businesses wary of recruiting staff. There is also a positive to consider though—a business can make itself highly desirable to work for and improve motivation and productivity levels if it is seen to be a caring employer. The organization may even pay well above the legal minimum wage and offer attractive maternal and paternal childcare rights. In the UK, Marks and Spencer plc was considered to be one such company, although the extra benefits have been eroded in recent years.

Consumer law

Consumer laws may include consumer protection concerning faulty goods or those not fit for purpose; and cooling-off periods for consumers who sign credit agreements, for example for cars and TVs, and then want to change their minds.

Impact on an organization's objectives and strategies:

Businesses will need to ensure that production quality is high and that product safety is outstanding because accidents caused by faulty goods could cost a business significant sums if it is found to be liable. Indeed, more and more businesses advertise for goods in certain batches to be returned by consumers or shops. One example is when there's a fear that food products are contaminated. Better to be safe than risk destroying your brand name completely by inaction and bad publicity when an accident or major illness occurs, as in the case of contaminated Chinese baby formula milk in 2008.

Theory of Knowledge

Is the rise in product recall by large businesses a sign that they are taking liberties with their customers?

Competition and tax law

Competition laws and government organizations set up to ensure that fair trading exists in markets need to be monitored by businesses. Tax law, such as changes to corporation and purchase tax rates, will also have an impact on organizations and their consumers.

Impact on an organization's objectives and strategies:
Competition laws may mean that a business will not be allowed to buy a competitor as its market share would be too high as a result. Instead it may have to look at organic growth. If corporate tax rates rise, people thinking about starting up in business in some countries may consider setting up as sole traders or a partnership rather than as a limited company.

Tax rate rises may also influence international location and how much future investment there will be as retained profits (see p. 149) may be reduced.

Economic factors

There are various economic factors that businesses should be monitoring. Interest rates, exchange rates, growth rates, inflation, and unemployment are the key variables to follow as all these will have an impact on a business, whether negative or by offering opportunities. Remember that an organization's objectives and strategies need thinking about when factors change in the external environment.

Interest rates

The cost of borrowing by businesses is determined indirectly by the national interest rate set by the central bank of the organization's home country, for example the Federal Bank in the US or the European Central Bank for the EU single currency zone. Changes in national rates will influence the rates set by banks to businesses and individuals seeking loans. If the central bank raises rates, this will lead to loans becoming more expensive and savings becoming more attractive.

Impact on an organization's objectives and strategies:
Businesses will see this rise as an indication that demand for certain products, for example luxury goods, may fall. Some businesses offering these products might perhaps consider changing their product portfolio to more basic lines, moving away from the luxury end. They might consider changing to cheaper materials to keep prices low and encourage consumption. An interest rate change also adds to the costs of borrowing so, for example, if one of an organization's objectives is expansion via bank funding, this may be put on hold.

Exchange rates

As you will know, the exchange rate is the price of one currency in terms of another, for example $1= €1.2. Changes to the rate of exchange between currencies will affect the demand for exports and imports as the effective price of these goods and services will change.

Impact on an organization's objectives and strategies: A rising exchange rate will make exports more expensive for overseas citizens buying an organization's goods or services, so a business may well seek to cut prices (and profits) in the short run, to ensure that there is no change in the effective price being paid by customers overseas. This is more likely if the goods or services are price sensitive or elastic. If a business buys materials or components from a country whose currency is falling, it will find the cost of imports reduced. There can therefore be a benefit and/or a cost to a rising exchange rate. A business worried in the long run by a high exchange rate and falling sales may consider relocating to that country if sales there are a very significant proportion of total sales. Alternatively, it may start to focus its marketing strategies on countries where the exchange rate has not risen.

Economic growth

The size of an economy usually rises over time as more and higher-quality factors of production are used. Improvements in productivity create more output, employment, and income. As an economy grows, it creates greater demand for goods and services, and businesses will assess changes to the growth rates when planning production levels and product mix.

Impact on an organization's objectives and strategies:

When economic growth slows, growth in demand for goods and services will also slow and businesses will respond by reducing stocks and production levels, making surplus staff redundant and holding back on investment, for example. The effect of this reduction in staff can snowball and cause further falls in demand for goods and services. Businesses that are flexible and responsive can adapt quickly to changed economic conditions like these. Businesses that can't change their plans easily will struggle.

Inflation

This is the tendency for prices to rise in an economy. If average prices rise and incomes remain constant then people are generally worse off and may well demand fewer goods and services, especially if they are income-sensitive. Inflation also occurs in raw materials and therefore adds to some organizations' costs (known as cost-push inflation). This in turn cuts their profit margin, unless they can pass on this cost rise to their customers.

Impact on an organization's objectives and strategies:

With cost-push inflation, businesses may seek alternative or cheaper materials for their products or change the country of origin for supplies. If businesses can find a supplier in a country where their own exchange rate is high, this will help to reduce cost-push inflation. If the demand for their goods or services is price sensitive, businesses may consider identifying and supplying products that are less price sensitive (elastic), so that when they put prices up they don't lose too much business.

Unemployment

If the level of people without work rises, this can be an indicator that there is more potential labour to choose from when recruiting and that wage rates may fall as the unemployed are more keen to get back into work. Equally, if the numbers without work rise demand for goods and services in the economy may well fall, especially for brands at the top end. So changes to unemployment can influence costs for businesses and demand for their goods and services. A fall in unemployment has the opposite effect—raising demand and also the costs of labour.

Impact on an organization's objectives and strategies:
If unemployment falls dramatically and businesses find it difficult to recruit staff, they may consider various options. They might: first, re-train existing staff to be more flexible and multi-skilled; second, poach staff by paying higher wages than competitors pay; third, substitute labour with investment in more machinery: finally, in the long run, relocate to where more potential staff are—either in the home country or another country.

Sociological factors

This category might include changing lifestyle and buying habits or preferences, more one-parent families, and changing demographics and life expectancy.

You can see how the answers to questions about changing lifestyles could affect businesses. For example, are more people living alone than people used to a generation ago? Are they eating out more? Are people buying less from retail outlets and using home delivery and the Internet more?

Impact on an organization's objectives and strategies:
Lifestyle changes will change a company's marketing objectives and strategies—perhaps it will spend more on Internet advertising than on billboards and radio.

Demographic changes

Businesses will need to consider whether the area they work in is suffering from de-population or is becoming an ageing population.

Impact on an organization's objectives and strategies:
A business may need to relocate or recognize that it might need to recruit older people and have a strategy for retraining older members of staff.

Technological factors

Technological factors include new products, like the latest MP3 player or pc, and also the improvements in the production process, for example from the development of CAD (computer assisted design), CAM (computer assisted manufacture), and robots.

New products

Technology is being harnessed to increase the pace and range of product innovation for consumers—which in so doing also shortens product life cycles.

Impact on an organization's objectives and strategies:
Businesses need to invest in research and development (R&D) and ensure that if they are market-led they review their product portfolio and ensure that they understand their consumers' needs.

Improving production processes

CAD/CAM has improved production processes and efficiency and the Internet has opened up the global market-place. Material resource planning (MRP) and manufacturing resource planning (MRP2) software systems help businesses in aligning stock purchases to orders received and machine scheduling—eliminating down time and high stock levels.

Impact on an organization's objectives and strategies:

- CAD/CAM can help businesses to improve design.
- CAD/CAM can reduce the number of staff needed to monitor machines.
- The Internet means that small businesses may seek out export markets or strategies for identifying low-cost suppliers.
- Businesses can plan to minimize stock levels and release more working capital.

Organizational planning and decision making

By the end of this chapter, you should be able to:

- analyse and interpret business plans
- compare and contrast scientific and intuitive decision-making processes
- analyse and apply business planning tools
- apply a formal decision-making framework to a given situation
- construct and interpret decision trees and evaluate the value of decision trees as a decision-making tool
- prepare a SWOT analysis and use it to analyse an organization's position

Organizational planning tools

Planning is key to any business throughout its life. The process of strategic planning is about determining the direction of a business and setting overall goals and targets. By contrast, a business plan provides the detailed route map to take that business in the desired direction.

A business plan

A business plan sets out how the organization will meet its corporate objectives. It involves stepping back from day-to-day operations and asking where the business is heading and what its priorities should be. The plan applies to a specific period, potentially over several years, and is a detailed statement of the short-term and long-term objectives of the business with an analysis of the resources needed to achieve these objectives. It should be regularly reviewed and, if necessary, updated.

Responsibility for delivering all the elements of the business plan will be allocated to key individuals in the organization, such as department heads. Success will be measured against clearly stated performance targets set out in the plan.

A business plan is usually combined with detailed budgets to finance the required activities.

The purpose of a business plan

A business plan is drawn up to:

- support the launch of a new organization or business idea
- attract new funds from banks, grant providers, or venture capitalists
- support strategic planning
- identify resource needs
- provide a focus for development
- work as a measure of business success.

Risk of new business failure is very high—up to 80% over the first two years in some sectors. Entrepreneurs may have plenty of original ideas, but they often lack business experience. If banks are to lend funds to new businesses, they want to be confident they will be paid back with interest. So they will only want to lend to those businesses with a low risk of failure. To persuade a bank to lend it money, a business needs to prove that it has done its homework, knows where it is going, and how it is going to get there. In other words, it needs a plan.

A business plan is likely to contain the following details and elements:

- the purpose of the business—where it is going, its mission, aims, and objectives
- a short description of the business opportunity—what will be sold, why, and to whom?
- market research on the need for the goods or services, the likely level of demand and evidence that there is a profit to be made—identifying who the target customer is and the level of competition for this customer
- a list of key personnel and their skills, and any recruitment and training needs
- financial plans outlining the financial security of the business, including a cash flow forecast, a budgeted profit & loss account, and any loan requirements
- marketing projections indicating estimated sales, and market share or market growth predictions
- the marketing mix with pricing strategies, plans for advertising and promotion and identified distribution channels
- business operations—an outline of the business location and premises, production facilities, and management information systems.

A good business plan may be of significant use to stakeholders. For potential investors it will provide a basis for assessment of risk by detailing how the business will use a bank loan or investment. For employees it will identify specific objectives and goals and provide a focus for action and a source of motivation. For suppliers, analysis of the business plan may identify whether there are likely to be long-term advantages from a commercial relationship with the business. For the local community and pressure groups, access to the business plan will provide the basis for assessing the organization's role in the community.

Decision-making framework

Decision making is at the core of business and management. Every decision is associated with a risk. Although risk can never be removed, the purpose of using business tools and techniques is to try to minimize that risk. This is really central to any business course.

Decision making is likely to involve one, or a combination, of:

- experience
- a hunch—using intuition or gut feeling
- scientific data or facts.

Experience

Decisions are made by every employee. If a decision is routine and familiar there is little point in further research as it would simply waste time. The experience of the decision maker is likely to be enough, because similar decisions have been made many times in the past. An example of a routine decision could be the ordering of supplies.

A hunch

Decisions based on intuition or gut feeling would seem to be rather risky and impulsive. Entrepreneurs may make decisions that appear to be little more than inspired guesswork, yet they often seem to work. Why should this be the case? In fact, the hunch is often built on a solid foundation of prior experience of similar situations and a thorough understanding and knowledge of the market-place.

There are several advantages of this more informal approach.

● It is useful where little scientific data is available.
● It may lead to creative solutions and the development of a USP.
● It may be necessary in dynamic, changing market-places.

Scientific data or facts

There are certain strategic decisions that are crucial to the success of the business, such as the development and sale of new products or services, expansion of the business, and relocation. These decisions guide the long-term direction of the business, are made by senior management, and involve significant risk. They tend to involve unfamiliar situations or problems and will require the gathering of research data to allow an objective approach. Scientific decision making provides a logical and rational basis for business decisions and, therefore, reduces risk.

Decisions based on scientific decision making are more formalized, involving a structured process, which may take weeks, months, or even years. As a result, the outcome is likely to be of a higher quality. The disadvantages are that the data may be inaccurate or out of date by the time it is collected and analysed, or possibly unavailable if the situation is unfamiliar or unique. The whole process of gathering data is likely to be very time consuming and potentially expensive.

Theory of Knowledge

1 Define intuition.
2 Should an entrepreneur ever rely on intuition when making strategic decisions about marketing approaches, HR, or financial requirements?
3 Discuss whether the five whys decision-making technique (see p. 64) can help explain the link between intuition and knowledge.

Extension

Prepare a plan for one of the following "Theory of knowledge" essays, but with a focus on the business environment.

When should we trust our senses to give us truth?

Evaluate the role of intuition in different areas of knowledge.

A formal decision-making framework involving the gathering of data and a scientific approach to this is shown in Figure 1.4 and described below.

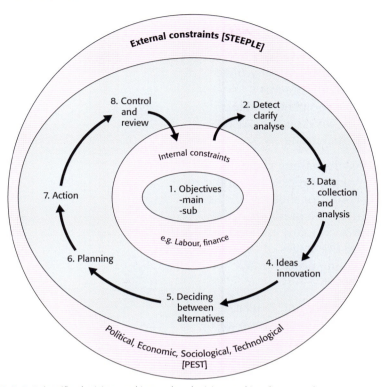

Figure 1.4 Scientific decision making – the decision-making framework

Phases of the decision-making framework

- *Set objectives.* Organizations set their main, strategic objectives, such as market growth, but also include less important sub-objectives, such as targets for specific products or product lines.
- *Clarify the present situation.* Before a decision can be made, a business needs to analyse its present position and identify any underlying issues and causes that need to be addressed. Ways of doing this might be to use methods such as the five whys technique (see p. 64) and the fishbone technique (see p. 57).
- *Gather information.* Collect relevant data to support decision making using primary and secondary market research. The data collected is then analysed using business techniques and tools such as ratio analysis (see p. 174), break even analysis (see p. 243–247) and SWOT analysis (see p. 66).
- *Gather ideas and innovation.* Involve relevant individuals and teams in the process of identifying possible tactical and strategic approaches to the problem. This can include creativity techniques such as brainstorming. This is a crucial stage in developing new product opportunities.
- *Decide between alternatives.* Analysis of data often results in several possible opportunities and options. Not all of these can be implemented as businesses possess limited resources. Therefore, businesses will have to select the options that provide the best return and/or have the least risk. Techniques that can be used at this stage include decision trees, forecasting, and investment appraisal.

- *Work on planning.* The business will need to decide how best to implement the chosen strategic option or options. This will involve activities including setting budgets, analysing workforce requirements, and marketing planning.
- *Take action.* Putting the strategy into action will involve implementing an effective market mix. The organizational structure is important here. Many responsibilities will have to be delegated. Change may be resisted by the staff, unless they have been adequately involved in the decision-making process.
- *Control and review.* Progress is checked against the plan. Budgets and forecasts are reviewed and variances are investigated. At the end of the year, the business will draw up final accounts.

Every time the organization completes a decision-making cycle, it acquires experience. The end of a decision-making process is also the beginning of the next as organizations will set and/or modify objectives in response to the success or failure of the previous cycle. If the organization has completed a similar process many times it will not have to spend as much time repeating the stages of the decision-making cycle. In fact the decision-making process may become intuitive, rather than formalized.

Most decisions are constrained or limited by internal and external factors. Internal constraints are controllable by the organization and include factors such as labour and finance shortages. To reduce, or even to remove, these constraints the organization can prepare a staffing plan and actively recruit new staff and train existing staff. To overcome a lack of finance, the organization can approach a bank for a loan, find a business partner, or sell assets.

External constraints, however, are uncontrollable by the organization and are the result of interaction with the external environment (STEEPLE factors). Although it is possible for the organization to make contingency plans to minimize the impact of the external environment, in practice there is nothing the organization can do to prevent the external changes happening. For instance, changes in the economic or business cycle cannot be influenced by individual organizations, however large.

Examiner's note

The decision-making framework:

- is an excellent tool to help structure examination responses, especially when answering the strategic questions on the case study paper

- is extremely useful to support business projects and coursework
- provides a perfect structure for preparing revision notes—the entire business course can be linked to at least one element of the framework.

HL
There are a number of other scientific techniques that may assist managers in making more effective decisions. For the business and management syllabus, we need to know the following:

- the fishbone (cause and effect) diagram—see p. 57
- decision trees (probability diagrams)—see p. 58
- force field analysis—see p. 84.

This section also considers the five whys technique (see p. 64) as this can support other decision-making methods.

The fishbone

The fishbone diagram (also known as an Ishikawa or cause-and-effect diagram) is a diagram that attempts to identify the causes of an event. It gets its name from the fact that the diagram resembles the skeleton of a fish (see Figure 1.5).

The diagram was created by Kaoru Ishikawa, who pioneered quality management processes in the Kawasaki shipyards, and became one of the founding fathers of Japanese modern management (see p. 255–257).

Fishbone analysis provides a structured way to help think through all possible causes of a problem. Causes in the fishbone diagram are usually arranged into four or six major categories, although this can be adapted to the individual situation. While these categories can include any factors, it is common to include:

- six Ms: manpower, methods, machinery, materials, mother nature (environment), measurements (recommended for manufacturing goods)
- equipment, policies, procedures, and people (recommended for delivering services).

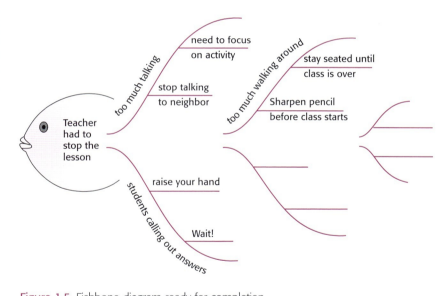

Figure 1.5 Fishbone diagram ready for completion

This is the stepped process for using a fishbone diagram.

1 *Identify and agree on the problem.* Write down the exact problem. Identify the staff involved, and when and where the problem occurs. Write the problem on the right-hand side of the diagram. Draw an arrow across the paper horizontally to the problem, providing a framework to develop ideas.
2 *Establish the major causal factors involved.* Identify the factors that may be root causes of the problem and merit further investigation. Draw lines off the spine for each of the factors and label the branches. These may include factors such as the people involved with the problem, machinery employed, methods used, and materials used. These factors may be established using a brainstorming exercise.

3 *Identify possible causes.* Where a cause is complex, there may be several sub-causes. For each root cause identified, ask: why is this cause happening? Establish possible related sub-causes. These are then shown as smaller lines coming off the "bones" of the fish. The five whys technique (see p. 64) would be useful here.

4 *Analyse the diagram.* Investigate the most likely causes identified on the diagram, which may involve further, more extensive and detailed research. This should help clarify whether the causes are correct.

Once the diagram is completed, the business will put into action policies to address the underlying causes of the problem identified. For an application of the fishbone to total quality management (TQM) see p. 254.

Decision trees

A decision tree is a diagram setting out the key features of a decision-making problem. Examiners really like decision trees. Setting a decision tree question is relatively easy and can be adapted to most papers and time frames. There are also two obvious follow-up questions. First, candidates may be asked to examine the advantages and disadvantages of using decision trees; second, they may be required to examine non-numerate or additional information, other than that on the decision tree, which can be used to support a decision.

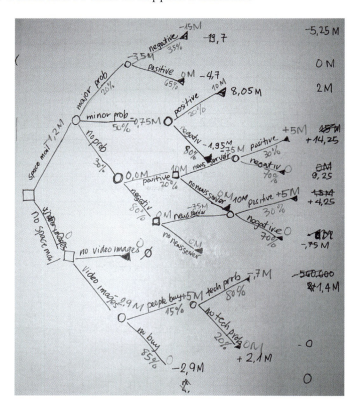

Students are sometimes worried by decision trees because they look complicated and can contain plenty of information and lots of numbers. The thing to remember when learning to construct and interpret decision trees is that, however detailed they look, they merely repeat the same process over and over again through the diagram. If we start with this basic process, the decision tree suddenly begins to look easier to manage.

Constructing a decision tree

Decision trees are particularly helpful in situations supporting complex business decisions or problems, involving more than one decision.

A decision tree is constructed **from left to right** with **events** laid out in the sequence in which they occur, but the **calculation of financial results** is always from **right to left**. There are two major elements in the diagram.

Squares represent decision points, which are under the control of the business. The lines that come out of each square show all the available options that can be selected at that decision point. In Figure 1.6, the business can chose between launching product A or product B. Along the line is the cost of that decision—in this case, the cost of launching each product.

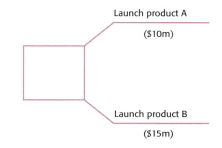

In most cases there will always be another possible decision option—that of doing nothing at all. Although this option may not have an immediate direct cost, it certainly may have a negative outcome. A failing business left to carry on failing may end up with bankruptcy of the owner and liquidation of the business, unless some miracle happens.

Circles represent probability or chance nodes. These show various circumstances that have uncertain outcomes. The lines that come out of each circle denote possible outcomes of that uncontrollable circumstance. In Figure 1.7 on p. 59, the possible outcomes are the success or failure of the new product. Above each line in the decision tree are the best estimates for the probability of each of the different outcomes happening—in this example, success or failure. These probabilities are shown either as a percentage or a decimal, for example 80% or 0.8.

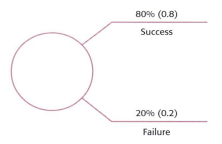

All the probabilities must add up to 100% or 1, as one of the outcomes must happen, for example the new product will fail or succeed. In other words, there is a 100% probability of something happening.

How does a business establish the probability of an event happening?

It is difficult to establish accurate probabilities of an event, especially if that event is beyond the control of the business itself. However, estimates of probability can be achieved through market research or experience. Despite this, the fact that probabilities may be little more than educated guesses is one of the weaknesses of decision trees.

Each branch of the decision tree will have an **outcome** or financial return. For example, the following outcomes are predicted for the launch of products A and B.

- Success of product A will increase profit by $20 million.
- Success of product B will increase profit by $30 million.
- Failure of product A will lead to a loss of $2 million.
- Failure of product B will only increase profit by $6 million.

Calculations are always made from right to left in the diagram.

A calculation is required of the average outcome given the probabilities. This is a weighted average, because the outcome is multiplied by the probability of that result happening. In decision trees, these are referred to as **expected values (EVs)** and are shown at every probability node. Figure 1.6 shows an example.

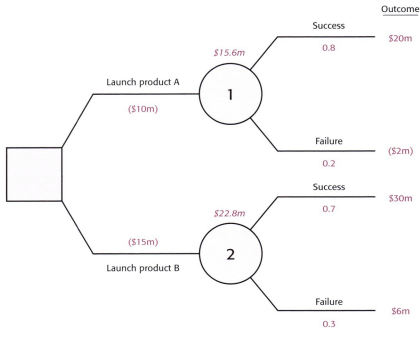

Figure 1.6

Node 1: Calculation of EV

> Outcome × probability
> $20m × 0.8 = $16m
> ($2m) × 0.2 = ($0.4m)

The EV (or weighted average) is shown by adding the two results together.

> EV = $16.0m + ($0.4m) = $15.6m

This result is put next to the probability node 1.

Node 2: Calculation of EV

> Outcome × probability
> $30m × 0.7 = $21m
> $6m × 0.3 = $1.8m
> EV = $21m + $1.8m = $22.8m

This result is put next to the probability node 2.

Finishing the diagram
The construction of the decision tree is almost complete.

Product A: To achieve an EV of $15.6m, the business has had to spend $10m. Therefore, the cost must be deducted from the EV to find the final profit:

$15.6m − $10m = $5.6m (net EV)

Product B: To achieve an EV of $22.8m, the business has had to spend 0$15m. Therefore the cost must be deducted from the EV to find the final profit:

$22.8m − $15m = $7.8m (net EV)

These net EVs are transferred to the diagram next to the appropriate line coming out of the decision node.

Examiner's note
Don't try to complete all your calculations on the actual diagram. Number the nodes and show your working below the diagram and transfer the final result to the diagram.

To complete the diagram, the decision maker indicates which of the decisions is to be rejected on purely financial grounds, by drawing two parallel lines through the rejected decision or decisions. The last important addition is a **key** explaining the major elements of the diagram. (This is shown in Figure 1.7, which is the final diagram.)

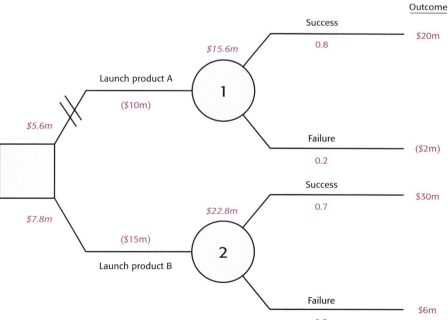

Figure 1.7

Student workpoint 1.14

Be a researcher—calculate

Copy the diagram below onto paper.

Then:

1 Fill in the missing probabilities on the decision tree (see next page).

2 Calculate the expected values at nodes 1 and 2.

3 Calculate the net EV for product A and product B at decision point A.

4 Reject the product that gives the lower net EV.

5 Complete the decision tree by adding a key.

Extension

1 Individually, construct a decision tree with all information included—this will be the model answer.

2 Delete some of the data, but leave sufficient information for a partner to complete the tree.

3 Swap the incomplete diagrams with a partner and then solve.

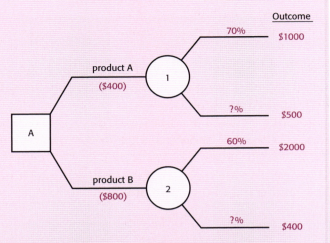

4 In your pairs identify as many other issues as you can that a business would consider when deciding whether to launch a new product.

Advantages of using decision trees

Decision trees encourage a rational, scientific decision based on hard data, for these reasons.

● The process tree requires a formal and thorough examination of an issue, including the identification of options, probabilities, and consequences.

● It forces managers to quantify outcomes.

● It presents a visual representation of decision options.

● It supports a logical planning process.

● Communication and cooperation between departments is improved.

● It can be used to generate new ideas.

Limitations of using decision trees

● The process can be time consuming and expensive.

● The information gathered may be inaccurate as the process relies on estimates.

● The external environment is constantly changing, which may invalidate findings.

● The results are purely quantitative and may ignore more important qualitative information, such as motivation.

● EVs are weighted averages of outcomes and the values presented can be statistical results which may not happen in practice.

● Not all alternatives may be identified.

Remember…

● A decision tree is simply a tool to help a business with its strategic decision making.

● To complete the analysis, additional financial and non-financial information needs to be considered.

Putting the pieces together

A decision tree can contain more than one decision and, therefore, more than one decision point. In this case, treat the section of the tree following each decision point as a separate "mini decision tree". Work backwards from right to left to each decision point. The net EV at the decision point becomes an outcome value for the preceding section of the decision tree.

So in Figure 1.8, treat the diagram as if it were three separate diagrams with decision points A, B and C as the three starting points. Work from the right and calculate the net EVs at decision points B and C. When you have calculated these values they become one of the outcomes for the first mini tree starting at decision point A.

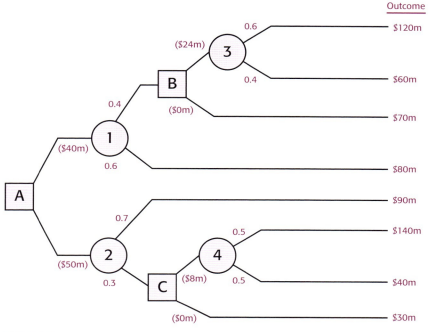

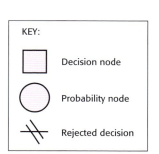

Figure 1.8

Examination questions

Exercise with more than one decision point

1 Using the decision tree in Figure 1.8, decide which option should be selected on purely financial grounds. Show full working to support your choice.   [*12 marks*]

2 Explain four limitations of using a decision tree.   [*8 marks*]

Case study

Primature Inc.

Following a 13% increase in orders over the last six months, Primature Inc. is considering the expansion of its production facilities. It is presently producing at 98% of its production capacity. The production manager is examining two expansion options.

Option 1—The construction of an extra production line in the present factory building at a cost of $1.5 million. This will increase capacity by 16%.

Option 2—The construction of an additional factory unit at a cost of $3.5 million. The new building could be designed to allow for cell production and just in time (JIT) management. This would cut costs and provide additional future production flexibility and HR advantages. Capacity could be increased by a maximum of 40%.

The recent increase in orders is a result of improved economic conditions. However, the finance director is not convinced it is wise to invest in either option before it is clear that the increase in economic growth will be maintained. He believes unit price and revenues can be increased at current output, provided economic growth remains constant or improves. Economists differ on their forecasts for the next five years. Of those asked, 40% believe that the economy will strengthen over the next five years; 30% believe that average growth over that period will remain constant; while 30% believe there will be a decline in economic growth. The production manager estimates the following profit or loss outcomes for each of these predictions.

	Option 1 (new line)	Option 2 (new factory)	Option 3 (no expansion, increase unit price)
	$ million	$ million	$ million
Economy strengthens	6	9	4
Constant economic growth	3	4	3
Declining economic growth	1	2	−1

1 **a** Construct a fully labelled decision tree showing Primature Inc.'s options with the financial costs and outcomes for each option.   *[3 marks]*

   b Using your decision tree, decide which option Primature Inc. should select on purely financial grounds. Show full working to support your choice.   *[4 marks]*

2 Describe three benefits of using decision trees.   *[3 marks]*

3 Evaluate the extent to which additional non-financial and financial factors may support, or not support, the choice of option selected for Primature Inc. in your answer to question 1b.   *[10 marks]*

The five whys technique

Decision making may first require an approach to problem solving. A frequent mistake in business is to try to solve the symptom of a problem, rather than find the root cause.

The five whys technique is an attempt to establish the root cause of a problem and to provide the basis for decisions to address that root cause. This technique is based on the principle that the most obvious cause of a problem may not always be the most important.

To establish the root causes of a problem we keep asking the question "Why?" until the cause is exposed. This can normally be achieved in five steps.

Why?
Why?
Why?
Why?
Why?

Case study

Five whys—an illustration

A student fails to meet the school deadline for the final copy of the business and management internal assignment. The head of department is angry and calls the student into her office. Various punishments are being considered, but the teacher is concerned, because the student is normally conscientious. What happens, though, if we use the five whys technique to consider the problem?

Why did the student miss the deadline for the internal assessment?

Because he was not happy with the quality of the finished project.

Why was the student not happy with the quality of the finished project?

Because he did not have the time to complete it properly.

Why did he not have the time to complete it properly?

Because he had three other assignments to complete in the same week.

Why did he have three other assignments to complete in the same week?

Because the teachers of these subjects did not know about the other deadlines.

Why did the teachers of these subjects not know about the other deadlines?

Because no plan of the entire programme had been made by the coordinator mapping these deadlines against each other, and the teachers had not discussed deadlines with each other or tutors.

As you can see from this simple illustration, at first it appears the student is solely to blame for missing a deadline. In fact, there were other contributory causes. It may not excuse the student from any blame at all, as he may not have planned his own time effectively. However, the difficulties for students could be reduced if all deadlines were identified, and if staff involved in setting deadlines ensured that deadlines did not clash or put too much pressure on students. Some of the blame appears to rest with the school and the coordinator.

Solution

After several meetings the teachers and coordinator produce a "map" of IB deadlines, published in the school calendar and available on the school website. Parents are also sent a copy. These deadlines are explained during the induction programme for IB Diploma Programme students.

Student workpoint 1.15

Be a thinker

Can you think of some problems at your school that may not be as clear cut as they appear? Identify them and use the five whys technique to see if you can reveal any underlying problems.

Many business problems could be examined in a similar fashion. Here are some examples from different businesses.

- Why have sales of a shop's best-selling line fallen for the last three months?
- Why has staff turnover risen?
- Why has productivity in one factory fallen 20% in the last year?

SWOT analysis

Decision makers must be clear about the organization's capabilities and what aspects make it distinctive. This requires a detailed examination of the market-place and the organization's position in it. One useful tool is a SWOT analysis. SWOT stands for strengths, weaknesses, opportunities, and threats. A SWOT analysis is an important but simple tool for auditing the strategic position of a business and then generating strategic alternatives from a situation analysis. It can be part of a business plan and may be used in conjunction with complementary business tools, such as PEST analysis and Porter's five forces analysis (see p. 190–2).

SWOT analysis provides a snapshot of the business position at a specific point in time and helps in the process of improving performance. The SWOT analysis headings provide an excellent framework and starting point for business in its strategic planning, competitor evaluation, marketing planning, and product development. For this reason, you will find further examples of the use of SWOT analysis in later chapters in this book.

	Positives	**Negatives**
Internal factors	Strengths * * * *	Weaknesses * * * *
External factors	Opportunities * * * *	Threats * * * *

Figure 1.9 SWOT analysis grid ready for completion

Examiner's note

It is common for students to identify correctly that strengths and weaknesses are internal factors, and opportunities and threats are external factors. However, it is also then a frequent mistake to include factors in the opportunities section that are, in fact, internal factors. For instance, a student may say that the business has the opportunity to enter new markets. The problem is that this is under the control of the business itself and is not an external factor. To make the answer more accurate, it can be split into two elements: the availability of new and growing markets (external factor) and the fact that the business has the financial strength and human resources to take advantage of the opportunity (internal factor).

Completing a SWOT analysis is very simple, and is frequently used in training sessions as it helps build teams and produce consensus on the way forward. A SWOT analysis is normally presented as a grid, comprising four sections, one for each of the SWOT headings (see Figure 1.9 on p. 66). Strengths or weaknesses are the internal aspects of the company and opportunities or threats are the external situational factors. Strengths and opportunities are positive factors. Weaknesses and threats are negative factors. For example, strengths can act as a basis for building competitive advantage, and weaknesses may hinder this. Opportunities can provide growth potential, whereas threats may lead to lower sales or even business failure.

As strengths and weaknesses are internal factors they are under the control of the business itself. They tend to describe the present situation. For example, one strength of the business may be an excellent brand image and one weakness a poor location. Both of these situations are controllable by the business.

On the other hand, as opportunities and threats are external factors they are outside of the control of a business. They tend to describe the immediate future. For example, an opportunity could be the growth of online shopping, which suits a business with a strong web presence. A threat could be a new competitor in an important existing market or a legal change that will increase production costs.

Adding weighting criteria to each factor in the SWOT analysis can increase the validity of the analysis.

Here are examples of issues contained in each of the four SWOT sections.

Strengths
These can be anything that is favourable for the business, such as:

- a stable financial position: good cash flow, profits, and few liabilities
- a skilled and motivated workforce
- brand and customer loyalty
- a reputation for quality goods and services
- excellent access to new technologies
- excellent location with good communications
- a dominant market position
- good relationships with stakeholders.

Weaknesses
These are areas of the business that require attention and an honest and realistic assessment, so that their effect may be minimized through strategic action. They could include things done badly or, alternatively, things done better by competitors. Some examples are:

- weak financial position restricting business options, for example high gearing (see p. 177)
- poorly trained workforce
- high staff turnover
- low productivity
- poor public perception of the business and its goods or services

- old and badly maintained machinery and no spare production capacity
- bad company location with inadequate transport links
- limited research and development with little innovation
- obsolete stock tying up capital
- high rejection rates caused by poor quality
- poor access to distribution channels
- weak management.

Opportunities

These are factors that provide growth potential. They include:

- increasing globalization and access to new markets
- technological changes that reduce production and marketing costs
- growing market demand resulting from positive economic conditions
- cuts in tax or interest rates
- demographic change positively affecting future demand patterns
- availability of skilled labour
- vulnerability or closure of the main competitor
- fashion changes that make the organization's products desirable
- liberalization of markets with fewer rules and regulations.

Threats

These are factors that have the potential to have negative effects on the business and are barriers to development. They are issues that the organization must protect itself from and include:

- changing customer tastes and preferences away from the organization's products or services
- new legislation that increases costs or limits production
- negative economic trends, possibly leading to recession
- technological advances that remove an organization's USP
- new competition in the market-place
- declining sales in the organization's target market
- rises in tax or interest rates
- new distribution channels
- demographic changes negatively affecting future demand patterns
- climate change
- increases in raw material costs.

The effectiveness of a SWOT analysis depends very much on how it is organized, managed, and prepared. It is possible that the individuals taking part in the process are unable to be objective and unwilling to confront some of the organization's weaknesses, especially if they might be responsible. In other words, like all business tools, it is only as good as the people using it.

A SWOT analysis can be used to assess an organization's:

- position in the market
- service level, product range, or brands
- new business, and new product ideas and innovations
- strategic opportunities, such as expansion or relocation
- potential for merger and acquisition
- investment opportunities.

Once a SWOT analysis is complete, managers can use it to generate strategic options. In the planning process, it is likely that the business will:

● use its strengths to take advantage of its opportunities
● minimize its weaknesses to reduce the significance of the threats.

Student workpoint 1.16

Business investigation

Conduct a SWOT analysis on one, or more, of the following.

1   your school or college

2   a well-known brand or product

3   an organization or company known to you.

You should research this thoroughly and produce supporting data to justify your findings, for example market share, competitors, economic facts and figures.

The relationship between SWOT and PEST analysis

PEST analysis is a method to group and classify the external environment (see p. 46–51). It is this external environment that provides the opportunities and threats for a business. To carry out a successful SWOT analysis, it is usually necessary to have conducted a PEST analysis first, especially with larger and more complex businesses. However, even when conducting a SWOT for a smaller, localized business, a PEST analysis can identify significant issues that might otherwise be missed.

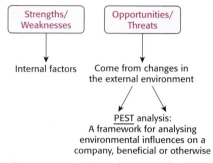

Figure 1.10 SWOT and PEST analysis

1.4 Growth and the impact of globalization

By the end of this chapter, you should be able to:

- apply the concepts of economies and diseconomies of scale to business decisions
- evaluate the relative merits of small versus large organizations
- explain the difference between internal and external growth and evaluate methods of achieving a firm's growth objectives
- apply a formal decision-making framework to a given situation
- analyse franchises and evaluate the use of franchises as a growth strategy
- explain the value of the Ansoff matrix and apply the growth strategies to a given situation
- analyse the role of multinationals in the global business environment and evaluate their impact on the host country
- explain the impact of membership of a regional trading bloc on business operating in the country

Growth and evolution

Economies and diseconomies of scale

As businesses grow in size they begin to benefit in a number of ways from falling average costs (unit costs). They can spread their costs, such as rent, over a wider range of units and therefore the average costs begin to fall. This is known as gaining benefits from **economies of scale**. Here are some other examples.

- If a business orders a lot from suppliers it may be able to get bulk purchase discounts.
- If more units are ordered from suppliers transport costs will be lower on average.
- As a business grows its managers are able to specialize in certain roles, so they become experts and therefore more efficient. When the business was smaller the managers probably had to take on lots of different roles. They may not have been very fast or skilled at doing some of these and so they were less productive.
- Banks may well give a large business lower interest rates on loans than they offer small businesses.

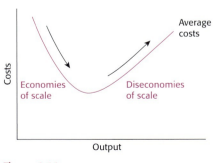

Figure 1.11

As businesses grow in size there is a point where average costs begin to rise—inefficiency begins to appear—because of **diseconomies of scale**. This could happen for these reasons.

- Communication breakdowns can arise in larger organizations.
- Decision making slows down as more people become involved, causing inefficiency and lost market opportunities.
- Motivation of workers falls and productivity drops causing costs to rise—often workers in large organizations feel they have no influence or importance and lose interest in working effectively.

Student workpoint 1.18
Business investigation

1 Explain what economies and diseconomies of scale may occur for:
 a the local newspaper shop
 b a regional radio company
 c a government-run bus company
 d a state-controlled airline.

2 What might happen to average costs if a business located in Argentina sets up a second factory in China? Explain the possible economies and diseconomies of scale from this decision.

The owner of a small business may think twice about whether to expand the business or stay small when he or she thinks about economies and diseconomies of scale.

Should I expand my business or stay small scale?
Here are some arguments for staying small.

- Many small businesses decide not to expand but instead to stay small because they prefer the friendly atmosphere of a work environment where everyone knows the boss and respects each other.
- There may well be more manageable levels of debt if the business is kept small. Large businesses need more funds so debt levels and personal investment may be much greater and more worrying for the owner.
- Small business people often make poor directors of larger organizations. Different skills are needed to lead a large organization. To take one example, can the person talk effectively in public, perhaps to large groups of investors?

On the other hand, there are arguments for expanding and growing the business.

- The business may become less dependent on one product or one market, for example the business might start to export.
- Career opportunities for the workforce grow and new managers appear who can help run the organization.
- If business conditions become tougher, there is less worry in a large business about sacking people (whereas in a small business the colleagues may be old friends).
- Owners of a business that expands can increase their wealth in the future. A larger and more successful company will sell for a lot more money when they want to retire.
- If a business doesn't expand, it may be squeezed out of the market completely. The argument is, "You can't stay still"—all businesses need to grow to survive.

71

Student workpoint 1.19

Business investigation

Should the businesses in the following situations expand or stay small scale? Explain your reasons.

1   A scientist in Brazil discovers a local plant makes a good headache cure and he now grows and sells it to a local shop. He is 51.

2   A café owner and shopkeeper in a small rural town in France is wondering whether to buy another café in the next town.

3   A director of a popular local newspaper is thinking of turning it into a national paper.

4   A driving instructor is thinking about expanding her business and hiring a second instructor.

Internal (organic growth) and external growth

Internal growth strategies will mean, for example, that a business can consider:

●   increasing sales by recruiting more agents, advertising more, or cutting prices—even if profits fall in the short run

●   developing better production techniques so that the business can produce its products at lower costs and therefore it can cut prices (but not profits) and win more market share.

Growth through external solutions

However, there is usually a limit to how much internal growth a business can achieve without also considering external solutions such as the following.

●   *Joint ventures.* A business can work with a partner to pool resources and develop business opportunities. One business may have a skill in producing one product and the other business in a complementary product; if they sell both products together they will win most of the market from competitors who can't offer both. In the UK, RBS plc (a bank) and Tesco plc (a multinational supermarket) formed a joint venture in personal banking. RBS plc had the required banking expertise and Tesco plc had the retail customers. The joint venture helped both sides grow their profits more quickly than if the two had operated separately in personal banking.

●   *Strategic alliances.* Sometimes two or more organizations will benefit from an alliance of convenience. "Oneworld" is an alliance between American Airlines, British Airways, Cathay Pacific, and several others. The purpose of Oneworld is for the airlines to share ticketing and make transfers at each other's main airports speedier. This reduces costs and is more efficient for customers. The companies will still compete on some routes but they will work together on others.

●   *Mergers and acquisitions.* Buying a competitor, supplier, or customer can help increase the pace of growth. If a business buys a customer or supplier we call this "vertical integration" whereas if a business buys a competitor we call this "horizontal integration" (see p. 347). If two companies of equal size join forces we call it a merger; if the two are very different in terms of size and profits we would generally say that this was an acquisition by one business of another. Time Warner and AOL merged in 2002, whereas Volkswagen acquired Skoda cars, and Vodafone plc acquired Mannesman AG of Germany in 2000.

There are risks with acquisitions. To start with, organizations often pay too much to buy a business. Then problems can emerge in the organization being acquired. One example might be asbestos claims involving the products being made. The different culture of the two organizations can mean that the workforces are never happy working with each other and productivity falls.

Various benefits can emerge though. There may be cost savings, for example from closing one factory down and moving the business to the other site. The businesses can share R&D knowledge, and skills. The businesses might also cross-sell to each other's customer list.

Student workpoint 1.20

Business investigation

1 Evaluate whether you think strategic alliances such as those in the airline industry can survive in the long term.

2 Using the Internet, research strategic airline alliances other than Oneworld. What advantages might there be for airlines operating in this way?

Profile

Michael Porter

Michael E. Porter is the Bishop William Laurence University Professor at the Harvard Business School. He has an almost "living legend" status in the world of management thinking. He has written 18 books and countless articles. In addition to his teaching, he consults widely with the Monitor Group which he helped establish. Above and before everything he is an educator, either by the spoken or by the written word. But he is not a performer or management superstar. *The Economist* once commented that he was as likely to write a best-selling management blockbuster like … (the reader can no doubt supply an example) as to give a lecture wearing a bra and stockings (what an awful image!).

Few of his books are available in paperback. He has advised both the public and private sectors throughout the world. Not only has he been showered with academic and business awards, he has even received civic medals usually reserved for military heroes or extraordinary sports people. Porter was for many years active in the US military's reserve and was a celebrated college footballer, baseballer, and golfer in his youth.

Porter was born in a university town – Ann Arbor, Michigan. His father was an army officer. He studied mechanical and aerospace engineering at Princeton and then switched to business, earning an MBA and a PhD in economics from Harvard. He later joined the faculty there.

Source: http://www.thinkers50.com

HL ⋮ Competitive advantage

An organization's relative position in its industry determines whether the organization's profitability is above or below the industry average. The fundamental basis of above-average profitability in the long run is sustainable competitive advantage. A business can have two basic types of competitive advantage: low cost or differentiation.

The two basic types of competitive advantage, combined with the scope of activities a business uses to try to achieve them, lead to three generic strategies for achieving above-average performance in an industry: cost leadership, differentiation, and focus. The focus strategy has two variants, cost focus and differentiation focus (see Figure 1.12 and p. 332–3).

		Lower cost	Differentiation
Competitive scope	Broad target	1. Cost leadership	2. Differentiation
	Narrow target	3a. Cost focus	3b. Differentiation focus

Figure 1.12

Franchises

Sometimes a business can expand more quickly by offering franchises to others. A franchise is a legal right for a second business to manufacture, sell, and/or market products from a company in a certain place or through a certain medium. The entrepreneur buying the franchise is called a franchisee, while the business selling the rights is the franchisor. McDonalds has in the past sold franchises to entrepreneurs who wish to set up and run a business format that is known to be successful. Franchisees have sole rights in an area, but must also comply with certain requirements about how the food is made, promoted, branded, and so on. Table 1.2 shows advantages and disadvantages of operating franchises, for franchisors and franchisees.

While McDonalds, Prontaprint, H&R Block, 7-Eleven and Radio Shack are well-known names, franchises are available in a wide range of industries. The list of over 3,000 companies covers some 150 different business categories and includes automotive, beauty and health, business services, fast food, home improvement, hotels, printing, publishing, retail, sports, travel, video, and many more.

Advantages for the franchisee	Disadvantages for the franchisee	Advantages for the franchisor	Disadvantages for the franchisor
Trading under a well-known brand name means that sales are almost guaranteed.	There are limits on how the franchisee uses the brand name and little freedom to change format, etc.	Franchisees have to buy the organization's products and related services.	The franchisor can't easily buy back the business from franchises.
There will be business support from the franchisor, for example help with the business plan.	The capital costs needed to buy the franchise can be high.	The franchisor takes a percentage of the franchisee's profits or sales.	There is less control of business performance.
Banks are more willing to provide start-up capital on favourable terms, as the franchisee is operating with a well-known brand and track-record.	If a problem appears in another franchise, or there is bad national publicity about the brand, it can affect the franchisee's sales and profits.	The franchisor can gain growth of the brand cheaply and quickly compared with internal growth.	A bad franchisee can damage the brand and business.
Usually the franchisee becomes a local monopoly, as it is buying sole rights to a geographic area.	The franchisee can only sell the franchise to someone approved by the franchisor.	The arrangement reduces management demands, as the franchisor supports rather than runs local operations.	Some franchisees focus on profits while the franchisor gets more royalties if they focus on sales.
Often the franchisee can buy lower-cost goods from the franchisor than elsewhere because of its buying power.			

Table 1.2 Advantages and disadvantages of franchises

The Ansoff matrix

The Ansoff matrix is a marketing tool created by Igor Ansoff[2] and used to help businesses explore possible growth strategies. See more on this on p. 333–4.

The Ansoff matrix has four quadrants.

1 Growth with existing products in existing markets. This is the **market penetration** approach, where the business is growing with its current goods or services in the current markets.
2 Growth with existing products in new markets. This is the **market development** approach, where the business is growing with its current goods or services into new markets.
3 Growth with new products in existing markets. This is the **product development** approach, where the business is growing with new goods or services in its current markets.
4 Growth with new products in new markets. This is the **diversification** approach, where the business is growing with new goods and services in new markets.

For a diagram showing the four quadrants, turn to Figure 6.8 on p. 332.

Case study

Example of Azore's use of the Ansoff matrix

Azore produces specialist bearings for the automotive industry in South America and has several products that dominate the market. It therefore decides that further penetration of existing markets is not likely to bring significant growth. The company uses the Ansoff matrix to explore the possible use of its bearings in the aerospace market and through this starts devising a new marketing strategy, aiming its products at market development. New product development would be more risky and costly for Azore as it is worried that it would struggle to find the necessary funding.

Case study

Tallyfood Computers

Tallyfood Computers, a Singapore-based software company, produces accounting packages for the restaurant industry. It has a 65% market share in the Far East and in addition about 25% of the Indian sub-continent. Its products are well known and have been the undisputed number one until the arrival of a small and more entrepreneurial company called Eatmoney Inc. Eatmoney has a more bespoke approach to software solutions and tailor make products for each client. →

[2] Ansoff, I. H. 1957. "Strategies for diversification". *Harvard Business Review*. September–October.

While its software development takes longer, the business employs cheap student labour who are well motivated and provide a fast and effective service for Eatmoney's new clients.

Tallyfood Computers feels that its products are proven in the market-place and although its premier product, Talisman, is considered a good accountancy package, both McDonalds and Burger King have decided to investigate bespoke solutions through Eatmoney Inc.

Tallyfood Computers has a strong cash flow and can borrow significant capital from its bankers for research and development.

Using the Ansoff matrix, analyse possible growth solutions for Tallyfood Computers.

Case study

The challengers

A new breed of multinational company has emerged

Tata Motors, the car making bit of Tata Group, India's biggest industrial conglomerate, recently acquired for Jaguar and Land Rover cars. The future of these two grand old badges will be shaped not in Coventry, cradle of the British motor industry, but in Pune, home of Tata Motors.

By 2004 the UN Conference on Trade and Development (UNCTAD) even noted that five companies from emerging Asia had made it into the list of the world's 100 biggest multinationals. In early 2006 Arcelor, a steelmaker of French, Luxembourgeois and Spanish extraction and Europe's biggest, faced a bid from Mittal, an international steel group largely owned by the family of Lakshmi Mittal. Thus was born Arcelor Mittal, the first steel company with an annual output of more than 100 million tonnes.

Even before Mr Mittal bought Arcelor, Corus, an Anglo-Dutch steel company, had approached Ratan Tata, head of Tata Group, about joining forces with Tata Steel, which owned plants in Singapore and elsewhere in South-East Asia as well as in India. Months of discussion led to the conclusion that the only efficient way to combine would be for the Indian company to take over Corus. Cemex, a Mexican cement company, has already taken over a big British group, RMC. Embraer of Brazil has become the world's third-largest aircraft company, specializing in regional jets.

The rationale

The new brigades are fanning out around the world using a selection of five strategies, according to BCG.

The first is taking brands from local to global. China's Hisense, a $3.3 billion consumer-electronics group, is a prime example. With over 10% of the market for TV sets at home, it has turned its attention to the wider world with a product range that includes air conditioners, PCs, and telecoms equipment. It now sells over 10 million TVs and 3 million air conditioners a year in more than 40 countries.

A second strategy is to turn local engineering excellence into innovation on a global scale, as Embraer has done. Supported by the Brazilian government and later largely privatized, Embraer has overtaken Canada's Bombardier to become the world's leading maker of regional jets.

The third path to international success is going for global leadership in a narrow product category. Johnson Electric, which though based in Hong Kong now produces chiefly in mainland China. It makes tiny electric motors for products such as cameras or cars.

Brazil's Sadia and Perdigão exemplify the fourth strategy: taking advantage of natural resources at home, and boosting them with first-class marketing and distribution. They have built sales organizations around the world to make the most of the abundant resources for producing pork, poultry, and grain in Brazil, complemented by ideal growing conditions and low labour costs.

The fifth strategy is to have a new or better business model to roll out to many different markets. This is the approach of Mexico's Cemex, one of the world's biggest suppliers of ready-mixed concrete. Its annual sales topped $18 billion in 2006. Industries such as cement are usually considered "territorial goods", meaning they are bulky, basic, and too expensive to transport long distances. But now this wisdom is being stood on its head: though it may not be worth shipping cement from Mexico to Europe, know-how and investment can be swiftly poured into any market. The secret of the company's success is the rigorous development of its own style of managing acquisitions, which it calls "the Cemex way". It has its own systems, very heavily dependent on standardized procedures built around highly developed IT systems.

The new multinationals have some distinct advantages in their sprint to the fore of global business. They are often family owned or family controlled (even when they are public companies), which helps them to make decisions quickly. They often enjoy cheap finance from state banks.

Business investigation

1   There are five reasons why multinational companies from the developing world are now succeeding. Identify these reasons and evaluate what this growth might mean generally for the economies of the developed world (especially the US or Europe).

2   Select one of the multinational companies from the article and undertake some personal research into the history and development of the business. Also consider what the advantages and disadvantages might be for the specific host countries from having this multinational company.

Source: Adapted from *The Economist* print edition, 10 January 2008

Globalization

Multinational companies are companies that have factories in more than one country; an organization that only has sales offices abroad would not be considered a multinational business. Walmart Inc (US); Tata Group (India); Exon (US); and Volkswagen AG (Germany) are examples of multinational companies.

Multinationals developed for a variety of reasons, including:

- saturation of domestic markets—this meant growth had to be in other countries
- wanting to move closer to their global customers
- wanting to benefit from lower labour costs
- the lower tax rates in other countries allowing for greater retained profits
- incentives from governments—monetary and non-monetary
- exploiting colonial power to grab markets abroad
- the opportunity to be closer to raw materials and energy sources.

However, the recent growth in multinationalism is from emerging markets to the developed world—as the case study highlights.

Problems

Here are some examples of problems in the host countries of multinationals.

In Bhopal, India, in 1985 Union Carbide operated a chemical plant that leaked toxic gases and killed thousands of local residents. It seemed that safety standards were not rigorous enough as the business had minimized costs.

"MacDonalization" is the term given to the impact of fast food outlets in countries where obesity was previously almost unheard of. This has an effect on health costs and also on cultural values.

Some people also think that multinationals are "footloose"—that they have no long-term loyalty to a country and will pull out if there are negative changes in the external environment, for example if the government increases tax rates, or if better locations emerge.

Finally, there are arguments that while multinationals create employment, the type of work they provide is low level and the wages are low. If the work is only very low skilled and is also poorly paid then that would be of concern. In many cases though, the wages paid are at least equal if not better than the local rates and there is also some local management created. Perhaps we should ask: If multinationals are all bad why are they warmly welcomed by so many countries?

Multinationals are the key mover of foreign direct investment in countries around the world; they are an important driver for globalization—which is the growing interconnectedness of the world we now live in.

Regional trading blocs

A trading bloc is a collection of countries that agree to certain rules regarding trade. There are various types of trading bloc:

- free trade areas
- customs unions
- common markets
- economic and monetary unions.

Free trade areas

A free trade area is where member countries trade with each other without imposing any taxes or restrictions on each other. However, each member is independent when it comes to determining restrictions or taxes on other countries outside of the bloc. NAFTA (the North American Free Trade Area, comprising the US, Canada, and Mexico) is an example.

Customs unions

In addition to the free trade area elements, a customs union has a common external barrier for imports. For example, it might impose a quota on the number of units of a product allowed in, or all countries in the union agree to a 10% tax on imports of certain goods or services. An example of a customs union is Mercosur (which includes Argentina, Brazil, Paraguay, Uruguay and Venezuela).

Common markets

As well as having the features of a customs union, a common market not only allows the free movement of goods and services but also of labour and capital between its members. In theory, labour can move across members' borders without restrictions. The countries involved may also introduce agreements on products, for example they might standardize what the ingredient proportions must be in chocolate for it to be called chocolate. The EU is an example of a common market.

Economic and monetary unions

In addition to the features of a common market, an economic and monetary union requires a single currency for its members. It will also require a single interest rate across the zone. The eurozone group in the EU is the best example.

The impact on businesses joining a trading bloc

This will depend on a variety of factors, such as:

- the type of trading bloc the country is a member of
- the proportion of business that the organization has outside the bloc and how this may be affected—for example, if there is a common tariff or tax on imports to the bloc from a country that

is not a member, that country might impose limits or taxes on exports in retaliation

- the number of competitors in the bloc that may now have free access to the organization's domestic market and customers
- the new opportunities for free entry into other member states' markets
- the likelihood of the country and bloc developing into the next phase, for example from common market to economic and monetary union
- the level of imported raw materials or components that the business buys from outside the bloc and the level and cost of any restrictions, quotas or taxes that may now appear.

Be a thinker

Is the possible expansion of the EU into non-European states, like Turkey and the Ukraine, a step too far?

Change and the management of change

HL

By the end of this chapter, you should be able to:

- explain the causes of change and factors causing resistance to change
- examine the dynamic nature of organizations and the relative importance of driving and restraining forces
- evaluate different strategies for reducing the impact of change and resistance to change

"Things alter for the worse spontaneously, if they be not altered for the better designedly."
Francis Bacon (1561–1626)

Change

Change and the management of change

This section on change is a higher-level extension. However, in reality change cannot be ignored by standard-level students and this is why change is considered extensively throughout this book and in most core topics on the business and management syllabus.

The rate of change is accelerating and no business is immune: there are new markets, new products and services, new production methods, new social values, and new technologies. Every change is a challenge to the management of a business. There are thousands of books on change and its management, which clearly reflects a desire by senior managers to have some methods to avoid the quicksand of a dynamic business environment.

Causes of change

Where does the impetus for organizational change come from? The simple answer is that the drivers for change come both from the internal and external environment. Effective managers understand that change in the strategic environment is a continuous process and that successful businesses are those that anticipate and plan for change. Therefore, managing change is about the long-term survival of the business.

Organizational change is especially necessary when external environments are uncertain, complex, and dynamic. Significant and/ or rapid change may require an organization to reconsider its structure, purpose, mission, and culture. The implementation of strategic change is clearly a period of significant danger for any business.

What are the pressures driving change?

External drivers of change

The external environment is in a state of constant flux. External factors driving change include:

- globalization
- new technologies
- demographic changes
- social and cultural change
- changes in legislation
- economic trends
- competition.

The next section looks at these issues, but as they are significant in all areas of business, you will find more on each issue in later chapters in this book.

Globalization

Globalization brings significant opportunities in terms of larger markets and growth possibilities. Global markets are converging, offering organizations the opportunity to produce standardized products and to benefit from economies of scale. However, globalization also brings threats resulting from greater international competition, and affects the range of goods and services that must be offered. Different nationalities and cultures will have different tastes, preferences, and buying habits. Businesses will have to be increasingly aware of, and responsive to, the growing and evolving needs of emerging economies, such as China, India, and the countries of Eastern Europe.

In addition, multinational companies are faced with a wider range of HR issues including differences in the skills, attitudes, and needs of their workforces worldwide. As a business grows internationally, there are more communication problems and it is difficult to maintain a common purpose. The challenge of expansion has intensified as more business functions are outsourced, often overseas.

New technologies

The rate of organizational change is accelerating as new technologies emerge and computer power and speed increases exponentially. In organizational terms the introduction of new technologies has allowed increasing decentralization and downsizing, with power shifting away from the centre to local or regional offices. As a result, organization structures have flattened requiring employees to develop new skills and take on extra responsibilities. The outcome is that power often shifts from centralized functions to local operating units, changing the management function as well.

Technological change affects all business functions from marketing to production. These changes are discussed throughout this book.

Demographic changes

Changes in the size and structure of the population affect a business in two significant ways—the nature and needs of employees change as do the needs and wants of consumers.

Most developed countries are facing up to an ageing population, which may cause skill shortages. This requires changes to recruitment, training, and retention policies. Working patterns are being reassessed and, as a consequence, more flexible working practices are being introduced.

Demographic change affects consumption patterns and purchase behaviour. This is already noticeable in growing markets catering for older age groups.

Social and cultural change

Over time, consumer behaviour, attitudes, and expectations change. For instance, in most developed countries the majority of women have jobs. Changes such as this have changed the way retailers offer their services, for example 24-hour shopping, in more convenient locations.

Increasing migration also changes the social and cultural mix of a country and the nature of demand. Fusions of different cultures, religions, and ethnic groups provides new market opportunities. This is noticeable in the food, entertainment, and clothing sectors.

Changes in legislation

Government legislation can force changes in business practice and activity. In many countries, laws on health and safety, working hours, and discrimination have affected both working conditions and the nature of the workplace.

Consumer protection laws can force businesses to change the way they market and sell their products or services.

Economic trends

Changes in the economic cycle will have significant effects on business activity. As organizations and countries have become more interdependent, crises like the US "credit crunch" in 2008 have had global effects, like ripples in a pond, causing worldwide recession.

Competition

In highly competitive markets, innovation and change initiated by one business will trigger a response from the competition to protect market share. For instance, in the game console market, each manufacturer attempts to gain competitive advantage over its rivals by frequently upgrading the functionality of its products. Additions like broadband access, Blu-ray disc players, wireless controllers, and portable models force other manufacturers to introduce updated models with similar, or improved, features.

Internal drivers of change

The internal resources of a business are constantly changing and management will need to respond to these. Internal factors driving change include:

● changes in human resources and skill levels
● new management approaches
● changes in employees' expectations, motivation, and behaviour
● new product development
● financial requirements and availability of funds.

Changes in human resources and skill levels

As markets and products change, so do the needs for specific HR skills. This will require changes in personnel and training needs.

New management approaches

The turnover of senior managers in most business fields is becoming more rapid. The desire for quick success is encouraging businesses to consider changing their management teams rather than waiting for improvements. This is particularly evident in sport, which has become "big business". For example, soccer club directors see managers as expendable, and in times of failure prefer to sack their off-field staff rather than the players, who are perhaps scarcer in supply.

Changes in employees' expectations, motivation, and behaviour
In most organizations, the "job for life" is gone. Very few organizations reward loyalty and, in return, employees are more fickle, moving between jobs more quickly and staying in positions for shorter periods. In economic boom periods, the bargaining position of skilled employees is stronger and managers will have to review and modify remuneration packages more often to retain their better staff.

New product development
The introduction of new products and services will require changes in the nature of an organization's production and marketing approaches. New products may require increased automation of production and new services may require different ways of selling. The target markets for new products may not be the same.

Financial requirements and availability of funds
Changes in goods and services will require additional investment and cash flow that a business may not have. Businesses will have to raise new funds through loans, share issues, or integration with other organizations.

Resistance to change

Individuals react very differently to change. Some people embrace change as it provides variety, opportunity, and excitement. As the pace of social and economic change has accelerated it has become an accepted part of many working environment. But there are individuals who fear change and resist it. This may be a rational reaction, because change can have negative consequences for the individual even if it's beneficial for the organization. It may involve higher workloads and longer hours, relocation, the breaking up of working groups, and possibly redundancy. Periods of stability create a sense of familiarity and therefore a feeling of security. When employees are confronted with the need or opportunity to change, especially when they perceive it as "enforced", they can become emotional.

All stakeholders of a business may resist change. This resistance can be attributed to a number of factors.

Personal reasons include:

● fear of the unknown
● a risk-aversive personality
● dislike of the person making the change or suspicion of the motives
● lack of skills to cope with new demands
● proposed changes to working hours and reduction in personal flexibility.

Explanation and communication of change can lead to people resisting change, for example when:

● the justification of the change is unclear
● the value of the change to the stakeholder is not identified and communicated in a simple manner
● the stakeholder is not involved in the decision-making process.

Examiner's note
Change runs throughout the business and management programme. It is an area that allows examiners to ask **evaluation** questions. When addressing change always look to cover these four key points.

● How significant is the issue?
● How likely is the change to take place?
● What is the size of the change? (Indicate this using supporting data.)
● What are the time frames involved? (What happens because of change in the short run will be different from what happens in the long run.)

Social aspects of proposed change include:

- concerns that change breaks up existing teams and friendship groups
- lack of confidence dealing with new colleagues and systems.

Financial reasons include:

- fear of redundancy or worse payment terms, for example less chance of overtime
- possible additional costs, for example for relocation and transport, or childcare.

Force field analysis

In 1969, Kurt Lewin developed force field analysis, a graphical tool that can guide change and help identify priorities for action. Individuals or teams can use this tool.

Lewin identified what he called a "problem situation", where there is a difference between the way things are and the way the organization wants them to be. The principle of force field analysis is that at any given time a problem situation may exist, because counterbalancing forces are keeping it that way. These forces are defined as:

- *driving forces for change*—forces that initiate a change and keep it going, for example new competition, cash flow crisis, rising costs
- *restraining forces for change*—forces that decrease the driving forces, for example apathy, lack of finance, or poor motivation.

Force does not imply physical pressure, but refers to the broad range of internal and external influences at a particular time. Equilibrium is reached when the sum of the driving forces equals the sum of the restraining forces. In essence, the technique is a specialized method of weighing pros and cons. By carrying out the analysis in a meeting or series of meetings, the team leading change identifies factors driving and restraining change and rates the importance of each.

To support the analysis, a force field diagram is drawn with a line representing each change force. The change force is then given a weighting to show how important it is. This is done by simply placing a number next to the force or by varying the length of each line with its perceived importance; more important being longer.

The force field diagram helps the decision maker to weigh the importance of change factors and decide whether a plan is worth implementing by:

- investigating the balance of power involved in an issue
- identifying the key individuals affected by a change
- identifying supporters and opponents of a change
- examining how to strengthen forces supporting a decision, while reducing the impact of opposition.

In Figure 1.13 the restraining forces are stronger in total, so there would be no change unless restraining forces could be reduced or driving forces increased.

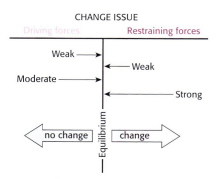

Figure 1.13 The force field diagram

This means that a manager desiring change has to increase the drivers or reduce the resisters to change. The choice of method is important. One potential method to increase the drivers is to push the change by autocratic leadership. But this may only lead to an acceptance of the change in the short term—in the long run, autocratic leadership may lower motivation and productivity and increase staff turnover. A better alternative could be to reduce opposition to a change by offering additional incentives or by better communication of the benefits of the change.

Case study

Change issue

The school council wants to remove the requirement for sixth formers to wear uniform

Driving forces

- This will provide an additional privilege for the sixth form.
- Not wearing uniform will distinguish sixth formers from the other year groups.
- The existing uniform is unfashionable.
- Other local schools have no uniform for the sixth form.

Restraining forces

- The headteacher is worried about security on the site as it will be difficult to distinguish between sixth form students and outsiders.
- Parents are concerned that this change will lead to falling standards in the school.

- Some students believe that the change will be more expensive and discriminate against those unable to afford fashionable clothing.
- Staff believe the uniform represents the culture of the school and all years should wear it.

At first the restraining forces are stronger, and no change seems likely. But the school council suggests the following to reduce resistance to the change.

- All students will wear a clip-on identity badge with a photograph.
- There is a dress code rather than total freedom of choice. The clothes on the acceptable list are smart casual and can be bought from most retailers.
- Uniform will be worn on special occasions, such as speech day.

After further discussion with the headteacher and consultation with parents, the change is agreed.

Student workpoint 1.22
Be a thinker

Examine a proposed change to your school environment, or to a business you know about, and identify the driving and restraining forces involved.

Produce an action plan to strengthen the case for change and to address some of the restraining forces.

The effects of rapid change

Modern businesses are responding to the changes in the external and internal environment by examining and changing some of the fundamentals of their operations, leading to changing priorities. Here are some examples.

- It is becoming more important to carry out market research to identify changing trends that will impact on the business and its products or services.
- There is an increasing emphasis on quality as a method of creating competitive advantage or maintaining a position in the market. Quality assurance at all levels and benchmarking against key competitors have become vital to survival.

- Product life cycles are getting shorter, requiring greater focus on innovation and research and development to keep one step ahead of the market and to provide the business with first mover advantage.
- Flexible workforces and working practices are being created. This has an impact on recruitment and training. Organizations are maintaining fewer core staff and look more to temporary and part-time peripheral staff.
- Organizations are developing a corporate culture that embraces change.

Managing change

Most organizations work in situations where they plan, implement and manage change in a fast-moving environment. Excellent leadership is about understanding when environmental change requires organizational change and when it doesn't.

There are three key questions associated with business change:

- Is the change anticipated or unanticipated?
- Have managers planned for change?
- To what extent is the change controllable by the business?

If change is anticipated it can be planned for, making management of the process more effective. Organizations can then produce corporate plans and budgets to support the changes and individual employees know their role in the process. Unanticipated change can be disruptive to the business and result in change leading the business, rather than the business initiating change. At worst, the business may move into a period of crisis management.

Key elements for successful change management

Management theorists, such as Mintzberg and Peters (see p. 105–106 and 107–108), have explored planning issues in dynamic markets. Their belief is that the formalized planning approaches used in the past have little benefit in modern markets, where change can make the best-laid plans obsolete. Mintzberg has talked about strategy that emerges from constant evaluation of the external environment. This is based on some of the following approaches.

- Only planning in a broad sense for the long-term. Managers should prepare a strategic vision, not a specific meticulous plan. In fast-moving environments, detailed five-year plans are out of date almost as soon as they are written. So organizations should focus more on establishing and measuring immediate actions, rather than preparing detailed medium-term to long-term plans.
- Developing channels of communication that allow immediate review and quick decision making. Those directly affected by decisions must be part of the decision-making process, enabling their input to be gained, their approval obtained, and their commitment secured.
- Delegating responsibility and power to managers operating at a local level. By empowering local teams, decisions can be made that address local issues and are far more immediate.
- Creating a climate that embraces change by appointing managers who are open to new and creative solutions.

● Developing ICT systems to support effective information management and team working.

Whenever an organization imposes new things on people, there will be difficulties. Participation, involvement, and open, early, full communication are vital factors when introducing change.

Change management entails thoughtful planning and sensitive implementation, and, above all, consultation with, and involvement of, the people affected by the changes. If change is forced on people, problems frequently arise. Change must be realistic, achievable, and measurable.

Before starting organizational change, it is useful for businesses to consider three questions:

● What do we want to achieve with this change and how will we know that the change has been achieved?
● Who is affected by this change and how will they react to it?
● How much of this change can be achieved by the organization itself, and what parts of the change will require external help?

John Kotter, in his well-respected books on change (1995, 2002)[3] outlines a model for understanding and managing change. Each stage acknowledges a key principle identified by Kotter relating to people's response and approach to change, in which people see, feel, and then change. Figure 1.14 shows Kotter's model.

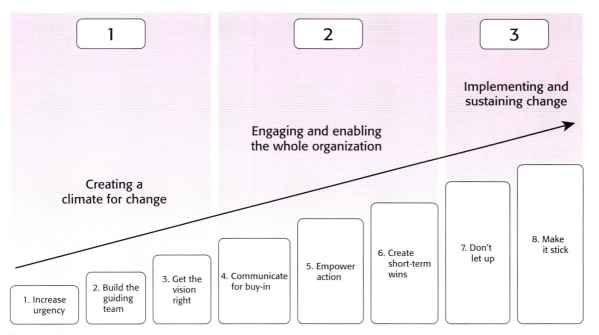

Figure 1.14 Kotter's model for understanding and managing change
Source: www.toronto.ca

[3] Kotter, J. 1995. *Leading Change*. Boston, MA. Harvard Business School Press; and Kotter J. and Cohen D. 2002. *The Heart of Change*. Boston, MA. Harvard Business School Press.

Let's look at what is meant by the eight statements given in the model.

- Increase urgency—inspire people to move. Make objectives real and relevant.
- Build the guiding team—get the right people in place with the right emotional commitment, and the right mix of skills and skill levels.
- Get the vision right—get the team to establish a simple vision and strategy, focus on emotional and creative aspects necessary to elicit the change.
- Communicate for buy-in—involve as many people as possible, communicate the essentials, simply, and appeal and respond to people's needs. Simplify communications.
- Empower action—remove obstacles, enable constructive feedback and lots of support from leaders—reward and recognize progress and achievements.
- Create short-term wins—set aims that are easy to achieve—in bite-size chunks. Have manageable numbers of initiatives. Finish current stages before starting new ones.
- Don't let up—foster and encourage determination and persistence about ongoing change, encourage ongoing progress reporting, highlight achieved and future milestones.
- Make change stick—reinforce the value of successful change via recruitment, promotion, and new change leaders. Weave change into culture.

Data response exercise

Read the text below and answer the questions that follow it.

Case study

Time is what you make of it

The Swiss were early adopters of the wrist watch and by the 1950s had perfected complicated watches renowned for their quality and workmanship. Swiss technology dominated the global watch market. However, in the 1970s, the Japanese perfected the quartz watch. The growth of Japanese watch producers and the emergence of Timex, the US jewel-free, throw-away multinational watch company, had a catastrophic impact on the market for traditional watches. Many Swiss watch brands disappeared almost overnight. In 1982 alone, sales of Swiss watches dropped by 25%, as newly formed competitors began to mass produce low-cost, technologically advanced watches. Economies of scale drove market prices significantly lower.

The visionary, Ernst Thomke, was appointed to develop a strategy to turn around the fortunes of the ailing Swiss watch industry. In 1983, Thomke and his partner Nicholas G. Hayek oversaw the creation of the Swatch brand, an abbreviation of "Swiss watch". Swatch was formed by merging two bankrupt watch-making groups. The merger gave the group ownership of many of Switzerland's dominant watch brands and helped regain much of the ground lost to the Japanese and Americans. The Swatch was a fusion of style and technology. It offered a quartz movement under an analogue dial. Swatch was technologically innovative in reducing the number of components to about 60% of those used by its competitors. Its product was a cheap watch produced on a fully automated assembly line. But the real genius of Swatch was in its marketing. Taking its cue from the fashion industry, the Swatch, as one commentator remarked, "put an artist's palette on the face of a watch".

Swatch signalled that functionality and time telling were no longer the primary selling points in a watch. Swatch became a fun, fashion accessory and wrested dominance from inexpensive watches from Asia. It became the fastest-selling brand in watch history.

Nicholas G. Hayek, Swatch's chairman, said, "We were convinced that if we could add our fantasy and culture to an emotional product, we could beat anybody. Emotions are something nobody can copy." Heyek went on to invent the Smart car for the Mercedes group, known affectionately as the Swatchmobile.

Source: Adapted from "The three outsiders who rescued the Swiss watch industry", Desmond Guilfoyle, 3 August 2006

Examination questions

1 Define these terms:
   a multinational company [2 *marks*]
   b merger. [2 *marks*]
2 Swatch's mission statement, is "Time is what you make of it". Explain the purpose of setting such a statement. [6 *marks*]
3 Analyse mergers and acquisitions as a method of achieving Swatch's growth objectives. [6 *marks*]
4 Evaluate the effect of the external environment on Swatch's objectives and strategy. [9 *marks*]

2.1 Human resource planning

By the end of this chapter, you should be able to:

- identify the constraints and opportunities provided by technological and demographic change
- compare present human resources with future requirements and evaluate strategies for developing future human resources
- describe methods of recruitment, appraisal, training and dismissal and discuss the advantages and disadvantages of each method
- examine how recruitment, appraisal, training and dismissal enable firms to achieve workforce planning targets.
- describe reasons for changing work patterns and practices and analyse reasons for these changes and their likely consequences
- apply Handy's shamrock organization

The supply of labour

The supply of labour is the total number of people who are willing and able to work. Economists view the supply of labour as a fixed stock which grows, for example when there is an increase in immigration, and shrinks, for example when more people retire than take up work. The stock of labour becomes increasingly difficult to measure because of changes in technology, work practices, and the economic and political environment. In some industries the supply of labour includes labour beyond domestic boundaries because it's possible to complete work using information technology (IT). Here are some examples.

- Some US hospitals are sending X-rays and blood tests overseas for doctors to interpret the results. There are considerable cost savings in doing this and results are often interpreted more quickly as the hospital is able to consult a large pool of doctors.
- Many small US businesses employ an offshore online service provider to complete their tax returns at a much lower cost than would be the case if a fellow citizen were employed.
- Students can find an online tutor, often on the other side of the world, to help them with whole subjects, such as mathematics, or with a difficult essay assignment.
- Music can be compiled and recorded online with artists from different parts of the world without the musicians ever meeting.

The supply of labour can therefore be described as increasingly global, informal, and impersonal.

While technological change can increase the reach and availability of labour, demographic change can provide constraints and opportunities for organizations. In many economically developed economies, organizations are faced with an ageing population because fertility rates are falling, life expectancy is rising, and the post-war baby boomers are getting older.

Older staff offer an organization rich life experience, well-honed skills, knowledge, and wisdom. Rising life expectancy and a growing dependency ratio may mean that the retirement age will need to be raised in some countries, so many organizations may need to reassess their attitudes and recruitment procedures.

Migration has provided opportunities and threats for businesses. At the same time as providing an economics bonus to countries experiencing labour shortages, migration can lead to a "brain drain" from countries with net emigration as skilled workers are the ones with greatest mobility. As these skilled workers return to their passport country they may also pose a greater threat in terms of competition since they are now equipped with the knowledge to take on their former employer—often at lower cost.

Data response exercise

Read the text below and answer the questions that follow.

Case study

Nordic countries experience labour shortages

In early 2008 Finland, Sweden, Norway, and Denmark introduced a number of measures to attract skilled foreign workers. Unemployment in these countries was lower than the European average and employers were complaining of labour shortages and rising wage costs that undermined export competitiveness.

The Nordic countries have responded to this by introducing a number of measures including promotional videos, and simplified and relaxed immigration rules and procedures. This made it easier and faster for prospective employees to work in those countries.

However, these changes have been largely unsuccessful, with most immigrants leaving within a year or so.

Examination questions

1 Identify four factors that could have contributed to skilled labour shortages in these countries. [8 marks]

2 Discuss additional measures that these governments could take to reduce labour shortages. [10 marks]

Workforce planning

Changes in the external environment mean that organizations have to anticipate and manage changes in their workforce. For workforce planning, an organization will:

- forecast the human resources it needs to achieve its objectives
- identify, develop, and maintain the skills its workforce needs
- need to bear in mind the work–life balance employees are looking for.

Workforce planning is likely to include assessing the current situation, then looking ahead to future workforce needs and addressing any shortfall or surplus.

Data response exercise

Read the text below and answer the questions that follow.

Case study

Ford Motor Company

Having laid off almost 34,000 workers in 2006, in early 2008 Ford Motor Company was offering buyouts and early retirement to 54,000 more employees. Ford also said that it would eliminate shift working at four US plants and lay off some 2,500 workers—or almost 5% of its remaining workforce—as part of an effort to cut costs and return to profitability in 2009. Ford said it would run its Chicago and Louisville, Kentucky, assembly plants on one shift rather than the current two shifts starting summer 2008. Ford reported a loss of US $2.7 billion in 2007.

Source: Adapted from www.reuters.com

Examination questions

1 Define these terms:

   a lay off   [*2 marks*]

   b buyout   [*2 marks*]

   c early retirement   [*2 marks*]

   d shift work.   [*2 marks*]

2 Discuss how the measures taken by Ford could help the company return to profitability.   [*8 marks*]

3 Using appropriate motivation theory, evaluate the short-run and long-run implications of this strategy on employee motivation.   [*10 marks*]

Recruitment

An organization that identifies a shortfall in its workforce, or can see one coming, will need to start recruitment. The most common methods of recruitment are to use recruitment agencies, job centres, specialist publications, and personal contacts.

Recruitment agencies keep records of potential employees and can save an organization the trouble of advertising, interviewing, and selecting candidates. However, this convenience comes at the cost of the agent's fees and the organization relying on the agent to provide the right person rather than selecting someone itself.

In some countries, local or central government offer job centres. These aim to help potential employees and employers match their requirements so that both parties' needs are satisfied. They advertise job vacancies, offer a room to interview potential candidates, and may help an organization to advertise and draw up a short list of interviewees. They will also inform jobseekers of potential vacancies.

While job centres will tend to focus on a wide range of vacancies, specialist publications enable an organization to target a particular profession. For example, producers of the latest Bond movie recruited a model airplane expert from *Model Airplane News* to shoot aerial movie scenes using a camera attached to a model airplane.

> "The world is full of willing people, some willing to work, the rest willing to let them."
>
> Robert Frost (1874–1963)

Given that recruiting employees involves a fair degree of risk, some organizations prefer to rely on friends and professional contacts to make recruitment recommendations. This takes the cost element out of the recruitment process and is likely to be based on professional and personal knowledge. The person making the recommendation is going to want to be sure that the recommendation reflects well on him or her and the person being recommended may well want to ensure that he or she does not let the friend down. However, a lot of upset or embarrassment for everyone involved can arise if the recommendation turns out to be disappointing.

Once an employee has been recruited, the organization will want to ensure that he or she settles in quickly and helps the organization to achieve its objectives. In many organizations an employee undertakes a probationary period of employment which, if completed satisfactorily, is replaced by a permanent contract.

Training and appraisal

Professional development through training and education can bring several benefits to a business:

- It helps existing staff adopt new innovations.
- It can be a source of motivation.
- It can help to build team spirit.
- It might be used to develop junior staff so that they are able to cover for the short- or long-term absence of senior staff.

For these and other reasons, professional development of staff through training and education can help an organization to achieve its objectives. The organization needs to be clear about the objectives, and the gaps, for example in knowledge or skill, that need to be filled to improve achievement of those objectives. Then managers can decide on a training programme. Once this has been done, the trainees have to be selected and their training needs analysed.

A summary of different types of training is given in Table 2.1.

Type of training	Description	Usually undertaken
Orientation:	introduces the organization's history, objectives, key staff, and the location of key facilities. It also explains how the business objectives are met and the expectations of staff.	In-house
On-the-job training:	includes apprenticeships, job rotation, job enlargement, and shadowing.	By supervisors, peers
Off-the-job training:	includes lectures, discussions, case studies, role play, and simulation.	By outside trainers

Table 2.1 Different types of training

Having made an appointment and given an employee a reasonable time to settle in, it is important that an organization undertakes regular evaluations of the person's performance. An appraisal system aims to assess the performance and value of employees in an organization.

"Success in business requires training and discipline and hard work. But if you're not frightened by these things, the opportunities are just as great today as they ever were".
David Rockefeller (1915–)

The appraisal is typically annual so that targets can be set and progress can be monitored. It may be upwards as well as downwards, meaning that employees may have an opportunity to comment on the performance of their supervisors or managers.

An appraisal record will often comment on a subordinate's ability to meet certain criteria and may suggest areas and action for improvement. An example is shown on Figure 2.1.

Criteria	Evidence	Rating	Future action needed
Ability to meet deadlines			
Contribution to organizational targets			
Work effectively with colleagues			
Work effectively with customers			
Work effectively with supervisor			
Respond appropriately to complaints or stressful situations			
Meet quality targets			

Figure 2.1 Example page from an appraisal form

Student workpoint 2.1

Be reflective

Using the criteria shown in Figure 2.1, make a self-appraisal of your performance in each of your IB subjects.

What rating system could you use?

Why might you be reluctant to show this to your teachers or parents?

After their appraisal, some employees may find that they are recommended for training and or promotion. In some cases though, employees may find that they face the prospect of having to show significant improvement by a given deadline, possibly enter a disciplinary process, and even have their contract of employment terminated.

A key area of employment law is the ability of an employer to dismiss an employee for unacceptable behaviour or poor performance. However, in many countries an employer may face prosecution for unfair dismissal if the termination of the employment contract has not followed appropriate procedures.

Theory of Knowledge

How reliable is archival evidence when making decisions about recruitment and appraisal? Can intuition be a more reliable source of knowledge?

Is logic or emotion likely to dominate when making decisions about recruitment, promotion, and dismissal?

Data response exercise

Read the text below and answer the questions that follow.

Case study

A sacked Eton College art teacher recently won a legal case for unfair dismissal against her employer. An industrial tribunal ruled that Sarah Forsyth had been unfairly dismissed after being bullied by her head of department. Eton College had argued that the reason it did not renew the contract of employment was that Ms Forsyth was a poor teacher.

The industrial tribunal was critical of art department head Ian Burke, who had a meeting with Ms Forsyth five months before her dismissal. The tribunal concluded that Mr Burke undermined and bullied Ms Forsyth, repeatedly changed his version of events and was inconsistent in his evidence to the tribunal and in the way he dealt with Ms Forsyth.

The school was criticized for failing to produce any written employee appraisal procedure for the tribunal. This led the tribunal to conclude that no appraisal procedure was followed. Eton College Headteacher, Antony Little, was also criticized by the tribunal for not looking independently at Ms Forsyth's case.

Examination questions

1 Define these terms:
   a industrial tribunal   [2 marks]
   b unfair dismissal   [2 marks]
   c contract of employment   [2 marks]
   d appraisal.   [2 marks]
2 What procedures would you expect to be in place before an employee is dismissed?   [6 marks]
3 Referring to the Eton College case study, explain the steps an employer could take to avoid a member of staff claiming unfair dismissal.   [10 marks]

Changing work patterns

While employment laws may vary from country to country and can be in the control of domestic governments, the external forces driving changes in employment patterns are largely beyond a government's control. To varying degrees most economically developed countries have experienced in recent years the trends in work patterns shown in Table 2.2.

Trend	Causes/driving forces	Implications for employees	Implications for employers	Other comments/ observations
Decline in				
manufacturing employment				
public sector employment				
average number of hours worked				
permanent work contracts				
Growth in				
individual employment disputes and legal action				
average age of the workforce				
immigration				
service sector employment				
educational qualifications				
self-employment				
portfolio work				
temporary and part-time work, homeworking and teleworking				
outsourcing and offshoring				
female employment				
workplace stress				

Table 2.2 Trends in work patterns

Data response exercise
Refer to Table 2.2 and answer these questions.

Examination questions

1 Define these terms:
   a homeworking   *[2 marks]*
   b teleworking.   *[2 marks]*
2 Use PEST analysis (analysis of political, economic, social, and technological issues) to identify and explain the forces driving employment changes in a country of your choice. Make a copy of Table 2.2 and fill in the gaps based on your analysis.   *[10 marks]*
3 Which of these forces have been the most important and why?   *[8 marks]*

The changes in Table 2.2 have led many to believe that the HR management function of an organization increasingly needs to get the best out of people through effective communication, motivation, and leadership. If this is the case, employees will have to be seen increasingly as knowledgeable individuals with learning and developmental needs rather than a collective resource that needs to be measured, managed, and controlled.

Data response exercise

Read the text below and answer the questions that follow.

Case study

Flexible work arrangements

The Manpower Research and Statistics Department in Singapore has published an occasional paper, "Flexible work arrangements". The paper describes various flexible work options and discusses the benefits and drawbacks of them.

Flexible work practices range from conventional part-time working to high technology teleworking. The more common ones include part-time working, temporary and seasonal working, flexitime, annualized hours, job sharing, term-time working, homeworking, and teleworking.

Singapore employers should consider offering greater flexibility in work arrangements because of the emergence of dual-income families, and the need to respond rapidly and efficiently to changes in demand. Flexible work arrangements also result in more women and older people being hired.

However, despite its potential benefits, flexible working has been slow to catch on in Singapore.

Source: Adapted from www.employmenttown.gov.sg

Examination questions

1 Define flexitime. [2 marks]
2 Discuss the forces driving the move towards more flexible working practices. [8 marks]
3 Explain why some Singapore employers might resist introducing flexible work practices? [6 marks]

Charles Handy on the relationship between workers and organizations

The business writer who is largely credited with anticipating changes in the workplace is Charles Handy. In his 1989 book[1] Handy uses the symbol of the shamrock (a three-leafed clover) to describe the changing relationship between workers and organizations.

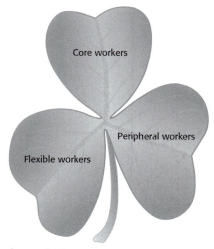

Figure 2.2 The Shamrock organization

Source: Handy, C. 1989. *The Age of Unreason*. London, Business Books.

According to Handy, a worker's relationship with an organization falls into one three groups. The first group is made up of **core** workers. These are often highly qualified professionals and managers. They set and implement the objectives and strategies for

[1] Handy, C. 1989. *The Age of Unreason*. London, Business Books.

the organization and have a detailed knowledge of how things get done. They are central to the survival and growth of the organization and receive a lucrative financial package and fringe benefits. In return they are expected to be loyal servants of the organization by working long hours, and to have the flexibility to fit in with the changing needs of the organization. The core is expensive and consequently tends to be shrinking since organizations want to keep costs down.

The second leaf of the shamrock represents the **contractual fringe**, consisting of workers who provide services such as advertising, catering, and transport. They are paid fees for doing a particular job. How they do it is pretty much left up to them. Their value to the organization tends to be measured in output and results. Many leading sports and clothes manufacturers, for example, have contracted out the production of their products to less developed economies. They have subsequently discovered that work practices in these factories can be harsh and unsafe, and have therefore received bad publicity. The contractual fringe therefore needs to be monitored since a business can be held to account for unreasonable work practices even though the contractual fringe is not one of its employees.

The third leaf of Handy's shamrock represents the **flexible labour force**. These workers do part-time, temporary, and seasonal work. Being poorly paid can be a way of life for them and since the organization typically demonstrates little loyalty to them they usually respond in kind. They tend to do their work and leave, often moving on to another organization and doing much the same. These workers will experience job insecurity and will usually be the first to lose their job in an economic downturn. Some may well like this kind of work since it is often varied and affords them the freedom to come and go because contractual and emotional ties are relatively weak.

Student workpoint 2.2

Be a thinker

Identify core staff, contractual staff, and temporary staff in your school.

Which functions at your school could be contracted out? Here are some examples to get you started:

- bus services
- cleaning
- teaching
- gardening
- maintenance work, such as painting and repairs.

Which functions would not be contracted out? Why?

Handy (1989) also describes the federal organization and federalism. Handy sees a great future for federalism in the workplace.

Federalism means reverse delegation. Delegation means passing authority to the outlying bits—so reverse delegation means passing authority to the centre. It is different from centralization because centralization implies *taking* authority away from the outlying bits while federalism implies *giving* authority to the centre.

The outlying bits of an organization recognize that certain functions are best controlled and managed centrally, so these functions are reverse delegated to the centre. In the federal organization senior management needs to provide vision, motivation, inspiration, and coordination. Initiative primarily comes from the outlying bits of an organization since these are closest to the customer and decisions.

"Subsidiarity" is an essential feature of Handy's federal organization. Subsidiarity means that it is inappropriate—even sinful—to take decisions away from another person. If you have ever felt strongly aggrieved that your parents have "stolen" your decisions then you will have a sense of the message that Handy is trying to get across. The outlying bits are closer to decision making—if the centre (in this analogy your parents) try to make decisions about how and when you should do your homework there is a high probability that they will make a bad decision. This of course assumes that you are able and willing to make the most of your abilities!

In a similar way, for a global fast food franchise it would make sense for marketing, managing corporate image, and purchasing to be controlled by the centre. These bits of the organization might sensibly be handed over to the centre because the centre could negotiate buying discounts and ensure that the brand image is managed effectively and consistently. The individual franchise would have local knowledge though, and it would make sense for considerable decentralization on issues such as recruitment and some modifications to the menu to cater to local tastes while maintaining the core identity of the franchise.

Handy argued (in 1989) that organizations would become increasingly federal in nature with decisions being made at the local level to provide flexibility and response to local needs. The outlying bits would recognize though that it makes sense for certain functions to be managed by the centre.

Handy suggested that portfolio working would become an increasing trend and full-time working for one employer for your working life would be seen as a thing of the past—even a bit odd or unimaginable— and this may already be the case in many countries. Handy thought that individuals would increasingly avoid working in formal organizations, which he said could become "prisons of the soul".[2]

Student workpoint 2.3

An investigation

Ask your parents and grandparents (or people of a similar age to them) the nature of their working life. For example, ask:

How many organizations did they work for?

When they started out, did they expect to work with the same organization for life?

---

[2] Handy, C. 1989. *Ibid.*

Data response exercise

Read the text below and answer the questions that follow.

Case study

Flexible trends

The Happiness at Work Index, a quarterly survey by recruitment consultant Badenoch & Clark of 1,000 UK office workers, found that 41% of employees cited flexible working as one of the most important factors when looking for a new job.

Additionally, a survey of more than 20,000 employees found that 35% of employers were taking responsibility for work–life balance in the workplace.

Organizations can benefit from a reduction in recruitment and retention costs and attract a more diverse and better-skilled workforce with flexible work practices. By allowing staff to manage their time and responsibilities more effectively, organizations can help them to be even more motivated and committed.

However, a common concern for employers when adopting such practices is the issue of trust. "The fear factor is that if you set employees free, they will abuse it, but the best employees actually react in a different way," says Keith Nash, who is the Human Resource Director of Badenoch & Clark. "We have found that even when employees have had the freedom to work flexibly and reduce their working hours, they still end up working long hours."

Nash explains that one simple way to introduce flexible work practices is to pilot a carefully structured employee survey to gauge how staff feel about it. Nash also argues that it is necessary to implement a robust performance management system, where quality and quantity of output from homeworking is measured through the use of technology that provides instant remote access. Appraisals should be more frequent if you cannot directly supervise staff.

Source: Adapted from www.personneltoday.com, January 2008

Examination questions

1 Explain why many UK organizations have introduced flexible working practices, whereas others have resisted them. [10 marks]

2 Evaluate the benefits to an employee and an employer of introducing flexible working practices. [10 marks]

2.2 Organizational structure and communication

By the end of this chapter, you should be able to:

- construct different types of organization chart and describe the nature of their structure
- explain and analyse how changes in organizational structures affect employee motivation, communication and performance
- discuss factors influencing the degree of centralization and decentralization
- discuss the development of flexible organizational structures
- evaluate the role and importance of informal organization
- identify and analyse methods of organizing human resources
- evaluate whether firms benefit from outsourcing, offshoring and the migration of human resource functions
- compare different forms of business communications
- identify types of ICT and discuss the effects of new technologies on communications

"There is no degree of human suffering which in and of itself is going to bring about change. Only organization can change things."
Susan George (1950–), author

Organizational structure

The formal organization

The term "formal organization" refers to the official structures of command and control that exist in an organization. In any organization there is a formal organization; this refers to the formal relationships of authority. In the formal organization, authority is delegated from senior to middle to junior management. Each level of management will tend to have written or unwritten rules that outline what can and cannot be done at each level.

At your school there will be a formal organization that features the board of governors, the senior managers, middle managers, student representatives, and so on. There is also likely to be an informal organization. This term refers to the unofficial organization of personal and social relations that develop in an organization. In the informal organization, power comes from informal groups in the organization. Since the informal organization does not officially exist it is difficult to identify and there are no rules or individuals that can be officially identified as representatives. Whether the informal organization works for the good or ill of the organization as a whole will depend on what it is trying to achieve and whether its aims and skills are more constructive than the official organization's.

The formal organization will feature delegation (passing authority to a subordinate) to those subordinates in a manager's span of control (those the manager has official authority over). It's worth noting that the person who delegated the work remains accountable for the outcome of that work.

What factors will determine the amount of authority the manager delegates? They include:

- the ability of the subordinate
- the expectations of the manager and the subordinate
- the consequences of getting the decision wrong
- the culture of the organization
- the amount of work the manager and the subordinate have to do.

student workpoint 2.4

Be a thinker—define, describe, and explain

1 Define delegation.   [2 marks]

2 Outline the activities or jobs that your parents have
   delegated to you now.   [4 marks]

3 Explain how the activities that have been delegated to
   you by your parents have changed over the last six years.   [10 marks]

Levels of hierarchy

As the formal organization grows, a hierarchy will become apparent. This hierarchy is the system of ranking people in an organization. It can link people either directly or indirectly, and vertically or horizontally.

Flat and tall organizations

As an organization grows it is likely that people become relatively more specialized, rules will need to be put in place and lines of command and control will become clearer. Individuals who work in large organizations may complain that it has become rules-based and that they are an insignificant cog in a large impersonal machine. These people will feel alienation to a bureaucracy—a system where there are standardized procedures, formal division of powers, rigid hierarchy, and formal working relationships. These large organizations often have a long chain of command and are therefore referred to as tall organizations. A stable business environment where the rules can be applied over time is more likely to be a tall organization. The buildings in which these organizations operate are often old and traditional and will probably be a major feature of your town or country.

In contrast, flat organizations have few levels of management. Decentralized decision making and employee participation are encouraged. This structure aims to create autonomous units that are close to the customer and can quickly identify and respond to changes in their internal and external business situation. In flat organizations the managers tend to be closer to subordinates and so more likely to have a more personal working relationship with them. While this may be the preferred organizational structure, decision making may be slow and frustrating. It can also be confusing as the source of power and decisions is less clear than in the tall bureaucratic organization.

Chain of command

The chain of command is the line of authority and responsibility along which orders are passed in a formal organization. Instructions are passed down the organization until they are received by those who are expected to carry them out. The extent to which this happens will depend on the culture of the organization—a feature we'll turn to later.

Organization charts

In this section we're going to construct different types of organization chart and describe the nature of their structure, for example flat or tall. An organization chart is a diagram that shows the official working relationships in an organization. Levels of hierarchy, chain of command, span of control, and scope for delegation in an organization can all be identified from the diagram.

In many large organizations the organization chart is complicated and so it is usually broken down into smaller, more manageable bits.

Let's imagine the organization chart for a typical school. The hierarchy will be as shown in Figure 2.3.

Extra elements may be needed, for example if there is subdivision into pastoral roles:

- principal
- vice principal
- head of year
- tutors

and academic roles:

- head of faculty
- head of department
- subject teachers.

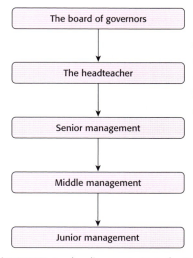

Figure 2.3 A school's organization chart

2 Human resources

HL

Centralization and decentralization

Centralization means concentrating decision making in a particular location or group. If the decisions in your school are predominantly made by one group or location then decision making could reasonably be described as highly centralized.

In contrast, decentralization is when decision making is largely dispersed to outlying bits of the organization. If your school allows different parts of the organization to make substantial decisions about things like uniform, activities, subjects and how they are taught, then decision making is highly decentralized.

Many economies have moved away from centralized command and control to decentralized systems. These systems have the advantage

"Watch out for the fellow who talks about putting things in order! Putting things in order always means getting other people under your control."
Denis Diderot (1713–1784)

that decision making is closer to the people making and understanding the decision. However, such a system is likely to result in greater variation in the decisions made and the process of decision making may be slower because more people are usually consulted. Of course, the reverse could be true since decentralized decision making will often involve fewer layers of hierarchy and faster decision making.

Data response exercise

Read the text below, then answer the questions and discuss the point that follows.

Case study

Hoover's free flight marketing fiasco

In August 1992, the UK division of domestic appliance manufacturer Hoover offered free airline tickets to any customer spending more than £100 on Hoover appliances. Initially, the offer was for return-trip flights to destinations in Europe, but it was soon extended to included free flights to the US. There was a massive customer response, as many of the flights were worth more than the £100 purchase required to get free tickets.

Hoover intended the promotion to sell vacuum cleaners and washing machines. The company also hoped to recoup some of the cost of the promotion by selling profitable extras. However, the promotion ended up costing Hoover around £50 million.

The travel agents Hoover was working with struggled to cope with the massive demand for flights and this led to a great deal of bad publicity in the national press about the promotion. Hoover found itself at the centre of one of the greatest marketing and PR mistakes ever made.

The matter was even raised in the UK Parliament. Customers formed pressure groups to take Hoover to court to ensure that it fulfilled its promise. Hoover found itself fighting legal battles for six years. Eventually, around 220,000 customers were given free flights.

At the time, some observers said that the real cause of the problem was decentralization: the decision to go ahead with the free flights promotion was made by the UK division of Hoover, rather than by the US headquarters.

Examination questions

1   Distinguish between decentralization and centralization, and between marketing and PR.   [*8 marks*]

2   Discuss the factors that will influence the extent of centralization and decentralization in an organization.   [*10 marks*]

3   Examine the safeguards that could have been put into place at Hoover's head office to avoid this situation arising.   [*10 marks*]

Discuss the problems that could arise if your school allowed complete decentralization of decision making for school expeditions.

Matrix structures or project teams

In your school you will probably find that some teachers work for two bosses. They may have a head of department who they are accountable to for their academic subject and a head of year who they are accountable to for their work as a class tutor. Such a system reflects a matrix structure. This term refers to the situation where individuals work across teams and projects. It is possible that such a system can lead to a clash, for example when a person is expected to be in two places at the same time. In this situation it may be that senior management will need to intervene to decide where and when the priorities should be.

Data response exercise

Read the text below and answer the questions that follow.

Case study

Bob was thrilled—his new school had decided to introduce flexible work practices and cross-functional teams. He would now be working with a team that was required to advise on the school's new building programme as well as reporting to the head of drama, head of English and head of TOK. On top of that he would have to attend meetings with the head of Year 12, since he would be required to write references for his IB students. Before long, Bob found that he was getting into trouble with everyone, despite being prepared to work after school hours and attending meetings at the weekend. He found it impossible to attend all the meetings since they were often scheduled at the same time. Despite this Bob found that he was popular with the headteacher since he worked such long hours and was involved in so may parts of the school. The conflicts and long hours caused Bob so much stress that he tendered his resignation and left the school.

Examination questions

1   With reference to the case study about Bob's changed work arrangements define these terms:

   a   span of control   [2 marks]

   b   delegation   [2 marks]

   c   line manager   [2 marks]

   d   lateral working relationships   [2 marks]

   e   functional management.   [2 marks]

2   Discuss the steps senior management could have taken to ensure that Bob could make this system workable.   [10 marks]

Henry Mintzberg

Professor Henry Mintzberg is a well-known academic writer on human resources. Mintzberg describes six frameworks, parts, and coordinating mechanisms for organizations.

The six organizational frameworks, or coordinating mechanisms in an organization are: "DOSPAN".

- Direct supervision: a boss tells a subordinate what to do. This is common in small businesses where there is little distance between managers and workers.
- Output standardization: standards are set for results. This is common in organizations that produce a wide range of outputs and where uniformity is important.
- Skills standardization: standards are set for the qualifications that employees must have. This is common in professional organizations such as those employing lawyers and doctors.
- Process standardization: standards are set for the way work is done. This is common in organizations with tight control on quality, such as producers of medicines.
- Adjustment: employees adapt and adjust to achieve organizational goals. This is common in entrepreneurial organizations where the environment is rapidly changing.
- Norms standardization: team "norms" are the standard by which someone is assessed, so an employee must fit in to established customs, traditions, habits, and practices if that person is to

succeed in the organization. This is common in religious or missionary organizations.

The six parts of an organization are: "MOSTIS".

- Middle management, which acts as a buffer between senior and junior management and ensures that policies are put into effect.
- Operating core, which produces the goods and services of the organization.
- Strategic management, which sets the strategic direction of the organization.
- Technostructure, which provides the systems such as IT and training, for organizational effectiveness.
- Ideology, which includes the values of the organization and the way things get done.
- Support staff, which offers back-up services such as catering and maintenance.

student workpoint 2.5
An investigation
Using examples from your school—or an organization that you are familiar with—suggest what might go in the gaps in these tables.

Framework	Description	Example
Mutual adjustment	Adapt to achieve objectives	
Direct supervision		
Processes		Fire drill
Outputs		Canteen
Skills		Teachers must have degree and teacher training certificate
Norms		Sports team members must adhere to a given dress code

Basic parts	Description	Example
Strategic		Senior management team
Middle		Head of department
Core		Teachers
Technostructure		Timetable manager
Support staff		Caretaker
Ideology		

Coordinating mechanisms	Description	Example
Direct supervision		
Mutual adjustment		
Processes		Health and safety procedures
Outputs		Number of students enrolling
Skills		School nurse must be a qualified medical practitioner
Norms		Sports team members must adhere to a given dress code

Tom Peters

Tom Peters is a prolific writer on organizations. His most famous book (written with Robert Waterman in 1982)[3] cites successful organizations and suggested reasons for their success. Peters and Waterman suggested eight features of organizations that achieved excellence.

- Get things done.
- Understand your customers' needs.
- Be independent and innovative.
- Achieve productivity through people.
- Be hands on—get involved in the organization.
- Only do what you do best.
- Have a simple organization structure and lean staff.
- Directly control core activities but delegate or outsource peripheral ones.

Peters provided seven pointers for analysing the set up of an organization: the "seven S" framework.

The "hard Ss" are:

- strategy—in broad terms, how aims are to be achieved over the long term
- structure —the management structure needed to achieve those aims
- systems —the operational systems, such as appraisal reporting, and IT.

The "soft Ss" are:

- staff—attracting, retaining and developing people
- style—the way things get done
- shared—values (the beliefs of the organization), subordinate goals
- skills—ensuring that staff are suitably qualified to achieve a given task.

---

student workpoint 2.6

An investigation

Select an organization that you consider to be effective or successful.

Based on the information that you can find from the organization's website and/or other sources, what would you put in the gaps in these tables?

Characteristic	Evidence
Get things done	
Understand your customers' needs	
Be independent and innovative	
Achieve productivity through people	
Be hands on—get involved in the organization	
Only do what you do best	
Have a simple organization structure and lean staff	

→

---

[3] Peters, T. and Waterman, R. 1982. *In Search of Excellence*. New York, Harper & Row.

Structure	
Systems	
Staff	
Style	
Shared values	
Skills	

Source: Peters, T and Waterman, R. 1982. *In Search of Excellence*. New York, Harper & Row.

Outsourcing, offshoring, and migration of HR functions

When an organization gets a sub-contractor to undertake part of its production process, it is outsourcing. Examples are when Nike gets another company to manufacture its products or Coca-Cola appoints a marketing agency to market its range.

Outsourcing enables an organization to cut costs and focus on what it believes it does best. Toyota Motor Company has been described as a car assembler rather than a manufacturer because so many of the components in its cars are made by sub-contractors.

The relocation of an organization's activities from one country to another is called offshoring. Many organizations have relocated their activities to India and China to take advantage of much lower production costs. (See more on outsourcing and offshoring on p. 280–281.)

In this section, we analyse the reasons behind, and the effects of, moving some HR functions to external organizations located nationally or globally.

The HR function in an organization typically includes the following functions:

- payroll—ensuring that employees receive the pay due to them
- work time—recording hours worked and holiday entitlement
- benefits administration—such as travel and accommodation expenses incurred while working away from home
- the HR management information system—recording qualifications, training, appraisal, experience, and disciplinary records
- recruiting—anticipating employee shortfalls and recruiting staff in preparation for this
- dismissal and redundancy—ensuring that appropriate procedures are followed
- PR—managing internal and external communication to project and maintain a positive image.

Many organizations have outsourced all or parts of the HR function and hardly any have reversed their decision once they have seen the benefits of outsourcing. The main benefits are cost savings and service improvements. An external HR services provider can focus exclusively on those functions and be fully conversant with legal requirements and labour developments. It also allows the outsourcing organization to focus on what it does best.

Data response exercise

Read the text below and answer the questions that follow.

Case study

Eighty per cent of companies that outsource HR functions would do so again

More than three quarters of executives at large North American and European companies that currently outsource one or more major HR functions said they would do so again, according to a survey released today by The Conference Board and sponsored by Accenture.

HR Outsourcing: Benefits, challenges and trends is The Conference Board's second study to track the benefits of HR outsourcing and changes in the HR market-place. Based on the results of a survey of executives at more than 120 companies in North America and Europe, the study found that outsourcing is now firmly embedded as part of HR service delivery.

The study found that:

- 76% of respondents surveyed said their organizations currently outsource one or more major HR functions.
- 80% of those said they would do so again.
- 71% of the surveyed companies that currently outsource HR said that they will extend or renegotiate contracts with their current outsourcing providers.
- 29% said that they will put their existing outsourced services out for a new bid.
- None of the respondents said they plan to take services back in-house.
- 91% of respondents reported either having achieved or partially achieved their HR outsourcing objectives.
- 9% of respondents said they are entirely against outsourcing some or all of their major HR functions, compared with 23% in an earlier survey.

The survey revealed notable regional differences regarding the acceptance of HR outsourcing, with US companies being the most accepting. For instance, 87% of executives at US companies surveyed said they currently outsource major HR functions, compared with 71% in Canada and 57% in Europe. However, European firms lead in outsourcing non-HR functions, with 70% of European respondents indicating that they outsource a significant business process other than HR, compared with 65% in Canada and 52% in the US.

"European companies are more likely to be confronted with challenges in standardizing HR processes across national borders due to differing in-country legislative requirements," said David Dell, author of the study. "North American companies do not face this legislative challenge, and are more likely to be driven to HR outsourcing by a need to streamline costs, improve service quality, and reap the benefits of new technologies without major capital investments."

HR programmes that are most often fully outsourced are:

- pensions/benefits (30%)
- stock options administration (30%)
- health benefits (29%).

Partially outsourced services are:

- health benefits (50%)
- training and development (48%)
- payroll (40%).

The survey concludes that companies are focusing on how to improve the outsourcing of the HR function rather than bringing the function back under their own operations.

Source: Adapted from: www.conference-board.org

Examination questions

1 Define these terms:
   a outsourcing   *[2 marks]*
   b HR function.   *[4 marks]*
2 Evaluate the advantages and disadvantages of outsourcing the HR function.   *[10 marks]*

Theory of Knowledge

To what extent can great military leaders of the past guide chief executive officers who are shaping the structure of their organizations?

Communication

"Send reinforcements, we're going to advance."

This was the apocryphal message sent by a British first world war officer along the trench line and then through a long chain of command to headquarters.

The final message received was:

"Send three and fourpence, we're going to a dance."

(At the time, three and fourpence was three shillings and four pence in British money.)

Communication is the process by which meaning is conveyed with the aim of creating understanding. The process of communication requires a number of skills so that collaboration and cooperation can occur.

Communication has the following features.

- Content—what information is being communicated?
- Source—who has sent the information?
- Form—how has the information been sent?
- Channel—what route has the information been sent through?
- Destination—who will receive the information?
- Purpose—what is the aim of the information?

Formal and informal communication

Formal communication is communication that is processed through a formal organization structure. In contrast, informal communication occurs through unofficial channels outside the formal organization structure. In your school it is likely that there will be formal routes through which you might, for example, request changes in the school uniform policy. You might make a request to student representatives who then pass this request on to the school administration. In contrast, if you bump into the headteacher at the local supermarket and casually mention that you think it's time to consider changing the school uniform this would be an example of informal communication.

Barriers to effective communication

When organizations experience a major problem, or crisis, commentators often say poor communication is the root cause. Here is a list of eight barriers to effective communication.

- *Language.* A message needs to use vocabulary and grammar that is understood by the receiver.
- *Overload.* It is cheap and fast to send e-mails to a large number of people. In this situation the receiver may simply be unable to cope with the sheer volume of information and therefore filters out certain data.
- *Noise.* Anything that can interfere with the reception of a message is referred to as "noise". This may be a poor Internet connection, or background noise in a busy office, or too many people speaking at the same time in a meeting.

- *Emotion.* If an individual has a poor working relationship with someone, that individual's feelings may act as a barrier to effective communication. Messages are likely to be ignored or misinterpreted.
- *Sensitivity to receiver.* A message needs to recognize the receiver's needs and abilities. For example, if a teacher speaks to teenage students in the same way as he or she talks to infants then the message is likely to be perceived as patronizing and the students may "tune out" of the discussion.
- *Specialist knowledge.* If the subject being discussed is technical or includes other specialist knowledge then the sender and/or receiver may not understand all or part of the message.
- *Inconsistent messages.* If people receive conflicting messages and instructions from managers they may chose to ignore both, or just select the bits of the message that suit them.
- *Gap.* The greater the distance between the receiver and sender, the higher the probability that a message will not be received or will be distorted or blocked as it passes from person to person. In a tall organization structure the geographical distance between sender and receiver may be quite small, but a message may be distorted—or not reach its destination at all—because the message has to be passed on by so many people.

Data response exercise

Read the text below and answer the questions that follow.

Case study

The space shuttle *Challenger*

This case study looks at the decision-making process and communications that led to the launch of the space shuttle *Challenger* on 28 January 1986, despite inclement weather conditions and the warnings of many engineers working both for NASA and for NASA contractors Morton Thiokol and Rockwell International.

The shuttle was destroyed as a consequence of the failure of one of the O-ring joints in its right solid rocket booster (SRB). After the loss of *Challenger*, the engineering decisions, organizational problems, and inadequate safety culture that led to its launch were criticized by the Rogers Commission and by the US House Committee on Science and Technology, as well as by independent commentators.

As originally designed by Thiokol, the O-ring joints in the Shuttle's SRBs were supposed to close more tightly due to forces generated at ignition. However, a 1977 test showed that when pressurized water was used to simulate the effects of booster combustion, the metal parts bent away from each other, opening a gap through which gases could leak. This made it possible for combustion gases to erode the O-rings. In the event of widespread erosion, an actual flame path could develop, causing the joint to burst—which would destroy the booster and the shuttle.

Engineers at the Marshall Space Flight Center wrote to the manager of the SRB project, George Hardy, on several occasions suggesting that Thiokol's design was unacceptable. For example, one engineer suggested that joint rotation would render the secondary O-ring useless. However, Hardy did not forward these memos to Thiokol, and the field joints were accepted for flight in 1980.

Evidence of serious O-ring erosion was present as early as the second space shuttle mission, which was flown by *Columbia*. However, contrary to NASA regulations, the Marshall Center did not report this problem to senior management at NASA, but opted to keep the problem within their reporting channels with Thiokol. Even after the O-rings were redesignated as "Criticality 1"—meaning that their failure would result in the destruction of the Orbiter—no one at Marshall suggested that the shuttles be grounded until the flaw could be fixed.

By 1985, Marshall and Thiokol realized that they had a potentially catastrophic problem on their hands. They began the process of redesigning the joint with three inches of additional steel around the tang. This tang would grip the inner face of the joint and prevent it from rotating. However, they did not call for a halt to shuttle flights until the joints could be redesigned. Rather, they treated the problem as an acceptable flight risk. For example, Lawrence Mulloy, Marshall's manager for the SRB project since 1982, issued and waived launch constraints for six consecutive flights. Thiokol even went as far as to persuade NASA to declare the O-ring problem "closed". Donald Kutyna, a member of the Rogers Commission, later likened this situation to an airline permitting one of its planes to continue to fly despite evidence that one of its wings was about to fall off.

In addition to these technical and communications problems, Challenger was beset by additional frustrations and poor decision making.

Challenger was originally set to launch from Kennedy Space Center in Florida at 2:43 pm on 22 January. However, delays suffered by the previous mission caused the launch date to be pushed back to 23 January and then to 24 January. Launch was then rescheduled to 25 January due to bad weather. Predictions of unacceptable weather at Kennedy Space Center caused

the launch to be rescheduled for 9:37 am on 27 January.

The launch was delayed the next day by problems with the exterior access hatch. First, one of the microswitch indicators used to verify that the hatch was safely locked malfunctioned. Then, a stripped bolt prevented the closeout crew from removing a closing fixture from the orbiter's hatch. When the fixture was finally sawn off, crosswinds at the Shuttle Landing Facility exceeded the limits so there were further delays. The crew waited for the winds to die down until the launch window finally ran out, forcing yet another delay.

Forecasts for 28 January predicted an unusually cold morning, with temperatures close to 31 °F (−1 °C), the minimum temperature permitted for launch. The low temperature had prompted concern from engineers at Morton Thiokol, the contractor responsible for the construction and maintenance of the shuttle's SRBs. At a teleconference which took place on the evening of 27 January, Thiokol engineers and managers discussed the weather conditions with NASA managers from Kennedy Space Center and Marshall Space Flight Center. Several engineers—most notably Roger Boisjoly, who had voiced similar concerns previously—expressed their concern about the effect of the temperature on the resilience of the rubber O-rings that sealed the joints of the SRBs. They argued that if the O-rings were colder than 53 °F (12 °C), there was no guarantee they would seal properly. They also argued that the low overnight temperatures would almost certainly result in SRB temperatures below their red line of 40 °F (4 °C). However, they were overruled by Morton Thiokol management, who recommended that the launch proceed as scheduled.

The Space Shuttle *Challenger* broke apart 73 seconds into its flight and its seven crew members died.

Examination questions

1 Evaluate the communication failures that contributed to the *Challenger* disaster. Your answer should refer to the seven barriers to effective communication listed earlier. [10 marks]

2 Write a report outlining the safeguards that could be put into place to avoid a repeat of a disaster like this. [4 marks]

Different forms of communication

In this section we look at preparing different forms of communication, for example, reports, and research proposals.

There are various forms of written communication in organizations. The most common are memoranda (memos) and reports. The layout for these may vary, but typically the features they contain are as follows.

Memos

There are five required elements for memos:

1. Subject:
2. From:
3. To:
4. Date:
5. Message:

The message will be brief and may often be written in a very informal manner. Now that e-mails are commonly sent, memos have been used less and less and in many organizations they are already a thing of the past.

Report

A report is a much more detailed written form of communication than a memo and will typically have:

- cover page: title, author, and date
- executive summary: a concise account of the terms of reference, techniques applied, data collected, main conclusions, and main recommendations
- introduction: likely to outline the terms of reference and the context in which the report is written
- main body: the real substance of a report, the facts applied to business techniques, such as ratio analysis (see p. 174)
- conclusions: the main ideas that are a logical result of the research that has been carried out
- recommendations: the action part of the report, which outlines what needs to be done to address the question or problem set out in the terms of reference
- bibliography: books, websites, and other sources cited in the report
- appendices: documents and details that are too bulky to be included in the main report – but can be referred to by the reader for more details.

Information and Communication technology (ICT)

You will know that ICT stands for information and communication technology and you will probably take for granted all the digital devices you use to process and share information. As a student of business you need to understand how these technologies can affect:

- the cost and speed of communication
- where and when people work
- the location of business (all or parts of the business)
- how organizations market their products
- how organizations recruit

- the hours people work
- how organizations project themselves.

Theory of Knowledge

Theory of Knowledge discussion

Discuss the validity, reliability, and credibility of knowledge communicated through formal and informal channels.

Data response exercise

Read the text below and answer the question that follow.

Case study

Our nomadic future

From *The Economist* print edition, 10 April 2008

Prepare to see less of your office, more of your family—and still perhaps be unhappy

Sometimes the biggest changes in society are the hardest to spot precisely because they are hiding in plain sight. It could well be that way with wireless communications. Something that people think of as just another technology is beginning to show signs of changing lives, culture, politics, cities, jobs, even marriages, dramatically. In particular, it will usher in a new version of a very old idea: nomadism—having the ability to wander around in search of food or work without being anchored to one place.

The broad technological future is pretty clear: there will be ever faster cellular networks, far more numerous Wi-Fi "hotspots" and many more gadgets to connect to these networks. Second, the social changes are already visible: parents on beaches waving at their children while typing on their BlackBerrys; entrepreneurs discovering they don't need offices after all (if you need to recharge something, you just go to Starbucks); teenagers text-dumping their boyfriends or girlfriends. Everybody is doing more on the move.

Ancient nomads went from place to place—and they had to take a lot of stuff with them (including their livelihoods and families). The emerging class of digital nomads also wander, but they take virtually nothing with them; wherever they go, they can easily reach people and information. And the barriers to entry are falling. You don't have to be rich to be a nomad. It is getting harder to find good excuses for being offline: the European Union allowed airlines to offer in-flight mobile phone service, and several carriers have Wi-Fi. The gadgets, too, are getting ever smaller and more portable.

A century ago some people saw the car merely as a faster horse, yet it led to entirely new cities, with suburbs and sprawl, to new retail cultures (megastores, drive-throughs), new dependencies (oil) and new health threats (sloth, obesity). By the same token, wireless technology is surely not just an easier-to-use phone. The car divided cities into work and home areas; wireless technology may mix them up again, with more people working in suburbs or living in city centres. Traffic patterns are beginning to change again: the rush hours at 9 am and 5 pm are giving way to more varied "daisy-chain" patterns, with people going backwards and forwards between the office, home, and all sorts of other places throughout the day. Already, architects are redesigning offices and universities: more flexible spaces for meeting people, fewer private enclosures for sedentary work.

Don't sweat, don't shower

Will it be a better life? In some ways, yes. Digital nomadism will liberate ever more knowledge workers from the cubicle prisons of Dilbert cartoons. But the old tyranny of place could become a new tyranny of time, as nomads who are "always on" all too often end up—mentally—anywhere but here (wherever here may be). As for friends and family, permanent mobile connectivity could have the same effect as nomadism: it might bring you much closer to family and friends, but it may make it harder to bring in outsiders. It might isolate cliques. Sociologists fret about constant e-mailers and texters losing the everyday connections to casual acquaintances or strangers who may be sitting next to them in the café or on the bus.

As for politics, the tools of nomadism—such as mobile phones that double as cameras—can improve the world. For instance, they turn practically everybody into a potential human rights activist, ready to take pictures or video of police brutality. But the same tools have a dark side, turning everybody into a fully equipped paparazzo. Some fitness clubs have started banning mobile phones near the treadmills and showers lest patrons find themselves pictured, flabby and sweaty, on some website that future Google searches will happily turn up. As in the desert, so in the city: nomadism promises the heaven of new freedom, but it also threatens the hell of constant surveillance by the tribe.

Source: Adapted from: www.economist.com

Examination questions

Use the information in the article from *The Economist* to:

a prepare a PEST analysis of the impacts of ICT [*8 marks*]

b evaluate the effects of new technologies on communication within and between organizations and their stakeholders [*12 marks*]

HL

Communication Networks

The term communication network refers to the route(s) through which messages travel within an organization.

The Chain Network

In a hierarchical organization it is likely that information will pass up and down the various levels. This can be time consuming and slow down decision making and organizational effectiveness. It is also more likely that the message could be distorted as it moves through the various levels. However, this system can ensure that all levels are informed and thus reduce the likelihood of errors.

The Wheel Network

The wheel network refers to the system whereby information passes through an individual at the centre (or hub) to various individuals surrounding him. The advantage is that information can be controlled by the individual and distributed quickly. The main problems are that he may become overloaded with information and organizational effectiveness may rely too heavily on this individual. A newspaper will often operate using a wheel (or wheels) so that one editor can control the information that goes out from his section.

The Web Network

The web network exists where anyone can communicate with anyone else in the organization to achieve their goals. Communication can thus be vertical, diagonal and horizontal. Although rather chaotic this kind of network can be useful to gain a variety of ideas and thus help deal with complex issues.

When assessing the effectiveness of a network it is important to consider its likely impact on speed, confidentiality, accuracy, and inclusiveness. For example, the chain network is likely to slow down communication and exclude those outside the chain, but it will be easier to keep the communication confidential and ensure the accuracy of the information communicated.

Examination questions

Suggest an effective network for each of the following situations and explain why you think it is the most effective.

Informing Regional Managers of new safety measures.

Getting ideas from the school community on the design for a new uniform.

Selecting a football team and making necessary changes during the match.

2.3 Leadership and management

By the end of this chapter, you should be able to:

- evaluate the effectiveness of various leadership styles and their implications
- apply the theories of Likert, Fiedler, Blake and Mouton and Tannenbaum and Schmidt
- explain the key functions of management, applying the theories of Fayol, Handy and Ducker

The difference between leadership and management

A manager is responsible for planning and overseeing the work of a group, monitoring the group's progress, and ensuring that the plan is put into effect. A manager therefore deals with complexity. In contrast, a leader's role is more emotional since a great leader will have the ability to inspire people to follow voluntarily. A leader therefore spends a great deal of time and energy building relationships.

Leadership styles

Four leadership styles are outlined below.

Autocratic leadership style

Autocratic leaders hold on to as much power and decision making as they possibly can. There is likely to be minimal consultation and employee input into decision making. Orders should be obeyed and employees should welcome the structured environment and the rewards they receive.

This style of leadership is most likely to be used when subordinates are unskilled, not trusted, and their ideas are not valued. It is also more likely in an organization that focuses on results and has to make urgent decisions that depend highly on the manager. The style is likely to be accompanied by very detailed instructions and close supervision. In some situations subordinates may expect—and like— to be told what to do since there can be no second guessing or uncertainty.

Autocratic leadership will probably be unsuccessful when employees have the opposite characteristics to those just described. Highly skilled individuals who have experienced democratic systems and who like to do things their own way are unlikely to tolerate an autocratic manager—and may well leave the organization.

Bureaucratic leadership style

In bureaucratic leadership a manager refers to the rule book when making decisions since procedure or policy dictate what should be done. This style of leadership can be effective when the operating environment is very stable or very definite procedures need to be followed because the consequences of a mistake may be very high.

The style is likely to be counterproductive in a situation when creativity and rapid decision making is needed.

Democratic leadership style

The democratic manager involves employees in decision making and informs them about issues that affect them. Consultation is central to the democratic process but, since the leader is ultimately responsible for the decisions of the team, the leader will have the final say.

Democratic leadership is probably the most popular style, possibly because the word democracy is seen by most people as having positive emotional connotations. The democratic leader can produce results in terms of quantity since many employees like the trust, cooperation, and sense of belonging that go with it.

The democratic leadership style may not always work out though. It is likely to be most effective when used with skilled, free thinking, and experienced subordinates who enjoy the relationships and chaos that can result from belonging to a highly effective team. Nevertheless, the democratic process may slow down decision making and may prove too costly. The style also requires a positive chemistry in the team and if this is absent, no amount of democracy can make the style work.

Laissez-faire leadership style

Laissez-faire means "to leave alone". In this leadership style the manager gives employees considerable freedom in how they do their work. Employees can set their own goals, make their own decisions, and resolve problems as they see fit.

This may be an appropriate management style to use when employees can be trusted to do their job because they are motivated, skilled, and educated. It may be appropriate when working with a culture based around the individual, and where people can work successfully on their own.

Other leadership styles include charismatic (where leaders use the power of their personality to manage a group) and benevolent (where leaders act as a parental figure doing what they think best for the team and handing out punishments and rewards as they see fit).

In summary, the style of leadership is likely to be influenced by:

- the subordinates (subordinates' skills, age, education, expectations, and motivation)
- the decision (whether urgent, important, or the consequences of an error)
- the leader (the leader's character, values, experience, and expectations)
- the environment (whether creative, standardized, repressive, democratic, or compliant).

2 Human resources

2 Human resources

---

student workpoint 2.8

An investigation

Select a leader you consider to be a "great" leader. He or she may be from any country, and may be living or dead.

● Why do you consider this person to be a great leader?
● What did this leader achieve?
● How did he or she achieve these things?
● What was his or her dominant leadership style?
● What did critics of this leader say were his or her main faults?
● Were their arguments valid?

Trait theory

"She's a born leader" encapsulates the idea behind trait theory, which argues that some individuals are born with the characteristics that make them natural leaders. Trait theory suggests that leaders are different from other groups of individuals in that they consistently demonstrate the following characteristics:

● intelligence
● self-confidence
● determination
● integrity
● sociability.

Interestingly, height and fluency in speech were often found to be common traits too, as were flat feet!

Critics of trait theory believe that it fails to take into account the life experiences that can affect leadership.

Fred E. Fiedler and contingency theory

Fiedler (1967) proposed the contingency theory of leadership and argued that effective leadership depends upon the situation that leaders finds themselves in.[4] Fiedler studied leaders in a variety of settings and made observations about which styles of leadership worked, and which did not, for a given situation.

According to contingency theory, leadership is predominantly either relationship-driven or task-driven. A task-oriented leader will focus on getting the job done, while a relationship-oriented leader will focus on interpersonal relationships.

Fiedler measured the leadership style that was adopted using his "least preferred co-worker scale" (LPC scale) which included the criteria shown in Table 2.5.

Unfriendly	1 2 3 4 5 6 7 8	Friendly
Uncooperative	1 2 3 4 5 6 7 8	Cooperative
Hostile	1 2 3 4 5 6 7 8	Supportive
Guarded	1 2 3 4 5 6 7 8	Open

Table 2.5 Fielder's LPC scale

---

[4] Fiedler, F. A. 1967. *A Theory of Leadership Effectiveness*. New York. McGraw-Hill.

If a leader's score is relatively high the person is likely to be relationship-oriented. A low score suggests a task-oriented leader.

Examples

In a crisis situation the task-oriented leader gets things done and is therefore more likely to be effective. Relations in the team are subordinate to the task since time cannot be wasted dealing with relationships if there is very real danger. Some workers may prefer to be given direct instructions and the task-oriented leader provides clarity and structure for them. It may also be the case that the culture of the organization demands a highly structured and disciplined working environment. Subordinates may also be happy to work for a task-oriented leader if that person is able to secure extra resources for team members and gain them pay increases and promotion—or simply job security. The task-oriented leader may therefore prove more popular than the relationship-oriented leader.

In contrast, the relationship-oriented leader may be effective when "position power" is weak (that is, there is no obvious hierarchy giving some people power—one example might be when all the team members are similarly qualified) and relations in the team are strong. It may also work if the way that things get done does not really matter. In other words, team members can achieve good results—but in different ways. For example, teachers can often achieve good results with students, but in very different ways. If leaders tried to impose their style and structure they would be unlikely to be effective.

Rensis Likert's four management styles

Likert argued that to be effective an organization should link together highly effective work groups in the organization. Likert identified four management styles.

The exploitive-authoritative system

Managers impose their directives with little communication and teamwork. Threats are often used as motivation. Managers make all key decisions.

The benevolent-authoritative system

As they believe they know best, managers make decisions with the best intentions for subordinates. Motivation is mainly by rewards, but there may be punishments too. Communication and teamwork is likely to be minimal.

The consultative system

Managers have substantial trust in their subordinates and therefore involve them in decision making. There is a reasonable amount of teamwork and communication.

The participative-group system

Managers have total confidence in employees and motivation is driven by rewards and the shared goals of the team or organization. All employees feel responsibility and empathy for the organization's goals and there is substantial communication and teamwork. This environment of trust, respect, and teamwork cultivates commitment and loyalty to the organization.

Robert Blake and Jane Mouton—managerial grid

Blake and Mouton proposed the idea of the managerial grid, which describes five management styles emerging from the relative concerns for people or production.

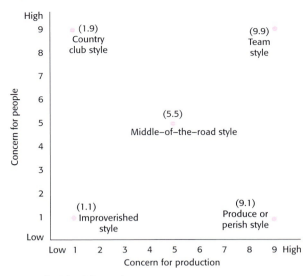

Figure 2.4 Managerial grid—Blake and Mouton

Source: Blake R. R. and Mouton J. S. 1964. *The Managerial Grid*. Gulf Publishing Company, US.

As shown in Figure 2.4, the following leadership styles emerge.

The impoverished style (1, 1)

Managers have low concern for people and production and just want to avoid mistakes. These managers do only enough to keep their jobs. They contribute little to their teams and are likely to get enjoyment in life from activities outside of work and from the idea that they will stay in the same position for quite some time.

The country club style (1, 9)

This management style combines a high concern for people with a low concern for production. Attention is paid to building relationships with employees in the hope that this will win them over and get them to contribute to the team. The working environment is thus friendly but may not be very productive if subordinates try to take advantage of the manager's good nature.

The produce or perish style (9, 1)

Managers place production as the main priority, with little concern for people. The needs of subordinates are peripheral to the needs of the organization. The employers provide money and expect performance in return—sanctions are likely to result if the employee does not perform.

The middle-of-the-road style (5, 5)

Managers hope to achieve creditable results by balancing some concern for both production and people.

The team style (9, 9)
Managers give high priority to both people and production.
Managers keep the team focused on the task but also nurture
good relations.

Robert Tannenbaum and Walter Schmidt—a leadership continuum

Use of authority   Freedom for subordinates

Tells → Sells → Consults → Participates

In a similar way, Robert Tannenbaum and Walter Schmidt (1973)
argued that leadership behaviour can be expressed along a
continuum ranging from boss-centered behaviour to subordinate-
centered behaviour.[5]

The leader must consider the forces in the manager, the subordinate
and the urgency of the task when choosing the most appropriate
style. For example, a manager who trusts the organization's highly
skilled employees, who are working effectively and look as if they
are going to meet a deadline, is more likely to be relationship-
centred than a manager where the opposite situation exists.

Theory of Knowledge

How can managers and leaders know that the business information they use
is reliable?

Leadership and management

Henri Fayol
Fayol's *Administration Industrielle et Generale* (1916)[6] is largely based
on his experiences as a manager at a large French coal mine.

Fayol outlined five functions of management:

- planning: setting a strategy for achieving objectives
- organizing: preparing resources to achieve given objectives
- commanding: instructing individuals to perform certain duties
- coordinating: bringing together the various resources to achieve
  objectives
- controlling: having power over a given situation to achieve
  objectives.

Fayol argued that these functions were universal, and could
therefore be applied to any organization. Read more about Fayol on
p. 328.

Charles Handy on handling organizational problems
Handy (1976)[7] likens managers to General Practicioners (GPs) in that
they are the first person to address a problem. They must first decide

"**Do, or do not. There is no
'try'.**"

Jedi Master Yoda, *Writers on Leadership*

[5] Tannenbaum, R and Schmidt, W. "How to choose a leadership pattern". *Harvard Business
Review*. May–June 1973.

[6] Fayol, H. 1916. *Administration Industrielle et Generale*—see Storrs, C. (translator). 1949.
General and Industrial Management by Henri Fayol. London. Pitman and Sons Ltd.

[7] Handy, C. 1976. *Understanding Organizations*. London. Penguin.

whether it is a problem and, if so, what sort of problem. Managers need to take the following steps in the search for solutions.

1 Identify the symptoms.
2 Diagnose the disease (the cause or causes of the problem).
3 Decide how it might be dealt with—decide on "strategies for health".
4 Start the treatment (start to resolve the problem).

Like GPs, managers may need expert assistance, or a second opinion, at any of the above stages, but, as Handy points out, responsibility for each of these stages lies with the local GP or manager.

Continuing the GP/manager analogy, problems come up when:

● the symptoms rather than the disease itself are treated
● the prescription is the same whatever the disease.

The skill of the GP and manager is to:

● correctly assess and interpret information and symptoms
● make the correct diagnosis (using specialist inputs where necessary)
● take the right decisions
● take the right courses of action to remedy the problem.

Peter Drucker

Drucker argued that the customer comes first, so a business should try to create a customer. He believed that internal structure, controls, organization, and procedures kept an organization on track but customers ultimately hold top rank because if they are not satisfied the business will not last very long.

Drucker (1954)[8] described eight areas of business in which objectives should be set and performance indicators established. They are shown in Table 2.3.

Area/performance indicator	Example
Market standing	Market share
Innovation	New products released
Productivity	Output per worker
Physical and financial resources	Capital employed and adoption of new technology
Profitability	Net profit margin
Manager's performance and development	Proportion of revenues spent on management training
Worker's performance and attitude	Staff turnover or attendance
Public responsibility	Code of ethical conduct

Table 2.3 Drucker's eight areas of business and performance indicators

[8] Drucker, P. 1954. *The Practice of Management.* New York, Harper & Row.

Drucker also identified seven tasks for managers, which are shown in Table 2.4.

Task	Example
Manage by objectives	Increase sales by 5% per annum
Take and encourage risk taking	New product developments
Make strategic decisions	Globalization
Build teams	Reward the team rather than the individual
Communicate and motivate	Regular and communication on key issues
See the business as a whole	Understand the impact of decisions on the whole business
Relate the business to the total environment	Understand the impact of internal and external changes

Table 2.4 Drucker's seven tasks for managers

Source: Drucker, P. 1954. *The Practice of Management*. New York. Harper & Row.

2 Human resources

student workpoint 2.7

Draw mind maps to outline the ideas of:

Henri Fayol

Charles Handy

Peter Drucker

Be creative and try to include images in your mind maps to help remind you of each writer's ideas.

Motivation

By the end of this chapter, you should be able to:

- analyse the intrinsic and extrinsic needs that have to be satisfied at work, and the financial and non-financial rewards that motivate individuals
- apply the content theories of motivation of Taylor, Maslow, McGregor, Herzberg, Mayo and McClelland
- analyse the effect of thought processes and expectations on individual motivation and apply the theories of writers such as Vroom and Adams
- evaluate the impact of financial reward packages on job satisfaction, motivation and productivity
- evaluate alternative methods of non-financial rewards in different circumstances in the workplace
- explain how non-financial rewards can affect job satisfaction, motivation and productivity

Motivation

Intrinsic and extrinsic motivation

In this section we will be studying the factors that influence a person to work. If managers can motivate employees it is more likely that those managers will achieve their goals. All the writers you will be reading about in this section will be referring to intrinsic and extrinsic motivators.

Intrinsic motivation occurs when someone gets satisfaction from an activity itself without threats or rewards from outside. Employees are more likely to be intrinsically motivated if they:

- can see that their success is a result of something they have done; if they put in more work they will achieve more positive outcomes
- have some control over their results—they are given a degree of freedom
- are interested in the work they are doing.

Rewards are extrinsic motivators—motivators that come from outside the individual. In the workplace pay is an obvious example. Extrinsic motivators provide satisfaction that the job itself may not provide and may compensate workers for the "pain" or dissatisfaction that they experience at work.

Frederick Winslow Taylor

Taylor was a mechanical engineer who observed the phenomenal contribution science had made to agriculture and the Industrial Revolution and wanted to apply scientific methods to management to achieve similar results. He is often referred to as the founder of scientific management since his ideas on management attempted to apply scientific methods of measurement under controlled circumstances to maximize output.

Taylor believed that standardization of work methods and enforced adoption of the best ways of working was the way to ensure that output would be maximized in the shortest possible time. It is worth recalling that Taylor's ideas were adopted when many poorly educated Americans were leaving agriculture and starting to work in factories. In this situation it is perhaps understandable that managers may have decided to take a more hands-on style in decision making. The introduction of his ideas and methods was often resented by workers though, and provoked numerous strikes.

Taylor is perhaps most famous for his time and motion study. This involved breaking a job down into its component parts and measuring how long it took to perform each task. One of his most famous studies involved shovels, but we'll take a different example. If you watch how a hamburger is prepared in a large and busy fast food restaurant then you will get some idea of the huge benefits that can arise if each "bit" of the system is managed precisely. The burger is cooked at a given temperature, for a precise amount of time on each side. The fries are also cooked at a given temperature for a precise amount of time. Each worker will have a specific role and will only move a few feet from his or her position to minimize time wasted in movement. The result of all this is consistent fast food cooked quickly and efficiently at low cost. Skill has been largely removed from the system so employees can be employed at low cost and with little training.

Abraham Maslow

Maslow is most famous for proposing a hierarchy of human needs to explain motivation.

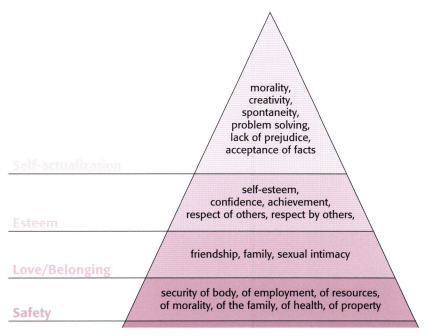

Figure 2.5 Maslow's hierarchy of needs

Source: "Hierarchy of needs", developed between 1943–54 and published in Maslow, A. 1954. *Motivation and Personality*. New York. Harper & Row.

Maslow argued that people have a number of needs and arranged these in terms of their importance.

The basic needs at the bottom of the diagram are most important and an individual will suffer anxiety if they are not met. The first four levels are considered basic needs. Once these needs are met they go away—or no longer cause anxiety.

The remaining needs are growth needs. Once these needs are initially fulfilled they do not go away. In fact the individual will strive to find new ways to satisfy these needs. These needs involve fulfilling your potential; being the best you can be in as many areas as possible.

One of the key issues for management is that once a need is satisfied, providing more of the same will not motivate a worker. So in Taylor's factories, workers will have initially been motivated by the need for food warmth and shelter, but the failure of his factories to satisfy higher-level needs may explain why his methods often resulted in labour unrest.

Douglas McGregor

McGregor proposed two theories of motivation: theory X and theory Y.

Theory X

A theory X manager assumes that employees are lazy and dislike work. Workers therefore need to be closely supervised and provided with a stable and disciplined work environment. This close supervision is best achieved through a tall organization structure with clear levels of responsibility. Employees in this theory will be motivated by financial rewards that compensate them for the pain of working. If employees fail to deliver they will be punished in the hope of modifying their behaviour.

Theory of Knowledge

What are the various ways of knowing that a person is motivated?

Theory Y

Theory Y pretty much assumes the opposite of theory X. A theory Y manager will assume that employees will enjoy their work and will seek opportunities to take on greater responsibility and do a good job. Employees can be trusted to get on with their work with little direction or supervision because they enjoy the mental and physical stimulation work provides. They have the desire to be creative and forward thinking at work.

With these assumptions about employees it is far more likely that the manager will adopt a "hands-off" approach. In some cases, theory Y managers will try to "get out of the way" and allow workers the freedom to do the job in the best way they see fit.

Theory Y managers believe that they do not have all the answers and try to feed off the pool of ideas their workers can share with the team.

Frederick Herzberg

Herzberg (1957) developed a two-factor theory of motivation based on hygiene needs and motivational needs.[9]

Hygiene needs are those factors that provide dissatisfaction at work if they are not attended to. At school you will probably be demotivated if the classrooms are not clean, or if the heating is not working properly. If these things are satisfactory, however, it is unlikely to lead to motivation. Hygiene factors are the things that are necessary for you to get started, but they don't drive you to succeed.

Motivators are the things that get you working because you get some intrinsic reward from them. For example, if you play in a football team you will probably be motivated by successes that you have notched up and the recognition you get for playing in the team.

Herzberg's "hygiene" needs are:

- company policy and administration
- relationship with supervisor
- work conditions
- salary
- company car
- status
- security
- relationship with subordinates
- personal life.

Herzberg's research identified that true motivators were other completely different factors:

- achievement
- recognition
- the work itself
- responsibility
- advancement.

Student workpoint 2.9

Draw a mind map to summarize the main ideas of each writer featured in the section on motivation.

Job enrichment and job enlargement

To motivate people at work, managers therefore need to eliminate the causes of dissatisfaction—by addressing the hygiene needs. After that the task is to create satisfaction. Herzberg suggested that this could be achieved through job enrichment and job enlargement.

Job enrichment entails giving employees opportunities to make use of the different skills they have, while job enlargement involves

---

[9] Herzberg, F. W., Mausner, B. and Synderman, B. 1957. *The Motivation to Work.* New York. John Wiley.

simply increasing the range of tasks a worker has to do. So, for instance, job enlargement could involve replacing an assembly line with modular work where an employee (or group of employees) carries out a job from start to finish. An enriched job differs from an enlarged job in that it involves a range of tasks and challenges of varying difficulty as well as a complete unit of work so that an employee has a sense of achievement. On top of this a manager will offer feedback, encouragement, and support.

Interestingly, Herzberg's ideas on job enrichment also tie in with Mihály Csíkszentmihályi's concept of "flow" which is achieved when a person simultaneously experiences interest, concentration, and enjoyment from an activity. If job enrichment can achieve this the work itself will be a major source of motivation[10].

Data response exercise

Read the text below and answer the questions that follow.

Case study

The King's School was established in Asia and became a prestigious, fee-paying international school with a reputation for sending its high school graduates to the best universities.

Teachers were employed on two-year contracts, which were renewed if performance was deemed to be satisfactory by the Chairman of the Board of Governors.

In 2004 the Chairman, Tom Jones, decided that the school needed to introduce radical changes to head off the challenge from new international schools. Tom Jones proposed to implement the following changes.

- The existing headteacher, who had been employed by the school for 15 years, would be replaced as soon as possible.
- A director of administration, who would oversee the non-academic operations of the school (e.g. catering, transport, cleaning), would be appointed. The director would have a business (rather than education) background and would receive performance-related pay.

- Existing teachers would take a 30% pay reduction.
- A major building programme would be initiated to distinguish The King's School from its rivals.
- Members of the union management committee would not have their employment contracts renewed.
- A rigorous programme of teacher appraisal would be introduced; underperforming teachers would not have their contracts renewed. Extra money would be given to teachers with a "good" appraisal.
- Heads of subject departments would be required to report regularly to the director of academic studies.
- Examination results would be monitored closely.

Tom Jones's proposals were strongly opposed by the teachers and management, but supported by the parents and students. However, since Tom Jones had complete control over the board of governors the opposition was largely ignored.

Examination questions

1 Describe Tom Jones's leadership style.   [2 marks]

2 Using Herzberg's theory of motivation explain the likely effects on teachers' motivation of the
   changes proposed by Tom Jones.   [6 marks]

3 Identify the interests of the stakeholders at The King's School and explain why conflict between
   them is likely.   [6 marks]

4 Evaluate the proposal to reward the director of administration on a performance-related pay basis.   [6 marks]

[10] Csíkszentmihályi, M. 1990. *Flow: The psychology of optimal experience.* New York. Harper & Row.

HL

Elton Mayo

Mayo is most famously known for describing the "Hawthorne effect" (1933)[11] which occurs when output of a worker—or team—improves because the people are being observed, or appreciated, at work. The most commonly cited example is when managers changed the lighting conditions at work in one factory. When they increased the lighting at the factory productivity improved. When the lights were dimmed productivity also improved! This result surprised Mayo, who concluded that people derive a great deal of satisfaction at work from social interaction in the workplace. Just the fact that the managers were taking an interest in the work conditions made employees feel important and established their cooperation. As a result, output increased.

In a similar way to Herzberg, Mayo believed that money and the physical conditions at work had little motivational value. Mayo believed that the value of social interaction at work and the content of work were far more important when it came to intrinsic motivation.

David McClelland

McClelland proposed that a worker's needs are acquired over time and are formed by life experiences. McClelland classified these needs as achievement, affiliation, and power, and argued that a worker's motivation are affected by these needs.

Achievement

People with high achievement needs like to succeed and will thus avoid easy tasks (because these tasks will not challenge them). They will also avoid high-risk challenges because the chances of success are low (and they do not like to fail).

Achievers like regular feedback so that they know that they are achieving. They also like to work on their own or with other achievers so that they can contribute to their success.

Affiliation

People with affiliation needs like to work in a harmonious work environment where they are liked and accepted. They like to work in an environment with considerable social interaction and they will go out of their way to contribute to make people feel needed. These individuals enjoy being team members and tend to perform well in roles where there is considerable social interaction.

Power

McClelland's final motivator is the need for power. Some people like to have power over an individual, while others may want to have power over a group. These individuals strive to direct the actions of others to further the goals of the organization.

Process theories of motivation

Process theory refers to the process that originally initiated a behaviour. For example, if a teacher praises a student for a good piece of work then that outcome (a good piece of work) will be repeated if the same process (praise) is repeated. Equity theory and expectancy theory (outlined below) come under the category of process theories of motivation.

[11] Mayo, E. 1933. *The Human Problems of an Industrial Civilization*. London. Macmillan.

2 Human resources

Victor Vroom and expectancy theory

Vroom argues that individuals strive to maximize pleasure and minimize pain. The most important features of his theory (1964) are expectancy, instrumentality, and valence.[12]

Theory of Knowledge

To what extent can motivation be measured?

How reliable is data on motivation likely to be?

Can observation and experimentation be used to acquire knowledge of the factors influencing motivation?

- Expectancy. This refers to whether or not people expect that they will be able to achieve a given role or task. If people expect that they can do a given job they will be motivated to do it. Highly confident individuals, who have the support of their superiors and colleagues, and the necessary tools for the job are likely to have a high perception of their expectancy.
- Instrumentality. This refers to the likelihood that workers will be rewarded in some way if they do a good job. If individuals see some kind of "carrot" for doing a good job then it is more likely they will perform well. So, if you believe that there is a good chance that your parents will reward you if you get good grades in your school report then you will view your work as having high instrumentality. Work paid largely on a commission basis is designed to make workers believe that there is a high probability that if they perform well they will be rewarded.
- Valence. This term describes the emotional connection people attach to a given outcome. If you like receiving praise then that outcome is positively valent. If you feel a job will cause too much stress or tiredness then you will avoid it. Those outcomes have negative valence. An employer could use positive valence to motivate employees and make sure that employees know what rewards they are likely to receive for good performance.

Vroom believes that an employee will have high motivation if the employee expects to be able to do the job (expectancy), believes that the job will give a positive reward (instrumentality) and has a positive emotional connection with the work (positive valence).

John Stacy Adams and equity theory

The second process theory of motivation is Adams's equity theory.[13] Adams argues that people who believe that they are rewarded too much (or too little) for their job will experience "pain" or dissatisfaction at work. They will therefore seek to redress the perceived imbalance. Workers do not have to all receive the same—they just have to perceive that what they get from the organization is consistent with the contribution they make to it. Of course, different people will have different views on this. That doesn't matter. The point Adams is making is

---

[12] Vroom, V. H. 1964. *Work and Motivation*. New York. John Wiley & Sons.

[13] Adams, J. S. 1965. "Inequity in social exchange". *Advanced Experimental Social Psychology*. Vol. 62. p. 335–343.

that if employees believe that, for instance, they are under-rewarded at work for the contribution they are making, they will be motivated to redress that imbalance. If, for example, you feel that you have been given an unfair report or assessment from a teacher, you will be motivated to get those grades changed—perhaps by negotiating with the teacher.

Motivation in Practice

Many organizations devise complex payment systems in an effort to reward and motivate their employees. Unfortunately there is no such thing as a perfect payment system and the table below identifies some of the major issues that need to be considered.

> **"Don't just stand there doing nothing you might be mistaken for a workman"**
> Anon

Method of Payment	Description	Job Satisfaction and motivation	Potential Impact on Productivity
Wages (time rates)	Employees are paid an hourly rate, or for a number of hours per week. It is possible that overtime rates of pay are used too.	The main benefit is likely to be the security of receiving a regular income and the opportunity to receive overtime pay.	It is possible that an employee will work slowly since his pay is not based on output. If overtime rates apply then an employee could benefit financially from ensuring that the work is extended to cover time over the usual hours of the working day.
Wages (piece rates)	Employees are paid for each unit (or batch) produced.	The main motivator is likely to be the fact that increased output will bring a measurable benefit. However this might involve tedious and repetitive work and the employee may not have control of his results (and this income) if he relies on others for example to supply materials.	An employee may work quickly to get as much money as possible. It may be that a system of checks will have to be put in place to ensure that quality standards have been met. There may be an emphasis on quantity rather than quality.
Salary	Employees are paid a sum of money per month.	The main benefit is likely to be the security of receiving a regular income.	The employer is typically relying on the professionalism of the staff to provide the quality and quantity expected.
Commission	Employees are paid by results for example a flat fee or a percentage for each item sold.	The main motivator is likely to be the fact that employees will be rewarded by results. However, employees may not have control over results (and this income0. For example during a recession sales commission will fall in many industries.	An employee may be tempted to sell products that are not in the best interests of the customer or business and this could create problems for the organization. For example, a bank employee that sells a mortgage to a customer will receive the commission, but the bank may suffer financially if the customer subsequently defaults on the loan.
Profit-related pay	The amount an employee receives linked to the amount of profit that the business makes.	Sharing the financial rewards of a business may encourage a sense of belonging and a desire to contribute to its success. If profits fall then the employee could experience a demoralizing loss through no fault of his own.	Productivity may be a consequence of the profitability of the business rather than the cause.

Performance-related pay (PRP)	The amount an employee receives is linked to the performance of the employee. The performance is typically assessed by a line manager.	The recognition and reward that this system can provide will be motivating. However, employee expectations may be unreasonable and resentment can result if an employee feels that his performance has been underestimated.	The impact is likely to depend on the line manager making a correct assessment of performance and the system being transparent, fair and substantial.
Employee share-ownership schemes	Employees may be issued shares or offered the opportunity to buy them at a discounted rate.	Owning part of the business may encourage a sense of belonging and a desire to contribute to its success. If share prices fall then the employee could experience a demoralizing loss through no fault of his own.	Productivity may be a consequence of the share price of the business rather than the cause.
Fringe benefits	Employees may receive benefits such as subsidized transportation, education, housing or health care.	The status and security that result from these schemes may be motivating. There may also be tax benefits for the employee. However, it is possible that the employee would prefer the cash rather than the benefit. It is also possible that employees may resent the fact that they do not qualify for certain benefits (for example if an employee does not have children then he will not qualify for subsidized school fees).	It would be extremely difficult to assess the impact of fringe benefits on productivity.

Examination questions

The IB pays examiners a fee for each script that is marked.

The above table suggests that IB examiners will focus on quantity rather than quality when marking papers. Discuss the measures that could be taken to ensure that examinations are marked to a consistent standard.

Suggest six performance indicators that could be used to assess the performance of teachers.

Discuss the problems that are likely to arise if these indicators were to be used as the basis of financial rewards for teachers.

Case study

The Fabulous Furniture Store introduced a commission scheme on top of a basic wage in an effort to motivate employees. Within three months the senior managers were receiving complaints from customers that they felt as if they were being encouraged to buy more expensive furniture and that they found the sales staff to be overly assertive. As if this were not bad enough, the managers also noticed that staff were neglecting other parts of their job - such as keeping the store tidy and answering telephone enquiries because they preferred to be in the store making sales. In addition some employees were unhappy because they felt that colleagues had taken their commission from them because they had completed the sale on paper but another employee had spent the time advising the customer when he initially came into the store. This had caused disagreements and some staff felt so aggrieved that they tendered their resignation. One manager suggested abandoning the commission system, but this proposal also created disharmony because employees felt that managers were trying to cut their pay.

With reference to the Fabulous Furniture Store, discuss the impact of commission based payment systems on motivation, productivity and performance.

Empowerment

The term empowerment describes the level of economic, political, and spiritual power that an individual holds. Disempowered individuals will feel economic, political, and spiritual inadequacy, while empowered individuals are likely to have confidence in their own ability. Empowered individuals will have power in decision making, access to resources and information, and a belief that they can be instrumental in changing things and learning new skills so that they can be part of the change process.

If managers can empower their employees they can make positive change a never-ending process in the workplace. In some countries the feeling of disempowerment may be very strong because individuals have been accustomed to repression and have been deprived access to resources, information, and opportunity. It is hardly surprising that these disempowered individuals do not feel motivated to take on new challenges, since experience suggests to them that there will be low levels of what Vroom called expectancy, instrumentality, and valence.

Teamwork

If you have ever worked cooperatively with a group of people to achieve a goal then you will have experienced the joy of teamwork. On the other hand, if you have worked with a group that can't "click" then you will have experienced the frustrations of team failure. Team members that can't help, listen, share, or communicate are likely to undermine the performance of the team.

The success of teams can be crucial to organizations' performance, so an organization will strive to have high performance teams.

R Meredith Belbin's team inventory

Belbin developed a personality test (1981)[14] to identify perceived roles that people have when they are working in a team environment.

Belbin identified the following character types that all perform a useful role in contributing to successful teams. Belbin developed a personality test to identify perceived roles.

Plants

In this context "plants" describes individuals who have lots of ideas and solutions and who look at things differently. They are usually bright and feel comfortable being separate from the crowd. A team made solely of plants is likely to be big on ideas but may not be so good at seeing them though to completion.

Resource investigators

Resource investigators are people who have the contacts outside the team to add resources that will get the job done. Resource investigators are therefore incredibly useful since their network of contacts and resources adds another dimension to the team. A team made up entirely of resource investigators will have lots of contacts but may struggle to get the job done because everyone is trying to add their contacts rather than do the work.

Student workpoint 2.10

Be reflective

If you search the Internet you will easily find a sample Belbin questionnaire and you will probably find it interesting to complete it and find out which of the roles are dominant for you.

You could then ask your teacher to compile teams to perform a given task, such as making a colourful paper chain. You could then assess which team performed best (and worst) and suggest why. It is best to do this exercise before you have read about the different team roles, which are described below.

---

[14] Belbin, R. M. 1981. *Management Teams: Why they succeed or fail.* London. Heinemann.

Coordinators

This term refers to the people in teams who see the big picture. Confident and mature, a coordinator recognizes the abilities of the others in the team and coordinates individuals to achieve organizational goals. The coordinator knows who should be given which task in the team. As they get other people to do the job, coordinators may be perceived as manipulative. A team made up of coordinators is likely to achieve little since everyone will be trying to get the others in the team to do the work.

Shapers

Shapers like to win and will push hard to achieve their goals. If this means challenging, arguing, and bullying, then so be it! A team full of shapers is likely to be focused but may disintegrate because there are too many dominant characters and the in-fighting becomes destructive.

Monitor evaluators

These people are the quiet brains of a team. They often say very little, but what they do say will be considered and valuable. They detach themselves from the team and reflect on what is going on. A monitor evaluator is almost like a helicopter—hovering over the team, watching what is going on and getting the big picture. A team full of these people would achieve little because they would spend all their time monitoring what is going on. They do not take risks and rarely have the ability to enthuse the team.

Teamworkers

Teamworkers like a team to be cohesive and working on the task. They will try to ensure that confrontations are smoothed over and that team members understand each other. A group that is made up exclusively of teamworkers is likely to be harmonious but may be slow and indecisive because members of the team do not want to dominate or offend.

Implementers

These are the "doers". They turn ideas into positive action and can be relied upon to get the job done. They are very loyal to the team and will happily take on jobs that others do not like. A team full of implementers will get the job done, but there may be a lack of imagination and some inflexibility in how things are done.

Completer finishers

These people ensure that the job is finished completely. All the loose ends will be tied off. Completer finishers are perfectionists who can be relied upon to make sure that everything has been double checked since they like things to be done properly. They may be highly stressed individuals since they are reluctant to let things go and may be checking up on other team members to make sure that others' work is up to their own standards.

Specialists

Specialists know their particular job really well and can be relied upon to be up to date in their given area of work. They also have a desire to share their ideas with the team. Specialists are extremely useful working in their given area, but will be disinterested in anything beyond it.

Corporate culture and employer – employee relations

By the end of this chapter, you should be able to:

- describe different cultures and explain the influences on organizational culture
- analyse the effects of corporate culture on motivation and organizational structures
- analyse the consequences of cultural clashes within and between organizations
- analyse the nature of relationships between employees, employers and their representatives
- examine methods employed employers and employees to achieve their objectives
- identify sources of workforce conflict and evaluate alternative approaches to conflict resolution
- explain the differences between crisis management and contingency planning and discuss how far it is possible to plan for a crisis

HL

Organizational and corporate cultures

The term organizational culture, or corporate culture, refers to the attitudes, experiences, beliefs, and values of an organization. For example, the ways that individuals in an organization dress, or treat each other and those outside the organization often reflect the culture of the organization. If an individual joins an organization and does not share its values and beliefs it is highly likely that person will not stay there long. This situation is described as a culture clash.

If you find that you are constantly clashing with the authorities in your school it is likely that you are experiencing cultural clash. This will probably be because your behaviour does not fit with the school's beliefs, expectations, ideas, and goals.

 Theory of Knowledge

Theory of Knowledge discussion

Discuss the cultural perspectives involved in gathering data and communicating conclusions to someone about that individual's role in the team.

Influences on organizational culture

Managers may try to influence the culture of an organization—but this can be extremely difficult, especially in established and old institutions with low staff turnover. Nonetheless, setting the values and the way things get done is a key role of managers so it is likely that new managers will spell out their beliefs and values to staff and will expect staff to behave in a manner that reflects the beliefs managers have set. In your school you will probably find that different cultural norms exist in different departments. The factors that will influence these will be the head of department, the members of the team, the senior management, the culture of the country in which the school is operating and the culture of the nationality of the department members.

Student workpoint 2.11

Be a thinker

- How would you describe the culture of the citizens in the country where you live?
- What factors have shaped this culture?
- Which countries have a similar culture?
- Which countries are very dissimilar?
- How easy would it be to change the culture of a country?

Charles Handy on organizational culture

Handy (1986)[15] introduced a highly memorable way of viewing organizational culture. Handy describes four distinct organizational cultures.

Power culture

The power culture describes an organization in which a few individuals retain the essential power. Control comes from these individuals and spreads out across the organization. Power cultures have few rules and procedures. People are usually judged by their results rather than how those results are achieved since ends are more important than means. Swift decision making can result, but the decisions may not be in the long-term interests of the organization. The collapse of Enron (see p. 36) and Baring's Bank are attributed to a dominant power culture by many who have studied their demise. Family businesses and merchant banks are often described as having power cultures.

The image Handy uses to represent a power culture is a spider's web. The power comes from the spider—and the web with no spider has no strength. The spider can reward or punish. If you work in a power culture and your face does not fit, you are unlikely to work there for long.

Student workpoint 2.12

Be a researcher

Research the collapse of Baring's Bank and/or Enron.

To what extent did a power culture exist?

Role culture

In a role culture, employees have clearly defined roles and operate in a highly controlled and painfully detailed organization structure. These organizations usually form tall hierarchical bureaucracies with a long chain of command. Power stems from a person's position and this position and the rule book play dominant roles in decision

[15] Handy, C. 1986. *Gods of Management*. London, Business Books.

making. Decision making is often slow and detailed and risk taking is often avoided. The Civil Service, The Army and nationalized industries are often said to have a role culture.

The symbol Handy uses to describe a role culture is a temple or building. These temples or buildings are likely to have been around for some time since they operate in stable environments. If you look at the oldest buildings in your town then the chances are that the organizations in them operate within a role culture—government offices and the main post office are often the oldest buildings in town.

Task culture

The task culture describes a situation when short-term teams are formed to address specific problems. Power within a task culture shifts from person to person since the team can be led at different times by different people with the requisite skills to work on a given project or task. Many people like the idea of a task culture because they work in a rapidly changing environment. A strong team spirit can emerge, but divisive decisions can have a seriously detrimental impact on the team since there is often a great deal of emotional energy invested in the team. This passion can be fantastically constructive, but the reverse can also be true. The task culture often features the crossing lines of a matrix structure.

Handy uses the image of a net to describe the task culture since the strength of the net relies on all its different strands. The task culture is often found in management consultancies where a team forms to enter an organization and work on a given project. Once the project is completed the team will break up and a new team (or net) will form for another project. In a school the drama department may resemble a task culture as teams form for a major drama production and then a new team emerges for the next one.

Person culture

A person culture exists where individuals believe themselves to be superior to the organization and just want to do their own thing. The organization is very much a place where they simply go to work and they see themselves as separate from it since they are free spirits. Some professional partnerships, such as architects and some university departments can be predominantly person cultures as each specialist brings a particular expertise to the organization.

The image Handy uses to represent the person culture is a constellation of stars. Each star (or person) is unique and different and operates on his or her own. Clearly the person culture can be difficult to manage. Individuals who prefer this culture will often find it difficult to work in organizations because the constraints they impose on these individuals can be unbearable.

Student workpoint 2.13

Be an enquirer

Why not find a sample of Handy's corporate culture questionnaire on the Internet.

Complete the questionnaire and see which culture "fits" with your school.

Student workpoint 2.14

Be a thinker

Take some examples of countries—the US, Japan, Italy, China, Cuba, Germany, France, Kenya, Singapore, Mexico, North Korea.

Could you place the culture of these countries (or others of your choice) under Handy's categories?

Theory of Knowledge

To what extent can observation be used to explain patterns of human behaviour?

Are globalization and the protection of national cultures mutually exclusive?

Edgar Schein

Schein described three levels of organizational culture.[16]

Organizational attributes

These are the things that you sense when you walk into an organization. As you enter a government building in a communist country you may often observe stern signs or warnings, there may be a picture or statue of a dominant leader. People may speak in hushed tones and dress in a conformist fashion. Outsiders may be viewed with suspicion. The things you see, hear, and feel reflect the culture.

Professed culture

When you receive a letter or brochure from an organization it may contain slogans, statements, or images that project a certain image. These documents give clues as to how things are supposed to be done. If you look at the websites of most large organizations they will give clear statements of what they profess to believe in, or value. There will be statements about their commitment to employees, customers, charities, and other stakeholders. All these things are what Schein would classify as the professed culture.

Organizational assumptions

If you talk to people who have been with an organization for a long time they will often talk about "how things really get done" as opposed to the "official" channels. These people are referring to the organizational assumptions. This aspect of the organization is the most ephemeral.

It is difficult to describe the organizational assumptions because people will often be afraid to talk about them or will not really be able to articulate them. The people most likely to understand the organizational assumptions in an organization are the ones who have been there the longest. They know how things really get done—even if the "official" organization structure and literature states otherwise.

This insight offered by Schein's organizational assumptions goes some way to understanding the difficulty that people new to an

---

[16] Schein, E. H. 1965. *Organizational Psychology*. Englewood Cliffs, NJ, US, Prentice-Hall.

organization often have in fitting in. The best way to get to grips with the third level is to work closely with someone who has been with the organization for some time. But even if that person knows how things really work, the truth may be "unmentionable". The existence of organizational assumptions also helps explain why some managers new to an organization may find it difficult to initiate change.

Data response exercise

Read the text below and answer the questions that follow.

Case study

When JW was appointed as the new chief executive of a software design and manufacturing company, the company had been through a period of significant losses due to lack of product innovation and the high cost of production.

JW has enormous personal energy and a clear bias for action. She is very keen to:

- deliver results immediately
- solve problems quickly and simply with the involvement of the people who ultimately carry out the decisions
- establish a new culture of trust, collaboration, and inspiration at the workplace that ensures maximum employee involvement and production output as well as minimum wastage of resources
- provide employees from both functions with individual short-term contracts that are renewable as long as performance targets are reached
- create a "boundary-less" organization, a concept that removes barriers between the functions.

Managers, therefore, have wide freedom to build and manage their units or departments.

JW believes that giving people self-confidence is by far the most important thing that she and other managers can do as this leads to action by employees. She feels that managers need to make employees believe that what they think and do is important.

Examination questions

1 Define corporate culture. [*2 marks*]

2 Discuss three policies that can be implemented by JW to create the culture that ensures "maximum employee involvement and production output as well as minimum wastage of resources". [*6 marks*]

3 With the use of appropriate theories and concepts, evaluate JW's belief that "giving people self-confidence is by far the most important thing that she and other managers can do". [*8 marks*]

4 Suggest and explain a suitable organizational structure that will enable JW to create a boundary-less organization. [*4 marks*]

Employer and employee relations

This section discusses employer and employee relations in the UK, but as an IB student you will know that labour laws vary from country to country.

Collective bargaining

When management and workers have representatives who negotiate on the terms and conditions of employment, this is called collective

> **"Don't be irreplaceable; if you cannot be replaced, you cannot be promoted."**

bargaining. It would be far too time consuming for a large organization to negotiate with each of its employees. It therefore makes sense for both parties to have employer and employee representatives to negotiate on their behalf.

Sometimes the collective bargaining system may not work and an industrial dispute may arise. Most students believe that the next sentence should contain the word **strike**. However, there are many other ways of resolving labour disputes other than strikes. Employee representatives may try to keep negotiating. They may start a **go slow**, which means they deliberately work below their potential. Alternatively they may **work to rule**, which involves working strictly by the company rule book—and following every rule in the organization would probably bring it to a standstill. An overtime ban occurs when workers refuse to work overtime. In this case, the organization may find it very difficult to operate. Finally, strike action occurs, that is workers withdraw their labour.

At the same time an employer can use a PR campaign to try to put forward its case. The employer might also threaten workers with redundancy or make changes to their contract of employment. It might also lock employees out.

Student workpoint 2.15

Be a researcher

Describe a major industrial dispute that has occurred in your country in the last 15 years.

- What were the causes of the dispute?
- What strategies did stakeholders adopt?
- Who "won" and why?

Conciliation and arbitration

Sometimes the employer and employee representatives will seek help from a third party to resolve a dispute. This process is often referred to as conciliation and arbitration. The aim of conciliation is to bring together the groups in dispute and help them to find a resolution.

An independent third party is usually called in to conciliate on the dispute. In this situation, both parties outline their positions by providing appropriate evidence. This evidence is then assessed and a judgment is made.

No-strike agreement and single-union agreement

A situation where a trade union has agreed not to undertake industrial action unless procedural steps have first been undertaken is a no-strike agreement. It can also mean that a union has agreed to rule out any possibility of taking industrial action. Such a union undertaking is likely to have been made if the management has agreed to certain conditions. For example, the management may have agreed to inflation-proof pay rises, or agreed to refer all disputes to arbitration should no agreement be made between management and unions.

Where one union is recognized as the only representative of employees it is called a single-union agreement. This situation saves managers the difficulties of negotiating with several unions and reduces competition between the unions to get a higher pay increase than rival unions. It also helps to avoid the disruption to the organization if one of several unions is in dispute with management, yet disrupts the production process for the whole organization.

Employee participation and industrial democracy

In industrial democracy there is partial or complete participation by the workforce in the running of an organization. At one extreme, industrial democracy implies workers' control over industry, perhaps linked with workers' ownership of the means of production, as with producer cooperatives. Another approach is the appointment of worker or trade union representatives to company boards or governing bodies. For others, industrial democracy takes the form of "worker participation", such as collective bargaining in which trade unions negotiate with managers. A fourth approach places less stress on power sharing and more on consultation and communication: managers are seen as retaining all responsibility for decisions but make arrangements to consult worker representatives before changes are introduced.

Data response exercise

Read the text below and answer the questions that follow.

Case study

Workers seize Hyundai plants in South Korea

Published 18 August 1987

More than 20,000 workers occupied factory buildings and a shipyard operated by the Hyundai group, the nation's largest conglomerate, in an industrial dispute in Ulsan.

At least 30 workers were injured in street battles with the police. Workers climbed over a barricade and seized the buildings after they had been locked out by Hyundai, which this morning shut its plants in Ulsan, in the south eastern part of the country. Hyundai, whose companies make heavy equipment and other industrial products as well as cars, blamed prolonged labor unrest and the failure of negotiations for its decision.

The workers left at the end of the day but leaders said they would return Tuesday. They have been demanding higher wages and the right to form an independent union. 20,000 workers paraded through the streets, cheered by their supporters. About 50 busloads of police stood by in a ring around some of the Hyundai plants. The auto plant at Hyundai Motors, where the Excel car is made, has been closed since Wednesday because of labor problems at parts suppliers. Production has also halted at plants of South Korea's other major car makers.

The turmoil has raised new concerns about the effects of labor unrest on South Korea's economy. Yet the labor

ministry said that apart from the problems at Hyundai, many other disputes were being resolved, including strikes by miners, electronics workers at the Gold Star group and shipyard workers at the Samsung group.

Most of the country's leading conglomerates—which account for 50% of South Korea's exports—have been forced to shut factories for at least a few days because of strikes by their workers or at their suppliers.

Analysts are divided about the potential effects on an economy that grew by 12.5% last year. Many government and private economists predict that growth will slow markedly, exports will drop, Korea's reputation as a reliable supplier will be badly tarnished and inflation could be rekindled if wages are increased.

But other analysts think that South Korea's economy is large enough and strong enough to withstand the disruption. They point out that strikes at individual companies are being settled quickly, even though fresh disputes are breaking out elsewhere.

Much depends, both camps agree, on how long the unrest continues.

Hyundai has been the most badly hit of the large conglomerates. At the heart of the struggle is the demand by Hyundai's workers to form a union.

Hyundai has long taken a tough anti-union stance, and until the recent turmoil, Hyundai employees had no union. After forming several company unions, employees have demanded that Hyundai negotiate with one union that would represent all companies within the group. Hyundai has refused.

Today, the group shut plants at five more of its companies—Hyundai Engine and Machinery, Hyundai Heavy Industries, Hyundai Electrical Engineering, Hyundai Precision and Industry and Hyundai Mipo Dockyard.

Low wages, long hours

Strikes, sit-ins and occasional violence have clouded South Korean workplaces since the government bowed to opposition demands for political freedom.

The workers are protesting low wages and anti-union policies of the government and company managers—policies that have helped Korean companies to enforce long working hours and make low-priced products.

The labor unrest has accelerated in the last three weeks, although the labor ministry indicated that many disputes were being settled. According to local press reports, 68% of the labor disputes since June 30 have been settled.

The Korea Development Institute, a government-financed study group, predicted on Friday that continuing labor unrest and agreements to increase wages could slow economic growth and lead to inflation. The institute said that if wages increased by 5% to 6%, economic growth

in the second half of this year could slow to 5.8% from its projected 9.5%.

The goal for economic growth this year is more than 11%. Wage increases could also trim the country's current account surplus and increase unemployment, the institute predicted.

Lee Phil Sang, chairman of the business department at Korea University, said: "This is much more serious than the student demonstrations in terms of economic impact. The international market is very competitive, and if there is any export cutback, Japanese or European exporters could squeeze in, or United States consumers may believe Korea is not reliable."

A prolonged work stoppage, he said, would hurt Hyundai. But a Hyundai spokesman said the amount of damage from labor unrest so far was "a trifle".

Other analysts said that fears of severe economic damage were exaggerated. "This is a fairly big economy at this point," said a Western diplomat who covers economic issues. "It's a hiccup in production." The diplomat, who asked not to be named, and Professor Lee said the work stoppages were a result of policies that kept wage increases low.

Source: Adapted from http://query.nytimes.com

Examination questions

1   Define these terms:
    a   trade union   [2 marks]
    b   single-union agreement   [2 marks]
    c   conglomerate.   [2 marks]
2   Identify the sources of conflict at Hyundai.   [6 marks]
3   Discuss the relative importance of factors that influence the bargaining power of each side
    in an industrial dispute such as Hyundai's.   [8 marks]
4   Evaluate alternative approaches to conflict resolution in industrial disputes.   [10 marks]
5   Evaluate the impact on four stakeholders of the actions taken by Hyundai and their employees. [10 marks]

Crisis management and contingency planning

Crisis management

Crisis management is an organization's systematic effort to avoid crises or to manage and limit the damage when a crisis occurs. This involves assessing, understanding, and coping with any urgent and serious threat to an organization.

When a major, unpredictable event that threatens to harm an organization and its stakeholders occurs, an organization faces a crisis. A crisis usually sets in quickly. Although crisis events are by

"Try to relax and enjoy the crisis."
Ashleigh Brilliant (1933–), artist and writer

2 Human resources

their nature unpredictable, they may not be totally unexpected. Memorable crises include currency collapse, natural disasters such as earthquakes and tsunami, and also mad cow disease, and bird flu.

Contingency planning

Contingency planning is an organization's attempts to put in place plans to deal with a crisis. It is the first step in crisis management. Crisis management teams can propose the most likely crises to face their organization and then simulate the crisis to use as a drill. The most obvious crisis to face your school is likely to be fire and you will certainly have simulated evacuating your school in the event of a fire.

Part of the simulation will often involve communicating with stakeholders. The best policy here is to have one spokesperson (so that a consistent message is communicated) and to ensure that accurate information is provided both internally and externally. The contingency plan should also guide the crisis management team to help make decisions that will limit both short- and long-term damage.

The obvious benefit of having a crisis management team and preparing contingency plans is that the plans can be put in place when minds are focused and working on a theoretical (rather than real) crisis. If a crisis emerges and there is no contingency plan in place it is likely that decisions will be made under great stress and urgency. In this situation there's a good chance that the wrong decision will be made.

While the crisis management team will not be able to anticipate every crisis, the fact that they are a team and have a contingency plan means that they will at least be prepared. If the crisis that occurs is similar to one that has been simulated then the chances of the damage being limited is even greater.

Student workpoint 2.16

Be reflective

Imagine there was an outbreak of a very virulent influenza virus at your school that was potentially fatal. The outbreak is totally unexpected and has occurred during the final IB examinations. All stakeholders want the school to remain open and for students to attend school and sit their examinations.

Discuss the steps that could be taken to minimize the spread of the virus and enable the school to remain open and students to take examinations.

Data response exercise
Read the text below and answer the questions that follow.

Case study

You think flying is bad now...

To fully appreciate the impact that soaring oil prices have had on the beleaguered airline industry in the US, consider that carriers spent around $60 billion on jet fuel in 2008—nearly four times what they paid in 2000. Airlines lose roughly $60 on every round-trip passenger, a slow bleed that meant losses of around $7.2 billion in 2008, the largest yearly loss ever.

Consolidation is likely

Experts believe that the crisis could profoundly reshape the industry in coming years. That means not only far fewer carriers than at present, but forcing the survivors to rethink every facet of how they operate, from ticket pricing to the very way they fly. "The problem right now is that no one knows where the price of oil is going to fall down, says Darryl Jenkins, an aviation expert at Ohio State University. "Your planning becomes 'What do we do to lose the least amount of money?'"

Experts believe that any carrier that falls into Chapter 11 [a form of bankruptcy] will likely have to liquidate. That would probably include one or more of the major airlines. Historically, airlines have attracted sufficient funding to operate while restructuring, and new capital when they exit. It's not clear that current market conditions—high oil prices and credit-squeezed lenders—would allow that. Airlines with the financial muscle to step in—for example Southwest (LUV)—would be interested. Southwest has avoided major acquisitions and considers them a steep risk but clearly recognizes potential opportunity in a bankrupt rival. "It just gives the acquiring carrier a tremendous amount of flexibility to impose change that would otherwise be very difficult," says Southwest CEO Gary Kelly, whose company has remained profitable because of long-term fuel contracts.

European buyers

Analysts say liquidations could well leave an industry consisting of two dominant carriers, most likely the combined Delta (DAL)-Northwest (NWA) and perhaps a combined American (AMR)-Continental (CAL), along with a couple of discount players like Southwest. "I think the industry is going to look more like Europe—a couple of far-flung carriers and then a bunch of little guys," says Roger King, airline analyst for CreditSights, a New York-based institutional research firm.

The oil crisis may eventually prompt Washington policymakers to drop their long-standing resistance to foreign ownership of US carriers, leading to the first generation of truly global carriers. "The US airlines badly need more capital to survive, and the only players with the resources to buy in are the [cash-rich] European carriers. Why would Congress object to that?" asks Robert Mann, an industry consultant in Port Washington, NY.

That could give British Airways the opening for the acquisition of American it has long coveted, and a similar move by Lufthansa on either United Airlines or JetBlue Airways, in which it already owns a 19% stake. For all its aviation woes, the US remains the largest, most lucrative travel market in the world. "Don't you think BA would fall over itself to buy American Airlines for $1.6 billion?" King says. "That's peanuts to them."

Creative pricing

This consolidation will come with a cost. Experts believe that if surviving carriers are to earn a profit it will require hefty fare hikes and a 20–25% cut in capacity. That means fewer routes, fewer flights, and even more crowded planes. The biggest losers would be smaller cities like Cedar Rapids, Iowa, and Baton Rouge, Louisiana, that became accustomed to dozens of daily flights, usually on 50-seat jets. But oil priced near $130 rendered those smaller jets uneconomical, meaning that carriers are likely to fly one much larger plane on marginal routes each day, but no more. "We might keep one flight just to keep Congress off our back," muses one industry executive.

Coast-to-coast flights will change, too. With roughly 30% of the weight of any transcontinental flight consisting of the fuel alone, carriers can be expected to replace many of those longer non-stops with one-stop flights, intended largely for refuelling.

The era of cheap fares will end, too. Since deregulation in 1978, fares have fallen by more than 50% in real, inflation-adjusted terms. Prices will rise, and airlines will become even more creative in how they set fares, and take other steps to wring more cash out of passengers, as American did when it announced plans to charge $15 to check a bag. Even more classes of service will be sold. A premium will be charged, for example, for window or exit-row seats, and for separate check-in, boarding, and baggage-claim service for travellers willing to pay more to save time.

Technical upgrades

The fee changes and higher fares are likely to cull millions of travellers from the ranks of regular fliers, ending an era of $99 cross-country fares and bargain-basement weekend flights. It is also likely that a far larger array of travel products will be sold at airline websites, such as aggressive hotel packages and travel insurance.

But airline executives know that they could get far more significant savings if they could lower the costs of operating their current fleets of fuel-guzzling jets. Engineers working on Boeing's X-48 Blended Wing Project designed a jet that uses nearly 25% less fuel but the design limitations (no easy exit, nor windows for passengers to look out) mean that the planes are likely destined for military use.

Congress is being prodded to fund the long-stalled modernization of the FAA's air traffic control system, which still relies on 1950s-era radar. Replacing it with a GPS-based system could cost the government and industry a collective $47 billion, but airline executives say it could save the industry billions in fuel costs each year. If pilots could fly point to point, that could cut some flight paths by a third.

A lovely bunch of coconuts

Developing a GPS-based system could take a decade or more, and in the meantime airline executives are exploring ways to reduce their reliance on jet fuel, a kerosene-based oil that in mid-2008 cost roughly $4.09 a gallon, up 98% in a 12-month period. But developing an alternative hasn't been easy: jet fuels have to pack enough oomph to power jet engines and at the same time be dense enough not to freeze in the air at −40°C—a temperature that turns most biofuels into solids.s

But progress is coming. The Pentagon, which buys more aviation kerosene than any other group, has successfully tested a jet fuel made from liquefied coal. Airbus, meanwhile, is leading a consortium on a project to replace a third of jet fuel with advanced biofuels extracted from algae and plant oils. The efforts will help lower fuel costs and reduce dependence on crude oil.

In February 2008 Virgin flew the first-ever commercial flight powered by biofuels—a Boeing 747 running on a blend of oils from coconut and Brazilian babassu trees, produced by Seattle-based Imperium Renewables. "Two years ago, we thought this was pie in the sky," says Billy Glover, managing director of environmental strategy for Boeing's commercial division. "But things have evolved very rapidly. Our guess is that in five years we could have commercial biojet fuels on the market." Projected cost: around $2 per gallon, or a third less than current prices for aviation kerosene. Coupled with higher fares, biofuels would be cheap enough for airlines to turn a profit. These days, that'd be enough to make many an airline executive go out and collect the coconuts.

Source: Extracts adapted from: www.businessweek.com

Examination questions

1 Define these terms:
   a crisis management   [2 marks]
   b contingency plan.   [2 marks]
2 Describe three crises that you would expect an airline to have contingency plans for.   [3 marks]
3 Outline the main contents of a contingency plan that an airline should have in place to deal with a major airplane crash.   [8 marks]
4 Explain how rising fuel costs will affect the profit & loss account of an airline.   [4 marks]
5 Outline two strategies that an airline could introduce to reduce costs.   [4 marks]
6 Outline two strategies to increase revenue.   [4 marks]
7 Discuss two strategies that airlines could put in place in anticipation of rising oil costs.   [6 marks]
8 Evaluate the strategies that an airline could put in place to cope with rising oil costs.   [10 marks]

Sources of finance

By the end of this chapter, you should be able to:

- explain the difference between internal and external sources of finance

- distinguish between long, medium and short term sources of finance

Sources of finance

All businesses require funding for their activities, for example a loan to purchase a new computer system, or a bank overdraft to pay suppliers before the receipt of customers' cash.

Just like people, organizations require a variety of funding for a range of purposes. There are a number of factors that should be considered when choosing one source of finance over another. The main issues are:

- that a business should match the source of finance to its specific use—in practice this means that a business should secure long-term sources of finance for long-term uses or needs, and short-term funding for more immediate needs
- the cost of the source
- the organization's objectives
- the flexibility and availability of the finance, for example how easy is it for a business to switch from one form of funding to another, or whether a particular form of finance is available for a new business with no trading record.
- the impact the new funding would have on the organization's current financial structure, for example its balance sheet (see p. 168–169)
- the state of the external environment, for example the economy, and consumer trends
- the type of business structure it is, for example a sole trader or partnership can't raise funds from a stock market!

Student workpoint 3.1

Be a researcher

Using the examples below, match the sources of finance for an individual to the best possible uses listed. Make short notes to explain your choices.

Research what the costs are for these personal sources of finance and what flexibility there is if you want to change a source of funding. (The websites of banks and shops should make a good starting point for your research.)

What advice would you give to a couple whose current financial situation meant they already had 50% of their income going out on loan repayments, but where interest rates in the economy are likely to fall?

Source of finance	Use of finance	What is the cost of each source of finance in your local area?
Savings in a bank	Buying a car	
Store card	Starting up a business	
Secured loan, for example a mortgage	Going on a holiday	
Bank loan	Buying new clothes	
Friend's cash	Buying furniture	
Bank overdraft	Buying a house	

You will now have discovered why individuals should use certain types of finance and not others when making a range of purchases. Did you identify all the costs associated with using savings?

Spanish firms and people are struggling to get new loans in 2009

The current global credit squeeze may exacerbate an economic slowdown in Spain, where borrowing by companies and consumers has fuelled rapid growth, according to analysts.

Tighter credit conditions will limit lending to firms that have borrowed money to finance acquisitions, pushing Spanish corporate debt to 105% of the country's GDP – the highest of any large European economy.

Spanish household debt is also among the highest in Europe at 130% of disposable income. Heavy borrowing means that Spanish banks are increasing credit restrictions despite expectations that the European Central Bank may be near the end of its rate-tightening cycle.

"Tighter borrowing conditions are beginning to be a worry due to the already high levels of debt", said Deloitte in a recent research note on Spain.

Now let's turn our attention back to business finance. Specifically, we will now:

● identify the variety of funding available to businesses
● evaluate the advantages and disadvantages of each source
● apply this knowledge using case studies and class activities.

Sources of finance can come from within a business (internal sources) or from outside it (external sources). We'll look at internal sources first, then external sources.

Internal sources of business finance

Retained profit
This is one of the most important sources of business finance and also one of the most difficult conceptually to understand. It represents the profits generated from sales once interest payments to lenders, tax to government, and dividends to shareholders have been accounted for. The remaining profit is then retained or ploughed back into the business and available for future spending by the organization.

Profit is intangible though—we can't touch it—so what do we really mean by this being a source of finance? Well, when we talk about retained profit we are really talking about the fact that, at the same time as profit is being generated from sales, cash should also be accumulating for the business. It is this associated cash, once received from customers, which if not spent on day-to-day needs is now, or in the future, available, for example to fund new machines. Perhaps if we called this "retained cash" it would be easier to understand it being a source of finance—though this isn't correct from an accountant's perspective.

The **advantages** of retained profit are that there are no associated borrowing costs and that businesses do not see a rise in debt levels (gearing). The owners' control is not diluted and decisions are not vetted by lenders (bankers). The **disadvantages** are that the owners may take out all the organization's spare cash and have no buffer if the business suddenly needs cash or another market opportunity arises. Equally, some businesses are more focused on investment decisions when borrowing money and are more lax when using retained profits, with no outsiders to be accountable to—especially small and family-run businesses with no outside shareholders.

Student workpoint 3.2

Be a researcher

Select five multinational companies based in your country and discover what level of retained profits they have in their business. It will be disclosed in their published accounts under "balance sheet" and may be available via the Internet or through searching through your country's business newspapers.

What conclusions did you draw about the size of retained profit in these businesses?

Theory of Knowledge

Is profit a necessary evil in a capitalist society given that it can be a lever for economic development and yet also raise income inequalities?

Is the "trickle-down" effect from the wealthy to the poorest in a capitalist system evident in the long run?

The sale of assets

Just like individuals who sell unwanted goods at car boot sales or even on the pavement outside their homes to raise extra cash, so businesses can sell machines that, for example, no longer match their needs or are inefficient given the existence of new technologies. Such funds can be used to part finance new machines or fund other requirements.

Many large retail businesses that own lots of property have decided to sell off their property portfolio and raise fresh expansion capital or cash. Supermarkets and banks are examples. They see themselves as retailers not property developers. However, there is a catch here:

they still need places to operate and sell from. So they sell the properties to property development or pension companies and then lease them back for a fixed period of time and rent.

The **advantages** of this include having no associated borrowing costs or debt. The **disadvantages** are that a business can only sell off the "family silver" once, so it needs to take care what it sells and how wisely it uses the cash. Also, when setting up a sale and leaseback situation it is imperative that the lease allows the business flexibility, for example if the new landlord wants to sell the site in 10 years' time or up the rent above inflation, what notice period is there in the contract?

Student workpoint 3.3

Be a researcher

Go to retailers' websites such as ikea.com, tesco.com, walmart.com, or victoire.au, or use a search engine and type in "sale and leaseback of properties" to find out how much cash has been raised this way and how the money was spent. Was it long-term or short-term use?

Utilizing working capital more effectively

Working capital is money tied up in the business and used to finance its day-to-day needs, such as buying raw materials. All businesses have a working capital cycle that identifies how this money moves around the business.

Let's say we're running a manufacturing business. The first part of the cycle starts with cash being spent on raw materials. These materials become our stock, so our cash is now tied up as unsold stock items. When the finished items of stock are finally sold to customers these consumers owe us (the business) money. They in effect become debtors of the business. When paid, the debtors' cash is returned to the business and the cycle carries on in funding new stock or in paying the expenses of our business, such as paying our suppliers or reducing our bank debts. If we are making a profit, some of this cash may be kept in the business as retained profit and not spent in the short run.

The working capital cycle is shown in Figure 3.1.

A possible source of finance is thus squeezing or reducing our own working capital needs, so that what cash we do need is more efficiently used. For example, if we minimize our stock levels we reduce the amount of money held as stock.

In modern consumer manufacturing, the concept of producing just in time and only to a specific customer order has grown dramatically. For example, when consumers order a bed or a dining table they often have to wait up to 4, 8, or even 12 weeks for delivery. This is because the goods are not held in stock by the retailer or manufacturer—they are both minimizing their working capital needs and the amount of money tied up in unsold stock. The consumer therefore pays upfront to the retailer and is in effect

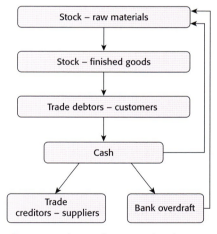

Figure 3.1 The working capital cycle

funding the retailing and manufacturing of the product. Equally, we can ask our customers to pay us more promptly, perhaps with a financial incentive, for example 5% discount for payment in 14 days, and this also helps reduce our funding needs from the bank or shareholders. Another example is that we could slow down payment to our suppliers or creditors, so we are using their raw materials for longer without having paid for them. Our suppliers are thus being asked to fund more of our operation.

However, better management of stocks can be done internally and without always affecting delivery dates—better ICT like material resource planning (MRP) and manufacturing resource planning (MRP2) systems are now making the ordering of stock materials more efficient and reducing the time that stock is left unused and therefore money is tied up.

The **advantage** of squeezing working capital as a source of finance is that you are not having to ask a bank or shareholder to give you more money and on terms that may be expensive. The **disadvantage** is that suppliers and customers may not be happy waiting for money or paying upfront for goods, especially when competitors may be able to offer a better delivery schedule for customers or better payment terms to their suppliers. Caution has to be exercised and communication with these two stakeholders is paramount.

Theory of Knowledge

Is there a moral dilemma if a business delays paying suppliers in order to avoid having to use more of its own cash to fund day-to-day operations? Or is this simply good business sense?

Depreciation

Depreciation is the reduction in value of our assets, which occurs naturally through wear and tear in the production process of a business. Measuring this fall in value over time is not always easy and so we have two normal methods of calculating the level of asset depreciation—the straight-line method and the reducing balance method. See more on this on p. 171–172.

Here is an example.

A plastic injection moulding machine that is used to extrude the outside of a ballpoint pen costs $500,000 to purchase. Its useful life in our manufacturing business is 10 years and after that we may be able to sell it to a second-hand dealer for $50,000. We work out the depreciation of the moulding machine like this:

$$\text{annual depreciation value} = \frac{(\text{cost} - \text{residual value})}{\text{useful life of asset in years}}$$

$$= \frac{500,000 - 50,000}{10}$$

$$= \$45,000 \text{ depreciation each year}$$

This method is easy to calculate and gives us a constant figure for each year. However, the problem here is that with some assets the drop in value is not constant, but is greatest in the early years and less in the last years of ownership. Assets where this is more common are cars and vans, which lose a high amount of value once they are driven off the forecourt of the outlet we buy them from. The second method, reducing balance method, attempts to take account of this problem and weights the depreciation more heavily in the early years.

How is depreciation a source of finance when it is really an intangible concept like retained profit, (which we discussed earlier)? By recognizing that our assets lose value and by attempting to identify how much each asset falls in value we can begin to set aside cash each year to replace each asset when it is no longer of use to us.

The **advantage** of this type of finance for purchasing assets is that it encourages the business to set aside money regularly for each asset's replacement and it also encourages the business to cost its goods and services correctly so that it takes account of all costs when setting prices for customers. The self-employed driving instructor who doesn't put money away each month for a new car may find he or she is unemployed when the current vehicle expires. The **disadvantage** is that depreciation doesn't take account of the fall in purchasing power of money over time—inflation.

External sources of business finance (long term)

Share capital

Share capital represents the monies that are put into a company by its investors, and who are then classified as shareholders. Note that sole traders and partnerships don't have shareholders and so this is not a relevant source of finance for these organizations.

Original investment by the owners is often used to fund the purchase of the organization's initial assets and sometimes to fund the working capital needs of the business while other funding is organized. However, it is a long-term source of finance and therefore should be used for long-term needs, such as purchasing machines or computer systems, or acquiring businesses.

When a business expands it can ask existing shareholders to put more money into the business and therefore new shares are issued in proportion to the size of the increase in share capital. Note that when people buy and sell existing shares, usually via a stock exchange, this does not help the business with raising new capital as it is simply swapping ownership between people.

The **advantages** with this sort of finance are that there are no interest payments and so no drain on company profits. If existing shareholders increase their investment by buying new shares in proportion to their current levels there is no change in control, but if new shares are bought by new investors this may dilute the control of the original shareholders. The **disadvantages** are that shareholders will still require rewards in the form of dividends, and this is paid for from profits. But unlike the arrangement with loan capital (see below), if the business doesn't make a profit and doesn't have a reserve of past profits it cannot be compelled to pay a dividend.

In some countries, such as the UK, the amount of share capital used to fund business activities is rather low relative to debt capital and therefore makes UK companies vulnerable to interest rate rises—which hit profits directly. In other countries, for example Japan and Germany, there is a tradition of investing in share capital and this makes for a more long-term and perhaps more stable financial structure.

Student workpoint 3.4

Be a researcher

Find out what the tradition is in your country or a neighbouring one for share capital and debt capital. Which is more dominant and why?

Loan capital

Funding provided by outside banks and other lenders is generally referred to as debt or loan capital. It is usually provided for a fixed period of time, with repayments evenly spread out over the length of the loan. Interest is paid on the loan at regular intervals, although interest rate holidays (where the lender agrees not to take interest for a short period of time) can be negotiated if the business is struggling to fund the debt. Loan capital is provided for more than one year and so is a long-term form of finance, anything shorter than this is classified as current liabilities or debt.

The **advantage** of this form of finance is that it is often easier to access and use for specific purposes like buying fixed assets, such as machines or property, and so payment is spread out over the useful revenue-earning life of the asset. If interest rates rise in the economy, businesses may find the loan becomes a very good form of finance as the loan interest is often fixed at the outset.
The **disadvantages** are that the lenders have to be paid even if the business doesn't make a profit; that any default often leads to the lenders controlling future decision making—in effect they call the shots. Equally, if the loan is secured against an asset then the asset can be seized if repayments are missed. Also, if interest rates fall the business may find that it has been caught with a high-interest bearing loan, although renegotiating loan interest is quite common for successful or profitable organizations.

Venture capitalists

These are specialist bankers who are more prepared to share the risks of business enterprise than high street banks, by investing in the share capital as well as providing loan capital for businesses with expansion potential.

The **advantages** are that they often provide business help and contacts—maybe for export drives or for identifying new technologies or partners. They sit as non-executive directors, protect their investments and ensure that there is a planned exit route for that investment in maybe five to seven years, possibly through a stock market flotation or via a trade sale. The **disadvantages** are many for the existing shareholders as venture capitalists impose profit or sales targets and if the businesses they invest in fail to expand as planned the venture capitalists automatically increase their equity stake, often from that of a minority investor to being the controlling one.

However, many organizations have used venture capital successfully and benefited from the business advice of their managers, as shown in the case studies below.

Case study

Venture capitalists at work

Scottish Equity Partners (SEP)

SEP has led a €26 million funding round for Kiala, an innovative pan-European delivery solutions business led by Denis Payre, one of Europe's most successful technology entrepreneurs.

Payre is co-founder and president of Brussels-headquartered Kiala, which allows people to pick up parcels when and where it suits them from more than 4,700 dedicated Kiala points across Europe including newsagents, dry cleaners, and petrol stations. Payre was co-founder and chief operating officer of Business Objects, the first European software company to float on NASDAQ, which he grew into a world leader in business intelligence software. He plans to build Kiala into a global leader in delivery solutions.

Kiala, which was founded in 2001, has built a unique technology platform incorporating a tracking system, delivery network, and scanners and hand-held personal digital assistants at every Kiala point, allowing customers to track their parcel and receive an alert via text, phone call or e-mail when it arrives. The company handles more than 10 million parcels a year and operates in Belgium, France, Netherlands, Luxembourg, and Austria. It has run successful trials in the UK and Germany and will use the new funds to expand in these countries and move into Spain and Russia.

SEP was joined in the €26 million funding round by other investors including funds related to La Post and TPG (TNT Post Group).

Kiala has more than 150 major international retail partners including Bertelsmann; Karstad Quelle Neckermann; Pinault Printemps Redoute; Yves Rocher; and Next Directory, which has participated in trials in the UK.

SEP's Andrew Davison said: "We believe Kiala can become the number one solutions partner in Europe for getting goods to customers when and where they need them." Kiala is also using its points' network for spare parts deliveries, particularly for time-critical items such as electronics parts for field engineers. The company already provides logistics solutions to leading players including IBM, HP, Nokia, and Unisys for spare parts and the return of defective items.

Young venture capitalists at work

David Mott, co-founder and investment director of UK company Oxford Capital Partners, has been named Young Personality of the Year (2008) at the Investor Allstars Awards. Oxford Capital Partners is the Oxford-based venture capital firm focused on emerging European science and technology.

The award recognizes individuals under the age of 35 who have made a significant impact on the early stage investment market. The judges were looking for evidence of the ability to source deals from a strong network, to assess opportunities, to manage the due diligence process, and to close deals in difficult circumstances. They were also looking for an individual with a reputation for providing valuable support to portfolio companies and who has played a significant role in driving the venture capital industry forward.

The panel commended David for "his professional work ethic and his entrepreneurial 'nose' for actively building the profile and reputation" of Oxford Capital Partners.

About Oxford Capital Partners

Oxford Capital Partners is a science and technology venture capital firm with extensive experience of commercializing science and technology and supporting businesses with high growth potential. Oxford Capital Partners seeks to identify the best opportunities for investment. We back exceptional entrepreneurs and invest across all stages of development from start-up to IPO, in the UK and internationally. Oxford Capital Partners manages the Oxford Gateway Funds and is currently investing its fourth fund in this series. We manage a portfolio of over 25 companies in the technology and life sciences sectors.

Grants from government and other philanthropic organizations

This is a growth area. Governments, successful entrepreneurs such as Bill Gates, and large corporations keen on promoting their social responsibilities are all increasingly seeking to help the smaller business sector with grants and soft loans (loans with more relaxed payment terms and lower than usual interest rates). While the sums may be small they can make a difference to a project's viability. Often the problem is identifying what grants are actually available, although the Internet has made this research easier.

Theory of Knowledge

Is it acceptable that business billionaires such as Bill Gates and JP Getty, who made millions from running their businesses by charging high prices and maintaining abnormally high profit margins, should now gain public adulation by putting a fraction of their wealth back into philanthropic charitable activities? Would it have been better if they had kept their prices a little lower for everyone and not been so aggressive in their market segment?

External sources of business finance (short term)

Bank overdraft

Banks finance the short-term needs of businesses by providing short-term monies called overdrafts. An overdraft is repayable on demand and so should be used for short-term funding needs, such as when a business is waiting for customers to pay, when it needs to pay suppliers upfront, or when staff have to be paid. When businesses find they are expanding very quickly due to a successful sales drive they may well find their overdraft rising as they await receipts from customers.

The **disadvantage** is that the cost of an overdraft will vary as interest rates change in the economy. This makes budgeting costs a little difficult. In some countries, for example the UK, bank overdrafts represent a very high proportion of the total funding of a business and this can be very dangerous as the bank may decide that the business is struggling or that a recession is due and cut back the overdraft limit without much notice. This can lead to a business failing. Overdrafts are often secured on a personal guarantee from the owners and/or on the assets of the business. The **advantages** are that changes in overdraft limits can be increased quite easily and it is a flexible source of finance.

Trade credit

Trade credit is where a business gains extended time to pay its suppliers—perhaps 30 or 60 days after delivery of the suppliers' goods. This means that the business can in effect use its suppliers as a source of finance.

Factoring

When working capital is tight or when a business is struggling to get paid by customers, it may consider using a third party agency to help. A factor agent is a company that buys the current unpaid invoices of a business at a discount of, say, 25%. The factor agent pays that cash immediately to the business and hopes that it can recover more than the 75% value of the debts in order to make its profit. The better the quality of the customers a business has, the greater the percentage that the factor agent may be prepared to offer upfront.

The **advantage** is that the business receives cash upfront and can use this money to fund expansion and working capital needs more generally. In addition, the administration cost to the business of chasing up its customers' unpaid bills is immediately removed.

Trade credit is the largest use of capital for a majority of business to business (B2B) sellers in the US and is a critical source of capital for a majority of all businesses. For example, Wal-Mart, the largest retailer in the world, has used trade credit as a larger source of capital than bank borrowings; trade credit for Wal-Mart is eight times the amount of capital invested by shareholders.
Source: www.en.wikipedia.org/wiki/trade_credit

3 Accounts and finance

The **disadvantage** is that the business is really giving up some of its profit margin by doing this. For example, if a firm is making a 50% profit margin already, giving away 25% of the sales value may be acceptable, but not if the business is only making a small margin. Equally, factors will not help very small businesses and those with very marginal and local clients. Also remember that a factor agent ringing up your biggest customer and demanding immediate payment otherwise the customer may be taken to court could mean that you lose vital sales in the future.

Leasing

When purchasing assets such as new machines or vehicles it can sometimes be useful to consider leasing as a source of finance. Many airlines lease purchase their aircraft. GE, large US finance company, is one of the largest leasing businesses in the world. Equally, leasing can be arranged with the firm's own bank.

The **advantages** are that the business does not need to find a large initial lump sum to buy the equipment, and can thus pay for the asset from its own revenue. The **disadvantages** are that the ownership of the asset does not pass to the business until the last payment has been made and the business will probably be paying a reasonably high level of interest.

Final thoughts on external sources of finance

Using external financing brings in much needed funding for expansion, but it has its problems or costs. Gearing ratios (see p. 177) rise as loans become a larger share of the total capital of the business; also interest cover ratios may worsen, unless profit rises proportionately as well. Equally, more long-term debt will dilute the owners' stake in the business and that of the lenders will rise, affecting to some extent business decision making. It is important to consider a variety of funding sources and not to become overly dependent on one.

Data response exercise
Read the text below and answer the questions.

Case study

Victoritz Bookshop

The business specialized in the retailing of travel and gardening books in São Paulo, Brazil. The original founders retired and sold the bookshop on in the early 1980s to two businessmen, Lopez and Gunnerson, for the sum of R$600,000. Sales grew and the business diversified into selling video books and also began supplying books to libraries in the south of Brazil.

By 1985 the owners had different views on how to move the business forward and Gunnerson, who had just passed 50, offered to sell his 50% share to Lopez for R$600,000. Lopez had little spare cash of his own, and his drawings from the business were just about enough to maintain his current lifestyle.

However, he had plenty of equity in his house in a fashionable part of São Paulo and some old savings policies which he had kept for funding his children's university education. As for the business, it was already highly geared having one development loan and an overdraft which represented some 80% of total capital employed; and operating profits were small at some R$140,000 on sales of R$4 million. In addition, the overdraft was growing as the business had developed, and currently stood at R$600,000.

Lopez recruited a business consultant as a non-executive director in order to help with strategy. Together they set out a new plan and vision for the business. They decided to computerize the old manual accounting system and also to push forward with a growth strategy for library supplies across Brazil. Equally, retailing was less important now as there was less passing trade and larger retailers were setting up nearby.

They subsequently purchased a small competitor in library supplies and brought it under their own roof in São Paulo. This was funded by a small upfront fee and a deferred payment or "earn-out" for the vendor based on sales over the next five years.

The three problems of low working capital, rising debt and also rising interest rates caused problems for the business in the early 1990s, especially when sales slowed through cuts in government funding to libraries. Of more significance, the computerization of the manual accounting system brought a hammer blow to the business when it was discovered that debts owed to publishers had been dramatically understated in the accounts for years—the current ratio was well below 1— and this all helped to explain why working capital was so tight and the overdraft was rising so quickly when sales were sluggish.

New funding was found through a corporate financier in 1993, but it would come at the price of liquidating the business and then establishing a new company. The new business had better funding and also few of the original debts, so it appeared to be getting off to a good start. The creditors of the original business (the publishers) were, however, reluctant to give trade credit and not unsurprisingly wanted payment upfront for supplies.

Final thoughts

Sadly, by 1995 Lopez couldn't see any alternative strategy and in the end the business went into liquidation for a second time in two years. The premises were closed, five jobs were lost, and Lopez lost his house and was all but bankrupt at the tender age of 59. The banks got most of their money back as they had secured their debt on his house and also on the company's stock, which could be sold on. The publishers lost out twice. There are now many fewer independent booksellers in Brazil, and the industry is dominated by a few national chains (who operate at very low profit margins) and the Internet sellers who are winning more market share.

Examination questions

1 In buying out his partner what sources of finance would you have recommended to Lopez and why? *[5 marks]*

2 What do you think are the advantages and disadvantages for the buyer of funding an acquisition through a sales performance formula as occurred here? *[8 marks]*

3 The business was now technically insolvent, but what other funding could have been secured to help it survive in the short term while it tried to expand sales? *[5 marks]*

4 This lack of credit brought new liquidity problems, so what else, if anything, could Lopez have done to fund the business? *[8 marks]*

5 Was there an alternative strategy no one had yet seen which would enable the core business of library supplies to prosper and at the same time remove the company's funding problems? *[5 marks]*

Data response exercise
Read the text below and answer the questions.

Case study

Voice & Vision Advertising Ltd

Voice & Vision Advertising Ltd was established by two would-be entrepreneurs in 1993 with the intention of selling audio and visual advertising space on the railway network in the UK. The idea was that adverts would be aired for five minutes four times an hour via the public address system on stations. Marketing research was undertaken and cash flow and budgets were prepared. The preliminary funding of £10,000 was paid for by the owners. Contracts with a variety of newly privatized railway companies were in progress though not yet signed. In addition, the technology and engineering firm that the owners had been working with on this project was prepared to offer some support with funding, in a variety of forms.

The owners identified that they needed £70,000 to fund the test equipment and feasibility work on the new technology. A further £1.5 million was required to fund equipment, advertising, and initial working capital needs in the first year. The owners had little capital of their own and could offer no collateral or security for any bank loans.

Conclusion

The venture ran out of steam in 1996 with no formal contracts signed, no capital injection, and no test run being undertaken even though various stations had been offered as test beds two years previously. The owners' expenses were lost, but not much else other than their time and energy—this is often the way when setting up new businesses; be prepared for lots of rejections before you eventually find the winning formula and success!

Published with permission from P. Golden and C. Fallows.

Examination questions

1 Discuss the possible sources of finance for both stages of this new venture, identifying strengths and weaknesses of each suggested funding method. *[10 marks]*

2 Apart from funding, what other issues do you think caused problems for these two would-be entrepreneurs and their innovative method of advertising on train communication systems? Why has this type of advertising still not been used? *[10 marks]*

By the end of this chapter, you should be able to:

- analyse the different investment appraisal technique
- describe the working capital cycle, construct cash flow forecasts and evaluate strategies for improving liquidity
- construct and analyse budgets

Investment appraisal

Once a business is up and running, and it is controlling its cash flow and making a profit, its directors' next thoughts turn to expansion. This often comes down to making choices about which project or opportunity to invest in; hence the term investment appraisal.

A variety of quantitative techniques are used to help explain which investment might be the best choice, but remember there are also qualitative techniques that are equally valid in helping inform decision makers.

Payback

This measures the time it takes to recover enough cash to cover an initial investment or outlay. For example, a new machine for a metal pressings business will cost $100,000 and generate $25,000 extra sales revenue each year. The payback is calculated as follows:

$$\frac{\text{initial investment}}{\text{annual cash flow from the investment}} = \frac{100{,}000}{25{,}000} = 4 \text{ (years)}$$

So the payback period for this investment is four years. This result can be compared with other projects, such as a new salesperson who might cost $100,000 and will generate $30,000 extra revenue per year.

The average (or accounting) rate of return (ARR)

An alternative measurement is the ARR (%). This measures the profitability or accounting of a project over its useful life. It therefore considers all data and not just cash flows up to the point of payback.

The formula is:

$$\frac{\text{net return (profit) per annum}}{\text{capital outlay (cost)}} \times 100 = \%$$

Here is an example.

Stilgitz Instruments AG is considering buying a new calibrating machine for €200,000. The extra costs and revenues over its useful life are shown in Table 3.1.

Year	Costs (€)	Revenues (€)	Net revenues (€)
0 (day of purchase and capital cost)	−200,000	0	−200,000
1	−5,000	100,000	95,000
2	−5,000	200,000	195,000
3	−5,000	100,000	95,000
4	−5,000	85,000	80,000
5	−10,000	70,000	60,000
Totals	−230,000	555,000	**325,000**

Table 3.1 Calibrating machine—costs and revenues

The ARR is calculated by adding up all the revenues (€555,000) and then taking away the total costs (€230,000). This results in a total profit of €325,000; which is then divided by the five years to get the average return:

$$\frac{325,000}{5} = €65,000$$

We can now plug our data into the formula:

$$ARR (\%) = \frac{\text{net profit per annum}}{\text{capital outlay}} = \frac{65,000}{200,000} = 100 = 32.5\%$$

Student workpoint 3.5
Business investigation

A company has to make a choice on how it spends A$40 million. There are three potential projects.

Project 1: Acquisition of competitor
ARR of 40% and payback of 4.5 years

Project 2: Investment in new computer system
ARR of 30% and payback of 3.5 years

Project 3: Sales offices set up in several countries in Europe and Africa
ARR of 50% and payback of 8 years

1 Which project is best and why?

2 Would your answer to question 1 be different if you knew that the company was very profitable, or that it was a loss-making business?

3 What other information and data might you want to have before being able to make a judgment about which project is best for the company?

Discounted cash flows and net present value

In our earlier calculation for ARR we assumed that revenues or cash flows of 100,000 in year 1 are worth the same as revenues or cash flows in year 3, but this isn't usually true. Inflation erodes the purchasing power of money and makes it worth less in year 3 than in year 1.

Discounting future cash flows is a way of calculating the effects of inflation on the value of future monies and is a more accurate method of investment appraisal. We use the rate of interest (or "discount rate") to determine the loss in value of money into the future.

Let's take an example. If we put £100 in a bank account today and earn 5%, then in a year's time our money will have grown in value to £105 (£100 plus £5 interest). On this basis our original £100 is therefore now only worth 95% of its value in a year's time. The "present value" of the money (£100) in year 2 has fallen by 5%. To calculate the present value of money we need to know the discount rates and the time periods. In the examination you will be given the discount table shown as Table 3.2 here for a unit of currency (for example £1), so you will not have to calculate the discount rates.

Years	Discount rates				
	4%	6%	8%	10%	20%
1	0.9615	0.9434	0.9259	**0.9091**	0.8333
2	0.9246	0.8900	0.8573	**0.8264**	0.6944
3	0.8890	0.8396	0.7938	**0.7513**	0.5787
4	0.8548	0.7921	0.7350	**0.6830**	0.4823
5	0.8219	0.7473	0.6806	**0.6209**	0.4019
6	0.7903	0.7050	0.6302	0.5646	0.3349
7	0.7599	0.6651	0.5835	0.5132	0.2791
8	0.7307	0.6271	0.5403	0.4665	0.2326
9	0.7026	0.5919	0.5002	0.4241	0.1938
10	0.6756	0.5584	0.4632	0.3855	0.1615

Table 3.2 Discount table (provided in IB examinations)

We can see that £1 in five years' time, where the discount rate is 20%, is only worth 40p.

Let's consider a project which costs £350,000 and which will produce net revenues over the next five years as follows.

Year 1: £50,000

Year 2: £80,000

Year 3: £100,000

Year 4: £150,000

Year 5: £130,000

Given that the discount rate is 10%, the data can now be put into net present value by multiplying the revenues by the decimals from Table 3.2.

```
Year 1  £50,000  ×  £0.9091  =  £45,455
Year 2  £80,000  ×  £0.8264  =  £66,112
Year 3           ?            =  £75,130
Year 4           ?            =  102,450
Year 5           ?            =  £80,717
```

This means that the net present value over the five years of all the income received is now £369,864. Given that the initial outlay was £350,000, this project produces a positive return, albeit that £19,864 over five years would only produce a very small adjusted ARR:

$$\text{ARR is: } \frac{19{,}864}{5} = \text{£3972.80}$$

$$\text{Therefore ARR} = \frac{3972.80}{350{,}000} \times 100 = 1.13\%$$

By now you will probably be beginning to appreciate the complexities of quantitative investment appraisal calculations, and the importance of understanding the objectives and context of a business before making a choice of project. If cash flow is more critical to a new business and profit to an established one, we might assume the project with the shortest payback is best for the start-up business, and the project with the highest ARR is best for the established and cash-rich business. In practice, businesses will often undertake a variety of measurements and consider issues such as the external environment—asking questions like these.

- How's the economy performing?
- What are the competitors doing?
- What might happen, for example to interest rates, or exchange rates?

Working capital

Working capital can be defined as the money needed by a business for its day-to-day or immediate needs. There is a balance between having too much working capital and too little, and businesses try to squeeze working capital by making it move quickly towards cash. This will also mean less new cash is needed to keep the business operational.

The working capital cycle (see Figure 3.1 on p. 150) will help you appreciate how cash is used by the business and how it moves from one stage to another.

Cash or working capital is used to buy raw materials, which are turned into finished goods and then sold to customers via invoice. The customer or debtor, on paying the invoice, returns cash to the business. This cash is then recycled into new raw materials and some of it is also used to pay suppliers' invoices and maybe even reduce the bank overdraft. Businesses who hold too much working capital in stock are in effect wasting their cash, as are businesses that don't chase customers who don't pay on time. The more efficient a business is at moving through the working capital cycle, the less new outside money (increased overdraft or investors' new capital) it requires for funding its next stage of growth and expansion.

Controlling the working capital cycle links closely with an accountant's role to manage cash and forecast cash flow needs.

Jan - May Sales, Being Collected Feb - June.

Rupees (000)	Jan	Feb	Mar	Apr	May	Jun	Totals
Sales: credit	45,000	40,000	50,000	65,000	55,000	50,000	305,000
Sales: cash	5,000	4,000	6,000	5,500	7,000	8,000	35,500
Total receipts (inflow)	50,000	44,000	56,000	70,500	62,000	58,000	340,500
Wages	25,000	22,000	25,000	25,000	35,000	35,000	167,000
Materials	10,000	10,500	15,000	18,000	19,000	20,000	92,500
Interest	1,000	1,000	1,000	1,000	1,000	1,000	6,000
Overheads	15,000	15,000	15,000	16,000	16,000	16,000	93,000
Total outflows	51,000	48,500	56,000	60,000	71,000	72,000	358,500
Opening bank balance	0	−1,000	−5,500	−5,500	5,000	−4,000	
Net cash for month	−1,000	−4,500	0	10,500	−9,000	−14,000	
Closing bank balance	−1,000	−5,500	−5,500	5,000	−4,000	−18,000	−18,000

Table 3.3 Cash flow forecast for Pedro Blanco Meats

In the example shown in Table 3.3 it is important to remember that the business is recording movements in cash flows not necessarily when sales are made but when payments are received. The business made sales on credit (invoice), as shown in Table 3.4.

Rupees	Jan	Feb	Mar	Apr	May	Jun
(000)	40,000	50,000	65,000	55,000	50,000	80,000

Table 3.4 Sales on credit for Pedro Blanco Meats

But payments were made 30 days after the sales invoice—therefore January's sales are received in February, February's in March, etc. December credit sales were R45,000.

Pedro Blanco Meats had a zero opening balance on the first day of January but it generated a negative net cash flow in that month of R1,000 (50,000 − 51,000) and therefore at the end of January its closing bank balance or position was minus R1,000. Later in the year the business is forecast to fall into a greater negative closing cash balance position of −R18,000. However, by undertaking a cash flow forecast a business can see what its cash requirements might be and arrange an overdraft or some other strategy to ensure that it doesn't face a liquidity crisis. It could also use any number of the following strategies to improve its cash flow. It could:

- offer prompt payment discounts to its customers
- delay paying its suppliers by asking for an extended credit period from them
- negotiate better interest rates on loans
- possibly sell off some of its non-core assets
- spread or smooth out quarterly rental or utilities bills to avoid sudden rises in overdraft position; cut back on wages, etc.

Many of these options have drawbacks or at least need careful management. For example, if a business delays paying its suppliers they may decide to stop deliveries to the business, so a key question might be whether there are any other suppliers the business could use if it ends up annoying its current ones. If the business is still struggling to keep its cash flow positive it may also consider looking for a business partner or investor and even selling the business to a competitor. By planning cash flow forecasts and considering its cash needs the business can at least avoid an unexpected call from the bank asking for its money back and suggesting that the business closes down. Most new businesses struggle to meet their original cash flow forecasts, not because they have unexpected costs, but because they are over optimistic about their likely sales. Existing companies like Pedro Blanco Meats should be better able to forecast their sales revenues—but even then a health scare like bird flu or mad cow disease might dramatically cut sales revenue and cause cash flow problems.

HL

Budgeting

Cash flow forecasts are one type of budget—a cash budget. Budgeting is a way of looking into the future and creating financial plans that help to control the business "going forward". Budgets create targets and underpin the objectives set by the business; they show what the business thinks is likely to take place over the next time period. The process of creating budgets links with business culture (see Chapter 2.5), for example are they imposed ("Taylorite") or created through consultation (see Mayo, p. 129)?

	Jan $000			Feb $000		
	Budget	Actual	Variance	Budget	Actual	Variance
Bearings	450	550	100 Fav	480	540	60 Fav
Bolts	33	40	7 Fav	50	45	5 Adv
Copper wire	850	600	250 Adv	900	800	100 Adv
Total	1,333	1,190	**143 Adv**	1430	1385	**45 Adv**

Table 3.5 Sales revenue budget for Aztec Engineering

Aztec Engineering set its sales revenue budgets for January and February (see Table 3.5). As we should expect, there were some differences between the budgets and the actual numbers. In this case the bearings product line saw favourable outcomes as the budget was beaten in both months. We describe this as a favourable variance ("Fav" in Table 3.5) because it was good news for the company. The bolts product line had a favourable outcome or variance in January, but missed the February budgeted figure by $5,000; this we call an adverse variance ("Adv" in Table 3.5) as it is bad news for the company. As for copper wire, the sales revenue was below budget in both months and therefore shows adverse variances of $250,000 and $100,000 respectively. Overall, the company missed its sales revenue targets by $143,000 in January and $45,000 in February. As a check, the product line variances can be added up to show that the total variances are correct.

The variance calculations are a management tool to allow the business to clarify why it has variances and whether there is something it can do to improve the situation. For example, with Aztec there are a number of possible follow-up questions that arise.

While bearings seem to have done well, why is the actual number for sales revenue falling in February ($540,000) compared to January ($550,000), especially when sales are expected (budgeted) to rise between the two months? Perhaps there was a large one-off and unexpected order received that distorted the actual sales revenue in January and also February.

Although there is an adverse variance in February for bolts, total sales did actually rise between the two months ($40,000 > $45,000). Was the adverse variance of $5,000 due to a pricing issue, for example discounts offered that were greater than planned for, or volume shortfall? If it was pricing, can Aztec improve its pricing for March or is it simply that the price elasticity (see p. 216) of bolts is very high and Aztec cannot do anything about this?

As for the adverse variances in copper wire, was it a price or volume issue? Was it due, for example, to an unfavourable exchange rate, or perhaps an imposed quota on import quantities by one of the customers' governments?

We have so far considered a sales revenue budget, but budgets also cover production areas and in fact all areas of the profit & loss account (see p. 166–167).

Student workpoint 3.6

Business investigation

Look at the production budget for Aztec Engineering shown in this table.

	Jan $000			Feb $000		
	Budget	Actual	Variance	Budget	Actual	Variance
Materials	300	350	?	330	340	10 Adv
Labour	?	350	50 Fav	420	?	40 Fav
Overheads	500	?	0	500	550	50 Adv
Totals	1,200	1,200	0	1,250	1,270	?

1 Identify the four missing numbers (indicated by question marks).
2 Interpret the production variances and suggest possible reasons for them.
3 Are the favourable labour cost variances an indication of a well-managed workforce or simply poor sales revenue? Discuss.

Budgeting is an ongoing business activity, not a one-off event. Businesses should learn from interpreting variance analysis and be able to improve their planning processes, perhaps by paying greater attention to the external environment and knowing what is happening with their customers (sales budgets) and suppliers (production budgets).

3.3 Financial accounts and ratio analysis

By the end of this chapter, you should be able to:

- construct and amend trading and profit & loss accounts for limited companies
- construct balance sheets for limited companies
- calculate and apply appropriate methods of depreciating assets
- explain the importance of intangible assets in the valuation of companies
- calculate and apply appropriate stock valuation techniques
- calculate and interpret profitability, liquidity, efficiency and shareholder ratios

Final accounts

Final accounts are financial statements that inform stakeholders about the financial profile and performance of the business. There are accounting statements for two areas of the business: one group of statements covers the year's trading, its profit or loss, and how that profit or loss was distributed at the end of the financial year; and the other is the balance sheet, which discloses what the business owns (assets); owes other people (liabilities); and how it has funded (the capital employed) its net assets (assets less liabilities). We'll look at this in more detail below.

The trading account, profit & loss account, and the appropriation account

The trading or manufacturing account looks at the costs of production. From this we can see how efficient this side of the business operation is. Note that labour costs in making the goods could also be included as a cost of sale.

	$000	$000
Sales revenue		1,500
Opening stock (at start of year)	340	
Additional purchases (during year)	950	
Less closing stock (as at end of year)	(290)	
Cost of sales		1,000
Gross profit (or contribution)		500

Table 3.6 The trading account for Copinicus for year ended 31st May 2008

In the Copinicus example gross profit ($500,000) represents 33.3% of sales revenue or, to put it another way, cost of sales is 66.5% of revenue. For every $1 of revenue, 66 cents goes on costs and that leaves 34 cents as gross profit. Copinicus would compare this with previous years' figures and also with competitors' results as a way of gauging its production efficiency.

The profit & loss account presents the sales revenue of the company for a given period of time. It also shows the related costs in making that sales revenue and finally it shows how the resulting profit is used or "appropriated".

In the example in Table 3.7, Copinicus' revenue is $1,500,000 and its related costs are $1,000,000 and also $250,000. The resulting net profit is the difference between revenue and all costs, that is, $250,000.

	$000
Sales revenue	1,500
Cost of sales	1,000
Gross profit	**500**
Expenses	250
Net profit before interest and tax	**250**
Interest	15
Tax	45
Net profit after interest and tax	**190**
Dividends	95
Retained profit	95

Table 3.7 The profit & loss account for Copinicus for the year ended 31 May 2008.

The appropriation account is part of the profit & loss account and looks at how the profit is distributed or appropriated. There are four uses of profit: interest payable to lenders, corporate tax due to government, dividends for shareholders, and finally what isn't given out can remain in the business for future investment needs—it is retained profit. The first two uses of profit are usually non-negotiable—in Table 3.7 these items are $15,000 interest to the bank for loans provided and $45,000 corporate taxes to the government—and the key issue is what to do with the profit after tax and interest. How much should the business give to shareholders today and how much should be retained by the business for investment or expansion, which will enhance future shareholder value? This decision relates to the objectives of the business and also of the directors and shareholders.

Student workpoint 3.7

Be a thinker—calculate

	$000
Sales revenue	3,000
Cost of sales	?
Gross profit	1,500
Expenses	?
Net profit before interest and tax	455
Interest	155
Tax	120
Net profit after interest and tax	?
Dividends	80
Retained profit	?

Complete this profit & loss account by identifying the missing numbers (indicated by question marks).

The balance sheet

The balance sheet tells us on a specific day what the business owns (assets), what it owes others (liabilities), and what the net assets (assets less liabilities) are. It also tells us how the net assets were funded or, in other words, what the capital employed is. The capital employed will always equal the net assets, and helps to explain why the account is called a balance sheet.

The balance sheet also gives an indication of the worth or value of a business on this particular day. However, this value is a very approximate estimation of value because, after all, the worth of a business depends on what a buyer is prepared to pay and in many cases this is well in excess of the net asset value as presented in the accounts.

Table 3.8 is an example of a balance sheet. First read the definitions of each part, which are given below the table and which will help you understand more fully what a balance sheet is.

	$000	$000
Fixed assets		1,500
Current assets		
Stock	32	
Debtors	60	
Cash	5	
Total		97
Current liabilities	25	
Creditors	12	
Short-term borrowings	8	
Total		(45)
Net assets		**1,552**
Share capital		1,000
Loan capital		350
Retained profit		202
Capital employed		**1,552**

Table 3.8 Copinicus balance sheet as at 31 May 2008

So what are the key terms in the balance sheet?

Fixed assets

These are long-term assets and remain in the business for more than one year, for example equipment, cars, fixtures and fittings, premises if owned by the business, and also patents and brands (known as intangible assets as we cannot hold them).

Current assets

These are assets that remain in the business for up to one year, hence "current". They include stock, debtors, and cash. These are all transitory items and are part of the working capital cycle.

Current liabilities

These are short-term debts that the business owes, such as unpaid bills to suppliers (trade creditors) and money owed to the bank (bank overdraft) and other lenders. All such liabilities are payable within one year.

If we add the fixed and current assets together (what we own) and deduct current liabilities (what we owe other people) we get to "net assets"—we "net off" the liabilities from our assets. This is one half of the balance sheet. We then want to establish how the net assets were paid for or funded and this is shown in the rest of the balance sheet under "capital employed".

Share capital

This is money invested in the business by the shareholders, and will include the original start-up funding and any subsequent investment by shareholders, perhaps for an acquisition or for purchasing new premises. Note that this has nothing to do with the buying and selling of existing shares on the stock market, which brings no additional capital into the business.

Loan capital

This is long-term finance (for more than one year) from a bank or other lenders. Loan capital is not a bad thing and helps to share the burden and risks of funding the business, although interest payments will take a share of the profits.

Retained profit

This is the profit over the years that has remained in the business and been used to help fund its development. Retained profit will be represented in the other half of the balance sheet in an asset category such as land and buildings, equipment, or even cash.

In the balance sheet example given in Table 3.8, Copinicus has a net asset value of $1,552,000. This means that the business is perhaps worth this figure—it is its net worth. How is this made up? Well, the business has fixed assets of about $1.5 million. Then if you take away all the current liabilities ($45,000) from the current assets ($97,000) you can add another $52,000. This results in a net asset number of $1,552,000. How this was funded is discovered by looking at the long-term loans and shareholders' funds (share capital and retained profits—which are the shareholders' even if the funds remain in the company). Here the majority of the funds came from the shareholders ($1,000,000, plus $202,000 retained profit), not from the bank ($350,000).

Student workpoint 3.8

Be a thinker

Look at where "cash" sits in the balance sheet and notice that those items furthest away from "cash" are at the top of the page.

Think about this for each type of asset.

1 Are there any assets that you would place in a different order, or not?

2 What about a car or machine that you might sell tomorrow—should that really be included as a long-term "fixed asset"?

3 Accounts and finance

How are accounts used by stakeholders?

Shareholders
Accounts inform shareholders of how efficient the organization is at investing their capital and making a good return (they would look at profitability and the level of dividends), how safe their investment is or if the business is likely to fail, and generally whether the directors are performing on their behalf or need to be replaced or possibly re-incentivized.

Directors, managers, and employees
Accounts inform these people about the financial viability of their employer and it may be useful to them or their trade unions to have profit figures when negotiating salary changes.

Customers
Some customers are highly dependent on their supplier, such that if the supplier struggles so might they. By reviewing the accounts, customers can appreciate whether their supplier is in trouble and what the effects might be on them. They might also be able to use this information to negotiate better discounts from their supplier or simply move to someone else to safeguard supply of materials, for instance.

Suppliers
Suppliers can check up on the financial profile of customers and use this to negotiate better terms. For example, a supplier might not have realized that it was such a significant supplier for a particular business and yet the supplier has always had to wait 90 days for payment.

Citizens or residents
Citizens can use this information to better understand the financial strength or weakness of a local business. They might be interested in questions such as these.

- Is the business likely to close and leave a lot of people out of work?
- Is it performing well and so able to support local community projects and charities?
- What expansion plans are likely and will they, for example, bring any noise pollution?

Competitors
Businesses will use published accounts to try and see how well their competitors are doing. Are competitors struggling or are their sales rising more quickly than their rivals'? This last point might confirm the view that a competitor is losing market share.

Bankers
They will want to know how safe their loans are and that the business can continue to pay both the interest and the capital back.

Case study

WorldCom

MCI WorldCom replaced Enron as a symbol for US corporate crisis when it revealed in 2001 that it had hidden expenses of $2.8 billion. The WorldCom deception became one of the biggest scandals in US corporate history.

For a while, WorldCom was the second largest US phone company after AT&T. However, between 1999 and May 2002 WorldCom used illegal accounting methods to cover up declining revenues by falsely recording financial growth and inflating profitability to increase the price of its shares. By the end of 2003, it was estimated that the company's total assets had been overstated by nearly $11 billion.

In 2005, Bernard Ebbers, the company's former CEO, was convicted of fraud, conspiracy and filing false accounts. He was sentenced to 25 years in prison. Other former WorldCom officials were charged with criminal penalties and also imprisoned. The company came out of bankruptcy in 2007, nearly $6 billion in debt, and was later acquired by Verizon Communications. Most of its debtors never received payment.

1 When published accounts mislead us over the real level of profits and debt levels, which stakeholders suffer and why?

2 If the British government is not showing in its public accounts the loans it provided Northern Rock plc (2008), can we really expect companies to be more honest? Discuss.

HL Earlier we indicated that a balance sheet is attempting to place a value on the business at a specific date. It is therefore important that the business values its assets accurately, but what value should it show for equipment, cars, or stock? And what about intangible assets like brands and patents? We will now look into how accountants and businesses have sought to improve and standardize the valuation of assets for the benefit of all stakeholders. This section covers:

● depreciation of fixed assets
● intangible assets
● stock valuation.

Depreciation

Take the example of a business buying a new car at a cost of $25,000. In one year the car's value has fallen by $10,000 due to wear and tear. As we've already outlined, this loss of asset value is known as depreciation and there are two standard methods of calculating it.

Straight line method

$$\frac{\text{original cost} - \text{residual value}}{\text{useful life of asset}}$$

Let's assume a delivery van costs £45,000 and has an expected life of five years and a residual value of £5,000. What is the annual depreciation charge and what is the value of the van in the balance sheet at the end of year 2?

Answer: $\frac{45{,}000 - 5{,}000}{5}$ = £8,000 depreciation each year

The value of the van in the balance sheet at the end of year 2 would be:

£45,000 − (2 × £8,000) = £29,000

Reducing balance method

This method is based on a fixed percentage depreciation charge and not a fixed annual sum that the first method uses, for example depreciation might be 40% per year. So the fall in value of the asset will be high in the early years and less as the asset reaches the end of its useful life.

Assume that a van is bought for £45,000 and it has four years of useful life. Its expected residual value is £5,832, so the business has chosen an annual depreciation charge of 40%* (see note below). Calculate the annual depreciation number and the value of the van in the balance sheet at the end of each year. Then look below to check your answers.

Note: *You wouldn't be expected to know the formula to find the

Depreciation of the company van—answers

Year 1: 40% × £45,000 = £18,000 depreciation in year 1 and net value of van £27,000

Year 2: 40% × £27,000 = £10,800 depreciation in year 2 and net value of van £16,200

Year 3: 40% × £16,200 = £6,480 depreciation in year 3 and net value of van £9,720

Year 4: 40% × £9,720 = £3,888 depreciation in year 4 and net value of van £5,832

percentage depreciation used in any example, but for those interested it can be found from the following equation:

Annual depreciation % = $(1 - \sqrt[n]{\frac{residual\ value}{price}}) \times 100$

where *price* is the purchase price of the asset, *n* is the number of years the asset is owned, and *residual value* is its value after that many years.

Intangible assets are defined as identifiable non-monetary assets that cannot be seen, touched or physically measured, that are created through time and/or effort and are identifiable as a separate asset from other company assets.

There are two primary forms of intangible assets—legal intangibles (such as trade secrets, for example customer lists, copyrights, patents, trademarks, and goodwill) and competitive intangibles (such as knowledge activities, for example know-how, knowledge, collaboration activities, leverage activities, and structural activities).

Intangible assets

Many businesses are sold for a premium over their net asset value and the reason is often to do with intangible assets, such as goodwill.

The problem accountants have in valuing intangible assets can be seen when one considers, for example, a multinational biscuit or chocolate business. Its brands are created through heavy investment in advertising and, quite rightly, the shareholders want to have this investment valued in the balance sheet, if only to avoid a competitor acquiring the business on the cheap. Indeed, the confectionery company Rowntree's in the UK was undervalued when two Swiss companies, Suchard and Nestlé, made hostile takeover bids for Rowntree's in the 1980s. But what value should we give a well-known brand? Should it be perhaps a multiple of sales revenue, for example five times annual sales? But what happens if sales fall or the brand gets bad health publicity—how would we adjust for this in the accounts? The complexities and subjective nature of intangibles has made this area of asset valuation fraught with difficulties and we tend to leave intangibles off the accounts.

Stock valuation

Stock valuation is a critical area to understand as using one method or another can make a significant difference to the overall current asset figure and also has an effect on profitability. When looking to value a business before acquisition the buyers will be very keen to ensure that stock has been valued accurately and does not include any old or obsolete items.

It is also an area where fraud can go undetected for a long time. There was an example of an oil company that had its large storage tanks regularly checked by someone climbing a ladder to the top and then reading a dipstick measurement of the volume of oil inside. For many years the value of stock was worked out by multiplying the cost or price of oil by the quantity in the tanks and it would be many millions of pounds. Then an accountant double-checked and discovered that there had been a big fraud over the dipstick measurements. Any ideas what he discovered? Well, there was an inner casing in the tanks which was only a few centimetres wide—so instead of holding a million gallons the tanks held perhaps just 10 pints of oil! Stock was seriously overvalued and the true worth of the business had been vastly overstated.

Stock valuation methods

FIFO is the "first in, first out" method—in other words the first items produced or in stock are used first. Table 3.9 shows an example.

Date	Stock received	Stock price ($)	Stock used/ issued	Stock price ($)	Movements in stock value	Total stock valuation ($)
01/08/2010	100	4			400	400
10/08/2010	150	6			900	1,300
21/08/2010			75	4	(300)	1,000
28/08/2010			50	5	(250) [(25 × 4) + (25 × 6)]	750
31/08/2010						**750**

Table 3.9 The FIFO ("first in, first out") method

Note that on 28/12/2010 issued stock consists of items arriving on both 01/08/2010 and 10/08/2010 and that therefore the price of these items is averaged out to the $5 stock price. At the end of August the valuation of stock is $750.

Now compare this approach to the next method, known as LIFO.

LIFO is the "last in, first out" method—the most recent stock arrivals are used or issued first. Therefore, remaining stock will tend to have the older and lower prices. Also, in times of inflation the stock valuation for the accounts will be lower than with the FIFO method.

Date	Stock received	Stock price ($)	Stock used/ issued	Stock price ($)	Movements in stock value	Total stock valuation ($)
01/08/2010	100	4			400	400
10/08/2010	150	6			900	1,300
21/08/2010			75	6	(450)	850
28/08/2010			50	6	(300)	550
31/08/2010						**550**

Table 3.10 The LIFO ("last in, last out") method

These tables show that stock valuation at the end of August would be $750 using the FIFO method or $500 using the LIFO method. Now put a few more noughts on the end of these numbers and you can begin to appreciate how significant the method is when valuing a company's assets and indeed when undertaking ratio analysis, for example current ratio (see below).

Ratio analysis

Financial accounts covering one year don't tell us much about trends and about relative performance in the industry that the business operates in. Equally, if we look at a large or small organization it can be difficult to appreciate which is doing better purely by glancing at the accounts; we use ratio analysis to help improve our interpretation of accounts. All the ratios below are given in the examination.

Ratios are often classified into groups covering: liquidity, profitability, operational efficiency, and investor areas.

Liquidity
The current ratio

$$\frac{\text{current assets}}{\text{current liabilities}}$$

Businesses need to ask: do our current assets cover our current liabilities or debts if we needed to liquidate them in a hurry? It is sometimes stated that this ratio should be around 2, but this is too much of a generalization—what is critical is the industry norm and the quality of the current assets; for example whether the business can sell its finished goods or stock quickly to someone else, and how easily it can turn all its current assets into cash.

The acid test ratio or liquidity ratio

The weakness of the current ratio is that it includes stock that can take a long time to liquidate and bankers (among other stakeholders) are keen to exclude this area when looking at an organization's ability to repay debt quickly; therefore the acid test excludes stock and is a more realistic way of assessing liquidity.

$$\frac{\text{current assets less stock}}{\text{current liabilities}}$$

As with the current ratio a generalization is made—in this case it is often indicated that the ratio should be at least 1 in an ideal scenario. But don't forget that the ratio is calculated on a balance sheet produced on one day of the year. So, for example, did the business spend a lot of cash on fixed assets near this date? Was it therefore really a typical acid test?

Profitability
Gross profit margin (%)

$$\frac{\text{gross profit}}{\text{sales revenue}} \times 100$$

This indicates what the return is after we take variable costs like production wages and materials from our sales revenue. For instance, if sales are £100 and variable costs are £75 we can see that gross profit is £25 (or 25%). Thus 25 pence from every £ of sales is gross profit. It also informs us how efficient the production process is at generating a surplus to help "contribute" towards paying the other costs of the business (fixed costs and overheads) and ultimately to leave it with a profit. Gross profit is therefore also known as contribution. Comparisons with industry norms are useful (for example service sector organizations would have very high gross profits as they have few if any raw materials and production staff), but when comparing a small and large business, the small business would probably come out worse as it wouldn't benefit from discounts for bulk purchases from suppliers.

Net profit margin (%)

$$\frac{\text{net profit}}{\text{sales revenue}} \times 100$$

This is the profit left after all costs, both variable and fixed, have been taken away from sales revenue. For example, for every £1 of sales revenue, 25 pence is taken up by variable costs, and overheads represent 50 pence, we are left with 25 pence net profit.

Return on capital employed (ROCE) or return on net assets (RONA)

$$\frac{\text{net profit before tax}}{\text{total capital employed}} \times 100 = (\%)$$

This is often referred to as the primary ratio. It informs stakeholders about how effective the business is at returning a profit from the capital it has. It is therefore a good ratio to use to compare the performance of small and large businesses. Equally, shareholders can compare the ROCE with alternative investments—one would hope that the ROCE would be substantially higher than the return from keeping your money in a bank account because of the extra risk of investing in an enterprise.

HL

Operational ratios

Debtor days

$$\frac{\text{trade debtors}}{\text{sales revenue}} \times 365 = (\text{days})$$

This indicates how long it takes on average for customers to pay a business. This can then be compared to the terms of business an organization sets and also compared to industry norms. If a business manages its debtor days sensibly it can minimize the amount of extra cash needed for developing the business. If a business can't get customers to pay promptly what should it do next?

Creditor days

$$\frac{\text{trade debtors}}{\text{credit purchases}} \times 365 = (\text{days})$$

This measures how quickly a business pays its suppliers during the year; you may think it would best for a business to pay its suppliers more slowly than it is being paid by its customers, but this has dangers. First, how will suppliers respond—does the business need the suppliers more than they need the business? Second, other stakeholders such as competitors and investors will think the business is struggling to pay and that it may collapse.

3 Accounts and finance

Stock turnover ratios

Our last operational ratio is to do with how well a business manages its stock. Is stock turning over quickly? If it is turning over too slowly this may indicate that the business is struggling to sell its finished goods.

$$\frac{\text{cost of sales}}{\text{average stock}} = \text{number of times}$$

It tells us how many times stock turns over in the period (year). Where needed, the average is calculated by adding "opening"and "closing"stock and dividing the number by 2 .

$$\frac{\text{average stock}}{\text{cost of sales}} \times 365 = \text{(days)}$$

This is another way at looking at stock. It tells us how many days it takes to sell stock or how many days' worth of stock are held by the business.

If you multiply the two answers from these stock turnover ratios they always add up to 365. Can you see why this is?

Investor ratios
Gearing

$$\frac{\text{long-term loan capital}}{\text{total capital employed}} \times 100$$

Gearing looks at the proportion of capital employed that comes from long-term loans, as opposed to coming from equity and retained profits. It is often indicated that gearing of 50% or more is dangerous and that this is a key benchmark. Not so! Consider two companies:

Company A: gearing 75%
Company B: gearing 35%

Now let's assume that company A makes profits of £100 million and pays interest on its debt equal to £50 million. It has covered its interest payments twice over. Company B has profits of only £20 million and interest payments of £18 million—it can just about cover its interest payments from this year's profits. Therefore be careful about indicating that high gearing is always bad news for a company—after all, if you share the risk between investors and bankers both can benefit and bank lending can help you grow a business more quickly than if you didn't borrow. The key point about borrowing and high gearing is: have the managers made the loan capital work effectively in generating extra profits?

Given the recent "credit crunch" and the difficulties of lenders, some firms with high gearing have been forced to repay loans early or had to pay higher interest than usual.

HL

Earnings per share

$$\frac{\text{profit after tax}}{\text{number of ordinary shares}}$$

This measures the amount that each share is earning for the shareholder or prospective shareholder, for example 10p per share held. This can be compared to the price of the share. Thus a £1 share price and a 10p earnings per share is showing a 10% return. Note that this doesn't mean that the shareholders received 10p per share, as this does not represent dividends per share, but simply looks at what profits are generated. Some or all of the profits may well stay in the business as retained profits.

Dividend yield

$$\frac{\text{dividends per share}}{\text{market price per share}} \times 100$$

This measure indicates the return to shareholders against the market price of the share. If the share costs £2 and the dividend is £1 then this would be a better return than a share that costs £10 and returns £3.

Student workpoint 3.9

Business investigation

Turn back to the section 'Final accounts' on p. 166. Use the ratios listed above to calculate the performance of Copinicus. You will find the data in Table 3.7 (the profit & loss account) and Table 3.8 (the balance sheet) on p. 167.

Interpret your findings and suggest any improvements the company should make, completing a table like this.

Current ratio	Answer	Suggested improvements
Acid test		
Gross profit margin (%)		
Net profit margin (%)		
Stock turnover (days)		
Debtor days		
Creditor days		
ROCE (%)		
Gearing (%)		
* Earnings per share		
* Dividend yield		

* The number of shares is 1,000,000 and the market price of each share is $1.

Redwood Materials Plc's financial ratios for the last two financial years, together with the industry averages, are shown below. Interpret these ratios and suggest what actions, if any, the company should take to improve its performance.

	Year 1	Year 2	Industry average
Current ratio	2.5	2.2	2.1
Acid test	0.8	0.7	0.9
Net profit margin (%)	15	18	14
Stock turnover (days)	85	101	90
Debtor days	106	95	75
Creditor days	81	96	55
ROCE (%)	18	22	16
Gearing (%)	40	60	45
Earnings per share (pence)	4	4	8

Websites

You may find these websites interesting.

- www.companieshouse.gov.uk (UK company accounts information)
- www.buergel.de (German company accounts information)
- www.handelregister.de (judicial register of company names in Germany)
- www.moc.go.th (Thailand company information/registers)
- www.sos.georgia.gov/corporations/default.htm (US—each State has its own registers and information on companies—this refers to corporations in Georgia)
- www.acci.gr/ (Greece's equivalent of company data/register)

By the end of this chapter, you should be able to:

- define and understand the concept of marketing
- understand how market size and share can be measured
- describe the concepts of market and product orientation
- explain the difference between the marketing of goods and services
- analyse the marketing techniques of non-profit organisations

The role of marketing

What is marketing?

Marketing is the process of getting customers interested in a product, through research of consumer needs, promotion, selling, and distribution of products (goods and services). Businesses need to ensure that their products will sell in order to be successful—the management of the operations, HR management, accounting and finance, and so on, are all secondary if the business cannot produce and market a product consumers will buy. This chapter will explain the key concepts and theory behind marketing at IB level and also outline practical application through examples, but you must remember that marketing is a real-life evolving topic that is all around us in our daily lives. The next time you buy a magazine or watch a TV advert, try to work out the reasoning behind the way a product has been sold or promoted—then you will start to understand how business leaders think and make decisions.

Market size

Market size represents all the sales of companies in a market. There are two main ways to measure this—by **volume** and by **value**. Market size by volume measures the amount of goods sold by quantity, for example litres of milk. Market size by value measures the amount spent by consumers on the total volume of goods sold and will be expressed, in terms of US dollars, euros, or pounds sterling, for example. Data from the UK crisps, snacks, and nut market for the year up to July 2008 is shown (see right) as an example.

It is important to think about the size of the market as it can tell you whether the market is growing or shrinking (and how fast) as well as being the basis for calculating market share data.

Market size by value	£1.99 billion
Market size by volume	9 billion bags

Source: www.thegrocer.co.uk

Student workpoint 4.1

Business investigation

Explain the difference between market size by volume and market size by value.

Given the information on the market for widgets shown below, calculate:

1 market share of Mega-widget by volume in 2007
2 market share of Superwidgets by value in 2008
3 market growth for the whole industry by value from 2007–08.

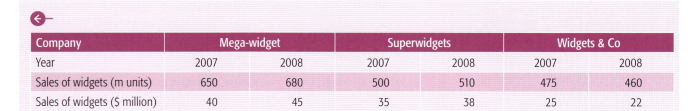

Company	Mega-widget		Superwidgets		Widgets & Co	
Year	2007	2008	2007	2008	2007	2008
Sales of widgets (m units)	650	680	500	510	475	460
Sales of widgets ($ million)	40	45	35	38	25	22

Market growth

Market growth measures how fast a given market is expanding. Let's continue with the example of the 2008 figures for the UK crisps, snacks, and nut market. According to *The Grocer*, this market is expanding at a rate of 5.9% annually. High growth rates mean that new products have a better chance of success. There will be approximately £117 million of new sales to fight for in 2009 in the UK crisps, snacks, and nut market. On the other hand, in a shrinking market, existing brands will compete fiercely for customers, making it extremely hard for new businesses or products to enter the market.

Businesses can exercise a small influence over the market size in that advertising Pepsi, for example, might not only get more people to drink that brand, but may also encourage consumers to switch to cola from other soft drinks. However, most of the growth or decline in a market's size is down to external factors such as the following.

- *The state of the economy*. Markets for luxury products, such as performance cars, will do very well in a booming economy, but are likely to suffer badly when recession (and higher unemployment) arrives.
- *Technology*. New inventions and products can dramatically reduce the size of an existing market. For example, the huge growth in iPods and other MP3 players has caused a large drop in demand for music on compact disc.
- *Demographic and social changes*. For example, more women in the workforce means that the market for pre-prepared meals has increased in size over recent years.

Market share

Market share measures what proportion of the total market's sales is held by one organization. As for market size, this can also be measured by volume but is usually measured by value. This is much more under the control of businesses; while they might not be able to control how much the overall market grows, they can gain market share at the expense of competitors, for example through a successful advertising campaign.

insignificant player on the global market, which reinforces the point that a business that has a strong reputation and high share in one market will not necessarily have the same success in all markets.

The success of Apple's iPod helped to bring about a large increase in Apple's sales of PCs in the US as the Apple brand became more and more fashionable. As shown below,

Apple's share of the US PC market increased from 3.6% in the second quarter (2Q) of 2004 to 7.8% in 2Q 2008, making it the thrid largest supplier in the US market. Despite this, it still remained a relatively insignificant player on the global PC market, which reinforces the point that a company that has a strong reputation and high share in one market will not necessarily have the same success in all markets.

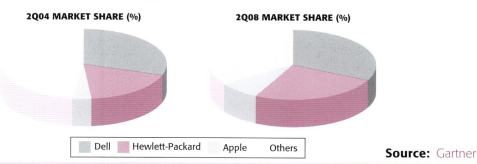

2Q04 MARKET SHARE (%) 2Q08 MARKET SHARE (%)

Dell Hewlett-Packard Apple Others

Source: Gartner

Market and product orientation

There are two main ways in which organizations can approach their business. Organizations that show **market orientation** will be very keen to analyse the market to find out what customers want. Once they have done this, they then put strategies in place to meet those needs and offer products that will appeal to a wide range of consumers. As a result, they will often tend to change and update their products regularly, for example with "special editions". They will offer a wide range of different styles in order to meet the expectations and needs of as many customers as possible. Given the changing nature of their product lines, market-oriented businesses will use lots of advertising and promotion to ensure that customers are aware of the numerous versions of products on offer.

Case study

Mobile phone suppliers—examples of market-led companies

One example of a market-led company is Nokia. The huge number of handsets Nokia offers are designed to ensure that all users of mobile phones can find a Nokia phone with the functions they desire.

But market research can be conducted quickly and relatively easily by any company with the resources to do so. This means that many companies will come up with similar offerings and there will be heavy competition in the market. Nokia's rivals, such as Samsung, will also have a model that covers the same functions. This helps to push prices down and reduces the amount of profit that can be made. For example, most mobile phone handset producers now offer a touch-screen based phone and music player to rival Apple's iPhone, such as the LG Prada.

Questions

Think about 3 companies in different markets. Are they more market led or more product led? Why do you think this is?

LG Prada phone   Apple iPhone

Source: www.macdailynews.com

By contrast, **product-oriented** businesses will be more worried about the concerns and convenience of their internal production than their potential customers. In a fast-changing market, companies like this will quickly lose market share as customers abandon their products in favour of rival offerings more tailored to customers' needs. However, product orientation can be successful in industries where change is very slow and the organization has a strong reputation.

Student workpoint 4.2

Be a thinker

1 Distinguish between product-oriented marketing and market-oriented marketing.

2 Give an example of an industry where product orientation may be successful and explain why this is the case.

3 What are the advantages of being a market-oriented organization?

Marketing of goods and services

Businesses selling goods, for example clothes, will often have a very different approach to those selling services, for example banking. This is because the products are very different in a number of ways.

- Goods can be taken back if you don't like what you've bought—but you can't return a haircut if it goes wrong!
- Services must be consumed immediately and can't be stored—you can't save your lawyer's time and use it later, you must listen to the advice when it is given.
- It is harder to compare the different offerings—one car can be directly compared to another, but different restaurants can't be compared in the same way.
- Services are intangible (they can't be handled).

The service sector in the developed world has been steadily increasing in importance as production of goods is outsourced to lower-wage economies. A TV can be manufactured anywhere and shipped to where it is needed, but service offerings need to be based close to the customer. Very few people can afford to pop to China for noodles one night, and to France the next day for some mussels—eating these different foods is only possible if shops selling them or restaurants serving them are based in your local area. Organizations offering services must focus on the image and quality of their reputation in order to attract customers. For example, hotels might try to indicate the quality of their product by having very smart and polite staff in the entrance lobby. A restaurant that looks shabby and unattractive will not attract customers, even if the meals are delicious.

Goods can be much more readily compared. Being able to handle a new camera and look at the detailed features enables buyers to choose one model or another. The customer can identify characteristics which are objective and businesses will therefore often focus marketing activity on the features of goods, such as the number of megapixels on a digital camera. An airline (supplying a service) may talk about the size of seats, but the angle of the marketing is usually about the comfort and relaxation of flying with the airline.

In reality, many products being offered now have goods and service elements to them (see Table 5.1 on p. 227). This means that all businesses must try to focus not just on the four "Ps" of price, product, place, and promotion but also on the other factors of people, process, physical evidence, and packaging. These factors are outlined on p. 187–8 and explored further later.

HL

Social marketing

Social marketing is applying the concepts of commercial marketing to the benefit of society or the "social good". The most common examples are public health campaigns, for example discouraging smoking or drink-driving. These have increasingly used "shock tactics" such as the recent EU anti-smoking campaign featured in the case study.

Case study

The 2004 EU anti-smoking campaign

Despite the message clearly being for the "social good", some campaigns do cause some controversy as many

people feel that the images are too graphic. This was the case in the UK "Get Unhooked" posters (pictured) and in the 2004 European Union - led campaign. In this case, the EU felt that the social problem of smoking out - weighed the distress caused to some people.

David Byrne, EU Commissioner for Health and Consumer Protection, was clear that the objective was to scare people into not smoking. He said: "People need to be shocked out of their complacency about tobacco. I make no apology for some of the pictures we are using."

Questions

Look at an example of social marketing you have seen in the past year in an area other than smoking. What tactics did the campaign use? How effective were these tactics?

Asset-led marketing

Most successful businesses actually adopt a middle ground between market and product orientation. Asset-led marketing involves being aware of consumers' needs and desires, but also taking into account where the organization's strengths are. This will mean that new products may be launched to meet changing customer demand, but these will be regarded as long-term opportunities, rather than short-term fashions.

Let's return to the example of Apple. The company has a very strong brand image and reputation for designing and making trendy products. This enabled Apple to move into the mobile phone market with its iPhone, which clearly traded on the success of the iPod music player. Apple was aware that customers wanted a fashionable, easy to use mobile phone that could also play music, but it was the company's own strengths in branding and design that ensured a successful launch and enabled Apple to charge a premium price above those of its rivals. Companies such as Apple will spend a lot of effort in image building to protect the long-term profitability of the brand.

Marketing in non-profit organizations

Non-profit organizations and charities are also increasingly using sophisticated marketing techniques to increase the donations they receive.

Contributors in the UK gave £43 billion in 2007 to non-profit organizations. Although this is a huge amount, it was a drop of 3% from 2006 according to the annual National Council for Voluntary Organizations and Charities Aid Foundation Giving Report. Furthermore, the report noted that 49% of the amount given was to just 0.39% of the UK's non-profit organizations, demonstrating the huge power that established names have in this market.

Did you know?

The increased importance of marketing in the non-profit organization sector has resulted in changes of tactics away from traditional mail-shots towards more modern methods such as e-mail marketing and the use of social networking sites such as MySpace.

A good example of this was Amnesty's "unsubscribe" campaign, which attracted more than 200,000 supporters. Amnesty asked donors to protest through "unsubscribing" to the war on terror by filling in an online form asking for more information.

Source: www.unsubscribe-me.org

Theory of Knowledge

Discuss the different uses of language in different types of marketing. What examples of different uses of language can you come up with? You may find that social marketing (for the common good) is likely to have a much more informative approach, with detailed text and use of language. It is much more likely to try to appeal to *reason* and convince its audience of an argument. Marketing for many other goods is likely to try to push an image or idealized lifestyle and appeal to *emotional* ways of knowing. For example, slogans such as "Just do it" (Nike) or "Where do you want to go today?" (Microsoft) do not tell you what each company does, but simply appeal to a positive emotional response.

Apply marketing issues to the following ToK essay title: *Does language play roles of equal importance in different areas of knowledge?*

A marketing plan

Marketing planning and marketing objectives

The marketing plan is a document that puts the company's strategic marketing aims into practice. It is likely to include:

- key marketing objectives
- strategic plans—an overview of how the objectives are be achieved
- specific marketing actions—details of the timings and types of marketing activity to be carried out
- marketing budget—detailed costings of the marketing activity.

Marketing objectives are goals and targets that must be met by the marketing department in order to meet the needs of the overall corporate objectives. For example, an airline may have the mission statement to "offer the best service possible in the sky". Marketing strategies and objectives based on a low-price, high-volume approach are clearly not compatible with the overall aims of this company. The marketing department will need to push for high prices, backed up by a campaign which emphasizes the quality of the service on offer.

For marketing objectives to be useful, they need to be SMART, for example see p 18 in Unit 1.

An example of a SMART objective might be to increase sales by 5% within 12 months. This objective is specific and measurable. The target of 5% is likely to be achievable and relevant to the organization's overall goals. Adding the time frame of 12 months provides a motivational focus and a point for feedback.

4.2 Marketing planning

By the end of this chapter, you should be able to:

- discuss the effectiveness of the marketing mix in achieving objectives
- examine the appropriateness of marketing objectives
- analyse and evaluate different methods of market research
- understand and evaluate different marketing strategies
- analyse a firm's products using tools such as product portfolio analysis and the BCG matrix
- analyse the appropriateness of different pricing strategies
- distinguish between different types of promotion and discuss their effectiveness
- discuss the effectiveness of different types of distribution channel
- evaluate the opportunities and threats posed by entry into international markets
- analyse the effect of e-commerce on the marketing mix

Marketing mix

A crucial aspect of successful marketing planning is in establishing the right marketing mix. The mix tries to cover all of the key elements needed in the marketing of a product. It is often referred to as the "four Ps" of price, product, place, and promotion. More recently, and particularly relevant to the service sector, the additional "Ps" of people, process, physical evidence, and packaging have been added. Here is a brief overview of the elements of the marketing mix.

- *Price*—how much the consumer is going to pay for the product. It can be changed, but consumers are far more sensitive to price rises than price falls. It can be a good indicator of the value of a product: for example products based on new technology, such as the latest games consoles, are usually priced at a very high level to start with, then the price is reduced over time.
- *Product*—involves the characteristics of the product or service being offered. New innovations in a market will be heavily relied upon to create a unique selling point for a product. Use of iTunes as a convenient download and music storage platform has allowed Apple to lock in customers to its products, for example.
- *Place*—where the consumer can buy the product. This usually encompasses not only the location, such as shops, the Internet or catalogues, but also the distribution channels (how the product actually gets to the consumer). On a more specific level, place can also refer to where a product is located in a shop. For example, supermarkets always put the higher priced, branded products at eye-level, with the cheaper ranges on the lowest shelf. Research tells them that, given similar products in a range, buyers are far more likely to take the first items they set eyes upon.
- *Promotion*—how the product is communicated to consumers. It will involve advertising, sales promotions, special offers, trade fairs, magazine articles, and more.

- *People*—use of human capital in bringing a product to market. All employees have an impact on the life of a product, from manufacture through to sales. Ensuring that employees are clear on the marketing objectives will help to attain a successful marketing mix. Customer interaction with employees will also affect their views of the product they are buying—friendly staff make a big difference to the success of a restaurant, for example. The skills of the workforce can also have a large impact on the success of a business; products based on a high-quality approach will need sufficiently trained and qualified staff to provide this.
- *Process*—the systems used to allow the organization to deliver the product. Customer loyalty may be increased by organizations able to use their processes to ensure that customer needs are met. For example, when you order your meal in McDonald's there is a set process in place to ensure that you get your burger in as short a time as possible. Waiting for ten minutes may mean that you will choose Burger King next time instead.
- *Physical evidence*—the element of the mix that allows a consumer to make a judgment on the organization. Consumers might ask themselves, for example: Is the hotel room really clean? Are the highest priced seats in the theatre are more comfortable, with a better view of the stage?
- *Packaging*—the look of a product can have a huge impact on consumers' buying decisions. Making products (including tangible items associated with delivering a service) stand out to potential buyers is a key part of any buying decision.

A business may have a wonderful product, but if the promotion is not targeted at the correct group of consumers, it may not be successful. Similarly, if an effective advertising campaign generates interest in the product, but the price has been set too high or the product is not available in the shops, then it will not sell as well as it should. Only when all of the elements above are combined in the correct way will the marketing objectives be met. It's like baking a cake—too much or too little of one of the ingredients will result in an end product that goes unwanted. Given the varied nature of products and markets, it is also important to realize that each product and market situation has its own individual marketing mix.

However, there are some limitations on the marketing mix that can strongly influence the final outcome.

- *Cost.* Does the business have the available resources to carry out its plans effectively? Small businesses may be forced to choose cheaper, less effective methods of marketing as they simply do not have the cash to run a huge TV campaign.
- *Competition.* Rival businesses will be doing their utmost to gain sales at their competitors' expense. For example, if a rival launches a huge advertising campaign, a business may be forced into running its own campaign to maintain its market share and avoid losing customers.
- *New technology.* Use of the Internet and social networking sites can allow businesses to use "viral" campaigns through social networking sites, offer a convenient "place" for the distribution of its product, and allow cheaper pricing through cost savings.

4 Marketing

Ethics of marketing

Ethics are a collection of principles that underpin decision making. Marketing can fall foul of accusations of unethical behaviour in a number of ways.

- *Pricing*. This includes businesses making misleading or false claims about prices, price comparisons with rival products, failing to mention important conditions of sale, and so on. Businesses often advertise on the basis of a short-term price but fail to state clearly when the price offer ends and that after purchase the consumer is tied into a much longer contract.
- *Promotion*. Businesses often sell their products on the basis of something other than the product itself. Sex appeal is commonly used in the marketing of deodorants and aftershave and fear can be used as a motivator. The smoking picture shown in the case study earlier is a clear example of trying to scare consumers into certain behaviour.
- *Product*. Using cheap suppliers can lead to health and safety issues. In 2007, US toy giant Mattel had to recall more than 18 million toys after lead was found in the paint used on some of its products, which could potentially poison young children. Mattel suffered a huge loss in terms of its reputation as well as the financial costs of the recall itself. (See more details in the case study on p. 255.)
- *Place*. "Doorstepping" practices of turning up at someone's home and trying, for example, to get them to switch gas or electricity supplier has come in for much criticism in recent years in the UK. The commission-based payment that the employees received encouraged them to bully homeowners, particularly the elderly, into signing up.

Similarly, children are a particularly vulnerable group, with young children not being able to understand fully the difference between TV programmes and adverts. There are strong guidelines in most developed countries now about how and when advertising to children is permissible. Indeed, advertising to children under 12 years old is banned in Sweden and sweets in shops must be placed out of the reach of little children to prevent "pester power"!

Businesses must also consider the international aspects of marketing ethics. This is particularly important as markets become more and more globalized. Businesses wish to save costs by running the same marketing campaigns across borders, but they must consider that what is acceptable in one country may not be perceived the same way in another part of the world. Nokia recognized this in 2004 with its first global marketing campaign. Although the words that were said were the same: "1,001 reasons to have a Nokia imaging phone", the adverts used local actors and settings to reflect the ethnicity of each region.

Be a thinker

1 Choose an industry you are interested in. Which of the elements of the marketing mix are most important to businesses in this industry? Why?

2 What limits an organization's ability to create the marketing mix it desires?

3 Do you think it is unethical for organizations to market directly to children?

Marketing audit

Businesses will want to assess the balance of their marketing mix continually. A marketing audit looks at the cost and effectiveness of marketing activity on a periodic basis. It will consider the internal and external environment in order to identify the organization's strengths and weaknesses and the opportunities and threats facing the business. As outlined in Chapter 1, a useful tool for this is a SWOT analysis.

Here's a reminder of the features of a SWOT analysis.

- Strengths and weaknesses are internal to a business. Strengths could include things such as a strong brand, highly qualified staff, or a good location. Weaknesses might be things like high production costs, or relying too much on one product.
- Opportunities and threats consider the external environment. Opportunities could be new markets opening up overseas, or using the Internet as a low-cost distribution channel. Threats could be a large business entering your market, or a price war erupting.

Businesses must consider their SWOT factors and try to find ways of using their marketing activity to maximize strengths and take new opportunities, while addressing their weaknesses and minimizing the damage caused by threats. By matching up strengths and opportunities, organizations can get a clear direction for the future success of the business.

Porter's five forces

Porter came up with a method for examining the competitive environment of a market[1]. His model analyses the five key factors that will enable an organization to understand how strong the competition is, and therefore how to devise a suitable marketing strategy. Figure 4.1 summarizes the model. The five forces are also examined on p. 66 in the context of strategic issues, but in this section we'll put more focus on their implications for marketing.

Threat of new entrants

New businesses coming into a market increase competition, resulting in lower prices and profits. Barriers that prevent entry into the market can limit this competitive pressure and allow existing businesses to make large profits. Porter established a number of strategies for businesses to help them increase the barriers in their markets.

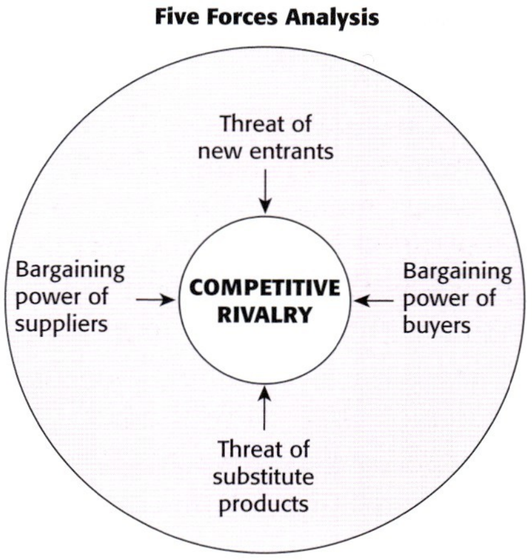

Five Forces Analysis

Figure 4.1 Porter's five forces
Source: www.marketingteacher.com

---

[1] Porter, M. E. 1980. *Competitive Strategy: Techniques for analyzing industries and competitors.* New York. Free Press.

- Create strong brands by investing heavily in promotion. Potential new entrants will face such high costs of entry that they will be deterred from entering the market.
- Spend lots on plant and machinery. New entrants will find it hard to compete without the same levels of equipment, but the expense of setting up will deter entry.
- Obtain legal protection for products and processes through patents and copyrights to prevent businesses simply copying your successful operations.
- Try to control distribution channels, for example by entering into exclusivity agreements. This will make it hard for new rivals to get their products to the end user.

Bargaining power of buyers

Buyers will try to force prices down as far as possible. If buyers are powerful, businesses will not be able to earn high profits. An example of this is livestock farming, where farmers in many countries struggle to earn a living due to low livestock prices. The buying power of supermarkets means that farmers have little choice but to accept the prices being offered to them as they have no other outlets for their meat. Porter felt that there were two main strategies for businesses to try to reduce the power of buyers.

- Merge or take over buyers to ensure that you have an outlet for your product. This is known as vertical forward integration (see also p. 347) and is common in the UK pub industry, where the majority of pubs are owned by breweries.
- Tie consumers in, for example by having service agreements. Buyers who find it very expensive to switch suppliers or products are far less likely to do so.

Threat of substitutes

If substitutes to a organization's products exist, consumers have a choice. The closer the substitute product, the more difficult the business will find it to raise prices, as consumers will simply switch to the alternative. Porter again offered some strategic options. These include creating barriers to entry through marketing, so consumers feel that your product is better than another (not a close substitute). Ways of doing this include:

- taking out patents and copyrights
- focusing on ensuring anti-competitive behaviour.

Bargaining power of suppliers

Just as buyers will use their bargaining power, suppliers will try to get the best deal they can. Suppliers with lots of power will be able to push prices up, increasing an organization's costs and reducing its profitability. Strategies to tackle this include the following.

- Businesses might use vertical backward integration—buying suppliers to ensure continuity of supply.
- Businesses can reduce the power of suppliers by not relying too heavily on one of them. By having a range of suppliers, a business can switch to an alternative easily if one supplier tries to raise prices.

Competitive rivalry

The more rivalry there is between businesses in a market, the more likely they will engage in price wars and push prices and profits for the whole industry down. Ensuring that price wars do not occur, perhaps by colluding with rival businesses, will allow all of the businesses in a market to increase their profitability. Bear in mind though that forming cartels is illegal in most markets and there are substantial penalties for businesses caught price fixing.

In the same way that marketing activity can help to reduce the threat of substitutes, it can also reduce rivalry with other businesses by particular companies ensuring that their products are perceived as better than their competitors'.

Market research

Market research is essential in creating a successful product and in marketing it effectively. It can be defined as the collection of objective data about a market, competitors, and consumers. Market research will be crucial in working out the size of the market, the growth rates, the market share held by rival businesses, and the needs of consumers. Market research falls into two main categories: primary and secondary research.

Primary market research

This is first-hand research, when data is collected directly from consumers. Large businesses often employ market research companies to help them organize and carry out this process, but it can be very expensive. Simple measures such as the feedback forms you get in hotels and restaurants are examples of primary market research on a much smaller scale. We have all seen examples of surveys sent out in the post or people asking for questionnaires to be filled in on the street, and these will all be used by an organization in some way to ensure that their marketing mix is correct.

Secondary market research

This is second-hand research—it is based on data that has already been collected. The data might be available from trade magazines, market reports, government surveys, and consumer groups. It is significantly cheaper than primary market research, but has a number of drawbacks.

- The data is likely to be general. Secondary research will not be targeted specifically to a particular company's needs. The company must therefore be very careful not to draw false conclusions from data that were intended for a different purpose.
- The data may not be current. Reports age very quickly in fast-moving markets and it is essential that businesses do not base marketing strategies on trends that have changed since the data was gathered.

Despite these problems, secondary data is useful in providing a good background picture. Once a business has this, it may decide to carry out some focused primary research to fill in the gaps.

Businesses that use market research effectively are likely to use a combination of primary and secondary research. This can minimize the cost, while maximizing the quality of information gathered. Spending time and money on the research can save far more in the long run if it results in the correct decisions on the organization's marketing activity.

HL

Quantitative market research

Quantitative market research aims to collect large amounts of data that can be analysed to identify trends. Surveys often ask long lists of pre-set questions with a limited choice of answers. These are fed into a computer for statistical analysis of the results. Given that it is impossible to survey the whole population, quantitative market research is usually based on a representative sample. There are a number of ways of conducting a sample survey, but here is a list of the most common.

- *Random sample*—trying to get a sample of a cross-section of society. This is harder than it sounds, as the time and place that you carry out your survey will have a huge effect on who takes part. For example, doing your survey at 10am will rule out a majority of those people who are in full-time work. As a result, random samples try to target people based on lists, such as one in every hundred names on the register of voters. The problem with this is that it takes time to contact these people and is therefore an expensive method of sampling.
- *Stratified sample*—involving products are clearly targeted at certain groups. For example, a company that makes electric shavers will only be interested in men who shave. As a result, women, children, and bearded men can be ignored! Once you have identified your key characteristics, you could try randomly to pick people who meet these pre-conditions (this is known as selecting a stratified random sample).
- *Cluster sample*—a very specific survey. This is not commonly used by large businesses. Small businesses based in a local area, for example restaurants, may want to focus their market research in a specific location. Surveys of local tastes and preferences would be of more use to them than a general survey based on the whole population.
- *Snowball sample*—involves using a group of targets to recruit future subjects for sampling. It is a very low-cost method of sampling and links in well with technology such as social networking sites. It is of particular use when trying to get data from subjects who may not be keen to respond to more traditional methods, for example drug users, or workers in the sex industry. However, because the respondents are recruiting their friends, it is strongly subject to bias and results must be treated with caution.

Irrespective of the method of sampling chosen, it is important that the sample is big enough to be representative of the population chosen. The greater the sample, the more confidence a business can have that its results are reliable. If a company asks only 20 people their views on a new package for its product, it may find that 15 of them like it. However, it would be a huge leap of faith to assume that this means that 75% of the population like the new design. Basing marketing decisions on a small sample runs the risk of getting key decisions of the marketing mix wrong, which can have disastrous effects on sales and profits.

You would therefore assume that businesses run huge samples to be as sure as possible, but the key limiting factor is cost. The larger the sample, the more it costs the business to carry out the research. As a result, businesses must strike a balance between the cost and effectiveness of their research. One way they do this is by looking at confidence levels. Confidence levels are simply a statistical measure of how likely a sample result is to be true for the population as a whole. For example, a 90% confidence level means that nine times out of ten the findings of the survey will be accurate. Of course this means that one in ten will be wrong, but businesses are usually happy to accept a confidence level of this magnitude, given that 100% confidence is impossible unless you survey everyone. Clearly, the larger your sample, the more likely that the survey will give representative results, that is they will have a higher confidence level.

Qualitative market research

Qualitative market research looks in far more depth at the buying process. Instead of formulating pre-set questions and answers, researchers will aim to get a more detailed view of consumers' behaviour by engaging in open-ended discussion and asking more general questions. It's important that discussions are carried out by professionals (usually psychologists) in order to be able to interpret findings fully. Long interviews and sessions with discussion groups take a lot of time and the process is expensive. However, it's useful for businesses to understand the thought processes behind buying decisions as this can add value and ideas in a way that quantitative research cannot.

Bias

For both quantitative and qualitative market research, there is always the danger of bias. Interviewers may consciously or subconsciously lead the person being interviewed in a certain direction. A dominant person in a group discussion may lead the other participants to that individual's point of view. The writer of a questionnaire may phrase questions in a way more likely to get one answer than another. As a result, it is crucial for the reliability of the research that a thorough review of the process is carried out to minimize the chances of participants being unduly swayed towards one answer or another.

Technology

Given the spread of the Internet in recent years, market research on a larger scale has come into the price range of many smaller businesses. It is relatively cheap and quick to send out an Internet survey, but the above points must still be considered by the business if it is to get useful results. One of the key issues with Internet-based surveys is the low response rate they can get. Without incentives to tempt people to fill in the survey, for example the chance to win a prize, it is likely that only a small percentage of people will respond. A way that businesses have been trying to get around this problem is by using information they have about consumers to target research more effectively. For example, many supermarkets run loyalty card schemes that record each consumer's purchases. If a supermarket wants to carry out a survey on ready meals, for example, through an e-mail survey, it could target those customers

> **Examiner's note**
> It is common for students to use sampling as primary research for extended written work. However, it should be noted that interviewing the first 20 people a student sees is *not* random sampling—it is actually convenience sampling. Random sampling must give all parts of the population being surveyed the same chance of being chosen.

who have previously bought pre-prepared products. In this way, it would focus on people whose opinions should be useful as they already have some knowledge of the product range, and it would be more likely to get a higher response rate as the people targeted would feel the survey is relevant to them.

Market segmentation

Segmenting a market refers to the process of dividing a market into smaller sub-groups based on some key defining characteristics of consumers. This will allow a business to better target its marketing efforts, using more specific promotional activity to better meet the needs of its consumers.

Businesses may decide to segment a market in a number of ways, such as by geographical region, age, and income. A good example of market segmentation can be found in the car industry.
The Volkswagen-Audi group own a number of popular brands in the industry, namely VW, Audi, Seat and Skoda. The group strongly markets these brands to different income groups of consumers, thus gaining coverage of the whole market. This approach is known as **target** or **niche marketing**, where businesses try to identify key sub-groups in a market and aim to generate profit by meeting the specific needs of those consumers.

Did you know?

The Volkswagen-Audi group has managed to target high-income customers with its VW and Audi brands, as well as lower income groups through SEAT and Skoda. Despite offering the whole range, it has managed to do this without devaluing the reputation or perception of quality offered by its upmarket models. (For more details, see the VW and Skoda case study on p. 366.)

Audi R8

Skoda Fabia

4 Marketing

The alternative to target marketing is **mass marketing**. This involves looking at a market as a whole, rather than segmenting it at all. Businesses will generate profits by being able to reduce their costs through huge volumes. Strong generic brands will enable a product to sell across the globe with very little differentiation. A good example of this is Burger King. The menu in Burger King restaurants around the globe will be by and large the same. This allows the business to save money in its promotional activity, product development, packaging, and so on, meaning that it can generate more profit per Whopper burger sold. Minor changes in some areas will exist, for example changing beef for lamb on the menu where a religion may prohibit eating beef, but the overall product mix will remain very similar.

Consumer profiles

So how does a business decide how to market its product? It is important to be aware of who its consumers are. To work this out, businesses try to create consumer profiles. These are detailed breakdowns of the demographic characteristics of the consumers of a particular product. It will include things such as:

- age
- gender
- income
- social group.

Once a business knows who its key consumers are, it can target its marketing activity specifically at those groups. For example, take a computer games manufacturer. If its main consumers are males aged 16–35 it will choose to advertise in places where the audience is likely to be similar—for many seasons Sony Playstation sponsored the European Football Champions League as the people watching the games were likely to consist of or be similar to Sony's targeted consumers.

Student workpoint 4.4
Be a thinker
1 Think of an organization you are familiar with. What are the advantages and disadvantages to the organization of:
  a primary market research
  b secondary market research.
2 Explain why consumer profiles are useful for businesses. See page 193.

Positioning

If a business wishes to target a niche, it will find it very useful to analyse the current state of the market. **Market** or **position maps** allow a business to see where existing brands are aimed and identify potentially profitable niches in the market. Looking at the car market, for example, you can see that most brands will have a consistent marketing strategy—those with a high price will strongly advertise their quality (promotion), have better standard features (product) and charge higher prices (price). Figure 4.2 shows some examples. Although theoretically possible to offer a cheap,

Did you know?

Sponsoring the Sony Playstation European Football Champions League for many seasons has allowed Sony to insist that Playstation branding is used on the billboards in the official champions league video game *for all consoles*. This means that rival products, such as Microsoft's Xbox, must essentially carry Playstation advertising!

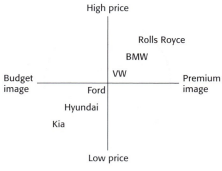

Figure 4.2 Position map

4 Marketing

high-quality car, the higher production costs would make it unlikely that it could compete with the likes of Kia. Clearly, an expensive car with a budget image is unlikely to sell well at all!

Some markets, however, will not be as saturated as the car industry. In these cases, gaps in the market can be identified and new products launched to meet the needs of consumers in each target market.

---

student workpoint 4.5
Business investigation

Choose an industry you are interested in.

1 Draw a position map, like the one given in Figure 4.2, showing different brands.

2 Why would companies in the industry you've chosen find it useful to have the information your position map shows?

Unique selling propositions (USPs)

USPs are key in protecting a niche once a business has identified it. If a product does not have something special or different about it, customers may be easily tempted away by rival products. Companies spend a lot of time and money ensuring that their product is clearly differentiated both in the design and the branding.

Did you know?

Dyson

Dyson created a unique product by introducing the first bagless vacuum cleaner. However, rival businesses quickly copied the idea once it was clear that it was a huge success. Despite this, Dyson has retained approximately 20% of the US market, due in no small part to the fact that Dyson cleaners are *perceived* as different. This is reinforced by advertising campaigns and the design of Dyson models in bright colours. Consumers are prepared to pay more for a Dyson as a result, meaning high profits for the business.

Dyson DC24 vacuum cleaner

Despite the success of its vacuum cleaners, Dyson was forced to quit the washing machine market because of the high costs of manufacturing its twin-drum model.

This illustrates the point that although you may have a successful brand and clear USP in one market, it does not guarantee that you can transfer this to other markets.

Dyson washing machine

HL

Sales forecasting

As well as knowing where sales are now, it is very useful for businesses to know what they are likely to be in the future. This helps businesses to decide the most appropriate marketing strategy to take advantage of the current situation and prepare themselves for future sales trends. Many businesses use **extrapolation** to help them get a better idea of what future performance is likely to be by finding trends from past data. The easiest way of extrapolating data is to plot previous sales figures on a graph and simply extend the trend line by hand. Sales figures are easily accessible for businesses and a line of best fit can be drawn very quickly and easily. This simplistic method can be quite effective for the near future, but it is very unlikely that an industry will have such stable growth patterns over the longer term. If you look at the bar graph below, which features data from Japan's GMO Internet group, you can see how the 2008 forecast was based on the trends in the previous data.

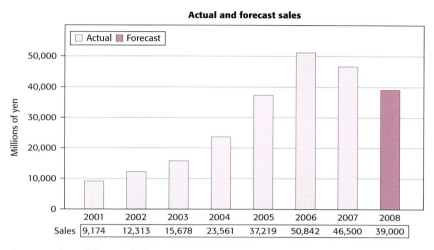

Source: http://ir.gmo.jp/en

Identifying trends is not always as simple as merely extending a line of best fit though. For example, many industries have seasonal sales, such as the ice-cream industry. It would be pointless to compare summer sales with winter sales, as you would clearly expect the hot weather to mean that more ice-cream is being purchased. Because of this issue of variations, many businesses use moving averages to try to isolate trends due to factors such as seasons and the economic cycle in order to understand properly how the business has performed, and is likely to perform in the future.

Let's look at some data to help explain this.

Year	Quarter	Sales €	4 quarter total	8 quarter total	Quarterly moving average	Seasonal variation	Average seasonal variation	Random variation
2006	1	**20,000**						
2006	2	**45,000**	**176,000**					
2006	3	**72,000**	173,000	349,000	43,625	28,375	29,958	−1,583
2006	4	**39,000**	171,000	344,000	43,000	−4,000	−4,333	333
2007	1	17,000	175,000	346,000	43,250	−26,250	−25,875	−375
2007	2	43,000	181,000	356,000	44,500	−1,500	−542	−958
2007	3	76,000	188,000	369,000	46,125	29,875	29,958	−83
2007	4	45,000	196,000	384,000	48,000	−3,000	−4,333	1,333
2008	1	24,000	203,000	399,000	49,875	−25,875	−25,875	0
2008	2	51,000	204,000	407,000	50,875	125	−542	667
2008	3	83,000	207,000	411,000	51,375	31,625	29,958	1,667
2008	4	46,000	209,000	416,000	52,000	−6,000	−4,333	−1,667
2009	1	27,000	211,000	420,000	52,500	−25,500	−25,875	375
2009	2	53,000	215,000	426,000	53,250	−250	−542	292
2009	3	85,000						
2009	4	50,000						

Table 4.1 Swimwear sales 2006–09

Sales figures for an imaginary swimwear company in France have been recorded in Table 4.1. In France, the sales for swimwear peak in the summer. This is shown as quarter 3 in the data (July, August, and September). As a result, the trend is distorted by these seasonal sales. In order to get a meaningful trend in sales, it is necessary to create an average. Although it's possible simply to take four quarters and calculate the average, this would pose the problem of which quarter to associate that average with, as there is no mid-point of four quarters (see Figure 4.3).

A statistical method called centring is used to solve this problem. Each set of four quarters is added together to create a four-quarter total.

In the example of the swimwear company, the €176,000 has come from the sum of the first four quarters in the data set. The second total (€173,000) comes from taking 2006 quarter 2 to 2007 quarter 1, and so on. Adding up adjacent four-quarter totals gives an eight-quarter total, but note that the data has come from just five different quarters.

The €349,000 is the sum of the €176,000 and €173,000 four quarter totals—comprised of two lots of 2006 quarter 2, quarter 3, and quarter 4 and one lot of 2006 quarter 1, and 2007 quarter 1. This means that the data now has a mid-point and the average of the eight-quarter total (the €43,625) can be assigned to it. This is the same as taking an average of the two four-quarter averages, as shown in Figure 4.4.

By continuing this process you can see the sales trend after the seasonal variation has been stripped out. Plotting this on a graph allows for the line of best fit to be extrapolated into the future (see Figure 4.5). The moving average line shows far more clearly what is generally happening to sales than can be seen by the wildly fluctuating sales figures.

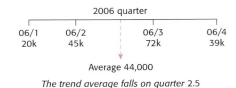
Figure 4.3 Mean of four-quarter average

Figure 4.4 Centring of two successive four-quarter moving averages

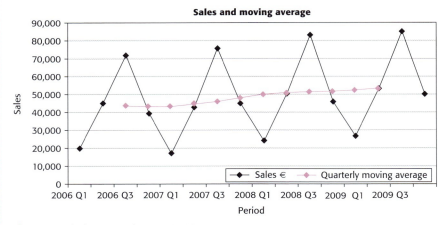
Figure 4.5 Swimwear sales 2006–09

You must remember, though, that if this trend is to be extrapolated into the future, it will not show actual sales figures, as the seasonal variations have been removed. To get predicted sales figures for the future, you must extrapolate the trend and add on or take away the average seasonal variation shown in Table 4.1.

This is calculated by averaging the difference between the actual sales and the trend in any given quarter. As a result, summer (quarter 3) sales could be extrapolated by extending the moving average line and adding €29,958 (the average seasonal variation for summer). For quarter 4 sales, you would need to extrapolate the trend and take away €4,333, as winter sales are lower than the moving average. To some extent, the extrapolation will also be subjective. If you have had booming sales growth, you may hope that this continues into the future, but it may well not. Therefore, many businesses give an optimistic (best-case) and pessimistic (worst-case) prediction of future sales to take account of the uncertainty involved in predicting the future.

Any variation not explained by the average seasonal variation is known as the random variation and is down to factors other than the seasonal boost in sales in swimwear. In quarter 3 2008, for example, sales were higher not only because of the summer weather, which accounts for €29,958 of the increase, but were in fact another €1,667 higher on top, due to other factors.

In a similar way, businesses can look at cyclical variations, which take account of the ups and downs in the business cycle, by extrapolating an average trend, and then adding an extra allowance for the extra sales in a boom, or take away the reduction in sales expected in a recession.

However the data is calculated, it is fundamental that a business acts on it. A falling trend will need to be remedied by adjusting the marketing mix by, for example, increasing promotional spending. Higher trend growth may indicate that the company could consider increasing prices to gain additional profit from a product in demand. The data in themselves will help in the decision-making process, but qualitative factors, such as customer perceptions and brand loyalty, will also need to be taken into account before the strategy is implemented.

Product

Classification of products

The **product mix** is the complete range of products produced by a business including product lines and individual products. A **product line** is a group of products within the mix that are closely related to each other. For example, Nestlé Rowntree make a large range of chocolate bars, such as Rolo, Smarties, and KitKat. This is the company's product mix, as well as the non-chocolate parts of its business such as baby food. Strong brands are often exploited by a company, leading to a product line. All the products in the line trade off the same brand name and reputation. The whole range is likely to appeal to many consumers, and the strong brand will encourage them to try the new versions of the product. This helps to increase sales and profits, while also keeping the brand new and fresh.

New product design and development

Product development involves determining what can be improved about a product by looking at how customer needs and wants have

Did you know?

Nestlé Rowntree has kept its KitKat brand new and fresh through a product line including the standard four-finger KitKat, dark chocolate and caramel versions, chunky and chunky peanut KitKats, and KitKat ice-creams. Chocolate eaters are encouraged by the strong brand to try the new products. In this case, keeping the brand new and fresh is a particularly successful strategy, given that KitKat was launched in 1935!

changed. This might be relatively minor, for example by adding another product to an existing product line, as described above. Alternatively, it may be a much larger task and involve designing a new product for the organization's product mix. Businesses will aim to ensure that any product development helps to increase the differentiation of its products and results in a USP wherever possible. Product development should always be market-led and driven by changing consumer needs as opposed to businesses looking internally. For example, Google has looked at how computer users are happy to use the Internet for many things, but still purchase software packages for tasks like word-processing (the most commonly used set of products being Microsoft Office). Google has launched "Google docs", an online software package, to do away with the need for Internet users to buy proprietary software. This may allow Google to dominate a new market based on the future needs of Internet users.

A company culture that allows for innovation and creativity is key if a business is to be successful in these areas. However, harnessing talents effectively can be difficult and it is useful for an organization to go through a clear development process to make the most of the creativity of its staff.

1 **Brainstorm ideas**. This is to encourage "blue sky" thinking to allow employees to come up with anything and everything that might help to meet a consumer need. This process may be prompted by market research that has identified a need or desire.

2 **Develop ideas**. Many ideas will not be possible or practical to work with, and these must be weeded out. The ones remaining will need to be developed into real business propositions.

3 **Create the product**. This will be on a prototype (one-off) basis at first to allow visualization of the design. It can be offered to control groups of customers who can feed back ideas and criticisms of the product.

4 **Refine and carry out final testing of the product**. Comments and problems are acted on to get a product ready for launch. However, the initial launch will be on a small scale, for example in one region only, to ensure that customers will demand the product and there are no unforeseen problems with it.

5 **Launch**. Assuming that the test launch has been a success, a full launch can go ahead. This will include full promotional activity, pricing strategies, and key decisions on distribution—the whole marketing mix.

6 **Ensure continual development**. Once a product has been launched, a business can't just stand back and admire it. Continual monitoring will allow for the product to be continually refined and modified to ensure that sales remain as high as possible for as long as possible.

The product life cycle

The product life cycle shows how sales are likely to be generated throughout the market life of a product. Products go thorough five main stages.

"The more original the discovery the more obvious it seems afterwards."

Arthur Koestler (1905–1983), author

4 Marketing

- *Development.* As discussed above, significant time, money, and energy must be spent making sure that a product is ready for market. Costs will be incurred by the business in research and development (R&D), but no sales will be made at this stage. This means that cash flow will be negative.
- *Introduction.* This is when the product is launched. Focus will be needed on the promotional part of the marketing mix, especially in consumer markets, to get the product onto the shelves and into consumers' minds. In this stage of the life cycle, cash outflows may well be greater than cash inflows to ensure that the launch is successful.
- *Growth.* This is when sales really start to take off. Different pricing strategies can be used, depending on the market and product being sold. A product based on new technology, such as the latest games console, is often sold at a high price to start with, as some customers will be prepared to buy the latest product at almost any price. Other products may need to be offered at a low price to start with in order to attract market share quickly. See the section on pricing strategies (pp. 212–19) for further discussion of these points. In this phase, cash flow will be turning positive and the product will start to make a profit as promotional costs are being spread over many more units than in the introduction stage.
- *Maturity.* In this phase, sales stabilize and the product has reached its level in the market. Because the product is now well known, there will be less spending on promotion and the business can benefit from repeat sales by satisfied customers. As a result, the cash inflows usually exceed the outflows in this stage and it is here that the business can reap the profits of its earlier spending.
- *Decline.* The final stage of the product life cycle is where sales start to fall, perhaps due to newer and better products coming on to the market. The business can choose whether to let the product die (if it feels that the product can't be revived) or to pursue some extension strategies to try to prolong the product's life. Extension strategies may be expensive, however, so the business must weigh up how much it is prepared to spend for the chance of future sales.

Figure 4.6 illustrates the stages of a product's life cycle.

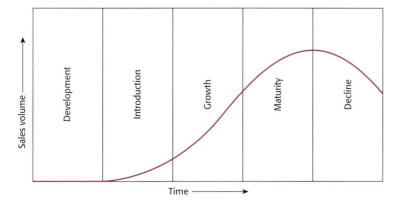

Figure 4.6 Example of a product's life cycle
Source: http://samueljscott.wordpress.com

Extension strategies

Product life cycles do not have a set duration. In fast-moving markets, such as those based on new technology, they may only last a couple of years. Think how quickly your mobile phone is superseded by newer models. Other products may have product life cycles lasting decades—board games for instance: many of the most popular offerings on the market were invented long ago, Scrabble was invented as Lexico in the 1930s, and renamed as Scrabble in 1948. Monopoly is another good example.

Case study

Monopoly

Monopoly was first published in 1936. Imagine if it had remained as the original version shown in this picture. Would it still be a top-selling game today? The answer is almost certainly "no", and Parker Brothers Games has been clever in ensuring that its product has remained updated. The company has done this in a number of ways, such as by producing many very localized Monopoly boards for smaller towns and cities, offering special editions based on popular films and characters (such as the Disney-Pixar version) and even dispensing with cash and offering an electronic card payment system on the latest release!

Questions

Look at a product you know which has had sustained success over a long period of time. Why is this? What extension strategies have been used to maintain market share when faced with newer competitors?

The reason Monopoly has been updated in the different ways outlined in the case study is to try to prevent the product going into the decline phase. The examples given are **extension strategies**—they try to extend the life of the product and delay or prevent its decline (see Figure 4.7).

Extension strategies can be changes to the product, or any other part of the marketing mix. They are critical to the long-term success of a business, as the maturity phase is when businesses gain the most net cash inflows and profit. However, devoting additional resources to a

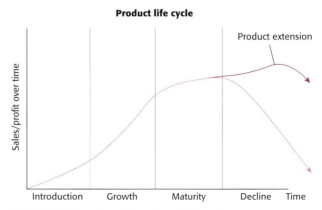

Figure 4.7 Extension of the product life cycle

Source: http://tutor2u.net

4 Marketing

product already in terminal decline will not show a return and businesses must know when to allow a product to die. For example, no matter how much marketing is put into typewriters, they are not going to replace word-processors in the office as the means of producing printed documents!

Perhaps the key issue with extension strategies, though, is the fact that it is not always easy to see exactly which stage of the product life cycle a product is in. External factors may cause a temporary drop in sales: assuming that this means that the product is going into decline may mean that the business takes the wrong marketing decisions. This can even become self-fulfilling. Let's say a business sees a drop in sales, so decides to cut back on marketing expenditure to save costs while the product dies. Due to the lack of investment the product actually does decline and die, and the business thinks that it has done the right thing. But if the drop in sales had been a temporary setback, maintaining marketing expenditure could have kept the product in the maturity phase for much longer, giving the business much higher profits in the long run.

Product diffusion curve

A useful addition to the product life cycle is the product diffusion curve. This groups customers according to how quickly they adopt a new product. Some people will immediately go out and buy the latest product as soon as it hits the shops, but others will wait a long time before buying new products.

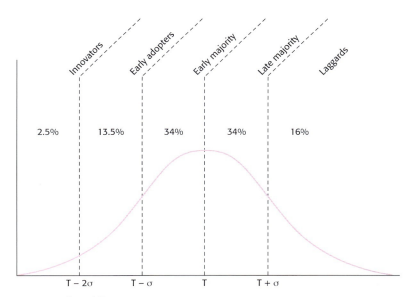

Figure 4.8 Product diffusion curve

Source: www.quickmba.com

The curve (shown in Figure 4.8) splits consumers into five groups.

- *Innovators*. These are the first to take the risk of buying a new (and therefore unproven) product. (They will buy in the introduction phase of the product life cycle.)
- *Early adopters*. Once the product has been launched and tried by the innovators, the well-informed leaders of opinion will buy it. (They will buy in the growth phase of the product life cycle.)

- *Early majority*. Once positive feedback has been received from the early adopters, these more risk-averse consumers will take the plunge and buy the product. (They will buy in the growth and maturity phase of the product life cycle.)
- *Late majority*. These consumers are more skeptical and will only buy a product once most others already have it. (They will buy in the maturity phase of the product life cycle.)
- *Laggards*. These are consumers who are happy to keep using existing technology and may only switch to the new product once their old product becomes obsolete. (They will buy in the maturity or decline phase of the product life cycle, if at all.)

Different groups will require different marketing strategies to entice them to make a purchase. Linking the groups with the different stages of the product life cycle allows a business to maximize sales by appealing to the different nature of consumers at the different stages.

Product portfolio analysis

Product portfolio analysis is looking at the range of products a business offers to ensure that it has products that are performing well and generating profit, but also has new products in the pipeline to replace existing products once they reach the decline phase of the product life cycle. The **Boston Consulting Group (BCG)** matrix or **Boston matrix** is the most common tool for businesses to analyse their product portfolios. It was developed by the Boston Consulting Group in the 1970s to help businesses decide where to best devote their scarce resources of time and money.

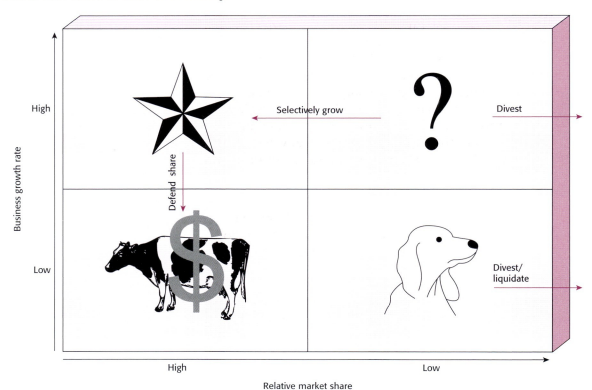

Figure 4.9 The BCG matrix

Source: www.theadvisoryfirm.com

The BCG matrix requires two pieces of information—how much market share a product has and how quickly the whole market is growing. Based on this, a product can be classified into one of four categories (illustrated in Figure 4.9).

Cash cow

A cash cow is a product with high market share and low market growth. Cash cows are to be milked. The fact that the market share is high means that the product is strong in that market and the business may be able to charge a high price for it. A cash cow's reputation allows it to get by on relatively little marketing expenditure as the market is not growing (mature). This means that increased market share is hard to come by as it can't be gained from new customers, but must be taken from competitors. Cash cows are very profitable for businesses to have in their portfolio.

Star

A star has high market share and high market growth. Stars are the dominant products in a market, but they must work much harder to retain that lead in market share. This is because the market is growing quickly and rival businesses can gain share by attracting the new customers who are entering the market. As a result, rising stars require high levels of marketing expenditure to retain their status. If they manage to do so, the benefits will come as they will be the cash cows once the market matures.

Question mark or problem child

This type of product has low market share and high market growth. Question marks pose a problem for businesses. Although many will fail to break through and earn high profits, the potential exists for them to become the stars of the future. This is because market growth is rapid, offering a business the possibility of growing its market share through new customers, which is far easier than trying to tempt them from a rival. If a business wants to develop a question mark, however, it will need to spend very large sums on marketing, and even then it may not succeed due to the fiercely competitive nature of the high growth market. As a result, businesses will selectively choose which of their question marks to develop, spending on the ones with the best chances and selling or dropping the others.

Dog

A product classified as a dog has low market share and low market growth. Very few businesses want dogs in their product portfolios. Not only do these products not have much market share, the chances of them gaining a greater share are very limited as the market itself is not growing. Because of this, businesses tend to get rid of dogs (divest) unless the products have secondary benefits, such as being a necessary part of a product line that is profitable overall.

HL : Using the BCG matrix in strategic decision making

Businesses must ensure that they have a good range of cash cows, stars, and a few question marks. This will help to ensure the long-term viability of the business, because when the cash cows eventually decline and die, there are plenty of rising stars to take their place. Selective investment in question marks will lead to a future supply of stars. Drug companies have been criticized in recent years by investors for having relatively few top products in the development stage, despite the fact that at the same time their cash cows are still earning high revenues and profits.

It is tempting to see the BCG matrix as the ideal way to make decisions on the marketing mix. It has the huge advantage for businesses in that it is quick and easy to do, meaning more management time can be devoted to the specific issues of the products on offer. However, some key issues with the model must be considered.

First, it assumes that you need a large market share to be successful. Many businesses operate extremely profitably by carving out niches in a larger market. Although not having anywhere near the sales of rival newspapers, the UK newspaper the *Financial Times* has a worldwide reputation for financial news and can operate profitably as a result.

Second, the model assumes that a fast-growing market is where the opportunities can be found. Although there's no doubt it's easier to gain new customers than poach them from rivals, there are many examples of slow-moving markets that have been revolutionized by new entrants. As we saw in the case study on p. 197, Dyson has shown how a company can come from nothing to dominance in a very mature market by clearly differentiating its products from those of its competitors.

As with all models, the BCG matrix is a useful tool that should be used in conjunction with other information, rather than as the sole basis for decision making. For further information on this, see p. 206–8.

Student workpoint 4.6

Be a thinker

1 Explain each stage of the product life cycle and give examples of products at each stage.

2 Explain what extension strategies are and why they are important.

3 Take the example of a small manufacturing business. Why is it important for this business to have products of different types in the BCG matrix, for example stars and cash cows, in its portfolio?

Branding

Brands are well-known names of individual companies or products. The most successful brands become synonymous with the name of the product itself; for example the brand name Coke is usually interchangeable with the generic (general product) name "cola". When people say that they would like a coke in a restaurant, they are usually prepared to accept Coca-Cola, Pepsi, or another cola, whatever the restaurant happens to stock.

A strong brand will allow a business to differentiate itself from its rivals. If people *perceive* a strong brand to be better than a rival product, it almost does not matter if it is *actually* better or not. Consumers will choose the branded product when given the choice. This can also mean that businesses owning strong brands can sell their products at higher prices than their rivals, making higher levels of profit and adding to the perception of quality. For example, Nike can sell trainers that cost them very little to make at extremely high prices because their brand has value—it is seen as cool to be wearing the latest pair of Nike basketball shoes, for example, and some people will pay for that privilege. Even without the Nike name, the fact that the swoosh logo is instantly recognizable means that the company can effectively brand all of its products and incorporate the logo easily into its latest designs. The logo also transmits the information and attributes associated with that brand, such as being good quality, fashionable, and reliable.

Building **brand awareness** is ensuring that customers recognize the offerings, name, and products of a particular business. This is particularly important in markets where there is not a massive difference in terms of product quality between rival businesses. For example, there is very little difference in terms of taste between Sprite and some other lemonades on the market. However, the fact that people instantly recognize the name and brand allows it to outsell its rivals.

As a result, businesses try to develop their brands. **Brand development** is trying to increase the power of a name or logo in order to increase the brand awareness and therefore gain higher sales. Spending on promotional activities, such as advertising, sales offers, and free samples can help to develop a brand and get it into consumers' minds. For example, Nescafé often offers free samples at busy transport hubs such as airports and train stations. Getting consumers to try Nescafé and pushing the logo and name at the same time can mean that consumers will gravitate towards Nescafé the next time they are buying coffee in a supermarket.

The better a brand is known, the more **brand loyalty** there is likely to be. Brand loyalty is the willingness of consumers to purchase the same brand repeatedly and even to act as a marketing tool by telling their friends how good a brand is. Given that consumers are far more likely to act on the advice of friends and family rather than on a company's promotional activity, this can be of huge benefit to a business. As we have seen, Apple is a good example of a company that has successfully built large brand loyalty among its computer users and has benefited from powerful word-of-mouth marketing. This enables Apple to charge high prices and still gain sales in the PC market, despite the availability of Windows-based models at significantly lower cost.

Theory of Knowledge

Theory of Knowledge discussion

Discuss how businesses communicate with consumers or potential customers. Is language (for example the wording of adverts) the only way businesses get their message across? What about the company logo—does that transmit a message? Businesses are far more sophisticated in their communication than you might think. For example, the Coca-Cola logo is recognizable not just in its entirety, but through the particular style of the lettering and that exact shade of red it uses. All these things are used in the complete range of Coca-Cola's marketing activity, with the result that the different factors all transmit the messages that Coca-Cola promotes in its adverts on a continual basis. Without you realizing it, you are being communicated to each time you see someone with a can of Coke!

An example of a past *Theory of knowledge* essay title is: "Are some ways of knowing more likely than others to lead to the truth?" To what extent can a business employ language, perception, emotion and reason to communicate its message to both existing and potential customers?

Types of branding

Family branding

Family branding is where an organization uses its strong name and reputation to launch new products under the umbrella of one of its existing brands. This can help sales early on as the products automatically have the associations of the existing brand.

For example, it is now common for confectionery to have an equivalent ice-cream. This trend was started by Mars in 1988 with the launch of their Mars ice-cream bar and has now turned into a huge industry. Use of the strong Mars brand and proven taste meant that the risk of failure in this venture was dramatically reduced and it allowed the company to enter a new market quickly at relatively low cost. All marketing and promotion for the Mars brand helped increase sales of both the chocolate bar and the ice-cream, resulting in higher overall sales and profits.

Product branding

Also known as individual branding, product branding is where a business assigns a new brand name to each of its products, with no clear connection between them. This does remove the key advantage of family branding when launching a product, but also avoids the negative effects that come about if the product is a failure. Product branding also makes it easier for businesses to sell off parts of their business without losing complete control of their brand image.

For example, Unilever owns many brands in numerous markets, such as Ben & Jerry's ice-cream, Persil washing powder and Dove bath and shower products. In November 2007, Unilever sold their Boursin cheese business for €400 million and the fact that it was not branded as Unilever made it far easier to separate that business from the rest of the organization.

Company branding

Company branding can have similar benefits to family branding, but across a whole company's range. The Virgin Group is a conglomerate that has a very large array of different products in different markets, from finance to holidays to music, and more. However, it strongly pushes the Virgin brand across all of these different lines.

For example, the young, modern image of Virgin has allowed it to enter the UK mobile phone market, despite having no previous reputation or image in that industry. Consumers will assume that the same qualities that they associate with other Virgin products will also be true of the mobile phone network, allowing the business to gain customers' trust quickly and build sales rapidly as a result. Other businesses trying to enter such a competitive market without this strong brand behind them will struggle to succeed against the established players in the industry.

However, it is important to note that any negative publicity for the brand in any of the areas of its business are likely to have an impact on sales across the business. For example, Virgin trains in the UK had a poor reputation for quality and this may have damaged consumers' trust in the complete range of Virgin products as a result.

Own-label branding

Retailers can brand products under their own names. This is particularly common in the supermarket sector, where own labels are becoming far more sophisticated. Supermarkets often now stock a range of different own-label ranges, each aimed at a different sector of the market. The UK's largest retailer, Tesco, offers own-label food and drink ranges in the categories Tesco Value, Tesco Healthy Eating, Tesco Kids, Tesco Organic, and Tesco Finest. Offering alternatives to branded products in these specific areas allows supermarkets to gain a greater share of sales for their products. This is important to them as own-label products are usually more profitable per unit for the supermarket than buying in branded goods. These products cannot compete in all markets though. For example, products that require high levels of spending on R&D, or have very strong existing premium brands, are hard to crack for own-label ranges. This is why you do not see them competing in upmarket clothing or in expensive cosmetics.

Manufacturers' brands

These are brands created by the producers rather than the distributors of a product. For example, Levi's jeans are reliant on other businesses for the distribution of their products, such as the iconic 501 jeans. However, there are clear advantages to Levi Strauss & Co of having created a strong brand as this can ensure that the business is resistant to buyers trying to force the price down. Levi Strauss & Co knows that any store selling jeans has to sell Levi's to be credible and so it can hold out for a higher price than its rivals. It also tries to control supply chains strictly to ensure that only designated supplies through official channels reach distributors. This resulted in a court case that reached the European Court of Justice in 2001, where a number of retailers (led by Tesco) were challenging Levi Strauss & Co's ability to restrict supplies through certain channels, claiming it was a restraint of the principle of free trade. In the end, Levi Strauss & Co won the case, keeping the power of its manufacturer's brand intact.

Global branding

As barriers to international trade fall and transport links improve, the world is getting smaller. As a result, many multinational companies try to set up global brands that can compete across borders. This can save large sums of money if, for example, the same advertising campaign can be rolled out worldwide. As we saw in the section on marketing ethics, Nokia used a global campaign tweaked for local regions to promote its imaging phones. Hollywood film stars are also increasingly used to market global brands, such as L'Oréal (advertised by Penelope Cruz), due to their international appeal. The international aspect is even apparent in every McDonald's restaurant with their "I'm loving it" catchphrase printed in many different languages all over the cups.

As people become more mobile and the Internet makes buying from all over the world a realistic option for consumers, it is vital for multinational businesses that they have a global identity and clear global brand. But it is also important that these businesses do not lose touch with their consumers. A generalized campaign that does not appeal strongly to any local group may end up damaging sales if local businesses offer a product and image that appeals more closely to regional tastes and trends.

Price

Pricing strategies

The pricing strategies adopted by businesses can be divided into three main categories: cost-based pricing, competition-based pricing, and market-based pricing.

Cost-based strategies

Cost-plus pricing

This method is very commonly used by businesses as it is easy to calculate and understand. It is also known as full-cost pricing or absorption pricing. It simply involves working out the average cost per unit produced (total cost divided by output) and then adding a percentage mark-up. For example, if a company makes 100 products at a total cost of $1000, its average cost per unit is $100. It may decide that it wants a profit margin of 25%, meaning that the selling price would be $125. The higher the percentage mark-up, the more profit per unit the business makes—but it is important to note that this assumes that the business can sell all of its output at that price. This is also known as full cost pricing or absorption pricing.

HL *Marginal-cost pricing*

The marginal cost is the addition to the total cost for producing one extra unit of output. Some businesses have very high fixed costs (costs that do not vary with output) and very low variable costs (costs that do vary with output), so once their fixed costs have been recovered, they can sell at any price above the variable (now the marginal) cost. This is because the extra units sold will only add a small amount to their total costs, so the business can still be profitable as long as those costs are covered. Utilities companies such as gas and water suppliers may do this as long as they have very low marginal costs of increasing output to one home or business.

However, it is important that this price is not well publicized as a business can't afford to sell its whole output at this low price—low prices for everyone would mean an overall loss.

Contribution pricing

This is similar to marginal-cost pricing in that it mainly considers the variable costs of production. Businesses will want to make sure that their variable costs, such as raw materials, are covered, but also need a contribution towards the fixed costs of the business, such as the rent on the factory.

Let's go back to the example given in the cost-plus pricing section above. The fixed costs may have been $400 and the variable cost $6 per unit (giving $600 of variable costs in total for the 100 units). The business may decide to price the product at $11. This gives a contribution of $5 per unit sold towards the fixed costs. The fixed costs of $400 will be covered by the first 80 units sold:

$$\frac{\$400}{\$5} = 80$$

and any more sold beyond that will each add $5 to profit. If 100 are sold, the total profit will be:

$$20 \times \$5 = \$100$$

A business cannot guarantee profit using this pricing method—it needs to sell enough units to cover its fixed costs before making profit. This method can be very useful when making one-off decisions though, such as a special price for a particularly large order. As long as the price contributes to fixed costs, it may be worth offering a special price, but if there is no contribution then the business is unlikely to take the order.

Competition-based pricing

Price leadership

Price leadership exists where a dominant organization in a market sets a price for its products and its rivals feel compelled to match that price. This may be because there is one large business in the industry coupled with lots of smaller competitors with far less market power to set prices. It can also often be seen in oligopolistic markets (markets with a few large businesses) where the leaders all tend to match each other's prices. For example, petrol and gas stations will often have policies where they agree to match local rivals' prices. This practice has brought about claims of illegal agreements by businesses to fix prices at an artificially high level and exploit customers, but it is notoriously hard to prove that this collusion has actually occurred.

Predatory pricing

Predatory pricing is deliberately selling a product at below average cost with the intention of forcing a competitor out of the market. In many countries this is illegal, but it is very hard to prove the intention of an organization's behaviour—it could be simply running a loss leader (see p. 215). Businesses often strongly contest

HL

4 Marketing

211

accusations of this in the courts—and even if they lose, they may not change their behaviour.

Going-rate pricing

Going-rate pricing is where businesses price their products at whatever the prevailing market price may be. This is likely to be because the market is highly transparent and the business would lose most of its sales by trying to charge a higher price. It will not want to drop the price below the market rate as it will earn a lower profit per unit sold and may even end up starting a price war. Agricultural markets are good examples of this—the prices of vegetables, fruit, and meat are quoted daily and farmers have little scope for affecting these prices unless they can strongly differentiate their products, for example by offering organic crops.

Market-based pricing

Price penetration

Price penetration is where a business sells its products at a low price to try to break into a market and gain market share quickly. The aim of this policy is to gain enough market share to be able to raise prices in the future once the business has become established.

Price skimming

This is most commonly seen with new and innovative products, such as new mobile phones and games consoles. The price is set high initially to gain those customers who will pay almost any price to get their hands on the latest gadget. Once the business has profited from selling to those customers, it drops the price to tempt other customers who may have been put off by the high price originally. It is only able to do this because there is likely to be almost no competition in this market due to the cutting edge nature of the product.

HL ⋮ *Price discrimination*

Most markets can be broken down into different sub-groups. It is likely that customers in some of these groups may be prepared to pay slightly higher prices than those in other groups. Ideally, the business would like to sell its product at different prices in the various segments, to take advantage by charging higher prices to customers who are prepared to pay more. Phone calls are a good example of this. It is usually much more expensive to make a call during the day than it is at evenings or weekends. This is because some users will have no choice but to use the phone during business hours (such as people who have to use the phone a lot in their work) and are therefore more likely to pay higher prices. Conversely, those people who just wish to call for social purposes are often prepared to wait to make their calls and so only pay the lower price.

Price discrimination is only possible if the product cannot be easily traded. For example, selling footballs in one town at a higher price than in another town would tempt entrepreneurs to buy up the cheap footballs and drive them to the first town to sell at a profit. If they did this, they would push prices down due to the increased competition so the opportunity for price discrimination would have been traded away.

Did you know?

In France, in 2004, Amazon was convicted of predatory pricing by offering free delivery on books. Amazon decided that it would not change its policy but simply keep paying the fine of €1000 a day!

Loss leaders

Loss leaders are products sold at very low prices to tempt customers into a store. Most supermarkets offer a low-cost range, which in itself may not be profitable. The supermarket knows, though, that someone coming in is unlikely only to buy products in the low-cost range, and as a result the supermarket will be able to earn profit overall on consumers' weekly shopping.

A business can use these loss-leading products as a part of its promotional activity as well, giving it a reputation for good value, which may in turn also increase sales and profits. In the US, Wal-Mart has managed to combine its huge buying power with a loss-leading strategy to offer new CD albums for sale at half their recommended retail price. This headline-grabbing strategy allows Wal-Mart to attract customers from far and wide, but has resulted in accusations of unfair market practices by music retailers where sales have been badly hit.

Psychological pricing

Psychological pricing is taking account of the fact that the price also gives a customer information about the characteristics of a product. For example, you would expect a luxury product to be priced at the higher end of the market. If a perfume is priced too cheaply, its sales may suffer as potential consumers perceive it as of poorer quality than higher-priced rivals.

Psychological pricing also refers to the practice of setting prices at just under the currency unit, such as $19.99 rather than $20. This is based on a number of assumptions, for example the following.

- Customers only take account of the "big number" rather than do the proper rounding.
- If a product is $19.99 it appears that it is offered at the lowest possible cost rather than being priced up to the nearest full currency unit.
- Psychological pricing pushes products into cheaper price bands. Examples of this are cars and property.

Whatever the reasons, pricing at amounts ending .99 has become commonplace. Prices that do not end this way can appear strange and this practice has become a permanent feature of the retail landscape as a result. Most bizarre are petrol and gas prices that often end in fractions of a penny or cent (as shown in the picture)—a price that is impossible to pay as we don't have small enough coins, so prices quoted need to be rounded up before we can pay!

Promotional pricing

Special offer or promotional pricing is used to clear excess stock quickly or to try and gain market share. The best example is "buy one get one free" ("BOGOF") offers, which are now commonplace across the world. This enables a business effectively to halve the price without it seeming that the product is of lower quality. It also ensures that those consumers who would only have bought one product at half price have to buy twice as much. Promotional pricing can also be used to boost sales in times of low demand, or to boost customers' awareness of a new outlet that has opened in an area.

Supply and demand

Businesses supply to a market and consumers demand products. Both parties will be strongly affected by the price. If the price increases, businesses will have an incentive to increase production to gain from the higher prices on offer. Conversely, higher prices are likely to reduce demand for a product as consumers choose not to purchase it or buy a cheaper substitute instead. Market forces work to push the price to an equilibrium level that satisfies customers and producers of goods or services. For example, suppose the price is too high: the plan of gaining a high price will incentivize lots of production by businesses, but they will be left with excess stock as there will be insufficient demand at the high price. The businesses with leftover stock will then drop the price to tempt customers to buy their products. They will keep dropping the price until they have managed to sell off all of their excess stock—where the price has fallen to where demand equals supply. This is known as "the invisible hand" of the market and was first discussed by Adam Smith, a Scottish economist, in the 18th century.

Other parts of the marketing mix will also affect supply and demand. An effective advertising campaign would be likely to increase demand for a product at any price level, which would be likely to push equilibrium prices up. Supply shortages can also lead to prices being bid up beyond the recommended retail price. For example, Nintendo Wii consoles were in very short supply in Europe in late 2007 due to huge demand for the product (see the case study on p. 296). In the run-up to Christmas 2007, some people who managed to get hold of consoles even managed to sell them to other customers on auction sites such as eBay at significantly higher prices than the consoles would sell for in the shops. The market forces were pushing the price to its true equilibrium, despite the shops only selling the consoles at the lower recommended retail price.

Elasticity

Price elasticity of demand (PED)

PED measures how sensitive the quantity demanded is to changes in the price. You would expect the demand for most goods to fall as the price increases, but PED measures how much of a fall is likely. If the price of this textbook increases by 10%, and as a result demand falls by 30%, demand is said to be elastic: a small change in price resulted in a relatively larger percentage change in quantity demanded. If, however, the price increases by 10% and demand only falls 1%, then demand is said to be inelastic: a relatively large change in price led to a smaller percentage change in the quantity demanded. The same is, of course, true for price drops leading to a rise in demand.

PED can be calculated using the following formula:

$$\frac{\text{\% change in quantity demanded}}{\text{\% change in price}}$$

In the example of the textbook price, PED is:

$$\frac{30}{10} = 3 \text{ in the first example}$$

$$\frac{1}{10} = 0.1 \text{ in the second example}$$

Demand is price elastic if the value calculated is more than 1 (as in the first example). This means that a change in price will lead to a relatively greater change in demand. Demand is price inelastic if the value calculated is less than 1 (as in the second example). This means that a change in price will lead to a relatively smaller change in quantity demanded. If the PED is exactly 1, this is known as **unitary elasticity**, which means that a change in price will lead to an identical percentage change in quantity demanded.

It is useful for businesses to look at PED when deciding whether or not to change the price. Revenue (price × quantity) will be affected by any change in price, but how it is affected depends on whether a product is price elastic or inelastic. Where PED is inelastic (less than 1), businesses can increase revenue by increasing prices. They will lose some revenue from the lower quantity demanded, but will gain more revenue from the higher prices, as demand changes less than proportionately to the change in price. Where PED is elastic (more than 1), businesses can increase revenue by lowering prices. They will lose some revenue from the lower prices, but will gain more revenue from the higher quantity demanded, as demand changes more than proportionately to the change in price. This means that businesses must be careful to interpret their sales data correctly before making decisions on price changes.

Income elasticity of demand (YED)

YED measures the change in demand for a product if there is a change in consumers' income. It can be calculated by the following formula.

$$\frac{\% \text{ change in quantity demanded}}{\% \text{ change in income}}$$

Just as with PED, YED can be elastic or inelastic. If incomes rise by 5% and demand increases by 20%, demand is elastic—demand is more than proportionately affected by a change in income. Very income-elastic goods are known as **luxury goods**. Expensive jewellery is a good example as demand for quality jewellery will be significantly affected by changes in income.

You would expect most goods to have a positive relationship to income, with demand rising as income rises. After all, if you have more money, you will spend more. This is true for most goods and they are known as **normal goods**. Normal goods will have a positive YED because more is demanded as income rises—both the top and bottom of the calculation will have the same sign. However, some goods are known as **inferior goods** because their demand actually falls as income rises. The best examples of these are the low-cost value ranges stocked by most supermarkets. As incomes rise, instead of customers buying more of these products, they may choose to swap to a higher-quality or branded alternative. These products are therefore extremely popular in times of recession and when incomes are falling, but are quickly abandoned once incomes and employment start to rise again. The success of low-cost chains across Europe such as Lidl and Aldi will increase as the global economy tips into recession. As demand falls when income rises, the top and bottom of the equation will have different signs and they therefore have a negative YED.

Cross-elasticity of demand (XED)

XED is a measure of the responsiveness of change in demand of one product to the change in price of another (a complement or substitute). One example is how the demand for coffee is affected by the price of tea. It can be calculated using this formula.

$$\frac{\text{\% change in quantity demanded of product A}}{\text{\% change in price of product B}}$$

Products that can replace each other (substitutes) will have a positive XED—for example, as the price of coffee goes up, demand for tea will increase as some people choose to swap to the option that has become relatively cheaper. Products that are linked (complements) have a negative XED—as the price of DVD players goes up and sales go down, the demand for DVDs will decrease as fewer people have the equipment needed to play the discs. Goods with no relationship will have an XED of zero—for example if the price of cars increases, demand for cheese will remain unchanged! The higher the number calculated, the stronger the relationship between the products, whether complement or substitute. Coke and Pepsi are likely to have a very high, positive XED as they are very close substitutes. Coke and Sprite will still have a positive XED, but it is likely to be lower, as Sprite is an alternative soft drink to Coke, but not quite as close a match as another cola would be.

Advertising elasticity of demand

Advertising elasticity of demand measures how sensitive the quantity demanded is to changes in an organization's advertising expenditure. AED can be calculated using the following formula.

$$\frac{\text{\% change in quantity demanded}}{\text{\% change in advertising expenditure}}$$

If the AED is more than 1, it is known as advertising elastic (the change in demand is more than proportional to the change in advertising expenditure). Conversely, an advertising elasticity of less than 1 is referred to as advertising inelastic. You would expect most products to have a positive AED as increases in spending should, all other things being equal, lead to more demand for a product. AED will be useful to businesses when deciding how to promote a product. Retail goods (products sold to the general public) tend to have a higher AED—changes in advertising expenditure are likely to have a significant effect on sales. However, the level of demand in industrial markets (transactions between two businesses) is likely to be less influenced by advertising as businesses will be more focused on the characteristics of the product itself.

Theory of Knowledge

To what extent is emotion important in decision making? There are numerous models and tools outlined in this book to assist businesses in making decisions based on *reason*. However, many businesses (particularly smaller organizations) often go with the manager or owner's "gut feeling" rather than a more measured, logical approach. There are advantages to this—it is a lot quicker, for one thing—but you would think that it would lead to the wrong decision more often than if a logical process had been adopted. Yet successful entrepreneurs like Richard Branson (of Virgin Group) or investors such as Warren Buffet (of Berkshire Hathaway) seem to be able to pick winning strategies based on an innate *emotional* view of a market. Is there still a place for risk-taking entrepreneurship in today's age of cheap data analysis by computer, or are the entrepreneurs mentioned the last of a dying breed?

An example of a past *Theory of knowledge* essay title is: "Evaluate the role of intuition in different areas of knowledge".

Student workpoint 4.7

Be a thinker

1 Analyse are the advantages and disadvantages of cost-based, competition-based and market-based pricing strategies?

2 Examine how revenue is affected by price elasticity of demand?

Promotion

Promotional activity is categorized into two types: "above the line" and "below the line". Above-the-line promotion is direct advertising through consumer channels, where the control of the process is passed to third parties, such as TV, cinema, newspapers, the Internet, and radio. Here the business can lose control of the promotion by passing responsibililty to another organization. All other forms of promotional activity fall into the below-the-line category and remain in the direct control of the business.

Above the line—advertising

Advertising comes in many forms and can vary greatly in expense. A global TV advertising campaign will cost a company huge sums of money, but an advert in a local paper may cost only a few pounds, dollars, or euros. Advertising tends to be of two types: persuasive and informative.

- Persuasive advertising is aimed to convince consumers to buy a particular product. It is the most effective form of advertising, but can be controversial, particularly if targeted at children.

- Informative advertising aims to make consumers aware of the key features and characteristics of a product to enable them to decide for themselves which product to buy. Many government-run campaigns, for example against smoking, are informative in nature as they aim to outline the risks of smoking tobacco.

What type of advertising and where to do it will depend greatly on the individual product being sold. It makes sense to target advertising towards your key consumer groups, hence the number of beer adverts at half-time of football matches. It would be a huge waste to run an advert for Barbie dolls at this time, given the low likelihood of young girls watching the game! Similarly, specific products may require specific channels to be most effective. For example, it makes sense to advertise a local grass-cutting service in the local paper or on local radio. Not only will this be cheaper, but is far more likely to have a positive response.

Below the line

There are a number of different methods of below-the-line promotion.

- *Price promotions*. This could be in the form of discounts on the selling price, for example 50% off, or offering more for your money, for example "BOGOF". The aim is to increase sales of a product, particularly to new customers who may then buy the product again in the future.
- *Direct marketing and direct selling*. Mailshots to your door or e-mail inbox are common examples of this. Direct mailing is successfully used, for example, by local restaurants, particularly those who offer take-away or delivery services, as consumers get access to the menu, prices, and contact details on one sheet of paper. Direct selling takes this one stage further, for example cold-calling arranged by insurance companies and double-glazing suppliers. Technology also now allows for "robo-calling", where a computer continually dials numbers and plays a message when the call is answered. However, businesses must be careful of the reputational risk, as cold-calling and e-mail "spam" (junk e-mails) can put consumers off a particular brand or product.
- *Loyalty cards and regular purchase discounts*. Many supermarkets now offer loyalty cards allowing consumers to collect points on their shopping that can be redeemed against future purchases. Apart from encouraging customers to remain loyal, it also allows businesses to create a useful database of buying habits which can be used to target direct mailing, or even be sold on to other businesses.
- *Point of sale displays*. Many products are arranged in attractive displays to draw consumers' attention to them. This will make consumers more likely to pick the product up and is often used for products that are impulse buys, such as sweets, drinks, and snacks.
- *Public relations (PR)*. Companies try to create brand awareness and a positive image association by activities such as sponsorship. Red Bull, the energy drink company, sponsors activities such as the Red Bull Flugtag for crazy flying inventions (based on its slogan "Red Bull gives you wings"), and a Formula One team, among other things.

Promotional mix

All of the forms of promotion in the list will be effective for certain businesses in certain situations. Each business must consider a number of factors.

● Who is the product aimed at—should I be targeting the whole market or smaller segments?
● How much will it cost—do I have the finance available for all the types of promotional activity I would like to use?
● How effective will my promotion be—am I sure that I will get a return from my investment?

In general, businesses will adopt a number of different methods of promotion for any given product in order to get a good balance between effectiveness and cost. The combination of activities is known as the promotional mix and businesses will be continually tweaking this mix to try to attract as many consumers as possible to their products.

student workpoint 4.8
Business investigation

1 Summarize the main differences between above-the-line and below-the-line promotion.
2 Select a local business that you believe is poorly promoted. Prepare a suitable promotional mix to improve the effectiveness of its promotion.

Place

Distribution channels

Distribution channels are the ways in which a business ensures that customers can gain access to its products. This is either done by directly selling to consumers or by using intermediaries.

Direct selling is where the producer of goods or services deals directly with the customer. Historically, suppliers may have found it hard to access the general public, but the growth of the Internet has meant that even small local suppliers can access customers worldwide. The reduction in transport costs also means that businesses around the world can be competitive almost anywhere as goods can be quickly and cheaply shipped to customers.

Traditionally, however, suppliers have tended to use an intermediary. This may have been supplying a retailer—for example Heinz supplying supermarkets with tomato ketchup—or alternatively supplying a wholesaler, who then distributes the products onto smaller retailers—for example Heinz supplying the wholesaler in bulk, who then splits the consignment into smaller quantities to sell to small local stores. Agents may also exist, particularly in service industries such as travel, insurance, or mortgage advice, who actively look for business.

There are a number of advantages and disadvantages of the main types of distribution channels, as shown in Table 4.2.

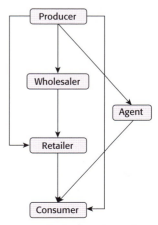

Figure 4.10 Distribution channels

Distribution channel	Key advantage	Key disadvantage
Direct selling	This carries very low cost	It can be hard to gain customer awareness using direct selling
Retail outlets	Retail outlets give customers confidence as they can bring goods back. Using these outlets them can also help build brand awareness	These outlets are expensive to staff and run
Wholesalers	Using wholesalers allows businesses to gain access to smaller retailers	Wholesalers add a further mark-up, increasing the retail price
Agents	Agents might be able to pass on better knowledge of customers' needs	Agents also offer rival products from other suppliers

Table 4.2 Advantages and disadvantages of different distribution channels

HL : Supply chain management (logistics)

Businesses will want to try to maximize the efficiency of their supply chains in order to reduce the cost and time that it takes to get products from the raw materials stage to the final point of sale to the consumer. Chapter 5.6 examines supply chain management, along with other operations management techniques, in greater detail. This section offers an introduction to supply chain management techniques and some examples.

Techniques such as just-in-time (JIT) production can reduce the amount of stock a business needs to hold, and therefore reduce warehousing costs. Better integration of its IT systems with those of its suppliers can allow a business to reorder quickly and efficiently to reduce the risk of stock-outs. Locating production facilities close to suppliers or end markets can massively reduce transportation costs. There has been a large growth in the number of specialist logistics businesses in recent years who make money by trying to streamline their clients' supply chains.

Many businesses now use specialist software packages to improve the efficiency of their supply chains. This allows for real-time monitoring of stock levels (both raw materials and finished goods) which can mean that the business is always able to keep production running at an optimum level without ever running out of supplies, or having bottlenecks develop, for example having no space for further production as finished goods are not being shipped fast enough. One system used to improve efficiency is barcoding. As you will know, barcoding is commonly used in large retail outlets to reorder products. When you buy a loaf of bread at the supermarket and it is scanned at the checkout, this automatically registers that the stock of bread is down by one. Once the stock reaches a pre-determined level, a computer automatically e-mails the supplier to order replacement loaves. Manual input is kept to a minimum, and the system can run almost by itself as long as it has been set up correctly. In practice, businesses will use a combination of software-based solutions and human oversight to manage the chain as effectively as possible without losing the human values of common sense and problem solving.

Managing the supply chain effectively can also have positive effects on consumer relationships. Businesses that can efficiently ensure that production is led by consumer demand are far less likely to suffer from stock selling out. If a product is not available, consumers will usually buy a substitute product from a rival company. This is a lost sale, but may also lead to future losses if consumers continue to buy the alternative product rather than their original choice.

Given the focus of many businesses on profit maximization through getting pricing right and sourcing cheap raw materials and components, supply chain management is one of the few areas remaining that present opportunities for large cost savings. As a result, it is likely to continue to grow in significance in the coming years.

Student workpoint 4.9
Business investigation

Choose three different industries.

1 Which distribution channels are likely to be most effective for each industry? Why?

2 How can IT help with supply chain management in each case?

International marketing

Businesses of appropriate size, offering suitable products, will want to expand internationally as this opens up a huge new potential market for their products. With approximately two billion people in India and China alone, any business that could sell its products in these markets and is not doing so is missing out on huge potential sales and profits. It is clearly not that easy though, and international marketing goes beyond simply exporting goods, but considers how the marketing mix needs to be adapted to fit the different cultural, political, legal, social, and economic issues of each new market. The main advantages and disadvantages of international expansion are shown in Table 4.3.

Advantages	Disadvantages
There may be a huge potential untapped market	Different markets may require significant product modification and cost increases
A successful business model in one country may be possible to replicate across the world	Strong local competition may already exist
International marketing reduces dependence on sales in the home market—for example if recession hits one country, there may well be other markets that are still expanding	Cultural and language barriers may make an organization less efficient

Table 4.3

Looking at each of the four main "Ps" of the marketing mix in an international context can help a business to decide what needs to be adapted to make the best of the opportunities and minimize the impact of the threats.

● *Product.* Some countries have very different needs, and products can't always be rolled out in exactly the same format.

For example, the Big Mac burger in McDonald's is identical in New York, Madrid, or Bogota. However, in India, where Hindus do not eat beef, the product was changed to a chicken burger to meet local customs and renamed the Maharaja Mac.

- *Place*. The distribution channel used may be different for various international locations. For example, when expanding into international locations, a business may try to increase its brand awareness by selling products through a partner before opening an expensive retail network.

- *Promotion*. Businesses may use different angles when deciding how to promote products in international markets. The Persil brand of washing powder is owned by Unilever in the UK and France. In the UK it is marketed as a premium washing powder, with advertising that focuses on its quality and a relatively high price. However, in France, Unilever markets Persil as a much more down-to-earth brand, because it does not want it to compete directly with another premium brand it owns there, called Skip.

- *Price*. Businesses will often have different pricing strategies in different markets. This is often due to the different buying power of consumers in different countries, but may also be affected by the promotional strategy used, such as in the Persil example.

Student workpoint 4.10
Be a thinker
1 Examine the reasons why do businesses choose to expand overseas.
2 Evaluate the potential dangers in doing so.

E-commerce

E-commerce means using electronic networks (principally the Internet) in the buying and selling of products. It can take two main forms: business-to-business (B2B) or business-to-customers (B2C).

B2B commerce involves one organization dealing with another organization. B2B transactions are far less visible to the general public, but there are many more of these than B2C transactions. This is because each product sold to the public has probably had a number of transactions go into its manufacture, for example the business has bought various components and the product has travelled through a distribution network involving producers, wholesalers, and retailers. Therefore the B2B market is larger and of more importance to most businesses than B2C transactions.

B2C commerce involves selling to the end-user. This is the experience that most of us have of the Internet in buying music online, for example.

All parts of the marketing mix are affected by e-commerce; some of these benefit businesses, others benefit consumers. Let's look at the four "Ps" in turn again, this time in the context of e-commerce.

- *Product*. The ability to tailor products to an individual's needs can increase sales. For example, buying a computer from Dell online allows the consumer to decide every minor detail from memory to speakers to the colour of the mouse. Dell's website is linked to its production facility so products are made to order from the range of base components available.

Online stores such as Amazon can stock huge ranges. This is known as the "long tail" (see more on this on p. 313). There is no way a local book shop can compete with the range of books on offer from Amazon as the storage space in the high street is far too limited (and expensive). Businesses selling through the Internet can afford to stock a wider range of goods and gain sales and profit as a result.

- *Price*. The ability to research prices quickly has made markets more competitive. Businesses are no longer just competing against local rivals, but against sellers from all over the globe. Consumers also find it easy to shop around, as it takes only a few clicks of the mouse. Increased use of shopping robots—sites such as "Google product search"—can make this even easier by comparing the market for you and allowing you to find the cheapest option quickly.

- *Promotion*. Promotion can be spread very quickly and cheaply through the Internet in pop-up adverts, through social networking sites and by paying for results to come up as the first results on popular search engines. Perhaps even more important, however, is the fact that the Internet is a two-way process. Online surveys can create consumer profiles—data that allows for specific targeting of certain customers and allows businesses to try to meet specific needs.

- *Place*. The Internet is an extremely low-cost alternative to traditional retail channels, but businesses must think carefully before deciding to give up other channels completely. Physical outlets generate consumer confidence that the enterprise is reliable. This is why banks traditionally had such impressive head offices—it was thought that a business with that level of investment in one location was unlikely to disappear overnight. The fact that a business has a high-street presence may also add to its reputation as a retailer and allow it to capture consumers who may not be keen to buy online. Also, many customers want to handle certain products before buying and may buy on the spot where they look, rather than waiting until they get home to order online.

Student workpoint 4.11

Business investigation

Choose a business that sells its products primarily using e-commerce.

1 How has e-commerce affected the different parts of the organization's marketing mix?

2 How do you think future developments will change the way this business and others market their products?

Data response exercise

Read the text below then answer the questions that follow it.

Case study

Maxi-burger

Alex Santiago owns a restaurant called Maxi-burger in a city centre location. He has made modest profits over his first year of trading, but Maxi-burger has some empty tables each evening and Alex wants to try to expand his consumer base. He tries to differentiate himself from other burger bars by offering larger burgers and a greater variety of sauces and fillings, and he is keen to continue to increase his range of products. Alex wants to carry out some primary market research to back up his views of customer tastes and preferences but his head chef believes that she is in the best position to decide what burgers and side orders should go onto the menu.

Examination questions

Standard level questions

1 Define the term primary market research. [2 marks]

2 Assuming that Alex Santiago's main marketing objective is to increase sales, prepare an appropriate marketing mix for Maxi-burger. [6 marks]

3 Analyse the appropriateness of two pricing strategies Alex Santiago could use. [5 marks]

4 Evaluate whether product or market orientation is most appropriate for Maxi-burger. [7 marks]

Higher level questions

1 Identify two cost-based and two market-based pricing strategies Alex Santiago could use. [4 marks]

2 Using at least one above-the-line technique and one below-the-line technique, prepare an appropriate promotional mix for Alex Santiago. [6 marks]

3 Analyse the usefulness of consumer profiles in helping Alex Santiago to increase the popularity of his restaurant. [6 marks]

4 Evaluate three methods of sampling that Alex Santiago may carry out in researching how to expand his range of burgers. [9 marks]

Production methods

By the end of this chapter, you should be able to:

- describe and compare the features and applications of each method of production and analyse the most appropriate method of production for a given situation
- explain the nature of cost and profit centres and analyse the value of cost and profit centres to a business
- analyse the role of contribution analysis in determining the viability of each product for a multi-product business

Every business is a producer of something. When we think of production processes, we tend to imagine big factories with long lines of sophisticated machines but it is worth bearing in mind that production can take a variety of forms. There are the large-scale capital-intensive production lines such as oil refineries or car plants. But a web browser, an airline or even a beach resort is a business with an end product too. The art of managing production to get the best end product is called operations management.

Production

Types of product
Production is typically described as the creation of physical products (**goods**) or non-physical products (**services**). For simplicity, earlier chapters have used this distinction but in fact it may not be so clear. Indeed, products can be goods or services, there can be a large range of products between the two types and there can be an overlap in definitions, as shown in Table 5.1.

Goods		Services	
Physical products	High physical content but some service	High service content but with some physical products	Service products
MP3 player	Cosmetic surgery	Airline travel	Music concert
Consumer gets the product but there may be after-sales service when the battery runs out or they need to load updates	Consumer gets the "new" nose/breasts/wrinkle-free face but there is extensive treatment before and after the operation	Customers travel from A to B but they have a meal, watch a film and get free drinks	Assuming that consumers don't buy the T-shirt or the CD or even the sponsor's soft drink, they only pay for the pleasure of the music

Table 5.1 Range of goods and services

Production methods

Similarly, there are some typical methods of production a business may use. And again there is a degree of overlap as many businesses do not rely just on one method but may employ many at the same time, especially if the market is segmented.

The methods of production are given in Table 5.2.

Type	Definition	Example
Job	Production of special "one-off" products made to a specific order	Custom-made cars with individualized accessories
Batch	Groups of a particular product made to order	Car models with differing features for each model
Mass/flow/Line	Standardized products made in large quantities, usually by assembly lines	Cars that are made to a standard design
Cell	An adaptation of mass production in which the flow is broken up by teams of workers who are responsible for certain parts of the line	Cars that are made to a standard design but produced by a number of different "cells"

Table 5.2 Methods of production

Job production

This is a production method normally associated with the top end of the market, where the emphasis is on quality and the producer can charge premium prices. Products are market oriented with the client deciding precisely what the product should be.

Some of the features of job production are the need for clear objectives and careful planning, which means there may be a longer development phase of the product life cycle. The client may require—and expect—greater consultation during the process and even after the product has been created. It is likely that the same format would be inappropriate another time. This can add to the time taken to produce the product as there may not be a successful "blueprint" to use.

Advantages
- The mark-up is likely to be high.
- Clients get exactly what they want.
- This production method is likely to motivate skilled workers working on individual projects.
- It can be a flexible production method.
- A special relationship can be developed with trend setters or role models.

Disadvantages
- This production method can be expensive, requiring skilled workers and non-standardized materials.
- It is likely to be time consuming as there is much more consultation with the client than when using other production methods.
- There is a possibility that the product might fail because of the lack of knowledge of the client but this may reflect badly on the business.
- This method can be very labour intensive and reliant on skilled workers.

Batch production

This is a production method normally associated with the middle of the market where the emphasis is on quality and affordability. Products are still market oriented. Customers are offered customized products but using a range of standardized options.

This method of production requires careful planning as the components for the products need to be interchangeable. Some consultation will need to be made with customers as their needs have to be taken into account, although the exact options may be limited.

Advantages

- Using this production method businesses can achieve economies of scale (see more on economies of scale on p. 70). There are many examples of economies of scale, from a small French manufacturer making savings on its budget for certain components by bulk buying, through to South African safari lodges making external savings by pooling resources.
- This method allows customers more choice—and so captures more market share.
- The product will be more organized when routing through the factory compared with a product manufactured using job production.
- This method may be useful for trialling products.
- Using this method it may be possible to deal with unexpected orders.

Disadvantages

- Businesses may lose production time as machines are recalibrated and/or retooled. This is known as down time.
- Businesses may need to hold large stocks of work in progress for just in case (JIC) scenarios.
- The sizes of batches are dependent on the capacity of the machinery (or labour) allocated to them.

It should be recognized, however, that increasingly sophisticated automation is now allowing greater customization, even in a mass production environment.

Mass production

This is also known as **flow production** as the business produces a high volume of standardized products using a continuous flow of raw materials along an assembly line. For this reason, it is known as **line production** too. This is perhaps our typical idea of a factory with long conveyor belts routing the product through the different stages of production without any pause in the whole process. Labour is unskilled and really there for quality control or robotic functions. Because of this there is a good argument for the automization of this method of production. Machines don't need toilet breaks and can be relied on to produce to the same standard every time they are set.

Mass production requires careful planning in order to synchronize all the stages of the production process. The production manager may well run a **critical path analysis** to calculate the right order of activities (see p. 291). For the process to be viable, the production must be driven by large reliable orders for the final product. There is likely to be a large **sunk cost** in setting up this method and this investment must be recouped by selling a high volume of the standardized products. The product is therefore sold at the low end of the market and in large quantities.

Advantages
- Once set up, the system needs little maintenance.
- The business can cater for large orders and so achieve considerable economies of scale.
- Labour costs may be low as the jobs required are relatively unskilled and with a fully automated process they are even replaceable.
- The business can respond to increase in orders very quickly as the process has already been set up.

Disadvantages
- Set-up costs will be high.
- Breakdowns are costly as the whole assembly line will be idle.
- The business is very dependent on a steady demand from a large segment of the market.
- The system is inflexible and if there are sudden changes in demand the business may well be left holding large stocks of unwanted products.
- The production process can be demotivating for workers doing robotic activities.

Comparison of the three production methods

Table 5.3 looks at several aspects of production to compare the three methods.

	Job production	Batch production	Mass production
Set-up time	Long set-up time as there is a new set-up for every new job	Can be reasonably fast as set-up is usually a modification of an existing process. Otherwise as for mass production	Very long set-up as it takes time to synchronize the whole process
Cost per unit	High	Medium	Low
Capital (machinery)	Can be flexible as it depends on specific use	A mixture of machines used, but this method is based on general purpose machines	Can involve large numbers of general purpose machines designed for a specific function
Labour	Highly skilled—may be craft workers	Semi-skilled and need to be flexible	Unskilled and need minimum training
Production time	Likely to be long	Once set up, production can be swift	Production is swift
Stock	Low raw materials and finished stock but high work in progress	High raw materials—buffer stocks. Medium work in progress and finished stock	High raw materials and finished stock, low work in progress

Table 5.3 Comparison of the three production methods

HL

Cellular production

This is a modern attempt to improve mass production techniques by allowing teams of workers to operate as a self-contained unit as part of the production run. The idea has parallels with the move away from **tall/flat** hierarchical organizational structures by creating a **matrix** or **project-based** organizations. A visit to many modern car assembly plants will show the difference between this approach and the more traditional assembly line method inspired by Ford in the 1920s.

However, not only traditional manufacturing businesses have been drawn to use this method but notably many of the newer industries using modern technologies—such as computing, mobile phone technology, or genetic engineering—have started off with this type of production.

Especially when cellular production has been combined with other elements of lean production (first developed by Toyota in the 1950s) this has led to a greater competitive advantage for many manufacturers. This advantage has been based on achieving the three main aims of:

- improving quality
- increasing productivity
- reducing costs of production.

Other features of lean production are **just in time** (JIT) stock control, *kan ban* supplies of stocks and *kaizen* (continual improvements) of quality management.

Quality improvements will come from the cooperative nature of the production with members of the team being directly responsible for their own quality checking. This should lead to less wastage and lower rejection rates. It is also easier to halt production in a cell compared with an assembly line. So if there is a quality problem it can be dealt with quickly and without affecting other parts of the production process.

Because the team is working together with all materials close at hand there is less distance for the **work in progress** to travel. By working as part of a close-knit team each worker is given greater responsibility compared with the robotic and repetitive job working on an assembly line. As Herzberg noted (1957)[1] responsibility can be a **motivating factor** so it can lead to improvements in quantity as well as quality.

"**Walking the job**" is a technique where workers follow the route a product takes as it passes through the various stages of production. In some cases this may be quite extensive, but with cellular production and having everything close at hand this represents a major saving for the business in time, energy, and money.

Changing production

Once a business has designed an appropriate production process it can be difficult and costly to change. At the very least this may involve retooling machines, redeploying human resources, and refinancing the new system. At its most drastic a business can opt to **reengineer** itself. This is where the company completely reworks itself by not only changing the production process but also the organization of the business. A fashionable management tool of the 1990s, business reengineering fell out of favour as the sheer difficulty of the task became apparent.

[1] Herzberg, F. W., Mausner, B. and Synderman, B. 1957. *The Motivation to Work*. New York. John Wiley.

5 Operations management

Changing production may have implications for the business in a variety of areas.

Marketing
- Production runs can reflect the orientation of a business and so the choice of product available to the consumer.
- Distribution will be affected. This may lead to differing response times.
- Changes in costs of production can be passed on to the consumer by changes in price.

HR
- HR will need to be carefully managed as workers may have to be redeployed, retrained, or even let go.
- The role and responsibilities of workers and middle managers requires careful planning.

Finance
- Changing production will have an impact on stock control, which itself will affect costs.
- Changes may take time and could interrupt current production.
- Any change will need financing whether it is short term or for significant developments that may require major long-term funding.

Which method of production is the best?

There is no one method that is best for business; it will depend on a number of different factors as to which system an organization may prefer. The factors include:

- the target market—for example is the business producing high-volume durable consumer goods?
- the state of existing technology—which can limit how flexible production can be
- the availability of resources—fixed capital, working capital, and human capital
- government regulations—for example waste emissions, working conditions, or quality standards.

Businesses that use more than one method

Because of the **opportunity costs** of setting up production processes and the difficulties of changing them, it may not be too much of a surprise that once a business has planned its production there is a reluctance to change and in many cases—especially with larger businesses—there are many advantages from combining different methods. Businesses that combine methods hope to reap the advantages of each different model and make the business more productively efficient. For example, a Thai restaurant might have a continuous supply of a staple food such as green curry but would produce batches of a less popular dish, say Tom Yam soup, and would even be able to make a special order on demand. Or Apple might produce the popular iPod classic "Video" and batches of "Nanos" and also special orders of the luxury gold-plated $23,000 models.

In this way the business can achieve economies of scale from the mass-produced product while satisfying the need for changes in demand for seasonal products. Similarly, flow production can be automated while the use of cellular production can help motivate workers, and indeed project teams can make sure that the business keeps ahead of product innovations.

Data response exercise

Read the text below and answer the questions that follow.

Case study

Wine industry in Argentina finding blend for success
Technology overhaul, marketing push spurs new exports
by Bill Cormier, Associated Press, 16 April 2006

Mendoza, Argentina—The wineries tucked beneath the distant Andes mountains nearly have it all: warm days and cool nights for growing the lushest of grapes, state-of-the-art technology and restless vintners bent on lifting Argentina's wine production to a point where it rivals the world's best.

Australia, France, the US and even neighbouring Chile still far outpace Argentina, but more than $1.5 billion in investments in the last 10 years to overhaul wineries, improve techniques and raise production standards—coupled with a tightly focused marketing campaign—is producing an international buzz about this country's up-and-coming grapes.

Many bodegas (wine producers) are overhauling old vineyards by planting new grape varieties, improving irrigation and harvesting techniques, and even upgrading fermenting, ageing, and bottling methods.

Argentina exported nearly $400 million in wines and grape juice concentrates to more than 70 countries. Grape juice and cheaper grapes cater for the **mass market** and the middle ground is met by the iconic Malbec varietal grape—which was brought to Argentina by European immigrants in the 1880s and first put the country on the wine map years ago—to suit the tastes of more knowledgeable customers. Now Argentinian vintners are experimenting with new blends of grapes for the discerning palate.

All of this is hoped to widen the scope of Argentinian wines and improve the country's image as having a poor **product position** as a producer of high-price, low-quality, unadventurous, and often overripe table wines served up to a large but captive domestic market.

Source: Adapted from www.washingtonpost.com

Examination questions

1 Define the terms in bold. [4 marks]
2 Explain how the same producer can position three separate products. [6 marks]
3 Evaluate the effectiveness for a bodega (producer) of splitting up production into the three areas. [10 marks]

5.2 Cost, revenue and break-even analysis

By the end of this chapter, you should be able to:

- define, explain and give examples of each different type of cost
- explain the meaning of revenue and comment on possible sources of revenue for different organizations
- explain and calculate the contribution to fixed costs
- use graphical and quantitative methods to calculate the break-even quantity, profit and margin of safety and to analyse the effects of changes in price on these three elements
- analyse the assumptions and limitations of break-even analysis
- calculate the required output level for a given target profit or level of revenue

Costs and revenue

Once a business has worked out *how* to produce, it needs to think about *how much* to produce. This will depend on a number of factors but in most cases production managers will focus on at least ensuring that they have covered their costs and not made a loss. The following simple formula can act as a **decision-making framework**:

profit = total revenue − total costs

Even if a business is a **not for profit** organization it must still abide by the formula, as although it may not make profits it must at least cover its costs and so not make any losses, which would mean:

total costs > total revenue = negative profits

In fact many **non-governmental organizations (NGOs)** need to make enough money not only to cover their immediate costs but also to ensure that they can reinvest for the future. For example, Greenpeace will need enough money to pay **lobbyists** or buy boats for **direct action** such as monitoring whaling "for scientific purposes" by Japanese vessels.

To understand fully what determines how much a business may want to produce we should look more closely at the right-hand side of the equation:

profit = total revenue − total costs   (1)

Revenue

Revenue is fundamental to all production decisions. It is the total money earned from selling the product. It is also known as **sales, sales revenue,** or **turnover** and appears in the top line on a **profit & loss account** or as a part of **cash in** on a business's **cash flow account**. To confuse matters even more these terms all refer to the "operational income" of a business—that is, money earned from its business operations. Sometimes a business can earn money from non-operational activities, such as selling shares in a subsidiary. This form of revenue is classified as non-operational income and appears below the **trading account** part of the profit & loss account.

However, for simplicity we can ignore this element of revenue (which was discussed on p. 169) and we can express total revenue as a simple formula:

$$\text{total revenue} = \text{price} \times \text{quantity, or:}$$
$$TR = P \times Q \quad (2)$$

For example, a car dealer in Singapore may buy BMW cars from the factory and then sell them to customers. If the car dealer was to sell 100 BMW 5 Series cars in 2008 for S$200,000 each, there would be S$20,000,000 in revenue: 100 × 200,000 = $20,000,000.

This looks good but it is very important to remember that revenue is not the same thing as profit. The annual "Fortune Global 500" league table published by *Fortune* magazine (see the top 12 entries in Table 5.4) can show this clearly for in 2007. Ford is number 12 in world companies but has a negative profit score!

In our example it depends on how much BMW sold the cars to the dealer for—and all the other running costs—as to what amount of profit the dealer will generate.

Rank	Company	Revenues (US$ million)	Profits (US$ million)
1	Wal-Mart Stores	351,139.00	11,284.00
2	Exxon Mobil	347,254.00	39,500.00
3	Royal Dutch Shell	318,845.00	25,442.00
4	BP	274,316.00	22,000.00
5	General Motors	207,349.00	−1,978.00
6	Toyota Motor	204,746.40	14,055.80
7	Chevron	200,567.00	17,138.00
8	DaimlerChrysler	190,191.40	4,048.80
9	ConocoPhillips	172,451.00	15,550.00
10	Total (Oil)	168,356.70	14,764.70
11	General Electric	168,307.00	20,829.00
12	Ford Motor	160,126.00	−12,613.00

Table 5.4 The top 12 entries in the "Fortune Global 500" league table of 2007 published by *Fortune* magazine

Source: Adapted from http://money.cnn.com/magazines/fortune/global500/2007/full_list/

Another way of looking at the distinction between the two concepts is to think of the difference between a fast food outlet and a Michelin five-star restaurant. With the fast food outlet there is a very low profit margin as the competition is very fierce and demand relatively elastic, so the business cannot afford to put their prices too high. Prices will not be much more than costs. This means that the business is dependent on a high volume of sales for standardized mass produced meals to generate sufficient profit to operate.

McDonald's only comes in at number 329 in the Fortune 500 for 2007. On the other hand, while a trendy top restaurant with five Michelin stars may not even appear in the Fortune 500, its profit margin may be 500 times more than McDonald's because it has less competition and **inelastic demand** for its "must be seen in" chain of restaurants. Of course, this does not mean it earns 500 times more profit—McDonald's at number 329 in the league table still generates over $3 billion worth of profit overall.

Revenue can take many forms:

- cash sales: money paid directly as cash
- credit sales: money paid on credit, for example using Visa or MasterCard
- debit cards (Chip 'n Pin, Switch or Nets, for example): money transferred electronically from a bank account
- cheques: money transferred from a bank account using a handwritten note
- loyalty cards: money transferred from a bank account into a special store account, for example Marks & Spencer's
- direct debit (Giro): money transferred electronically from a bank account for regular payments, such as a mortgage, or a cable TV monthly fee
- annual fees: money paid once a year, for example subscription to a tennis club, or car tax.

The only difference between each of these is the means by which the money is transferred to the business from the customer or client. Some businesses prefer one form of payment to another, for example an Internet company such as Amazon finds it much easier to accept credit card payments whereas the local baker would prefer cash. Many banks and businesses are moving away from using cheques towards electronic transfers of money as it is easier, quicker, and more secure.

Costs

The other part of the right-hand side of our original equation (1) is made up of the costs a business faces. These also appear in the profit & loss account as **cost of goods sold** and **expenses** and also as **cash out** on the cash flow account.

There are in fact five categories of costs and they can often overlap each other. They are:

- fixed costs: costs that do not change as output does
- variable costs: costs that do change as output does
- semi-variable costs: costs that are made up of fixed and variable, so there is an element that is fixed relative to output and there is also a variable element
- direct costs: costs that are directly related to output
- indirect costs (overheads): costs that are indirectly related to output.

As confusing as this may be, there are similarities between the types of cost. As the definition in the list says, fixed costs are simply those costs that do not change as production does.

For example, our car dealer may have to pay for the rent of the car showroom even if there are no customers. Businesses often refer to these "must pay" costs as **overheads** and they appear as **expenses** in the profit & loss account, because they are **indirect costs** of production. A business must pay them whether it makes any sales or not. They can be for many things such as the salaries of administrative staff, the sales manager's expenses, or interest payments on a bank loan, all of which are necessary for the business to be maintained but do not contribute directly to production.

Variable costs, on the other hand, are costs that do vary directly with production. For instance, in our car dealer example, if more people want to buy a BMW 5 Series the business will need to buy more of these cars from its supplier, BMW, to sell to those customers. Businesses often refer to these as **direct costs** of production and they appear as **costs of goods sold** in the profit & loss account because they are specifically linked to how much of the product is sold.

So in practice the five costs is our list can be categorized as:

> fixed = indirect
> variable = direct
> semi-variable = partly direct and indirect

Fixed/variable and indirect/direct costs

For simplicity, if we ignore semi-variable costs for the moment, we can return to equation (1):

> profit = total revenue − total costs

And if we take total costs to be composed of two elements (fixed costs + variable costs or indirect costs + direct costs) then we can write this as:

> total costs = fixed costs + variable costs
> TC = FC + VC (3)

And to return to our car dealer example, if we find that the business faces fixed costs of $3,500,000 and variable costs of $15,000,000 then we can see that total costs for the business are:

> $3,500,000 + $15,000,000 = $18,500,000

Using our first formula we can see that the business is making quite a healthy profit:

> total revenue = $20,000,000
> total cost = $18,500,000
> profit = $1,500,000

This is good, but not quite as fantastic as it seemed with the original total revenue!

Semi-variable costs

The **semi-variable** costs (also known as **quasi-variable costs**), as noted above, are a combination of fixed and variable costs. For example, the salary of the car salesperson is typically made up of two parts—a fixed element (the basic wage) and a variable element (the commission) which is dependent on the number of cars sold.

Another example might help to explain the distinction: electricity bills are usually split into a fixed element—the standing charge, and a variable element—which is taken from the electricity meter and indicates how much electricity has been used.

Student workpoint 5.1

Be a researcher

A mobile phone is a must-have accessory for many students and there are various payment options.

Why not conduct some research to find answers to these questions.

1 What type of costs are typically paid?

2 Is there a preferred payment plan? Why?

The following example might help explain the relationship between all these costs and also why fixed and variable costs cannot be directly translated as indirect and direct costs. Remember our car dealer recorded the costs as shown in Table 5.5.

These can either be described as fixed/variable or indirect/direct costs (see Table 5.6).

Costs (S$)	
Fixed costs	3,500,000
Variable costs	15,000,000
Total costs	18,500,000

Table 5.5 Costs for the car dealer

Fixed/variable costs (S$)		Direct/indirect costs (S$)	
Fixed	3,500,000	Indirect	3,500,000
Variable	15,000,000	Direct	15,000,000
Total	18,500,000	Total	18,500,000

Table 5.6 Fixed/variable costs and direct/indirect costs for the car dealer

But in reality part of the fixed costs are the salaries of the showroom attendants and total S$1,000,000; and also a proportion of their salaries are paid as commission depending on the number of cars sold. Let's say that this cost is equal to S$2,000,000 from the total of S$15,000,000 incurred by the business.

Then we can redraw our table as shown in Table 5.7.

Fixed/variable costs (S$)		Direct/indirect costs (S$)	
Fixed	2,500,000	Indirect	3,500,000
Semi-variable	3,000,000	Direct	15,000,000
Variable	13,000,000		
Total	18,500,000	Total	18,500,000

Table 5.7 Example of salary and commission as part of fixed costs

This helps explain why indirect costs do not always equal fixed costs and direct costs do not always equal variable costs.

Student workpoint 5.2

Business investigation

Create the trading account for our car dealer.

1 What is the gross profit?

2 What is the net profit?

Contribution to fixed costs

An important business tool is the **contribution** a product makes to the overall profitability of the business. When it knows this, a business can decide which product to focus on so as to expand production, increase investment and ultimately improve sales.

This is particularly useful for a business that has a range of products as the business will be able to judge whether one is outperforming another. In the terms of the Boston Consulting Group (BCG) matrix this can be the difference between a **star, cash cow** and a **dog** product. (If you need a reminder of the definitions of these terms, see p. 207.)

Contribution can be calculated in two ways.

- We can calculate the **total contribution** for a company. We use the following formula:

$$\text{total contribution} = \text{total revenue} - \text{total variable cost} \quad (4)$$

In our car dealer example this comes out at:

$$\text{total contribution} = \$20,000,000 - \$15,000,000 = \$5,000,000 \quad (5)$$

This tells us that the sales of BMW 5 Series cars contributes $5,000,000 to the overall profitability of the car dealer's business, which covers all of the fixed costs of $3,500,000 with a spare $1,500,000 as profit.

- Or we can calculate the **contribution per unit** for the business by using the following formula:

$$\text{contribution} = \text{price} - \text{variable cost (per unit)} \quad (6)$$

The contribution of the BMW 5 Series cars is:

$$\$200,000 - \left(\frac{15,000,000}{100}\right) = S\$50,000 \text{ per car.}$$

That means each car contributes $50,000, which can be discounted from the fixed costs to generate the eventual profit of the business. If the car dealer was to find that another range of cars, for example the BMW 7 Series, has a contribution of $30,000 per car then the dealer should concentrate on selling the more profitable 5 Series model.

Data response exercise

Read the text below and answer the questions that follow.

Case study

Carphone Warehouse cleared out of 8GB iPhones

by Tony Smith, 25 April 2008

The move made by O2 and Carphone Warehouse (CW) to offer Apple's 8GB iPhone for £100 less than the standard price at £169 has proved successful—in a week. CW has no more left to sell, and O2 is apparently down to the last few.

Last week, when it announced its cut-price iPhone package, O2 did warn that the £100-off deal would end when stocks ran out. CW said it was now reviewing its iPhone plans. It wouldn't say whether it will be restocking the 8GB handset.

Both O2 and CW are still offering the £329 16GB iPhone. And also a new generation of 3G iPhones is expected to be shipped soon.

Source: Adapted from www.reghardware.co.uk

Examination questions

1   If the variable costs of the 8GB were £40 and the 160GB were £50 respectively, what are the contributions of each model? [4 marks]

2   How might contribution have helped Carphone Warehouse and O2 to decide to reduce the price of their 8GB model iPhones? [6 marks]

HL

Cost and profit centres

Contribution analysis is a tool by which a business can monitor performance of the production process. The starting point for these calculations is to specify cost and profit centres that generate the sales. A cost or profit centre is an easily identifiable production unit that either generates costs or profits for the business.

A **cost centre** is just a production unit that generates costs but no revenues. Using our car dealership; these production units can be physical units, for example BMW regional headquarters or the marketing department. They can also be non-physical, for instance the web page or advertisements. The important thing is for the costs to be split up according to these units.

A **profit centre** is just a production unit that generates profits where both revenues and costs can be identified and quantified. Again, these centres can be physical units, for example the different car dealers in different parts of the city. Or they could be the different car models. And again, the important thing is for the profits to be split up according to these units.

These are the benefits to businesses of dividing production up into cost and profit centres.

● The business can monitor costs, revenues and profits more effectively.

● It can focus production on a particular unit.

- It can discontinue production on failing units.
- It can switch resources more easily to cope with changes in demand.

Case study

Sodexo

Another example of cost and profit centres is where universities have outlets run by fast food franchises. One example is Sodexo, operating in the UK and Ireland. The company's fast food outlets cater for the student clientele by offering cheap prices and products most in demand for hungry students who missed breakfast or who are on the late night essay shift.

However, the work is strictly seasonal so during vacation time, when there is not so much demand, the workers are redeployed to work in other outlets in the surrounding area.

Contribution analysis for multi-product businesses

Contribution analysis can be very useful for a business that has a range of products or a number of production units or, in fact as in many cases, both. For example, if BMW wanted to know which was its most profitable type of car in which country, it could use contribution analysis to find out.

A simpler example may be to consider our original car dealer, who on a closer look at the showroom reveals the figures shown in Table 5.8 for all cars sold in 2008.

	3 Series (S$000)	5 Series (S$000)	7 Series (S$000)	Totals (S$000)
Price	150	200	300	
Variable cost (per car)	120	150	220	
Contribution (per car)	30	50	80	
Demand (sales)	80	100	20	
Total contribution	2,400	5,000	1,600	9,000
Fixed costs				3,500
Net profit				5,500

Table 5.8 Breakdown of the car dealer's sales in 2008

This information is very useful for the car dealer because if things change then the business can plan accordingly. Say, for instance, that as a result of problems in the factory BMW can only deliver 150 cars in 2009 instead of the 200 required. The car dealer still wants to sell all the types of car so decides to keep a minimum of 10 of each model so that all market segments are still covered. By using contribution analysis we can evaluate the various options open to the car dealer.

The dealer could go for Option A, shown in Table 5.9—focus on keeping stock of the cars that generate the most contribution per car.

	I Series (S$000s)	S Series (S$000s)	K Series (S$000s)	Totals (S$000s)
Contribution (per car)	30	50	80	
Demand (sales)	30	100	20	
Total contribution	900	5,000	1,600	6,500

Table 5.9 Option A—stock cars that make the highest contribution per car

Or Option B, shown in Table 5.10—focus on keeping stock of the best-selling cars.

	I Series (S$000s)	S Series (S$000s)	K Series (S$000s)	Totals (S$000s)
Contribution (per car)	30	50	80	
Demand	40	100	10	
Total contribution	1,200	5,000	800	7,000

Table 5.10 Option B—stock the best-selling cars

Or even Option C, shown in Table 5.11—stock cars in the same proportion as the cut in deliveries — $\frac{3}{4}$ for each type of car.

	I Series (S$000s)	S Series (S$000s)	K Series (S$000s)	Totals (S$000s)
Contribution (per car)	30	50	80	
Demand	60	75	16	
Total contribution	2,400	3,750	1,280	7,430

Table 5.11 Option C—stock cars in the same proportion as the cut in deliveries

Of course, the car dealer has to add to this information various qualitative factors, such as changes to the external environment and how that may impact on future demand. But contribution analysis can be a useful tool to help in the evaluation process.

The same idea could be applied if we were to look at the corresponding figures for different car dealers. The figures might reveal which products sell best in which location. Remember cost and profit centres can also be actual production sites and not just the product itself.

It is also worth bearing in mind that just as there are several advantages for businesses in dividing up production into different cost and profit centres, there may be disadvantages too.

● Calculating costs and profits can be complex.
● The "bigger picture" is lost.
● There may be unhealthy competition between centres.
● The focus on figures may hide other qualitative issues.

Case study

Virgo Air

Passengers flying with Virgo Air are seated either in business or economy class. Because demand for business travel is increasing—and the contribution of business class is so much greater than that of economy—Virgo Air is considering replacing some rows of economy seats with business class seats. The company has the following information.

● Each row of business class passengers has four seats.
● Each row of economy class passengers has eight seats.
● To fly a business class passenger means that two rows of economy class seats have to be removed to make way for the reclining seats that also form beds in business class. ➔

	Business (US$)	Economy (US$)	Totals (US$)
Contribution (per passenger)	1,000	250	
Original demand	20	120	
Total contribution	20,000	30,000	50,000
Fixed costs			40,000
Net profit			10,000

A change in demand for business travel has risen to 32 passengers so Virgo Air wants to calculate the cost of changing the seats over.

	Business (US$)	Economy (US$)	Totals (US$)
Contribution (per passenger)	1,000	250	
Original demand	32		
Total contribution	32,000		
Fixed costs			
Net profit			

1 Should Virgo Air make the switch? (Use the tables in the case study, filling in the missing figures to show your answer.)

2 What other factors should the company take into account?

When you've answered these questions, look at the box below to check the figures you've put into the table.

Virgo Air case study—financial situation for the new business scenario

	Business (US$)	Economy (US$)	Totals (US$)
Contribution (per passenger)	1,000	250	
Original demand	32	72	
Total contribution	32,000	18,000	50,000
Fixed costs			40,000
Net profit			10,000

Break even analysis

Another important tool to help production decisions is **break even analysis**. This is especially relevant for new businesses or for businesses starting a new venture. The idea is to calculate the minimum product that would have to be sold for the business to break even; that is, just to cover its costs and no more than that. If a business manages to produce and sell more than this, it earns a profit.

To calculate break even output, we need to use our formula (1):

profit = total revenue − total costs (1)

If we rearrange this, we can get the following:

profit + total costs = total revenue (7)

And if profit is 0, break even is:

total costs = total revenue (8)

Using this we can calculate the break even level of output using the following three methods:

● creating a table
● drawing a graph
● using a formula.

The third method is the easiest but very often we use at least two of the methods to check that we have made the correct calculations.

The table method

Remembering formula (8):

total costs = total revenue

we can expand this by using our earlier calculations:

total costs = fixed costs + variable costs
total revenue = price × quantity

Then:

fixed cost + variable cost = price × quantity (9)

Note: For break even analysis we do not consider semi-variable costs because this would make things much too complicated, so we must always divide costs into either fixed or variable proportions.

Using a simple example may help explain this method. While on holiday in the Philippines, I got talking to a vendor selling fake Rolex watches. He told me that he had to pay a sum of US$1,000 to secure the rights to sell his watches outside the tourist hotels on the beach. He paid this to the local "enforcers" (mafia). He then told me that on average a tourist would pay US$50 for a watch and that the watches typically cost him US$25 from his supplier.

From this information I could work out how many watches he would need to sell before he started making a profit. Table 5.12 gives the details.

● Note that fixed costs (the fee for the right to sell the watches) had to be paid "up front" before he had sold any watches—the sum was a one-off payment, no matter how many watches he sold.

Examiner's notes

Remember the important thing here is **break even output (quantity)** and not break even price, break even revenue, or break even profit. It is the **number of products sold** not their price, revenue, etc. that we want to find.

In examinations many students confuse this point—don't be one of them!

- Variable costs are 0 if nothing has been sold. He could take the unsold watches back to his supplier. He only pays an amount on the watches he sold at $25 a watch.
- The price stays the same throughout. Yes, some tourists were good at haggling and some were not. The average price was $50.
- If nothing has been bought, total revenue for 0 is 0. After this, total revenue goes up by multiplying price and quantity.

Quantity/output (watches sold)	Costs (US$)			Revenue (US$)			Profit/loss (US$)
	Fixed cost	Variable cost	Total cost	Price	Quantity/output	Total revenue	
0	1,000	0	1,000	50	0	0	(1,000)
10	1,000	250	1,250	50	10	500	(750)
20	1,000	500	1,500	50	20	1,000	(500)
30	1,000	750	1,750	50	30	1,500	(250)
40	1,000	1,000	2,000	50	40	2,000	0
50	1,000	1,250	2,250	50	50	2,500	250
60	1,000	1,500	2,500	50	60	3,000	500
70	1,000	1,750	2,750	50	70	3,500	750
80	1,000	2,000	3,000	50	80	4,000	1,000
90	1,000	2,250	3,250	50	90	4,500	1,250
100	1,000	2,500	3,500	50	100	5,000	1,500

Table 5.12 The watch seller's costs, revenue, break even and profit/loss when selling watches for $50

We can clearly see from Table 5.12 that the watch seller breaks even by selling 40 watches. For every watch sold after this he makes a further $25 profit.

The graph method

We can transfer some of the information in the table to a graph. The vertical axis will have costs and revenue on it and the horizontal axis will have the quantity of watches sold (see Figure 5.1).

To this we can add the fixed costs, which we can draw as a line parallel to the horizontal axis starting at $1,000 (see Figure 5.2)—the line is parallel to the horizontal axis because these costs do not change as more watches are sold, the costs are fixed.

We can then add the variable cost line by starting from 0 where there are no sales and then fixing another point (at, say, sales of 40 units, variable costs of $1,000) and simply drawing a line through these two points (see Figure 5.3).

We know that total costs are just fixed costs + variable costs so we can draw a line parallel to the variable cost line but starting at US$1,000 to get the total costs line (see Figure 5.4). Notice that this should tally with the column of total costs in our table.

Finally, we can draw the total revenue line (see Figure 5.5). As there is no revenue if there are no sales, this also starts at the origin. Once we have this line, we can fix another point (at, say, sales of 40 units, total revenue of $2,000) and simply draw a line through these two points.

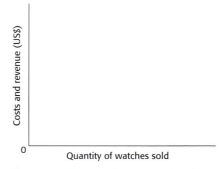

Figure 5.1 Costs and revenue related to quantity of watches sold

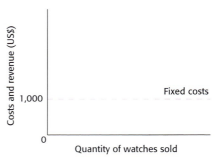

Figure 5.2 Fixed costs added to the graph

Our completed graph shows us that the break even quantity is indeed 40 watches.

We can see this more clearly on Figure 5.6, which is made simpler by only having the total costs and total revenue lines.

Here we can see that if the watch seller does not sell 40 watches he makes a loss, and the more he sells after 40 watches, the better things get as his profit builds up. The amount of profit or loss is given by the vertical distance between the total cost and the total revenue lines—and this should tally with the Table 5.12, which we looked at earlier.

Notice that as he sells more watches, first the watch seller's losses get smaller (the distance between total costs and total revenue gets less) and after breaking even the distance between total costs and total revenue increases, which means he makes more profit the more he sells. But he must sell a minimum of 40 watches before making a profit at all.

A further point is that if, for instance, the watch seller actually sells 60 watches then as well as earning profit he is also said to have a **margin of safety** of 20 watches (see Figure 5.7). The margin of safety is just the difference between actual sales and break even sales and is in effect his safety net.

> **Examiner's notes**
> Remember it is **margin of safety output (quantity)** we are interested in, not revenue, profits, etc.

The formula method
The final method we can use to find break even quantity is actually the simplest. This is the formula:

$$\text{break even quantity} = \frac{\text{fixed costs}}{\text{contribution per unit}} \quad (10)$$

Remember our contribution per unit is formula (6):

$$\text{contribution} = \text{price} - \text{variable cost per unit}$$

Using our example of the watch seller, we would have:

$$\text{fixed costs} = \$1,000$$
$$\text{contribution} = \$50 - \$25 = \$25$$

And so the break even quantity is:

$$\frac{1,000}{25} = 40 \text{ (watches)}$$

Note: There is no need to use US$, we just use the raw figures themselves.

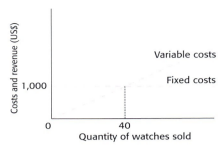
Figure 5.3 Variable costs added to the graph

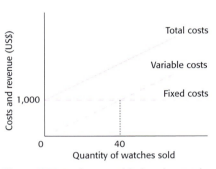
Figure 5.4 Total costs added to the graph

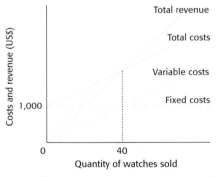
Figure 5.5 Total revenue added to the graph

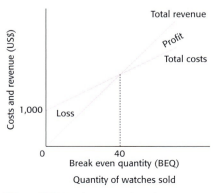
Figure 5.6 Total costs and total revenue

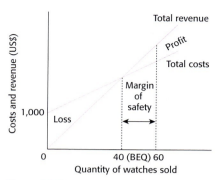

Figure 5.7 Margin of safety

Student workpoint 5.3

Business investigation

Money matters

A school's economics and business department publishes a magazine prepared by students. The department prints 400 copies. The costs are as follows:

Fixed costs	$600
Variable costs	$2 per magazine

The department will charge $4 for a copy of the magazine.

Using the three different methods, produce a table, a graph, and the equation to show the break even quantity of magazines.

HL

Changes in break even quantity

Changing the price
Break even analysis doesn't only tell a business how many units it has to sell before it makes a profit, but can also be used to see the effect of a change in any of the variables. For example, if the watch seller was able to sell his watches for an average of $75 a watch the formula would be:

$$\text{break even quantity} = \frac{1{,}000}{(75 - 25)} = 20 \text{ watches}$$

This makes sense because if the revenue coming in is increasing and costs stay the same then the watch seller will not need as many sales to start covering his fixed costs. This also would have the effect of increasing his margin of safety and of course his profit if he was to sell as many watches as before. Figure 5.8 shows this.

The total revenue line is now much steeper, and we can confirm this by returning to Table 5.12 (on p. 245) and changing the total revenue column to reflect the increase in price. This is shown in Table 5.13.

Of course the reverse would be true if the watch seller was only to get $25 a watch—he would need to sell more to break even.

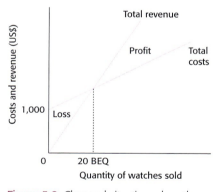

Figure 5.8 Changed situation when the watch seller increases the price of watches

5 Operations management

245

Quantity/output (watches sold)	Costs (US$)			Revenue (US$)			Profit/loss (US$)
	Fixed cost	Variable cost	Total cost	Price	Quantity/output	Total revenue	
0	1,000	0	1,000	75	0	0	(1,000)
10	1,000	250	1,250	75	10	750	(500)
20	1,000	500	1,500	75	20	1,500	0
30	1,000	750	1,750	75	30	2,250	500
40	1,000	1,000	2,000	75	40	3,000	1,000
50	1,000	1,250	2,250	75	50	3,750	1,500
60	1,000	1,500	2,500	75	60	4,500	2,000
70	1,000	1,750	2,750	75	70	5,250	2,500
80	1,000	2,000	3,000	75	80	5,000	3,000
90	1,000	2,250	3,250	75	90	5,750	3,500
100	1,000	2,500	3,500	75	100	6,500	4,000

Table 5.13 The watch seller's costs, revenue, break even and profit/loss when selling watches for $75

Changing the fixed costs
On the other hand, if the local mafia were to increase the sum the watch seller needs to pay to trade on his patch of beach, this would also have an effect on break even quantity, margin of safety, and profit.

Let's assume that the watch seller now has to pay $1,500 as a retainer (the right to sell his watches), but his watches can only be sold at the original price. Our formula is now:

$$\text{break even quantity} = \frac{1,500}{(50 - 25)} = 60 \text{ watches}$$

Again, this makes sense because the watch seller has to sell more watches to cover his overheads, as we can see from Figure 5.9.

As you can see, compared with the original diagram the margin of safety has entirely disappeared. Our poor watch seller has no safety net if he wants to avoid unpleasantness because he can't pay his retainer.

Changing the variable costs
Of course, there is another possible change that could affect the performance of our watch seller, if his variable costs were to increase—say he has more problems getting the fake watches because of increased police vigilance. Again, let's revert to the original situation but now increase the variable costs to $40 a watch. This is likely to affect his break even quantity, margin of safety, and profit as follows:

$$\text{break even quantity} = \frac{1,000}{(50 - 40)} = 100 \text{ watches}$$

And we can also see this in Figure 5.10.

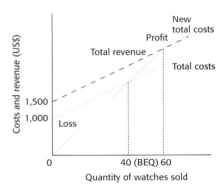

Figure 5.9 Changed situation when the watch seller has to pay a higher retainer

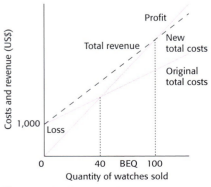

Figure 5.10 Changed situation based on increased variable costs

In this case if our poor watch seller can still only sell 60 watches he has no margin of safety and he makes a loss of $400! $50 × 60 watches sold—($40 × 60 + $1,000).

Target profit

Another use of the break even analysis is for the watch seller to calculate how many watches he would have to sell to make a certain amount of profit. He can do this by adapting the formula for break even quantity. So, for example, if he decides that he wants to make $2,000 profit then he can use the following formula:

$$\text{target profit quantity} = \frac{\text{fixed costs} + \text{target profit}}{\text{contribution}} \quad (11)$$

Which from our original calculations gives us:

$$\frac{1,000 + 2,000}{25} = 120 \text{ watches}$$

This is significantly more than both his original break even quantity and his margin of safety.

Break even revenue

We said earlier that you should not consider break even price, but it is possible by rearranging the formula to calculate the price necessary to break even if you know the total sales and costs. By itself this number is not that helpful but it would be the minimum price a producer would charge before making a profit. Ideally, the producer would want to charge a higher price but of course if the producer does that the **law of demand** comes into play and the business may lose some potential customers. It will depend on the **price elasticity of demand**.

To return to our watch seller; what if he knew his costs, decided how many watches he wanted to sell and wanted to know what price to charge to break even? The following formula would give him the break even price:

$$\text{break even price} = \frac{\text{total costs (fixed costs + variable costs of selling 40 watches)}}{\text{total quantity to sell}} \quad (12)$$

$$= \frac{2,000}{40} = \$50 \text{ a watch}$$

If he wanted to know what price to charge if he wanted to sell 100 watches and earn $2,000 profit, we can extend this formula to:

$$\text{target profit price} = \frac{\text{total costs}}{\text{total quantity to sell}} \quad (13)$$

or:

$$\frac{3,500 + 2,000}{100} = \$55 \text{ a watch}$$

Limitations of break even analysis

Of course by this time the watch seller might have decided that this is an awful lot of trouble to go to just to try and make some money and keep away from the bad people! He should be aware that although break even analysis is a very useful business tool there are many problems associated with it too.

- It assumes that all that is sold is actually bought. This may not be the case.
- It also ignores changes in stock, and stock that is used up and sold straightaway—**just in time** (JIT).
- Costs are often very difficult to calculate and divide up accurately per unit because of overheads and expenses.
- Price, revenue, and costs are assumed to be constant but the reality can be quite different.
  — For example, it would be pretty unusual for our watch seller to sell 1,000 watches for the same price as 10. He might well offer a "special price" to a customer who will buy a lot of watches.
  — Similarly, he may be able to buy up a lot of stock more cheaply if he **buys in bulk**. This is an example of **economies of scale** that large producers often experience.

If we take these final two points into account then the reality for many businesses is that the costs and revenue lines may not be constant—as shown in Figure 5.11.

In this example there is not just one break even point but two (a maximum and minimum) and there is a range of profits that a business can aim for. There is also an optimal level of sales. At point X the business is making the most profits because this is the greatest distance between the total revenue line and the total cost line—if the business tries to sell any more beyond this point it may well make more money but its profit per unit is decreasing. This is because the business is becoming less efficient as it is experiencing **diseconomies of scale** and having to sell at cheaper prices, perhaps because of **over trading**.

However, drawing accurate curves, calculating accurate figures and working with changeable variables is of course much more difficult, so most break even analyses ignore these and only deal with the simpler examples shown above.

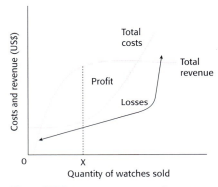

Figure 5.11 Inconstant cost and revenue lines

Examiner's notes
All IB examination questions will only ever use the simpler straight line models.

Did you know?

The Indian Premier League (IPL) was launched in 2008 at an estimated cost of over $1 billion and straight away courted controversy. National cricket boards lost players to play in this lucrative tournament rather than for the national team. The use of US-style cheerleaders was also controversial!

Indian Premier League: Will it break even?

R. Venkatesan Iyengar, 28 February 2008

The question that is uppermost in many cricket observers' minds right now is whether the IPL will ultimately end up as a costly misadventure. Industrialists and film personalities have paid "ego premiums" to buy teams and players. Mind-boggling amounts have been invested in the IPL in the hope that the cricket-crazy Indians would make it a huge success.

However, the success of the IPL in the long run depends on whether the team owners would be able to break even in the near future. While some of the franchisees have expressed the confidence that they will break even within two to three years, doubts remain.

Source: Adapted from: www.merinews.com

Examination questions

Enrique's establishment

Enrique Santa Cruz runs a café in the suburbs of Buenos Aires close to a railway station. Enrique has noted that Argentina has a strong chance in the 2010 Football World Cup in South Africa and wants to take advantage of this.

He is planning on hiring a huge, wide-screen plasma TV and a data projector for the month-long finals. He will need to pay the subscription to the cable provider too. The matches will be televised live in the afternoons and early evenings and so he is also planning special themed events to coincide with the games. To do all of this he will need to hire extra staff for the 30 days of the schedule.

All these extra costs will be a significant investment for Enrique and he has to consider his options very carefully. He has a maximum seating capacity of 50 people every afternoon/evening.

He has calculated his costs in US dollars:

Fixed costs	US$
Hire of data projector and TV	6,000
Staff salary for the month	2,000
Variable costs for a typical meal	
Food, wine, beer and extras	50

He has also calculated that on average every customer will spend $60 a night.

1 Draw a diagram to show how many people Enrique needs in order to break even. [4 marks]

2 Enrique has a target profit of $10,000. Calculate whether it would be possible for Enrique to make this profit over the month. [4 marks]

3 Enrique has another plan too. He wants to ask every customer to pay a "cover charge" of $10 a person to come into the restaurant. Assuming that the football-crazy Argentinians are happy to pay this, how will it affect Enrique's target profit and his break even quantity? [6 marks]

4 If this works what would his margin of safety be? [2 marks]

5 If disaster happens and Argentina are knocked out of the World Cup in the first round (as in 2006), Enrique is sure that his customers will lose interest and he will be lucky to get more than 15 people a night for the month. How will this affect his plan? [4 marks]

By the end of this chapter, you should be able to:

- analyse the move from traditional quality control methods to total quality management (TQM)
- evaluate different approaches to quality improvements, and explain the role of *Kaizen* in quality improvement
- explain the role of local and national standards in assuring quality for consumers

Profile

William Edwards Deming (1900–1993)

William Edwards Deming was a US statistician, college professor, author, lecturer, and consultant. Deming is widely credited with improving production in the US during the second world war, although he is perhaps best known for his work in Japan. There, from 1950 onward, he taught top management how to improve design (and thus service), product quality, testing, and sales (the last through global markets) through various methods, including the application of statistical methods. Deming made a significant contribution to Japan's later renown for innovative high-quality products and its economic power. He is regarded as having had more impact upon Japanese manufacturing and business than any other individual not of Japanese heritage. Despite being considered something of a hero in Japan, he was only beginning to win widespread recognition in the US at the time of his death.

Quality control versus quality assurance

A key component of operations management is the issue of quality. In the past this was very much a matter of **quality control** but thanks to the "**quality revolution**" that has sprung from Japan since 1945 there has been a move towards **quality assurance**. This change in quality management came about largely due to the work of one man: the US management theorist Deming. He worked alongside Kaoru Ishikawa in Japan after 1945 and in doing so achieved widespread acceptance of his "**14 points**" on how to produce quality products—incredibly his ideas only started to gain ground in his home country—and Europe—in the 1980s and Japan still leads the way. The results are clear to see with the big US car producers going the way of the British by losing market share to the Japanese.

Quality is important for a producer as it can lead to:

- increased sales
- repeat customers (brand loyalty)
- reduced costs
- premium pricing.

From a marketing point of view a product need not actually be a high quality product to bring all of these rewards but as long as the **consumer perception** is one of quality then that can often be enough. So league tables showing "top" business schools, airlines or MP3 players can be hugely important for businesses even if the product voted "the best" is not actually so.

The term quality suggests that a product is:

- reliable—it is not going to break down
- safe—it is not going to fail
- durable—it is going to last
- innovative—it is leading the way in terms of functionality or design
- value for money—you pay for what you get.

The quality revolution showed that even businesses not at the top end of the range could benefit from producing good-quality products. While a Honda car may not have the same brand image as a BMW there is still a huge amount to be gained by producing good quality cheaper cars. This is a fact that GM and Ford are only just starting to realize, and Rover and British Leyland never did work out.

Figure 5.12 shows a way of mapping products based on scales of quality and price.

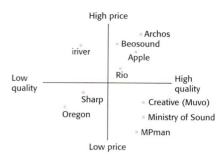

Figure 5.12 Products mapped according to quality and price

Student workpoint 5.4

Be an enquirer

A class did some research to find the best quality MP3 player. They initially did a survey then used *What hi fi?* magazine for a professional judgment to produce a product positioning map. They concluded that quality does not have to come at the expense of price.

Why not try the same exercise for a product of your choice?

The move towards quality assurance away from the old-fashioned system of quality control can be summarized as in Table 5.14, which shows the major difference between the two systems.

Quality control	Quality assurance
Concept Quality is "controlled" by one person (the manager) by inspection after the production run has been completed	Quality is "assured" because no one person is in overall control of quality; the whole business is focused on ensuring quality production
Costs A certain % reject rate is set, for example 2% of products are allowed to fail Wasteful production	Zero rejects are expected—every product is expected to pass inspection Lean production
Processes It is rare to halt production—as it is costly do so Associated with assembly line, flow production Quality stops with the job. The focus is only on the job at hand.	The company expects to halt production to fix errors Associated with cellular or modular production Quality includes suppliers and after-sales servicing
People Quality is the responsibility of one person—a quality inspector "Role culture" Autocratic leadership Top–down, one-way communication	Quality is the responsibility of the team—quality circles Total quality culture Democratic consultative leadership 360-degree communication

Table 5.14 Quality control versus quality assurance

In order for quality assurance to work effectively the whole business has to embrace a total quality cultural shift. This is difficult and costly to achieve in the short term but may well prove beneficial to the business in the long run. The main focus of this approach to quality is known as total quality management (TQM) and the main features are set out below.

Features of TQM	
Lean production	The business aims to reduce wastage at all stages of production by eliminating delays, stock hold-ups and maintenance issues. It includes techniques such as *kaizen*, *kan ban* and JIT.
Quality chain	The quality chain is linked to lean production but it is recognized that the quality of a business also depends on the quality of its suppliers and after-sales services. It is expected that at all stages of the production process, the business imagines that the next part of the chain is the final customer and considers the product from that point of view.
Statistical process control (SPC)	Volunteer groups meet regularly to discuss and suggest ways of improving quality. Volunteers are not paid and are from all levels of the business hierarchy.
Statistical process control (SPC)	All stages of production are monitored and information is given to all parties, usually in the form of easy-to-understand diagrams, charts, and messages.
Mobilized workforce	All members of the business are expected to "buy into" TQM and so the workforce are encouraged to feel pride in their work, given responsibilities and recognition, for example through employee of the month schemes, and so are included in the quality decision-making process.
Market-oriented production	By focusing on what the customer wants, the business can make sure that it is innovating and continually reinventing its products. This can lead to improved sales (as people buy the latest version) and brand loyalty.

Table 5.15 Main features of TQM

Implementing TQM has many advantages for businesses.
- It can motivate the workers.
- It can significantly reduce long-term costs.
- It can improve recognition of quality products.
- It can create closer working relationships with all stakeholders.

However, there are some disadvantages too.
- It is costly.
- Staff may need significant training.
- It may take time to change a corporate culture.
- It can create a lot of stress on formal relationships in the business.
- It is difficult to maintain over a long period of time.

Perhaps then it is no surprise that TQM is more commonly used by businesses that are new or are looking to make significant changes to retain their competitive advantage. However, many businesses are now registering the fact that the old-fashioned way of controlling quality may be too costly in the long term, so even if they are not embracing the vision of TQM they can still apply some of the elements of quality assurance.

Data response exercise
Read the text below and answer the questions that follow.

Case study

Mattel in China

Mattel has recalled more than 18 million toys worldwide, the second such recall in two weeks.

Chinese-made Sarge die-cast toys from the Pixar film *Cars* have been recalled because their paint contains lead. Mattel has also recalled toys containing small magnets that can come loose, including Polly Pocket, Batman Magna, Doggie Daycare and One Piece playsets. Previously the company had recalled Dora The Explorer dolls' houses.

The Consumer Products Safety Commission (CPSC) said it had no reports of any injuries from the recalled products.

Recalled toys:

- Sarge die-cast car
- 11 Doggie Daycare sets
- 44 Polly Pocket toys
- 4 Batman Magna toys
- 2 Barbie and Tanner sets
- 1 One Piece toy.

Examination questions

1 Identify what may be the costs to Mattel of recalling its toys. *[2 marks]*

2 Explain what may be the costs of not recalling its toys. *[4 marks]*

3 To what extent will a system of TQM help Mattel overcome this type of problem in future? *[8 marks]*

Theory of Knowledge

The announcement of the recall of Mattel toys and the media hype that this generated seemed to have unleashed some anti-Chinese feeling in the US by seeming to confirm the poor quality of Chinese production.

In a later statement Mattel announced that the problem was not of Chinese origin. The problem stemmed from the design of the toys and not from the manufacturing in China.

1 Who is responsible for the problem?

2 If no one has been injured hasn't Mattel overreacted by recalling so many toys?

3 How might distance and culture have an impact on our understanding of issues like this?

HL

Approaches to quality improvement
There are many different possible approaches that have been used to try to improve quality. Within the general TQM framework there is plenty of scope for introducing some of the most popular tools, which are set out below.

Ishikawa—the fishbone diagram
The original Ishikawa diagram was designed to show the **cause and effects** of qualitative problems. It was designed with 4 "Ms" (to be used with manufacturing) but has been followed by the "Ps" (for service-based industries) and "Ss" (for administration) and of course there are much more loose combinations of all of them. The general

idea, though, is to provide a tool to help brainstorm the causes of and the effects of a quality problem. It is particularly useful when running a quality circle.

For example if a business—let's take the example of a call centre in Bangalore—has a very high labour turnover, then it could help the business to try to work out why this might be so.

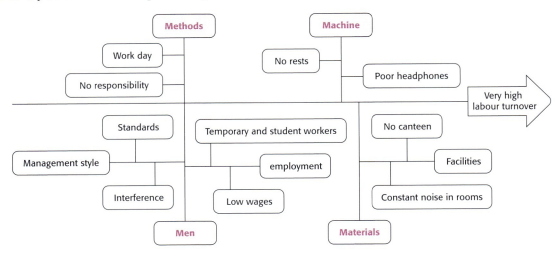

Figure 5.13 Ishikawa fishbone diagram—call centre example

After identifying key areas of concern, a brainstorming session may reveal that the constant interference by management, long hours worked, and poor-quality sound proofing may be the main causes of the high labour turnover at the call centre.

Benchmarking

Benchmarking is a tool that many businesses use and, perhaps more surprisingly, with **collaborative benchmarking** many competing businesses can act together to use it to help themselves keep up to date.

The idea is very simple—businesses take the best players or the market leader in their industry and follow those organizations' "best practices". This idea is also surprisingly open and it is not so much copying the rivals' products as their management practice and production processes in order to improve quality. Benchmarking can be used as part of the SPC process. In fact, open benchmarking can have advantages for both parties—the company that acts as the benchmark benefits because with this recognition comes a good PR opportunity and acceptance, often by other stakeholders, that it is an innovator.

Formally, benchmarking should involve the following process.

1 Identify the area that has quality problems.
2 Find other businesses in the industry that have similar processes.
3 Work out who the leading businesses are in the industry.
4 Conduct market research on those businesses' practices.
5 Visit the businesses.
6 Implement measures and practices learned from the businesses researched.

Of course, the success of benchmarking relies on the business wishing to solve its problem having the ability to "think outside the box", trying to introduce something new and not to carry on as it always has. And also what works for one organization may not necessarily work for another.

Kaizen

We have seen that the concept of *kaizen* is central to TQM and lean production in particular. The term means in effect "continuous improvement". The idea was developed by Toyota and the emphasis is on continuous change not one-time changes. This process may involve suggestion boxes or competitions to find suitable areas of improvements in the simplest form. However, *kaizen* formally requires certain key principles.

- It must be inclusive of all levels of the hierarchy.
- There should be no blame attached to any problem issues raised.
- Systemic thinking is needed to think of the whole production process not a small part of it.
- It focuses on the process and not the end product.

Kaizen is a great idea but the reality is that it is very difficult to maintain over a long period of time the momentum and focus that *kaizen* needs. To do so would require high levels of commitment and a sense of loyalty by the employees and so this is closely tied to **human relation** or **behaviouralist** motivational theories. It would not work under an autocratic leadership or bureaucratic corporate culture.

National and international safety standards

An excellent way for businesses to assure the consumer of the quality of their products is by gaining certification for recognized safety standards. At local, national or, even better, international level a safety certificate is a mark of assurance that the product has met certain minimum requirements. The problem of certification is quite a complex one. For example, in 2007 a Chinese producer manufacturing toothpaste for an international brand satisfied both local and national regulations but failed international safety standards as the toothpaste was found to contain elements of anti-freeze.

Meeting recognized safety standards and so assuring the consumer that the product is safe can be very favourable to a business because it can:

- give a competitive edge
- save on the costs of withdrawing products
- act as an insurance
- bring better profit margins.

Some of the most common international standards are set out in Table 5.16.

Standard	Organization	Example
ISO 9000	International Organisation for Standardisation	Quality of design in airplanes
ISO 2200	International Organisation for Standardisation	Quality of food
ISO 1400	International Organisation for Standardisation	Quality of environment
CE	European Union	Household appliances and toys
EN	European Union	Overall quality
BSI	British Standards Institution	Overall quality
JIS	Japanese Standards Association	Overall quality (in English)

Table 5.16 Common international standards

Of all of these the ISO is the recognized world leader in terms of accepted standards.

 The BSI "Kitemark" is the most famous since it was established in 1903.

 The European Union, as the world's biggest trading bloc, has many products that have the immediately recognizable "CE" label.

Safety symbols are designed to convey specific information at a glance. Can you say what each of these safety symbols means?

LION MARK

5.4 Location

By the end of this chapter, you should be able to:

- explain the causes and consequences of location and relocation, both domestically and internationally
- consider the effects of globalization on location
- analyse the impact of location on different areas of business

Location of production

Of course, one of the most important decisions a business has to make is where it will **locate** or as the business grows where it should **relocate** to. In this section we'll leave aside the ideas of **outsourcing (subcontracting)**, **offshoring** or even **inshoring** which we will discuss later (see p. 281) because they are transfers of part of the business. In terms of the whole business, organizations have to bear in mind many factors when deciding where to start up or where to move to.

Figure 5.14

Source: www.shannonburns.com

There is a distinction between setting up a business for the first time and moving the business on to a new location. However, many of the factors have a bearing in both cases. The only difference might be the objectives of the company. Setting up may be simply to get started but relocation can be for a number of reasons, such as chasing the market, gaining room for expansion, or the business might be a merger and need a neutral new venue. A further distinction is of course the question of whether a business **relocates domestically** or **internationally**.

The next section outlines factors related to location or relocation.

Costs

Costs will be a big determining factor and will largely depend on the type of business that is being started.

- *Land.* If the business is a large-scale manufacturer it may need a large, flat surface area.
- *Labour.* If the business is a technical one (such as a laboratory) requiring skilled workers the biggest cost may be labour.
- *Transport.* If the business is producing large quantities of a physical product transport costs can be crucial. There are two options.
  — If the business is bulk increasing—that is it buys in lots of components and builds something bigger (such as TVs or cars) then it makes sense to set up the business close to the market, as transporting the finished bigger items is likely to be more expensive than bringing in lots of small components.
  — If the business is bulk decreasing—that is the business buys in lots of big quantities of raw materials and turns them into smaller end products (businesses such as paper mills or slaughterhouses), it makes sense to set up the business close to the source of the raw materials.

Competition

There is a balance that needs to be made between finding a gap in the market physically and setting up near to your direct competition. Retail outlets, theatres, law firms, and many more businesses set up close to their rivals as the chances of getting passing trade increase if the area becomes known for a particular product.

In the most extreme form of this, companies such as Starbucks allegedly are infamous for a system called **cannibalistic marketing** whereby they set up one franchise in a location and then set up more and more units in the same area to flood the particular sector. They will keep on doing this even though each new franchise eats up some of the profits of the existing outlets, until eventually there are so many outlets that there is no more possible extra trade to be generated. This is shown in Figure 5.15.

Type of land

The type of land will be important, not only in terms of costs but because of its suitability. For example, ski resorts in the French Alps may have done good business in the early parts of the 20th century but with the onset of global warming and glacier shrinkage the snow covering has changed. The company Chamonix has at times had to import artificial snow because the level of natural snow is too low to guarantee consistent coverage throughout the ski season.

5 Operations management

The outer circle is a city. The small circle is the first franchise and its sphere of influence (where its customers come from).

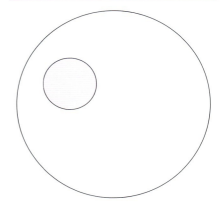

So another outlet is opened and as yet there is no problem—so another outlet is opened…

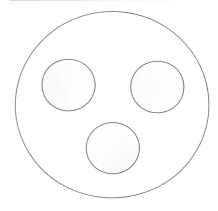

… until eventually although the franchisor (for instance, Starbucks) is doing OK—the company is covering lots of the market—the individual franchisee find themselves losing custom.

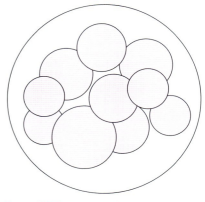

Figure 5.15 Cannibalistic marketing

Markets

In the past many businesses had to set up close to their customers. There were even special markets set up for special products so, for instance, you might find the corn exchange, the gold bullion market, or a general market-place (such as the great bazaars) in North Africa and the Middle East, for example Damascus, Marrakesh, Aleppo, or Istanbul.

With **e-commerce** the need for a physical market-place has changed and this can bring huge advantages for start-up Internet companies. Rather than depending on a physical market, they may only require an efficient **distribution system** through which to provide their products (see p. 221–2 for more on distribution systems).

Inertia

Very often businesses set up in the place that the owners are familiar with—Bill Gates and the Silicon Valley entrepreneurs spring to mind. Setting up in your garage may cut down on costs but will restrict your ability to expand. On the other hand, relocating to new areas where you don't have so many contacts may act as a drag. For Bill Gates, the pull of Berkeley and Stanford counteracted the push of expansion for quite some time.

Labour pool

Key to any business are the workers to do the work. Whether this requires university graduates or school leavers, most businesses need to take account of the type of workers available and balance this with the skills and qualifications the business requires.

Most importantly, **demographic change** can make huge differences to the type of workers available. For example, the increasing number of women in the workplace—and higher up in the workplace—means that more and more businesses have to adapt to part-time working, job sharing, flexitime and the provision of crèche facilities.

A final point worth taking into consideration is the level of unemployment as this can be a good indicator of savings on salaries—the more there are unemployed the more those people may want to become employed.

Infrastructure

This not only means the communication network for transporting products but also urban transport for workers and the provision of networks for phones, faxes and all forms of digital communication.

Also, infrastructure covers a much wider field as it includes facilities that support industry and this may mean the provision of services such as education, healthcare and all sorts of local utilities such as power, phones, water, post, housing, and police.

Transport may include road, rail, air, and water networks. And, as we are becoming more environmentally conscious, the extent of a product's carbon footprint has to be weighed against ease of distribution.

Services are important for the business as they will affect the welfare of staff. In particular, if staff have to be relocated this becomes a big issue.

Utilities are also important for the business, not only in terms of cost but also reliability.

Suppliers

The availability of a range of good local suppliers may be very important for the business, especially if it is using the JIT system of stock control, which implies a greater degree of coordination than is normal.

Government

The role of both local and national government can be crucial for a business, especially one that is starting up or one that is considering locating in a deprived area.

- *Support.* This can be anything from promises by politicians to some significant savings. A government can often be a big purchaser so securing a tender to a government department can bring secure and profitable contracts. At the very least many British companies have the right to promote their product with a "supplier to the Queen" label which may impress certain consumers.

Not only this but government support can come in the form of grants (non-returnable, one-time only funds) or subsidies (funds to be offset against the cost of production), soft loans (loans at preferential rates of interest or even tax rebates (a cut in the tax to be paid).

- *Laws.* From labour laws and health and safety regulations, to rules on advertising, and restrictions on sales government, laws are crucial for businesses. And businesses have to be careful because laws can change. Even if there is no regime change, there may well be a change in government policy. To this end many businesses keep political lobbyists on their payroll but even so changes in, for example, traffic rules can have a major effect on deliveries for a business.
- *Taxes.* Of course, the amount of money a business is liable to pay in tax will have a major effect on where a business may wish to locate. In the UK, businesses need to be aware of a number of possible taxes—national corporation tax and local council taxes for the business, income tax for their employees, capital gains tax for their owners, and even *ad valorem* taxes and duties payable by their customers—all of these will have a major impact not only on the amount of business the company can conduct but also how much profit can be retained and reinvested.

The huge changes in communications over the past 100 years have seen remarkable changes in where businesses set up. In the past, businesses were very much local and serving the immediate vicinity. However, as it has become easier to communicate and transport large volumes of materials many businesses don't only think in terms of their own locality when **relocating** somewhere. There may well be regional differences which still ensure that domestic businesses can locate within a certain area, but the distinction between local, domestic, regional, and even international is changing. The increasing importance of **regional blocs** (such as the EU and NAFTA) has had a major impact on location decisions. For example, Nissan built a car factory in the north of England to circumvent the EU import duties. A final factor is the growth of **trading hubs** such as Hong Kong, Singapore, or Dubai and these can seem good options for a business wanting to set up a regional base.

Data response exercise

Read the text below and answer the questions that follow.

Case study

Chicago, offering big incentives, will be Boeing's new home

by David Barboza, the *New York Times*, 11 May 2001

Seven weeks after announcing that it would move its headquarters out of Seattle, the Boeing Company selected Chicago as its new home. Boeing, the world's largest maker of commercial aircraft, chose Chicago over Dallas and Denver after it was promised tax breaks and incentives that could total $60 million over 20 years by the city and the State of Illinois.

The move from Seattle is part of a Boeing effort to transform itself into a more diversified company and separate its corporate offices from any one division. Along with its aircraft unit, the company is expanding into military and satellite equipment.

In its new home, the company says that it will operate a leaner corporate center with about 500 employees, down from about 1,000 in Seattle, with the displaced workers largely being absorbed into other divisions.

In Seattle, where Boeing was founded in 1916 by William Boeing, the company has more than 70,000 employees, largely tied to the company's commercial aircraft unit, which makes Boeing 737, 747 and 767 airplanes. The company said it had no plans to move those operations.

"Our decision to move was a strategic business decision," Philip M Condit, the chairman and chief executive, said at a news conference this afternoon on the tarmac at Midway Airport in Chicago. "We believe that having a headquarters separate from any of our businesses will help us grow."

The decision to move was clearly a blow to Seattle. Many in the Seattle area, where Boeing is the largest employer, were worried that relocating the headquarters might signal a scaling back of Boeing's operations in the Puget Sound region. Union officials were concerned about that prospect. But Boeing maintains the move is strategic and signals the company's desire to be a global company focused on growth.

At the news conference today, Mr. Condit, who had been behind Boeing's attempt to transform itself into a more diversified company, said he decided about nine months ago that Boeing needed to move its headquarters.

Source: http://query.nytimes.com

Examination questions

1 Identify two factors that led to Boeing relocating to Chicago. [*4 marks*]
2 Explain how the move might be a "strategic decision" by Boeing. [*6 marks*]
3 Discuss the likelihood of the move being a success for Boeing in the future. [*10 marks*]

HL

Impact of globalization on location

Globalization is a huge topic and there are many different aspects of it, covered throughout this book. In this chapter we will only look at the **push** and **pull** factors of globalization on location decisions and then also the impact of globalization on:

- production
- marketing
- HR
- finance.

From a business perspective, whether it is right or wrong, the process appears to be largely irreversible and it is important that we look at the reasons why businesses may want to set up operations in another country.

Pull factors

There are many external reasons why setting up or relocating globally is an attractive option for many businesses. These can be seen as **pull factors** and include:

- improved communications
- dismantling of trade barriers
- deregulation of the world's financial markets
- increasing economic and political power of multinational companies.

Improved communications

As we've already noted, it is far easier not only to transport products around the world—I live in Singapore and the bulk of the milk I buy in the local supermarket comes daily from Australia—but also with "Skype", e-mail and other digital devices it is far easier to communicate in real time than it ever has been. In fact, the only obstacles seem to be our body clocks, and time zones.

Dismantling of trade barriers

More than three quarters of the world's countries are signatories to the World Trade Organization (WTO) whose commitment to reducing trade barriers makes it far easier for trade to take place. China became a member of the WTO in 2000 and since then it has really exploded onto the world stage with US and European companies setting up in China. With the money earned, China is now starting to acquire foreign banks and manufacturers, and it is even sponsoring football teams.

Deregulation of the world's financial markets

This has made the transfer of vast sums of money very easy and in doing so has facilitated quicker start-ups for many businesses. Again, the rise in Internet banking has made it much easier to keep track of company finance and, allied to the digitalization of the world's money markets, it is much more common for investors to cross borders. This again helps to build up collaboration such as forming joint ventures, strategic alliances, or working with venture capitalists.

Increasing size of multinational companies

In the past there might have been companies like the East India Company which effectively ran India for 150 years, but now the size, and consequently the influence, of the world's biggest

"Globalisation is a new word to describe an old process: the integration of the global economy…"
www.newint.org

companies makes it easier for them to persuade countries to allow them to set up. In many ways the attraction for multinational companies is that they can. The enormous power and influence of multinational companies can create momentum for other businesses in the same field. For example, the impressive growth of the Chinese influence in Africa may have been driven by the need for raw materials but itself has generated interests in other areas.

student workpoint 5.5
Be a thinker

Here's the result of a very simple exercise. We took the world's biggest companies according to *Fortune* magazine's annual "Global 500" survey and compared the results with the national income of the world's countries, sourced from the United Nations development report.

1 What do these figures tell us about the power of multinational companies?
2 Is there an intra-national organization that could regulate them?
3 Should there be?

Rank	Country/company	$ billion	Rank	Country/company	$ billion
1	United States	12,416.5	26	Poland	303.2
2	Japan	4,534.0	27	Norway	295.5
3	Germany	2,794.9	28	Indonesia	287.2
4	China	2,234.3	29	BP	274.3
5	United Kingdom	2,198.8	30	Denmark	258.7
6	France	2,126.6	31	South Africa	239.5
7	Italy	1,762.5	32	Greece	225.2
8	Spain	1,124.6	33	General Motors	207.3
9	Canada	1,113.8	34	Toyota Motor	204.7
10	India	805.7	35	Ireland	201.8
11	Brazil	796.1	36	Chevron	200.6
12	Korea (Republic of)	787.6	37	Finland	193.2
13	Mexico	768.4	38	DaimlerChrysler	190.2
14	Russian Federation	763.7	39	Iran (Islamic Republic of)	189.8
15	Australia	732.5	40	Portugal	183.3
16	Netherlands	624.2	41	Argentina	183.2
17	Belgium	370.8	42	Hong Kong, China (SAR)	177.7
18	Switzerland	367.0	43	Thailand	176.6
19	Turkey	362.5	44	ConocoPhillips	172.5
20	Sweden	357.7	45	Total (Oil)	168.4
21	Wal-Mart Stores	351.1	46	General Electric	168.3
22	Exxon Mobil	347.3	47	Ford Motor	160.1
23	Royal Dutch Shell	318.8	48	ING Group	158.3
24	Saudi Arabia	309.8	49	Citigroup	146.8
25	Austria	306.1	50	Venezuela	140.2

Country = nominal GDP 2005 (sourced UNDP *Human Development Report* 2007)
Company = *Fortune* Magazine—Global 500 (2007)

Push factors

As well as these external factors working for multinational companies, there are a number of internal factors that may help push multinational companies and other businesses to operate overseas. They may be able to:

- reduce costs
- increase market share
- put extension strategies into place
- use operating overseas as a defensive strategy
- increase others' awareness of them.

Reduce costs

By setting up production facilities abroad, businesses may be able to reduce costs by moving closer to the raw materials or using cheaper labour. As such they may be able to achieve **productive economies of scale**. Also, businesses may be able to take account of more favourable tax regimes and so achieve **financial economies of scale**.

Increase market share

By opening up business in a new region many organizations hope to tap into a new market. The potential is huge but of course so are the risks, which include:

- language barriers
- cultural practices and etiquette
- local law and politics, especially labour law
- time and complexity
- being unable to find trustworthy partners.

However, the rewards can be extremely high, especially if the business has **first mover advantage** in a large market. Hence the rush to China—with its 1 billion potential customers—and the costs incurred the first time round by many big name companies.

Extension strategies

Some businesses may have even reached the saturation point for their product and may be looking to extend the **life cycle** of the product. McDonald's, one of the leading players in the US fast food industry, has found increasing competition not only from other burger outlets but from pizza suppliers, sandwich bars, Mexican and other fast food outlets. This increased competition has had a major impact on McDonald's profits and, being a market leader, McDonald's has also been one of the hardest hit by bad publicity as a result of films like "Supersize Me" and by increasing awareness of obesity and the dangers of overindulging in fast food. To counter this, McDonald's has made major strategic changes. The company has introduced healthy food options, diversified into coffee, published its nutritional values, and reduced the fat and salt content in its foods. Besides these general strategies, McDonald's has also targeted areas were people are more likely to appreciate the service they provide. Of the 30,000 or more McDonald's stores worldwide more than two thirds are outside the US.

Defensive strategies

Many businesses make the decision to move overseas not because they need to but because they don't want their rivals to corner the market if they don't go for it. Growth and expansion are main drivers for businesses and the fear that rivals might steal a lead can act as a catalyst for many. The rush for oil companies to set up in Central Asia to secure oil and gas reserves is a recent example. In fact at times this resembles the "scramble for Africa" by European powers in the late 19th century. Perhaps in fact a modern equivalent is the emergence of China as a big player in Africa today, as China has felt the need to secure the supply of raw materials to feed its growing industries.

Data response exercise

Read the text below and answer the questions that follow.

Case study

McDonald's bets on Chinese growth

In 2005 fast food outlet McDonald's said it was planning almost to double its outlets in China ahead of the 2008 Beijing Olympics.

The burger chain also agreed a fresh eight-year deal to sponsor the games for an unrevealed sum.

"It's an investment we obviously think is worth it for the long term," said McDonald's chairman Jim Cantalupo.

The company is currently trying to widen its global appeal and target young people, its officials have said.

Young appeal

McDonald's will sponsor the 2010 winter games in Vancouver, Canada; and the 2012 summer games, and it has sponsored the Olympics in Beijing.

Less than 10 years ago McDonald's was operating 580 restaurants in China and expecting that number to increase to 1,000 in preparation for the 2008 games. McDonald's has more than 30,000 outlets worldwide.

In 2005 McDonald's executive Charlie Bell was planning to build more restaurants in China than any other country.

China is one of the few big growth markets.

Increasing awareness

Awareness can come in many forms but as well as penetrating into a new market and gaining a new customer base many businesses can benefit from extending their potential investors. This is particularly true for multinational companies that are joint stock companies. The closer integration of the world's financial markets makes it easier for potential investors to buy shares in a non-domestic business. Of course, awareness is a double-edged sword. The downside is that protestors are just as liable to react to the penetration into the market as investors. However, of course, protestors don't provide funds that allow further expansion.

Impact of globalization on business functions

Globalization is not a one-way process. Businesses can learn as well as teach. Interacting in a new business environment may bring a number of opportunities for both the business setting up in another country and also for those external to the business.

Production

Globalization can lead to cheaper costs as business can locate closer to their source of raw materials, or where labour costs are lower, or indeed where there is a more favourable tax system. Multinational companies can stimulate training and introduce new production techniques to other countries—or they can offload obsolete practices that they would not be able to continue in their home country.

Marketing

Businesses can make creative marketing campaigns to make use of the "global village"; for example HSBC's popular advertising campaign "the world's local bank" cleverly played on local cultures with a global backdrop. However, businesses should also be wary of simply transferring existing marketing ploys to a new location—for example when Chevrolet introduced the "Nova" car to Spain it failed miserably—try the car's name in Spanish! Or, for that matter, the Toyota "MR2" in French! Different markets have different cultures, and the need to be careful and perhaps to use local parties is important. A final bizarre mistake was reported by Reuters in January 2008. A Wrigley's chewing gum advert in Russian offended sections of the Chinese community in Guangzhou because the backing music was the Chinese National Anthem. Sales of chewing gum in Guangzhou fell by up to a quarter.

HR

Many businesses fail to take account of cultural differences when setting up business in a different location. One of my favourite extended essays was on the topic of why US bosses working in China could not understand why their workers would not talk to them and tell them their problems—because this is common practice in the US the bosses expected it in China.

Distance learning, exchange programmes and easier access to information about the world's universities has made more people more geographically mobile. In fact even for semi-skilled and manual workers it is easier to move and work in other countries. Parts of the UK, for instance, have been transformed since the influx of Eastern Europeans since the 1990s. The same is true regarding people originally from Latin America now in the US, Africans in France and Spain, and Asians in Australia. Local societies can often benefit from the absorption of different cultures and practices. Globalization is both a cause and effect in this case.

When deciding on locating a business overseas a key decision is how to staff it and what proportions of expatriate and local staff to have. Expatriates can bring expertise and transferable skills but they are more expensive and they will need much more support, for example with family issues such as schooling, than will local staff. However, they may have wider contacts and a better appreciation of the "big picture".

Finally, there is the idea of a **third culture** where children who have lived out of their home countries all their lives, and have little identity with one place, find themselves looking for opportunities. In the same vein, as they will have acquired language skills from living overseas they may have advantages over others.

Finance

As we've noted, the global financial system is much more integrated these days. This can have advantages and disadvantages. It is easier

Did you know?

Apart from the Mongol Empire (which never used a single administrative language), the administrative languages of the other six largest empires by land area in world history (the British, Russian, Spanish, Arab, Qing Chinese, and French empires) have also become the six official languages of the United Nations.

to finance start-ups outside a home country but it is also easier to lose money too. The "credit squeeze" of 2008 is a case in point. The transfer of funds is much quicker because of deregulated markets, the computerization of the world's stock exchanges and the introduction of Internet banking, but just as the process has speeded up so too has the practice of fraud. Businesses need to be wary about financing a project in another location if they do not have local knowledge. Also, one system that has not been integrated is the world's accounting system and although the Enron scandal forced the US market to tighten its practices, this may not have been the case elsewhere.

Data response exercise

Read the text below and answer the questions that follow.

Case study

Globalizing the car industry
by Steve Schifferes, globalization reporter

Sheafali may represent the car consumers of the future

Sheafali is very pleased that, at age 25, she has just been able to buy her first car, a small Hyundai.

She plans to use the car to go on weekend trips to the hill country to escape the heat of Delhi, where she lives.

Sheafali is able to afford a car because she works in a call centre run by the US multinational Convergys—which is not only well paid by Indian standards, but also gives her the weekend off. She may be typical of the new breed of consumer—young, savvy and Asian—who represents the future of the car industry.

Saturated market

For many years, the model for the global car industry was the US—the single largest car market in the world. But now the US represents less than one quarter of the world industry, and its market share will decline further. The US car market has already reached **saturation point**.

Stephen D'Arcy of PricewaterhouseCoopers believes all the growth in the global auto industry in the next decade will come from emerging market countries such as India, China and Eastern Europe. And that means the fastest-growing segment in the car industry will be the small car, the only size that will be affordable to the burgeoning middle classes in these countries. The Tata "Nano" is a prime example of what the future may hold—and this was built by an Indian company!

Examination questions

1	Define globalization.	[2 marks]
2	Define saturation point.	[2 marks]
3	Explain how the change in demand around the world for cars may affect car producers.	[4 marks]
4	Evaluate the ability of US car producers to compete with Asian producers.	[10 marks]

5.5 Innovation

By the end of this chapter, you should be able to:

- explain the importance of R&D for a business
- explain the role and importance of intellectual property rights for a business
- analyse the factors affecting innovation

Innovation is a key function of any business. As we have seen, *kaizen* can improve the quality of the product and most businesses do not simply develop a product and then leave it as it is for ever. Coca-Cola has changed even the secret formula it uses, for instance. If businesses do not innovate then they may lose market share and their products may stop being the cash cows of the BCG matrix and become dogs—and that leaves the business open to takeover.

Innovation is not, however, restricted to marketing. Many businesses look to find new ways of financing projects, planning production, motivating their workers and setting administrative tasks. Management theorists such as Charles Handy and Kurt Lewin have argued that change is healthy and energizing for a business and if managed correctly can improve overall performance.

Profile

Charles Handy (1932–)

Charles Handy was born in Kildare, Ireland, in 1932 and was educated in England and in the US. He graduated from Oriel College, Oxford, with first-class honours in "Greats", a study of classics, history and philosophy.

After college, Handy worked for Shell International in South-East Asia and London and then entered the Sloan School of Management at the Massachusetts Institute of Technology. Here Handy met Warren Bennis, Chris Argyris, Ed Schein, and Mason Haire, and became interested in organizations and how they work.

He returned to England in 1967 to manage the Sloan Programme at Britain's first Graduate Business School in London. In 1972, Handy became a full professor at the school, specializing in managerial psychology. From 1977 to 1981, Handy worked at a conference and study centre in Windsor Castle that was concerned with ethics and values in society.

Bibliography:

Understanding Organizations. 1976. London, Penguin *The Future of Work,* 1984. Oxford, Basil Blackwell *Gods of Management.* 1986. London, Business Books *The Making of Managers.* 1988. London, Longman *The Age of Unreason.* 1989. London, Business Books *The Empty Raincoat.* 1994. London, Hutchinson *The Hungry Spirit.* 1997. London, Hutchinson

There are many forms of innovation in business. Here are some examples.

- **Product innovation** is where new products are created or improvements to products are made, for example producing flat-screen TVs or new models of mobile phones.
- **Process innovation** is where some part of the process is improved to bring benefit. The JIT system is a good example.
- **Positioning innovation**—Lucozade used to be a medicinal drink but the pharmaceutical giant GlaxoSmithKline decided to reposition it as a sports drink.

● **Paradigm innovation** is where major shifts in thinking cause change. During a period of increasing air travel, in the 1980s, Cathal and Declan Ryan (of Ryanair) and others saw the gap in the market for "budget" air travel. This itself has created a massive change in thinking by travellers, airports, and established airlines and has also spawned a whole set of opportunities from increasing the practicality of buying property in various countries (because travelling to them is much cheaper than in the past), to "despididas" (trips where students go as a group) by final year high school students.

Research and development

R&D is one form of innovation and is directly associated with development of existing products or creating new ones. Many businesses spend vast sums of money on R&D (especially the pharmaceutical industry) as this can extend the **product life cycle** by developing new ways to use existing products (such as increasing the functionality of a mobile phone) or by indicating new directions for the company (such as Apple—branching off from PCs to iPods and iPhones). If successfully applied, R&D can allow the business to find gaps in the existing markets or of course open up new markets entirely.

However, R&D is expensive, time consuming, and, if in the wrong direction, can be quite destructive for a business. The examples of Enron, where the creed was "innovate or die", or the banking crisis in 2008 serve as examples of innovation that was inappropriate and badly managed.

There is no single best way of conducting R&D but to be at its most effective R&D requires good planning and leadership. There are a number of stages between thinking of an idea and launching a product, as shown in Figure 5.16.

> **"The guy who invented the wheel was an idiot. The guy who invented the other three, he was the genius."**
> Sid Caesar (1922 –), US comic actor and writer

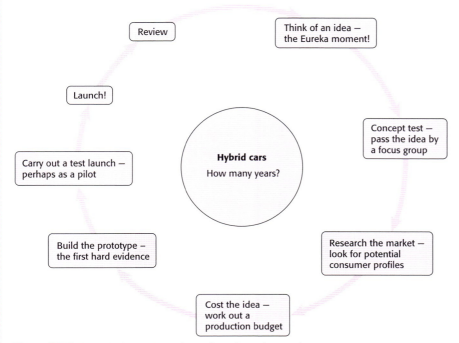

Figure 5.16 From thinking of an idea to launching the product

The process can take a great deal of time and indeed many brilliant ideas don't get to production stage because the product is deemed too costly or there is not enough of a market to be viable.

There does seem to be a different approach between US and Japanese producers to R&D and the next stage in the process of **new product development**.

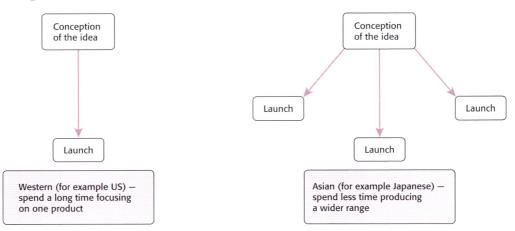

Figure 5.17 Different approaches to new product development

However, successful R&D can lead to many advantages for a business.

- It can give the business a competitive edge over the competition.
- It can extend the life of an existing product.
- It can open up new markets.
- It can enhance the prestige of the company—being a known innovator.
- It can motivate the workforce—designing new products.
- It can lead to improvements in quality.
- It can reduce costs.

But of course there may be several problems with R&D.

- There may be a huge opportunity cost—what else could the money be spent on?
- R&D may be in the wrong direction—for instance, take R&D for edible deodorant!
- R&D can be time consuming—think Windows Vista, which took over six years to launch.
- It can be fiercely competitive—work on Blu-Ray versus HD-DVD, for example.
- It can become bureaucratic and non-productive—despite extensive R&D, how many new products do drug companies actually produce?
- There may be ethical issues involved—for example with R&D involving GM crops, stem cell research, or animal experiments for cosmetics and tobacco.

Patents, copyrights, and trademarks
Patents, copyrights, and trademarks are important **intellectual property rights** for the business and the original inventor of an idea. As outlined in Chapter 3, for a business they appear in the **balance sheet** as **intangible assets. T**heir ownership by the

Did you know?

These products were actually launched:

- edible deodorant
- canned whole chickens
- children's toothpaste in an aerosol
- tissues impregnated with vitamin C
- smokeless cigarettes
- garlic cake.

They didn't sell. Why do you think they didn't?

5 Operations management

business constitutes a valuable asset that needs to be protected; for without this protection the business could lose its edge and the competition may be able to develop identical products.

Patents

When individuals or businesses invent a product or a production process, they should take out a patent to protect their idea. Once the patent has been bought, it gives the individual or business undisputed rights to exclude anyone else from making the product exactly to the specifications laid down in the patent for a period of up to 20 years. After that time, the individual or business can of course renew the patent.

A patent on one product does not stop anyone producing similar products, but they must not be exactly the same and/or they must have different features. For example, Apple had to fight for the right to produce the iPod because Apple was alleged to have used the touch wheel technology from another producer, Quantum Research Group.

Effectively the patent gives the inventor **first mover advantage** in the market and because of its head start the Apple iPod has become the iconic market leader. As such the iPod has spawned many clones such as the Microsoft Zune but it still holds the biggest market share.

Copyright

Copyright is similar to a patent. It originally applied to written material but has now been extended to cover other artistic forms of media presentations such as cartoons, music, and films. Again, the individual or business is protected for a period of time (in this case 50 years) from the unlawful copying of the material.

Since the digital age this has become a major source of concern for major record and film producers, especially with the introduction of file sharing sites on the Internet.

Trademarks

A final form of intellectual property rights is that of trademarks. These are split into two general forms. Conventional trademarks include logos, slogans, designs or phrases. The name Coca-Cola is protected by the symbol ™. Then there are non-conventional trademarks, which are qualities that are distinctive to the design, for example the Coca-Cola label, including the exact colour, match and shape of the letters, or even David Beckham's hairstyle, the unconventional trademark for which is based on the shape, smell and colour of the hair.

All these intellectual property rights ensure that individuals or businesses inventing something can:

- have first mover advantage
- earn greater profit margins
- ensure continuity in production
- develop brand loyalty
- have time to develop new products
- reap the rewards for their intellectual output.

However, it must be remembered that protecting the individual or business can have a negative side too. There are many famous disputes between singer songwriters and their music producers—one example involved the Beatles—and of course by excluding production of an invention, many patents may be bought up with the specific objective to "not produce"—oil and automobile companies are sometimes accused of allegedly holding back production of alternative forms of cars because if these were readily and cheaply available the companies would lose the profitability based on the internal combustion engine.

Factors affecting innovation

There are many factors that can affect the ability of an individual, a team, or a business to innovate successfully.

- *The corporate culture.* If an organization had a low-risk, role-based, bureaucratic, or autocratic culture then the fear of failure can outweigh the rewards of success. On the other hand, democratic or collaborative cultures may foster risk taking and view creative input as a valuable resource.
- *Past experience.* A proven track record of innovative practices can help develop the expectation for future change and can act as an archive of "what has worked in the past".
- *Available technology.* Technology can play a leading role in the development of ideas—especially CAD (computer assisted design) and the use of the Internet. For example, the collaborative nature of freeware has been largely a result of ease of sharing ideas and practices in a supportive environment—hence the success of Mozilla Firefox and other freeware.
- *The market.* Some markets are more responsive to change than others. The technology sector is one in which businesses may be less able to stay ahead of the market for long as the pace of development is so fast. Compare this to the market for traditional weddings—in whichever culture.
- *The level of competition.* Monopolies don't have to innovate—why should they? There is no competition. The more competition there is, the more of an incentive there is for businesses to create that competitive edge brought about by innovation.
- *Finance.* The amount of finance available, and particularly the R&D budget, can limit the amount of innovation a business may be able to achieve.
- *HR.* Tied into the availability of finance is the related field of available workers to innovate. Not only the number of workers, but their skill sets and the amount of time allocated to innovation will have an impact on the ability of workers to innovate.
- *Legal constraints.* Whether in the development stage or indeed in the implementation of a product there are many legal concerns that a business must take into account. For example, whether it is possible for airlines to reduce the turn-round time of planes on the ground is dependent on labour practices.

Given all of the above, the possibility for businesses to innovate successfully may be limited. Certainly the number of businesses that come out with radical market-changing inventions may be limited. However, any business has the capacity to make small-scale adjustments to improve productivity by adopting new techniques and innovative practices, as long as the **resistance to change** can be addressed.

"Discovery consists of seeing what everybody has seen and thinking what nobody has thought."
Albert Szent-Gysrgyi, Hungarian Nobel Prize winner in medicine

5 Operations management

Theory of Knowledge

Theory of Knowledge discussion

The mosquito alarm is an electronic device which emits high-frequency sounds, similar to the buzz of a mosquito. Because the ability to hear high frequencies deteriorates in humans with age, the noise is most commonly audible only to younger persons.

The device is marketed for use as a safety and security tool for preventing antisocial behaviour, such as gang loitering, which can often lead to graffiti, vandalism, drug use, drug distribution, and violence. It is very popular in the UK, with some 3,500 in use, mostly by shopkeepers and police authorities. The device is also being sold in Canada and the US. Even though it is currently legal for private citizens to use, the distributors and resellers of the product do not typically sell the device for home use.

Questions

1 Are there any ethical issues related to this product?

2 Is this the best way of dealing with antisocial behaviour?

3 Would you buy a mosquito alarm?

By the end of this chapter, you should be able to:

- explain the difference between just-in-case (JIC) and just-in-time (JIT) stock control
- recognize the need for optimum stock levels; prepare and analyse appropriate graphs
- explain different stock control methods and analyse the appropriateness of each method in a given situation
- explain outsourcing and subcontracting, compared with provision by the firm itself
- make appropriate calculations to support a decision to make or buy

Stock control

Controlling inventory levels is very important for a business. The business has to get the balance between not holding a certain level of stock because of emergencies (just in case, or JIC) and holding minimal levels and only ordering stock (just in time, or JIT). There are arguments in favour of each method but the trend at the moment is in favour of JIT methods.

JIT	JIC
Stock is only brought in from suppliers as and when it is required. The aim is to hold low (even zero) levels of stock.	Stock is brought in and stored with a reserve (the buffer stock) kept back from daily use just in case of need.
JIT:	JIC:
improves the cycle of money that the business needs for its day-to-day activities, which is known as working capital	reduces pressure on the cash flow
reduces costs (storage and wastage)	reduces costs (by buying in bulk)
reduces the chance of holding obsolescent or unsellable stock	means that you can meet sudden changes in demand
means less chance of damage or ruined stock	provides spare parts should the need be to cannibalize
creates more space for alternative production plans	means that all stock is stored—ready to use. There are no delivery issues.
creates a closer relationship with suppliers—they need to run JIT too!	has the advantage that suppliers don't charge a premium price for the outsourcing of stock holding.

?

Table 5.17 Comparison of JIT and JIC

Data response exercise

Read the text below and answer the questions that follow.

Case study

Building a Boeing 747

The manufacturing of a Boeing 747 is done in seven stages, which take on average six months to complete in total. The engines are bought from a supplier (Rolls Royce) in time for the sixth stage as buying them and storing inventories for five months would be expensive. The engines cost approx $10 million each.

Generally, Boeing can sell a 747 for $200 million.

Examination questions

1 Define inventories. *[2 marks]*

2 Explain how delaying the purchase of the engines might affect Boeing's cash flow. *[4 marks]*

3 Evaluate the effectiveness to Boeing of using this system of stock control. *[8 marks]*

HL As the debate over whether to use JIT or JIC goes on, many businesses continue to use the more traditional methods of stock control. While a lot of stock control is now computerized there is still a need to understand the process—and anyone who has worked in a warehouse will know that what it says on a computer screen may not be what they will find on the shelves.

As we've seen, there are two sides to the question of holding stock. On the one hand, there is the cost of not having stock when required—the cost of lost orders and emergency deliveries. And on the other hand, there is the cost of holding too much stock—the cost of storage and damage.

We can combine these two sets of costs in Figure 5.18.

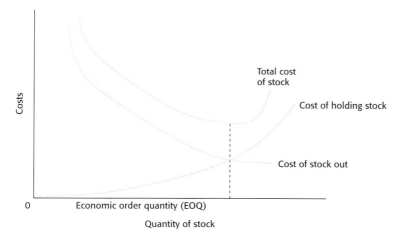

Figure 5.18 Costs of holding stock and of stock out

- *Cost of holding stock.* If we do not have any stock there is no cost but then the cost rises as we store more and more units.
- *Cost of stock out.* If we have a small amount of stock then the cost of having a sudden surge in demand can be huge but this will go down the more stock we buy in.
- *Total cost.* By combining the two sets of costs we can see that the minimum point of the total cost is what we call the **economic order quantity** (EOQ) and this is the amount that should be ordered for a given time period. Usually the calculations are made on an annual basis.

Traditional stock control diagram

Together with the EOQ the process of controlling stock is shown by using the following terms.

- The initial order: the first amount of stock delivered, say at the start of the year.

- Usage pattern: how much stock is used over a given time period. Usually the pattern is considered to be regular or at least to have predictable highs and lows (Christmas, Chinese New Year, school holidays, etc). In general, the stock is depleted over time and so is shown by a line with a negative slope.
- The maximum stock level: the maximum amount of stock held at any one time.
- The minimum stock level: the amount of stock that is kept back as a reserve, sometimes called the buffer stock. The amount of stock never goes lower than this level.
- The reorder level: when the stocks are depleted to a set level which is then the signal to order a new amount of stock
- The reorder quantity: the amount of stock that is ordered each time.
- Lead time: how long the stock takes to be delivered.

A typical stock control diagram may look like Figure 5.19.

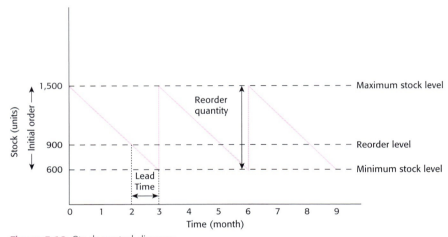

Figure 5.19 Stock control diagram

In the example shown in Figure 5.19—let's say it's a company making phones for Nokia—the factory staff may order an initial delivery of 1,500 hand phones and they want always to keep a reserve of 600 phones just in case. The factory's production manager has calculated that, barring unforeseen changes in usage patterns, he will run through 900 phones over a three-month period.

After two months he knows that stock will run down to 900 phones and that is when he arranges for a new delivery of phones to be made from their suppliers. It takes one month for that reorder quantity of 900 phones to arrive and when they do the whole cycle is continued.

Of course this is a simple example, but we can alter the usage patterns to take account of seasonal differences and odd surges in demand. Indeed, many businesses will also have the software to do this but the basic diagram remains as shown in Figure 5.19. And it is a very useful tool for production managers to see where the stress points are likely to be and how to resolve them.

Optimal stock levels

In order for a business to calculate the optimal level of stock, there are a number of factors that need to be taken into account.

- *The market.* Is it growing? Is the business increasing sales? Are there any new organizations coming in to the market?
- *The final product.* What type of product is it? Is it a cheap, single-use, fast-moving, high-volume product or is it the opposite? Is it a complex product requiring many individual components?
- *The stock.* Is it perishable? Is it likely to be out of date? Is it big—will it take up much storage space?
- *The infrastructure.* Is it reliable or is there a need to stockpile? Will, for example, the weather have a bearing on the ability of suppliers to meet demand?
- *The finance.* Does the business have the required money at the right time? What possibilities for credit do the suppliers allow? Are there going to be significant savings from buying in bulk?
- *The human resources.* What are the implications for resourcing changes in stock holdings?

Using the EOQ and stock control diagrams, businesses may get some idea of the correct amount of stock to order and when, but overall it is difficult to judge precisely. They should be aware that many factors can change and this creates more pressure depending on the system that they are using. It is for this reason that the JIT system requires greater coordination and cooperation with the suppliers than the JIC system which, although it may tie up a lot of funds, can be safer.

Capacity utilization

Production managers often want to know: How efficient is the facility? Is it being used to its maximum capacity? For example, a hotel may want to know what the occupancy rate of its rooms is, a factory may want to know how often a machine breakdown affects the work done, or a school principal may want to know whether there is a chance to use the school's facilities more at weekends and holidays by renting the site out.

Of course, it would be theoretically possible for a hotel to be full all year round, or a factory to work at full capacity—that is 24 hours a day, 365 days a year, or in fact a school to house a day school and a night school in the same buildings. But the reality is that even then (using one of our examples) there will be times of year when it is impossible to fill all the hotel rooms, and in fact the hotel may use some slack time to update or otherwise overhaul the facilities. Similarly, slack time will be used in factories if machines need to be "rejigged" or the site needs to be cleaned and maintenance done. The same is true of cleaning and maintenance in schools—and even teachers will need to sleep sometimes. So in practice it is often not possible to achieve 100% capacity utilization but many businesses would still aim to get as close as is possible to this figure.

There is a simple formula to calculate capacity utilization:

$$\text{Capacity utilization} = \frac{\text{Actual production}}{\text{Productive capacity}} \times 100 \quad (14)$$

Improving your supply chain—the Australian way

1. Check your inventory levels—produce to order, rather than for stock.
2. Consider smaller production runs with greater customization.
3. Conduct a survey of customers and suppliers.
4. Use the available advice from governments and professional associations.
5. Look for ways to expand your customer base.
6. Examine the available logistics technology to see what is most suitable for you.
7. Review your payments procedures to ensure stable cash flow.

Source: www.theaustralian.news.com.au

For example, if a hotel has 100 beds and on average 80 are filled then the capacity utilization is 80%. Similarly, a factory might be able to make 100,000 pairs of shoes in a year, but it only has orders for 40,000. Its capacity utilization is 40%. Finally, a school with sufficient space for 3,000 students which has 2,900 students on the register has a 96.6% capacity utilization.

Businesses that should aim for a high capacity utilization will be ones where profit margins are low, for example budget airlines or fast food outlets. These businesses cannot afford to lose any opportunity to sell the product and so will need to market their product accordingly. At the other end of the range, business class travel or Michelin five-star restaurants will not need and may not wish to aim for high-volume sales.

Outsourcing and subcontracting

A business can cut costs and so lower prices in order to earn a competitive advantage using **outsourcing** (also known as sub-contracting or contracting out work); which is where a business cuts back on its operations to focus on its core activities. There is an extension of outsourcing known as **offshoring** whereby a business can outsource outside the home country. With improved global communication this has been a growth area in the modern business environment. India, for example, has seen a huge growth in IT offshore contracts such as call centres and help desks signed up with Western businesses.

Traditionally, a business may have had a number of activities happening on a day-to-day basis, many of which may not have been part of the core business skill sets, so they become transferable and thus a saving for the business. By buying in these peripheral services from producers who can achieve economies of scale because they are specialists in that particular service, the main business can reduce costs.

Imagine that the costs of a business can be represented by circles and comprise the two different elements—core and periphery. The change can be clearly seen in Figure 5.20.

Let's return to an example used on p. 98—when we looked at what functions a school could contract out. For example, the school might have as its core activity the teaching but it can then outsource such services as:

- catering
- transport
- duties and invigilation
- coaching
- expeditions
- staff training
- recruitment
- security
- maintenance
- cleaning.

All of these could probably be provided at a lower cost and with a better result than if the school tried to complete all the tasks itself.

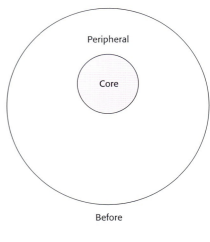

Before

After

Figure 5.20 Core and peripheral elements

5 Operations management

In the wider business environment typical, activities that are outsourced are:

- marketing—for example using an advertising agency
- production—for example licensing a producer to make your product
- HR—for example employing an agency to "headhunt" potential staff
- finance—for example hiring accountants to run an external audit.

Outsourcing can bring many advantages.

- It can reduce costs by losing employees and other assets.
- Costs can be restructured by reducing the fixed asset element.
- It can allow the business to focus on its core activities.
- The quality of the product that is produced should improve.
- It can lead to improved capacity utilization.
- Delivery time can be reduced.
- It can lead to transfer of expertise.

However, there are some very real risks involved by outsourcing and these problems can especially be made worse if the business offshores some of its production.

- There will be a different corporate (and national) culture, but for outsourcing to work there has to be "**synergy**".
- The business becomes more dependent on the supplier (reliability, for example for deliveries, can be an issue).
- The business has less control of the final product (there may be issues of quality and ethics, for example use of sweatshops).
- Communication can be difficult (especially when people are having to deal with different languages and time zones).
- Dilution of the brand can be a problem—if the consumer realizes that product "x" is not produced by company "y".

There are many reasons why businesses still prefer to produce at source rather than by outsourcing and especially by offshoring. In fact, there is also a new idea beginning to gain ground in the business environment—**insourcing**, that is, reversing the trend by taking back jobs lost to offshoring overseas by focusing on the quality end of the market. Particularly with service-based products, there is a lot to be said for local knowledge.

Make or buy decisions

Very often the decision about whether to outsource or not hinges on costs and at the root of this is the idea that it can be cheaper for a business to buy a product made elsewhere than to make it themselves. The decision can be shown very clearly by using the costs and revenues formulae in the section on costs and revenue (p. 234–235) to create cost to buy (CTB) and cost to make (CTM) equations:

$$CTB = P \times Q \quad (15)$$
$$CTM = FC + (VC \times Q) \quad (16)$$

For example, imagine that a small international school in South East Asia has to decide whether to subcontract the bussing in of students or to provide the service themselves. What if the school requires 20 buses and a company called School Run charges $10,000 a bus for the year? Then according to the formula

$$CTB = P \times Q$$

this service would cost the school:

$$\$20 \times \$10,000 = \$200,000$$

On the other hand, if the school could buy the 20 buses from Dodgy Dealers Inc. for $100,000 but faced variable costs of $10,000 a bus for fuel and the driver's wages over the year then the cost to make the service using the other equation

$$CTM = FC + (VC \times Q)$$

would be:

$$\$100,000 + (\$10,000 \times 20) = \$300,000$$

In this case CTB < CTM so the school should outsource.

Of course, this example ignores many of the factors that may have a bearing on the supply chain. For example, how reliable are the buses bought from Dodgy Dealers? What are the implications of the school employing drivers as opposed to someone else doing so? When deciding on what action to take, a business would take qualitative factors such as these into account as well.

Data response exercise
Read the text below and answer the questions that follow.

Case study

Supply chains should be kept on a short leash
Simon Caulkin, the *Observer*, 27 April 2008

The big business idea of the last 20 years is going rancid. Last week, Boeing's embarrassed chief executive announced the third major delay to its much-hyped 787 Dreamliner project.

Unbelievably, although nearly 900 of the aircraft have been sold, its profitability is in question as the firm's global **supply chain** cracks up. At the heart of the problem is the "Dell model" (after the computer manufacturer), applied to the project's funding and management. Industry researchers say that Boeing's attempt to minimise financial risks by maximising the number of development partners has had the opposite effect: outsourcing on this scale (80 per cent, including large and complicated components) has actually increased the risk of project and management failure.

Boeing should have paid heed to the experience of Dell, which posted a powerful warning on the dangers of paying more attention to the supply than the demand chain: being good at giving customers what they get is not the same thing as being good at giving them what they want.

But it's not only computer and aerospace companies that are learning these lessons. One automotive component maker was shocked to discover that parts arriving for final assembly in the US had spent up to two years shuttling between 21 plants on four continents—when it had only actually taken 200 minutes to make them. Much of the work was done in China to benefit from lower labour costs, but any advantage was more than offset by the costs of managing and scheduling inventory in the tortuous supply line. With hindsight, the China move was rated "a disaster".

Yet undeterred, service industries are now making exactly the same mistakes. In theory, since there is nothing physical to make or transport, services are ideal candidates for disembodied processing and reassembly by low-cost labour in foreign parts. But state-of-the-art call centres and distant graduates are quite often the wrong answer to the wrong question. A friend [in the UK] trying to get to Norwich [from the north of England] over Christmas spent ages on the phone to India working out how to do it without taking 24 hours [because of delays and cancellations]. When he got to Liverpool Street the man on the spot told him: "Go to King's Cross, mate: trains to Cambridge aren't affected, then change for Norwich." Similarly, when your cable broadband is down, you don't need someone thousands of miles away reading from a script, but a spotty youth around the corner who will sort it out for £60 and a supply of cola or coffee.

Why do companies—and public-sector organisations—continue to get this so wrong, pursuing the will-o'-the-wisp of cost reduction with measures that end up increasing them? Aided and abetted by consultants and computer firms that should know better, they are prey to three management myths.

- One is **economies of scale**. Manufacturers and service outfits alike think they can cut costs by mass producing processes in vast specialist factories. They can't, because of all the unanticipated costs noted earlier: carrying and transport costs (for physical inventory) ramifying the possibility and consequences of mistakes, re-work (mopping up complaints about things not being done or being done wrongly), knock-on costs up and downstream, and finally the management costs of sorting it all out.
- The second myth is that there's no alternative because **quality costs more**. Yet quality—in the sense of giving customers what they want, no more, no less—costs less, not more. This is because if you do just that, a) you don't incur the cost of giving them what they don't want, and b) indirect costs fall too, since there are fewer mistakes to rectify.
- Third, companies habitually overestimate the coordinating power of markets (and thus the attractiveness of short-term outsourcing to India and China) and underestimate the role of organisation. But while the internet can undeniably cut the cost of some market coordination, for any complex task a good organisation can still out-compete what can be supplied unaided by the market—which is why we still have organisations in the first place.

For both products and services, the principles are the same. Supply chains should be as short as possible in both time and distance; small and local, from police stations and GPs' surgeries to banks and computer firms' call centres, almost always beats large and remote. Expertise should be upfront, whether on the production line or the phone, where it can respond immediately to the customer. The title of a report from the Cambridge Institute for Manufacturing, "Making the Right Things in the Right Places", says it all: in a globalised, virtual world, location and supply-chain decisions are more critical, not less.

Examination questions

1 Define the terms in bold.   [*6 marks*]

2 Explain how Boeing can "minimise their risk by maximising their development partners".   [*4 marks*]

3 Discuss the costs and benefits to Boeing of outsourcing the 787 plane.   [*10 marks*]

Case study

Christer Fuglesang will do two spacewalks on the mission

Swede prepares for critical mission

by Irene Klotz, Kennedy Space Center, Florida

With the arrival this week of space shuttle Discovery at its launch pad, NASA has begun the final round of preparations for a critical space station assembly mission that promises to test the mettle of the seven-member crew.

In the thick of a complicated series of tasks to rewire the station—hopefully without serious interruption to the resident crew aboard—will be Sweden's first astronaut, Christer Fuglesang. He is a 49-year-old particle physicist who joined the European Space Agency (Esa) astronaut corps 14 years ago.

Though this will be Fuglesang's debut space flight, he will have his hands full. Fuglesang is paired with veteran Nasa astronaut Robert Curbeam for the first two spacewalks of the mission.

During the first outing, the pair will install a new external truss segment onto the station's structural backbone. Two days later, another spacewalk is planned to begin critical work to hook up the station's permanent electrical and cooling systems.

The work scheduled for the Discovery crew must be finished before any more station assembly missions can be flown. Nasa is under a strict deadline to complete construction before the shuttle fleet is retired in 2010. There are no other spaceships designed to carry and install the station components.

5.7 Project management

By the end of this chapter, you should be able to:
- construct and interpret a network, identify the critical path, and calculate the free and total float
- evaluate the value of a network in the management of projects

A final tool to help planning for production managers is that of the **network** or **critical path analysis**. This was designed to help project managers plan complex projects that have multiple interrelated tasks. It is a mathematical tool and of course carries the usual provisos about relying too heavily on numbers but nevertheless it can be a great help in breaking down a complicated production process into clearly manageable units. The aim is to identify which of the tasks are so "**critical**" that they cannot be altered without having an impact on how long it takes to complete the whole process; or by extension the likely effect of a change in any inputs such as HR or finance.

To create the network diagram we need to know a few variables:

- the number and order of all the tasks
- the dependencies of each task (which one cannot be started until another one has finished)
- the time that each task takes.

And then we have to follow a few simple conventions.

Conventions
- The process is drawn starting on the left of the page and working towards the right.
- A task is identified by a start and finish **node** that looks like Figure 5.21.
- The task is shown by drawing a line between the two nodes. We put the code for the task above the line and the duration below it. So we would show task A, that takes three minutes, as given in Figure 5.22.
- More than one task can start at the same node, as shown in Figure 5.23.
- More than one task can finish at the same node, as shown in Figure 5.24.

Figure 5.21 Start and finish node

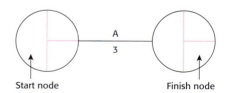

Figure 5.22 Task A

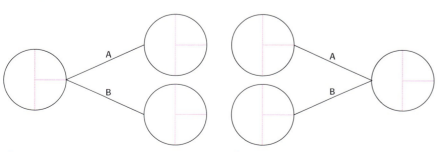

Figure 5.23

Figure 5.24

Sequences

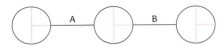

This means that task B cannot start until task A has been completed

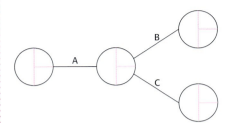

This means that neither task B nor C can start until task A has been completed

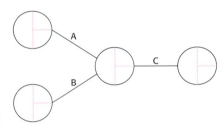

This means that task C cannot start until either task A or task B has been completed

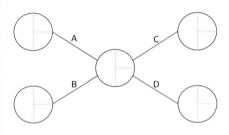

This means that neither task C nor D can start until tasks A and B have been completed.

Figure 5.25

Note: Drawing a diagram like this is not allowed as the tasks starting at the same time may have different durations so they cannot finish at the same node too. In this case there has to be at least a different start or finish node for the tasks.

Calculations

You may have noticed that each node is split into different quadrants. This is because we can fill these in with numbers that show the starting time and the finishing time of the task and these will depend on what comes before the task, how long that task takes and what will follow on from the task.

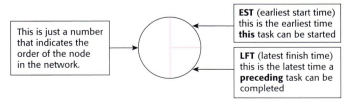

This is just a number that indicates the order of the node in the network.

EST (earliest start time) this is the earliest time **this** task can be started

LFT (latest finish time) this is the latest time a **preceding** task can be completed

Figure 5.26

- Every task therefore has two nodes attached that will look like Figure 5.27.
- The very first node on the diagram—the start of the whole process—always has an EST and LFT of 0.
- The very last node in the diagram has an EST and LFT equal to the total duration time of the whole project. Again the two numbers will always be the same.
- We calculate the ESTs by working from left to right and finding when is the earliest time that we can start each task in the process.
- We calculate the LFTs, on the other hand, by working from right to left and finding out when is the latest time each task can be finished by.

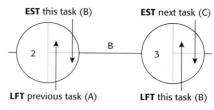

Figure 5.27

Example 1

Imagine it is the last lesson of the school day. The teacher won't let you go until you have finished your work and the class has tidied up. This process is shown in Table 5.18.

Code	Task	Preceded by	Duration (minutes)
A	Finish work	–	30
B	Tidy up	A	7

Table 5.18

Which we can represent by drawing a network diagram (see Figure 5.28).

Now this is a simple process, so apart from ending up with something that looks nicer than a table, there may be no advantage in drawing it. Either way, we can easily tell that it will take you at least 37 minutes to escape school.

Figure 5.28

Example 2

Now imagine that the teacher says that, after finishing your work, some of you should tidy up and the rest put away the laptops. After tidying up, those students put all the chairs on top of the desks. Nobody can leave until all these tasks are completed. The process now looks like Table 5.19.

Code	Task	Preceded by	Duration (minutes)
A	Finish work	–	30
B	Tidy up	A	7
C	Put away laptops	A	15
D	Put chairs on top of desks	B	6

Table 5.19

In this case it is not quite as clear how soon everyone could escape. So we can draw a new network diagram as follows to show this (Figure 5.29).

- As with our simpler example we start with the ESTs. At node 1 it will be 0, node 2 will be 30 and node 3 will be 37 (30 + 7) minutes. However, for node 4 we have to make a decision. We can't leave the school until both tasks C and D have been completed so the rule is that when there is more than one task at

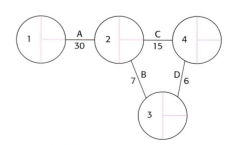

Figure 5.29

a node **the EST always takes the highest number**. In this case the EST for node 4 will be 45 (30 + 15 > 37 + 6).

● As with our earlier example, we work from node 4 for our LFTs. They will start at 45 and then node 3 will be 39 (45 − 6) but again when we have a node at which there is more than one LFT we must make a decision. This is that we **take the lowest number**. So for node 2 the LFT will be 30 (because 45 − 15 < 39 − 7).

So our network diagram should look like Figure 5.30.

● We can distinguish between a task that is critical (that cannot be altered without affecting the other tasks) from tasks that are not critical. We do this by indicating a critical task as shown in Figure 5.31.
● We can then show the **critical path**—which is all the linked tasks that cannot be altered without affecting the whole production process—by adding these symbols.
● All critical tasks will have **ESTs** equal to their **LFTs**.

What this tells us is that if you want to escape on time then you must make sure that the work is finished on time and those of you putting the laptops away must not muck around! However, those doing tasks B and D have a little spare time.

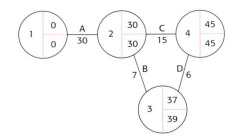

Figure 5.30

Figure 5.31

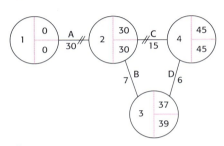

Figure 5.32

Student workpoint 5.6

Be a thinker

Imagine you have an interview for university in your home town. You want to know how much time to allow to get to the interview on time.

Having woken up you have a series of tasks to perform. First you must have a shower, then you will have breakfast, but being a multi-tasking teenager you can also text your friends and get dressed at the same time as you eat. However, your worrying parent says you can't leave until you have got dressed smartly and you have had all your breakfast. You can then drive to the interview.

Your table of precedence will look like Table 5.20.

Code	Task	Preceded by	Duration (minutes)
A	Take a shower	−	10
B	Have breakfast	A	15
C	Text friends	A	6
D	Get dressed	C	10
E	Drive to the interview	B, D	25

Table 5.20

1 Draw the network diagram.
2 What is the critical path?
3 How long should you allow yourself to get to the interview on time?

Floats

Spare time is known as a **float** and is important because it may be useful to know how much time a task can be delayed without having an impact on the whole process.

There are two main floats.

- *Free float.* This is the amount of time a task can be delayed without having an impact on the following task. It is calculated by the following formula:

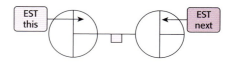

Figure 5.33

> EST of next task − duration of this task − EST of this task

- *Total float.* This is the amount of time a sequence of tasks can be delayed without having an impact on the whole process. It is calculated by the following formula:

Figure 5.34

> LFT of this task − duration of this task − EST of this task

Note: Because the total float is for the whole process and the free float immediately affects the next activity alone, the total float will always be at least the same as the free float and often times it will be a bigger number.

> total float ≥ free float

Example

So for our example above, see Table 5.21.

Code	Task	Preceded by	Duration (minutes)
A	Finish work	0	0
B	Tidy up	0	2
C	Put away laptops	0	0
D	Put chairs on top of desks	2	2

Table 5.21

We can see the following from this.

- Critical tasks always have 0 floats.
- Task B cannot be delayed as long as the next task (D) starts after 37 minutes; that is directly after the task has been completed. But also if we were to delay task B by two minutes this would delay everyone leaving school.
- Task D cannot be delayed by more than two minutes as this will affect the whole process as it is the last activity.

The dummy task (variable)

Sometimes it is necessary to include in the network a task that doesn't actually exist. It is needed though to make sure that the whole process is completed logically.

Example

Imagine that the teacher decides that the students putting away the laptops must sing their favourite pop songs as they do it. Remember when drawing the network we can't have two tasks taking the same time starting and finishing from the same nodes. So we'll have to add another intermediate node in the network and our new network will look like the one in Figure 5.35.

The table of tasks will look like Table 5.22.

Code	Task	Preceded by	Duration (minutes)
A	Finish work	–	30
B	Tidy up	A	7
C	Put away laptops	A	15
D	Put chairs on top of desks	B	6
E	Sing pop songs	A	15
F	Dummy task	E	0

Table 5.22

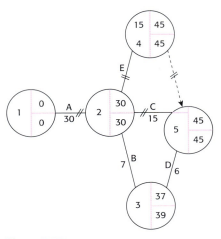

Figure 5.35

There are certain characteristics of a dummy task.

- As the task does not physically exist we cannot allocate time to it—its duration is therefore zero and we need not put this on to the network.
- The task is shown by a dotted line—with an arrow to show the direction necessary.
- The EST for the task following it will be EST start + 0 = EST start.
- The LFT at the start of the task will be the LFT at the end – 0 = LFT at the end.
- We indicate criticality for this task too.

Student workpoint 5.7

Be a thinker

Imagine it is the end of the week. You come home from school and your parents say you can't go out with your friends until you have finished your homework. So you go to your room and do your homework on your laptop, but at the same time you are chatting with your friends. Your homework takes you 40 minutes to do but you don't finish chatting until 50 minutes have passed.

Your table of precedence will look like Table 5.23.

Code	Task	Preceded by	Duration (minutes)
A	Do homework	–	40
B	Chat to friends	–	50
C	Go out	A, B	240

Table 5.23

1 Draw the network diagram.
2 Which activity is critical?

Summary

Critical tasks (activities)

The point of the network diagram is to show those tasks that are so critical the manager has to focus on them as any delay will have an immediate impact. **Critical paths** therefore have some characteristics.

- They must have EST equal to LFT at the start and finish nodes.
- They must therefore have zero floats.
- They cannot be altered without affecting the whole network.

Critical path analysis

A production manager can make a great deal of use of a network diagram.

- By distinguishing from critical and non-critical tasks the manager can decide on which task to focus attention.
- The manager can calculate the effect of diverting resources from non-critical activities to critical ones and so reduce the overall time of the whole process.
- The manager can factor into the calculations the effects of delays to specific tasks and the impact on the whole process.
- The manager can also cost the various tasks and so be able to calculate the most efficient funding for the process. This is very important for complex projects that may require funding over a long period of time. The manager can therefore determine an effective **cash flow** for the whole process and identify critical points in the whole process.
- The manager can test crash the process to see the effect of a change in circumstances.
- There are many computer programs that can run the process for speedy calculations.

However, of course, there are many limitations to using critical path analysis and a good manager will always be aware of these points.

- Critical path analysis focuses only on quantitative data and it ignores the qualitative aspect of production, such as in our school example whether or not the students are good singers.
- It can be confusing to create the network diagram, especially if dummy activities are required.
- The assumption is that all activities are sequential with a definite start and end to the whole process. In reality, many business tasks are continuous and independent of each other.
- Sometimes projects can be really complex and involve too many different specific jobs to be easily broken down into a clear diagram.
- The network is dependent on reliable data and this may be inaccurate or wrong.

student workpoint 5.8

Be a researcher

Why not try this simple experiment?

Baking a cake

Try to draw the diagram.
And does this work?

Node	Task	Preceded by	Duration (minutes)
A	Warm oven	–	10
B	Measure ingredients	–	5
C	Mix ingredients	B	3
D	Bake	A, C	25
E	Clean up (1)	C	5
F	Cool	D, E	10
G	Add topping/filling	F	2
H	Clean up (2)	G	2

Examination questions

Max's cottages

Max has made plans for building two cottages. He thinks that planning permission will take another 60 days to come through. Assuming the permission will be granted, a local building firm has given him the following breakdown of the building process and an estimate of the total time necessary.

Given this information the quote for the total building project was $150,000 based on materials and the following tasks

Code	Task	Preceded by	Duration (minutes)
A	Clear ground	–	30
B	Build access road	–	45
C	Lay foundations	A	60
D	Lay cables and water pipes	A	30
E	Put up structure	C, D	90
F	Put in windows	E	20
G	Put on roof	E	30
H	Wire for electricity	F	20
I	Paint	G, H	20
J	Hook up to utility supply	I	5
K	Put in fittings and furnishings	J	15
Total time			**365**

1 Max is convinced that the building firm is overestimating the time it should take so he draws up a network diagram to see whether the cottages can be built in less than a year.

Draw the diagram and show whether Max can make the building project shorter. Indicate on your diagram the total time taken and the critical path. *[6 marks]*

2 After seeing the diagram the builder comes back with a new quote of $120,000 but he says he underestimated the time taken to complete activities D, E and F.

The revised times are:

Code	Task
D	45
E	120
F	30

Redraw the network diagram and show the new time for the whole project. Indicate whether the critical path has changed. [6 marks]

3 Using this new information and evidence from the case itself evaluate whether Max should go ahead and build the cottages. [8 marks]

6.1 Introduction to business strategy

By the end of this unit, you should be able to:

- define strategy and describe its holistic nature
- identify different types of strategy
- outline the model of strategic management

Strategy is the only topic on the IB Diploma Programme Business and Management course that is examined specifically at higher level. There is a compulsory strategy question in section C on higher level (HL) paper 1, and strategic approaches are expected in the preparation and presentation of the research project for the HL internal assessment. To be successful in these components, students are required to show higher-order skills such as analysis and evaluation, the integration and synthesis of ideas, and evidence of critical thinking. In addition, an extended essay in business and management needs to show understanding of strategic approaches.

The strategy topic does not add subject content. The theories and techniques expected in a strategy question all appear in previous topics. This topic does anticipate a different and more sophisticated level of thinking though. Students will be expected to apply business concepts to a range of real-life situations and to analyse and evaluate data to support business decisions. This strategic overview topic is intended to provide a framework for students to think in an integrated and holistic fashion about the future strategy of an organization, given a range of information about the present and the past. It is natural that strategic approaches should be the focus for study at the end of the programme and form part of the revision process.

Note: Remember that products can be goods or services—there can be a large range of products between the two types and there can be an overlap in definitions. Because of this, "product" is used in places in this chapter to include services as well as tangible products such as manufactured goods.

Why strategy?

Business courses tend to be taught in a linear fashion, one unit at a time. For example, marketing may be the first topic taught on your course, followed by accounting, HR, and then the remaining topics. However, business decisions are multi-faceted. They normally require the decision maker to think in an integrated or holistic fashion—to see the whole picture. Senior managers, for instance, would be extremely unwise to make a significant decision, such as rapid business expansion, without considering the financial implications of this approach or the extra demands on personnel.

A decision in one department of the organization may have considerable effects on other departments. For example, if the marketing department is planning a major new advertising campaign, it should liaise with the production and distribution departments to ensure that any extra demand for the product can be met, and with the finance department to confirm that there are sufficient funds available to purchase the required stock or fund what's needed to deliver the service.

Strategic decisions may also have significant effects on an organization's internal and external stakeholders. Relocation, for instance of manufacturing, is likely to affect employees, suppliers, the local community, and possibly customers.

Although these issues may appear obvious, the business world is full of examples of organizations undertaking growth programmes without adequate funding, promoting products when demand can't be met, or simply selling products that customers don't want.

General Motors

For most of the second half of the 20th century, one automobile company dominated the global industry: General Motors. With its traditional brands—Chevrolet, Pontiac, Oldsmobile, Buick, and Cadillac—it held close to 60% of the US car market in 1960.

However, in the second quarter of 2008, GM reported a loss of $15.5 billion and announced large job cuts. As the price of gasoline at the pump topped $4 a gallon, GM was surprised by a dramatic shift toward smaller, more fuel-efficient cars and away from the pickups and sport utility vehicles that served as its mainstay. By July 2008, overall US sales had fallen 20%. Stock plunged more than 31%. GM said it lost had $6.9 billion in negative cash flow and could run out of cash early in 2009.

Source: Based on: USA Today, 6 November 2008, The New York Times, 25 November 2008

Student workpoint 6.1

Business investigation

Examine the decisions given as bullet points and explain what effects they will have on:

1 other business functions

2 other stakeholder groups.

- The ICT manager decides to buy a new computer program, which is very powerful, but incompatible with the existing system.
- The operations manager plans to replace batch production with a continuous flow production line.
- The marketing manager decides to rename and rebrand one of a company's established product ranges.

Extension

A brand is a valuable asset, communicating a clear set of values to its stakeholders. Rebranding is an important strategic decision requiring careful planning.

Investigate and evaluate the decisions by:

- Mars (UK) to rebrand the Marathon bar as Snickers, and Opal Fruits as Starburst, and its more recent decision to bring the replaced brands back
- Andersen Consulting to rebrand as Accenture
- any local, national, or international organization you know of, to rename the organization or rebrand any of its products or product lines.

In your discussion, concentrate on the effects that these rebranding exercises will have on the organization's stakeholders.

Data response exercise

Read the text below then answer the questions and discuss the points that follow.

Case study

Nintendo Wii

'Nintendo offers a raincheck for Wii shortage,' 14 December, 2007

Nintendo [has] underestimated the demand for the red-hot Wii since its launch in November 2006. The company has sold more than 6 million Wiis in the US since its release, and in November 2007, for example, it saw more than double the sales of the Sony (SNE) PlayStation 3.

While Nintendo increased production by 80% following the launch, Nintendo president Reggie Fils-Aime said the company did not expect such a craze for the Wii.

In November 2007 Nintendo sold a record 1.53 million units, and there were not enough of the portable consoles to go around at Christmas. "We went into the launch of the Wii with very high expectations. We had expected to be in the upper range of console launches," Fils-Aime said, "but this is unheard of". Thousands are still paying a premium on sites like eBay, and in shops, to get an actual Wii. Some retailers packaged extra controllers and games to mark up the cost of the console by more than $200–$300.

In November 2006, many retailers sold out of Nintendo's new Wii video game console on launch day.

Source: Adapted from http://techland.blogs.fortune.cnn.com/2007/12/14

Business investigation and class discussion

Investigate examples of product launches that have not gone to plan, such as New Coke, Concorde, Mercedes A Class, and Dasani bottled water, then answer the examination questions below.

Examination questions

1 Identify what caused the problems   *[4 marks]*
2 Examine whether the problems could have been anticipated and prevented   *[6 marks]*
3 Evaluate the consequences of businesses failing to meet customers' expectations.   *[10 marks]*

What is strategy?

Strategy was developed on the battlefield, where generals planned and directed large movements of troops and equipment with the aim of winning an individual battle or a war.

One of the earliest writers on strategy was Sun Tzu, who wrote *The Art of War* in China during the 6th century BC. The book has been translated into many languages and has influenced thinking beyond the military realm. Sun Tzu's ideas have been applied to many competitive situations, including the world of business. It is quite possible to regard the market-place as a battlefield, with winners and losers. Like war, business requires the effective and efficient use of scarce resources in dynamic environments, the development of good leadership, and the motivation of teams. In the business world there is also a high risk of failure and premature death.

In essence, a strategy is a declaration of intent, defining where you want to be in the future. It's like using a map to make a car journey from one point to another. You have directions and there are a number of signposts along the way. There may be alternative routes if your chosen route turns out to be blocked or appears too risky. However, the success of the journey can be affected by a number of variables, some of which are controllable and some of which are not.

You may have planned your route, but you get lost because you are tired and are not paying enough attention. Or you may run out of fuel because you didn't calculate the mileage correctly. These are faults that could have been avoided and no doubt you will try hard not to make the same mistakes again in the future. However, the journey can also be delayed or disrupted by external factors beyond your control. Traffic congestion and road closures can delay you for hours. Severe weather may make the journey completely impossible. These external factors are not controllable by you—unless you have special powers! True, travelling may be made easier by new technological innovations, such as satellite navigation, but the external environment has become ever more complex and "crowded" at the same time. Also, not all technology can be relied upon.

Businesses face similar problems getting from one point to another. They have:

● limited resources
● constraints on their decisions, both internal and external, which restrict or prevent progress
● imperfect knowledge
● a dynamic external environment.

All these factors mean there is a risk of failure. The purpose of a business strategy is to minimize that risk. Businesses may choose different routes to their destination, have the use of advanced technologies, and hire the most talented individuals, yet still fail to achieve their objectives. For smaller and newly formed firms, the risks of failure are particularly high. This is because these firms lack both experience and resources.

A strategy is a comprehensive plan stating how the organization will achieve its mission and corporate objectives.

There is a hierarchy detailing three types of strategy.

● *Corporate strategy:* the organization's overall direction through management of all of its businesses and products, for example portfolio analysis. Corporate strategy is usually focused on objectives related to corporate growth and diversification, but in difficult times may include reductions in operations and staffing.
● *Business strategy:* related to the strategic business unit or product level. Business strategy focuses on the competitive position of the organization's brands and products.
● *Functional strategy:* the management approach taken at a department level, such as marketing or production. The focus here is often on maximizing use of resources to create competitive advantage, for example examining alternative distribution channels to reduce costs through methods such as direct selling.

Long-term business success requires a company to build and sustain a blend of products that are different from those of competitors and unique in a way that is valued by customers. In other words, a business needs to develop a distinct competitive advantage to ensure that each of its products possesses a unique selling proposition (USP). An organization also needs to create a culture of success among its employees, which encourages independence and the desire to exceed

"If your enemy is secure at all points, be prepared for him. If he is in superior strength, evade him. If your opponent is temperamental, seek to irritate him. Pretend to be weak, that he may grow arrogant. If he is taking his ease, give him no rest. If his forces are united, separate them. Attack him where he is unprepared, appear where you are not expected."

Sun Tzu

Did you know?

Satellite navigation systems are being blamed for 300,000 road accidents each year, according to research by the insurance company, DirectLine. The research found that over half of drivers now use satellite navigation devices that are causing increasing problems on the road.

One in ten drivers said that the systems had caused them to make an illegal turn, double that number had lost track of traffic, because they were distracted, and one in four had been sent the wrong way down a one-way street.

customer expectations and create a real "wow" factor. The business must be flexible and responsive to its external environment. It needs to learn from its mistakes and build on its successes. With quickly changing external environments and changing customer expectations, the business must constantly adapt to its market to remain competitive.

When faced with change, managers will be tempted to look for options that are familiar to them. These changes may make operations more effective, but involve only little-by-little improvements; a process referred to as incremental change. Under normal circumstances this may be enough to maintain a competitive position, but over the long period it can make the business vulnerable to significant changes in the external environment. If the business does not embrace change, it may suffer from what is called **strategic drift**—a form of "organizational inertia". This is a slow movement away from the desired route, which can be catastrophic in the long term. To avoid strategic drift, businesses must develop flexible and responsive systems to promote change. In other words, firms need to plan for change (see more on this in Chapter 1.5).

The strategy topic—an overview

The strategic topic of the business and management syllabus considers the **strategic framework** set out in Figure 6.1.

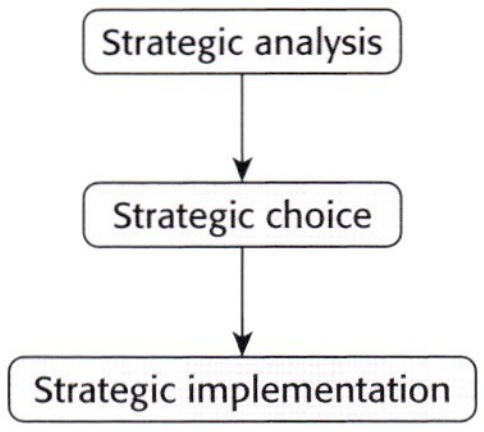

In simple terms, we are asking three questions.

- Where is the business now? **(strategic analysis)**
- Where is the business aiming to be? **(strategic choice)**
- How is the business going to achieve its objectives? **(strategic implementation)**

Added to these questions, **we will consider how a business controls its operations and the success criteria it uses to evaluate its performance** (*how will a business know whether its strategy is successful?*).

We can develop the syllabus approach into a more detailed model that will form the basis of this unit.

Figure 6.1 The strategic framework

A model of strategic management

Stage	Activities or issues related to this stage are:
1 Strategic analysis and environmental scanning	• preparation of a SWOT and PEST analysis examining the internal and external environment • identification of internal strengths and weaknesses and research into trends in the external environment, both general and specific • identification of existing competitive advantage
2 Strategy formulation	• development of a long-term plan to exploit environmental opportunities and to defend against threats in light of strengths and weaknesses—this requires agreement on the business mission and the identification of achievable objectives
3 Strategy implementation	• the process by which strategies and policies are put into practice through the development of programmes, budgets, and procedures
4 Evaluation and control	• measurement and monitoring of business activities, comparing actual performance to desired performance. This may identify weaknesses leading to a review of objectives and strategy.

Figure 6.2 Model of strategic management

As you will notice, Figure 6.2 sets out a model similar to the decision-making framework introduced on p. xxx.

6.2 Strategic analysis

Strategic analysis and environmental scanning—where is the business now?

The business and management syllabus outlines some of the questions that should be asked to create a picture of where the business is now—a situational analysis—and what business theory, tools, and techniques can support this analysis.

> The starting point for this analysis will probably be SWOT and PEST analysis.
>
> - What are the present aims, objectives, and core principles of the business?
> - Is it a new or established business?
> - To what extent has the business planned for its future direction?
> - What are the objectives of the organization and its stakeholders?
> - How does the vision or mission statement reflect what the organization is doing now and where it is heading?
> - What new market opportunities are available?
> - What are the resources available to the business?
> - What are the attitudes of the business to risk?
> - Is entrepreneurship or intrepreneurship encouraged?
>
> The aims, objectives, and core principles will be influenced by an analysis of the present market and the organization's competitive situation.
>
> - Porter's five forces market analysis (see p. 190).
> - How can the business expand and this expansion be financed (if this is desirable)?
> - Does the organization operate in the private or public sector?
> - Is the business in the profit or not-for-profit sector?
> - Is the business purely operating in a domestic market or is it presently, or aspiring to become, multinational?
> - What is the organization's present financial situation and is it conducive to change?
>   — financial and ratio analysis
> - Is the present product portfolio adequate and appropriate?
>   — BCG matrix (see p. 206–207).
>
> **Source:** Adapted from the IB Diploma Programme Business and Management guide

Before any business can plan a future strategy, it is essential it understands its present position. Many of the techniques and tools that have been examined in this book will provide a basis for identifying the strengths and weaknesses of the business as it presently exits. So far we have looked at these as individual techniques, but it is the combination of them that provides a broader and more holistic understanding of the business.

To identify strengths and weaknesses, the business will review its internal position to identify what it does well and what it does badly. It will need to ask some of the following questions related to each of its business functions.

● Has the business got staff with the skills it needs to address future demands? If not, can it retrain workers or will it need to recruit? This is the role of workforce planning (see p. 91).
● Does the business possess the financial strength to take on new challenges? Has it the profit to reinvest? If not, can it borrow the finance it requires and does it possess the cash flow to ensure the successful completion of any venture (see p. 160)?
● Has the business got the necessary production facilities, technology, expertise, and capacity to meet market demands for its products, especially if it is undertaking a growth strategy (see p. 333)?
● Does the business have the products required to remain competitive (see p. 73)?
● Does the business have the necessary ICT to support the efficient operation of the business and its functions (see p. 113)?

Having done an internal audit, the business must undertake research of the external environment. The business has to establish whether it has the internal strengths to take advantage of market opportunities, and the ability to reduce its weaknesses to minimize external threats to its success.

Environmental scanning

This is the monitoring, acquisition, and use of information about events, trends, and emerging issues in an organization's internal and external environment. Anticipating emerging issues allows organizations time to consider a range of possible options (contingency planning, see p. 143), rather than having to react quickly to a crisis. It assists management in the development of suitable longer-term strategies to achieve **sustainable competitive advantage**.

Objectives of environmental scanning are:

● detecting political, economic, social, and technological (PEST) trends and events important to the organization
● identifying the potential opportunities, threats, or changes for the organization created by those trends and events (swOT)
● providing "strategic intelligence" to inform decision makers in formulating strategic plans in light of internal strengths and weaknesses (SWot).

The internal environment (SWOT analysis)

Successful organizations assess their internal skills and capabilities. A SWOT analysis (see p. 66–69) holds a mirror up to a business and highlights what it does well, its strengths, and the opportunities it can exploit. It also examines what it does not do well, its overall weaknesses and, therefore, what its competitors can exploit. The SWOT analysis represents the start of the planning framework.

Strengths
- What are the organization's core competences?
- What does it do really well?
- What makes it stand out from its competitors?
- What proprietary tools, technology, or processes does it possess?
- What do competitors see as its strengths?
- What do customers see as its strengths?

Weaknesses
- What does the business do badly?
- What does it need to improve?
- Where is the business behind its competitors?
- What do customers say they do not like about the organization?

Opportunities
- What changes are taking place in the external environment?
- What do customers want the organization to deliver?
- What are its competitors' weaknesses?

Threats
- What is the competition doing?
- Do competitors possess better capabilities?
- Could any changes in the external environment threaten the organization?

Ultimately, what decides the success or otherwise of an organization will be the products it offers and whether these meet the wants and needs of its existing and prospective customers. Also crucial is whether the benefits offered by the organization exceed those offered by its competitors. At the start of the strategic process, a business must evaluate its products and the benefits these provide to customers.

A product audit

Here a business prepares a description of the important features of its main products, together with the technology that lies behind them. It then decides whether there are features, or aspects of the technology, that are not currently important but might be useful in future.

Then it examines the products in terms of what the customer sees in them. The brand that counts is the one that customers see, not the one the organization wants them to see. These are some of the factors that need to be analysed in this review.

- What is the target market or target segment?
- Who are the existing customers?
- Who are prospective customers?
- What benefits are existing and prospective customers looking for?
- How well do the existing products meet customers' needs and wants?
- How do existing products compare with competitive products?

Benefit analysis—the customer, the customer, and the customer

This is an analysis of the benefits that each product offers to customers in terms of their needs and wants.

The list of benefits should prioritize the ones that customers consider most important rather than those the company finds easiest to produce. However, it is essential to match the choice of products to the organization's strengths (asset-led marketing, see p. 184), so that the organization can differentiate its brands from the competitors'. There is no point in a business concentrating on products valued by the customer if it cannot produce these more efficiently or cost effectively than its competitors.

A good place to start the process of creating or sustaining competitive advantage is to establish just what the customer thinks about the business now. Market research will enable the business to understand its place in the market. For example, do customers see the organization's products as high or low quality, expensive or cheap? What image does the business have—is it fashionable or traditional? The business can use this information to place itself on a grid or perception map (see p. 335). Having done this, it will then be in a position to ask whether customers' perception matches its own and whether this perception is appropriate as the business moves forward.

The business must also go beyond an examination of the "core product"—that is, simply what the product does—to the other elements that influence customers' final buying decisions, such as credit facilities, service quality, and after-sales support.

There are three levels to a product, as shown in Figure 6.3.

1 **Core product.** The core is the functional benefits of the product, for example transport in a car.
2 **Tangible/actual product.** This involves the actual features of the product, for example what it looks like, its quality and style.
3 **Augmented product.** Features will include additional services or benefits, for example servicing, delivery, and guarantees.

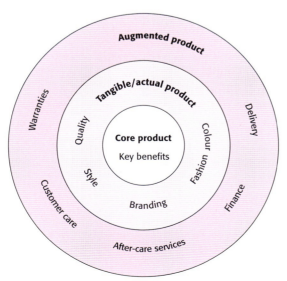

Figure 6.3 The three levels of a product

> "This may seem simple, but you need to give customers what they want, not what you think they want. And, if you do this, people will keep coming back."
> John Ilhan (1965–2007), founder, Crazy John's mobile phones store, Australia

> "There's a saying in the United States that the customer is king. But in Japan the customer is God."
> Tak Kimoto, Sumitronics Inc. Japan

> "A market is never saturated with a good product, but it is very quickly saturated with a bad one."
> Henry Ford (1863–1947), US entrepreneur and car maker

Three product levels

Organizations should establish customers' perception of their core products relative to competitors' core products, for example whether customers think the products are cheap, high quality, or luxurious, as well as examining customers' perception of the benefits offered by the actual and augmented product. A purchase decision may be based not just on the core product. Customers may be prepared to buy a product and pay more for it if they value other elements, such as the quality offered and the range of after-sale services available. The actual and augmented products can provide a business with its competitive advantage.

Using the BCG matrix

Businesses will normally have a portfolio of products available, rather than individual products or brands. These products can be categorized using a BCG matrix (see p. 206–207).

Comparisons of BCG matrices of competing businesses will provide valuable information about the viabilities of those businesses, as well as providing the basis for strategic decision making.

For each product in the matrix, the area of the circle represents the value of its sales. This means that the BCG matrix offers a very useful visual representation of the product's strengths and weaknesses in terms of profitability and cash flow. Relative market share shows where the brand is positioned against its main competitors. The creators of the BCG matrix believed that the higher the relative market share, the more cash will be generated. It is assumed that as a result of economies of scale (see p. 70), the higher the relative market share, the faster earnings will grow.

Use of cash is linked closely to the market growth rate. This is because the growth is the result of high investment in the product or brand. Firms will want to move their question mark products on to be stars and then cash cows, but the marketing costs to achieve this may be substantial.

In the BCG matrix shown in Figure 6.4, the business represented appears to have a solid and probably profitable product portfolio. It has two large generators of cash in its cash cows with a star close to converting to a cash cow. The business also has two question mark products that have the potential to be converted into stars. The investment for this can come from the cash cows. The business only has a single product regarded as a dog. On the basis of this portfolio a strategic plan can be put in place to map the future marketing and financial strategies necessary to develop the stars and question marks.

Clearly, on its own the BCG matrix can only provide basic information about the business. To support the analysis further, the business needs to examine other measures of performance, the financial accounts, sales forecasts and trends, profitability and liquidity ratios, and economic data such as economic growth.

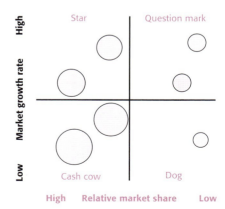

Figure 6.4 Example of a BCG matrix

6 Business strategy

The external environment (PEST/STEEPLE analysis)

PEST analysis is more accurately a **business environmental analysis**, but the acronyms PEST, STEP, PESTLE, or STEEPLE are easier to remember and are used as shorthand to classify the external environment.

For business and management, what is important is not the external environment in itself, but the impact that external change has on business activities, whether positive or negative. For example, we are not concerned with the mechanisms that lead to currency fluctuations, but how those fluctuations will affect the operations of businesses that export and import, or have branches in other countries. In particular, we are concerned with the opportunities and threats that result from changes in the external environment.

What key PEST variables are considered in business and management? The following list may not be comprehensive, but it covers the major external factors:

● political or legal factors (**P/L**)
— consumer protection legislation
— employee protection legislation
— taxation
— trade regulations, for example quotas and tariffs
— environmental protection
— terrorism
— government stability
— immigration
— competition laws
— data protection
● economic factors (**E**)
— inflation rates
— unemployment levels
— interest rates
— economic growth and gross domestic product (GDP)
— balance of payments and trade barriers
— trade blocs and international groupings
— exchange rates
● social or cultural factors (**S**)
— population growth
— demographic changes and age distribution
— lifestyle changes
— healthcare standards
— levels of education and training
— population movements within the country
— immigration and emigration
— fashion and customers' purchasing behaviour
● technological factors (**T**)
— new product development
— R&D
— patents, trademarks, and copyright
— ICT
— production techniques
— government finance for R&D

Each of the PEST factors will contribute to an organization's overall business environment. To maintain an understanding of the external environment, a business must research its markets on a continuous basis (see p. 192–5). A crucial part of competitive and market intelligence is ensuring that the information the business uses is relevant, objective, and up to date. Knowing the target market today underpins strategic success.

For more comments on the factors below, see p. 47–50.

Political or legal factors

For a multinational company, political or legislative changes may affect it in very different ways in each of the countries in which it operates. Consumer and employee protection and environmental legislation may be stricter in some regions. For example, countries in the EU often have more stringent animal welfare rules than other countries, which will increase the costs of production in some industries. Tax rates will differ across the world, which will also affect decisions on location and pricing.

As a result, firms may look to locate their businesses in countries that have beneficial laws and regulations for their type of operations. This may mean a low tax environment or one where planning regulations allow the construction of factories or offices at low cost and with few restrictions.

Multinational companies have often been accused of putting pressure on governments in less economically developed countries to allow certain business practices that would never be tolerated in more developed economies.

Economic factors

Most strategies depend on what is happening in the local, national, and global economy. Economic factors include unemployment rates, inflation levels, exchange rates, recession and economic growth. Issues such as the availability of skilled labour or the cost of raw materials will affect revenue and profit levels.

Membership of trading blocs and other regional allowances will have both positive and negative effects on those businesses in the bloc. Positively, a trading bloc offers a much larger market and therefore the opportunities for economies of scale, higher sales, and ultimately higher profits. But greater competition is a less positive consequence of free trade patterns in the bloc. In Europe, the introduction of the single European currency altered trading relationships within the eurozone and also with countries outside of it. Businesses in countries outside the eurozone face additional transaction costs, such as currency conversion, when trading in the eurozone.

Some changes in the economic environment are so significant that an organization will find it almost impossible to counteract their effects even through the most detailed use of planning and effective strategic management. For example, organizations with energy costs that make up a large percentage of their total costs will struggle to deal with sudden supply side shocks forcing up the price they pay for their energy, even if they have contingency plans in place.

6 Business strategy

The stage of the economic cycle will influence the strategic approach of businesses. A recession is normally considered a bad thing. In a recession, GDP growth is negative, leading to lower consumer demand, higher unemployment, and increasing business failures and individual bankruptcy. Some businesses are particularly susceptible to recessions. Many that offer expensive, luxury items are likely to be badly hit by falling consumer incomes. Some customers are liable to postpone purchases or substitute less expensive items.

Data response exercise
Read the text below and answer the questions that follow.

Case study

Fuel costs squeeze US airlines

Faced with jet fuel prices more than twice as high as they were in January 2007, major US airlines have announced nearly $1 billion in losses for the first three months of the year, a financial toll that is forcing carriers to slash flight schedules, cut jobs, add passenger fees and even seek potential merger partners. United Airlines became the latest company to reveal the pain of rising fuel prices, reporting a loss of $537 million in the first quarter.

There has been a run of such announcements, American Airlines in April 2008 posted a $328 million first-quarter loss, and Continental Airlines announced it lost $80 million. Frontier, Aloha and Skybus have sought bankruptcy protection in recent weeks and airline stocks have fallen sharply. Delta and Northwest Airlines announced a merger deal that executives said would help them better weather high fuel prices. Both carriers were expected to report substantial first-quarter losses in 2008.

To survive, US airlines have raised fares, added new fees and surcharges, cut jobs, and reduced services and capacity. American Airlines, for example, has announced hiring freezes, flight reductions and the accelerated retirement of its gas-guzzling fleet of MD-80 jets.

However, even those steps are probably not enough to offset fuel prices and falling demand. Executives at United are to trim spending by $400 million and are examining potential fee increases to boost revenue. They are going to cut about 1,100 management and front-line jobs and boost the number of planes they are grounding, selling, or returning to leasing companies. By the end of 2008, executives expect to ground about 30 of the carrier's 460 planes. Among extra fees under consideration are passenger charges to select seats during booking, and a $25 one-way charge to check a second bag.

Although fuel bills are a major headache, they are hardly the industry's only challenge. New international agreements are expected to spur more competition between US carriers and overseas rivals. A weakening dollar may start hurting demand for lucrative transatlantic flights. And regulators appear to be taking a tougher stance on safety, forcing airlines to undertake costly reviews of their records and planes. JP Morgan has estimated a collective loss of $7.2 billion for US airlines in 2008.

Source: Based on the *Washington Post*, 23 April 2008, and Reuters, 30 May 2008

Examination questions

1 Identify four changes in the external environment of the major US airlines. [4 marks]

2 Analyse the advantages and disadvantages of the projected merger between Delta and Northwest Airlines. [6 marks]

3 Evaluate the measures introduced and proposed by the airlines to address changes in their external environment. [10 marks]

A SWOT analysis can identify what competitive advantages a business possesses, even in times of a recession, and what opportunities poor economic trading conditions provide. For example, supermarkets that stock value-based, lower-price products may perform well in a recession, while demand for more exclusive supermarkets fall. Customers will often postpone certain luxury purchases and instead substitute these with lower-value purchases.

Industries and/or products that perform well in recessionary times are referred to as **counter-cyclical**.

Strategically, businesses must monitor the external environment and audit their internal strengths and weaknesses to see if they can take advantage of apparently negative situations. In simple terms, one organization's threat may be another organization's opportunity.

Data response exercise
Read the text below and discuss the question that follows.

Case study

UK economy heads for recession as growth slumps

After years of boom, official figures on the UK economy published in July 2008 show that growth has slumped to nearly zero, leaving the nation close to recession. Retail sales are down 3.9 per cent on the month—the worst figure since 1986.

Domino's Pizza beats slowdown as diners choose to eat at home

Online sales of Domino's pizza have surged ahead of its forecasts, as its half-year 2008 profits and sales were boosted by diners shunning restaurants in favour of eating at home. Its half-year online sales grew by a record 85.1 per cent. Domino's said the performance was "very positive, especially given the overall backdrop of what is going on out there [in the economy]". They added: "A lot of that is due to trading down. People are eating at home and eating out at restaurants is on the decline."

Car repair and bike sales help Halfords buck retail downturn

Halfords steered clear of the retail downturn when it posted better-than-expected first-quarter profits for 2008, driven by a focus on costs and sales of car maintenance products. While Halfords is not immune to the retail downturn, its average transaction value of £20, growing sales of bikes as customers embrace a healthier and greener lifestyle, and essential spend on car maintenance gave it a degree of protection.

The retailer said that its car maintenance division, boosted by demand for products such as windscreen wipers, batteries and oil, has "continued to perform strongly". Halfords accounts for one in every three bikes sold in the UK.

Credit Suisse analyst Assad Malic said: "Halfords in our view exhibits a more defensive product set than its peers with a mix of product categories playing to both discretionary and more needs-driven consumer spending categories."

Source: Adapted from the *Independent* online, 22, 24 and 25 July 2008

Be a thinker

Why have Domino's Pizza and Halfords been able to withstand recessionary pressures better than many other retailers?

Social and cultural factors
Ultimately, the various PEST factors are all governed by the socio-cultural factors. These are the elements that build society. Social factors influence people's choices and include societal beliefs, values and attitudes. So understanding changes in this area can be crucial, as they lead to political and societal change. When looking at socio-cultural factors, an organization needs to consider:

● demographic changes
● consumers' views on its products and industry
● environmental issues (especially if its method of production involves hazardous or potentially damaging processes)
● lifestyle changes and attitudes to health, wealth, age (for example attitudes to children, or the elderly), gender, work, and leisure.

Workers of the future will have an average of 19 different jobs in their lifetime as people increasingly change careers.

As the traditional "job for life" becomes less and less common, the typical individual will retrain several times for a new career, switch employers more readily, and even hold down different jobs at the same time, a new report has predicted. The study by City & Guilds found young people are more individualistic than their predecessors and will be less hesitant about shifting professions. The development of education over the Internet will make it easier for people to retrain for a new career. No longer will people have to give up their day job to retrain or take part in courses away from their home.

Rising life expectancy will give the average employee a longer work life span of 50 plus years, while pension underfunding will also have a significant impact as people decide to work longer, said the report.

These societal and cultural changes will result in a more fluid job market, according to the research. This will lead to 19 jobs for the average person as a result of career switches, internal promotions and structural change.

Source: Adapted from www.nijobs.com/forum

Be a thinker

What effects will constant changes in careers and jobs have on the way that individuals live and work?

As populations become more mobile and the numbers migrating from one country to another increase, demand patterns will reflect greater multicultural and ethnic diversity. These diverse groups will have very different lifestyles and attitudes, which influences how they view and purchase products and services. This provides the opportunity for firms to exploit new markets. It may, however, pose a threat to more traditional products and services where demand may fall.

Technological factors

Advances in technology have a major impact on business success, with companies that fail to keep up often going out of business. Technological change also affects political and economic aspects, and plays a vital part in how people view their world. For example, the development of the Internet has influenced the ways consumers and businesses research and purchase products. It is increasingly common for consumers to consider purchases from overseas. Electronic commerce (e-commerce) has boomed, with the result that even small businesses can now operate in the global market.

E-commerce is often defined as buying and selling using the Internet, such as consumer purchases from companies like Amazon.com. However, e-commerce involves more than this simple definition, because it also includes any electronic transactions between an organization and a third party, such as customer requests for further information or orders from suppliers made electronically (see more on e-commerce on p. 224).

Even before e-commerce emerged, marketers had begun to concentrate on relationship marketing as the key to long-term success. There is where businesses develop a relationship with their customers by following them from "womb to tomb", offering products that match customers' wants and needs at every stage of their life cycle. The new electronic media enables businesses to communicate on a truly personal basis —interacting with customers as individuals— across the globe. The Internet and electronic capture of information and e-commerce has refined this process further.

This growth of the Internet has seen the development of significant *e-tailers*—such as eBay and Amazon—businesses that primarily use the Internet as the medium for customers to shop for their goods or services. The launch of such businesses involves a very different business model from the typical high street retailer. Early on in the development of e-commerce, many firms attempted to set themselves up on the Internet without appropriate goods or services, but most importantly without an adequate distribution system. The so-called "dot-com bubble" referred to a speculative boom in investment during 1995–2001, when stock markets across the world saw their values increase rapidly as the result of the founding of thousands of Internet-based companies commonly referred to as "dot-coms". Although some of the new entrepreneurs had realistic plans and administrative ability, many based their businesses on ideas which, although novel, would not have been sustainable in conventional markets. As a result, few of these businesses survived online either, resulting in the dot-com crashes of the 1990s as investors suddenly realized that the Internet businesses were worth only a fraction of their share capitalization.

In the US, the dot-com bubble crash wiped out $5 trillion in market value of technology companies from March 2000 to October 2002. This led to the establishment of the mythical "99% club"—dot-coms that had lost more than 99% of their original value!

Data response exercise
Read the text below and answer the questions that follow.

Case study

Jeff Bezos, founder of the e-tailer Amazon.com, launched the business online in 1995. Amazon.com began life as an online bookstore, but soon diversified into other products such as music, computer software, electronics, toys, and clothing.

Amazon's initial business plan was unusual: the company did not predict a profit for the first four to five years of operations. Amazon grew steadily in the late 1990s while other Internet companies expanded considerably faster. Amazon's "slow" growth provoked shareholder complaints at the time that the company was not reaching profitability quickly enough. When the dot-com bubble burst, and many e-companies went out of business, Amazon survived and reported its first profit at the end of 2002.

Amazon has websites in many countries, such as Canada, the UK, Germany, France, China, and Japan. It provides a comprehensive global shipping and distribution network.

Examination questions

1 Define the term e-tailer. [2 marks]

2 Examine the main differences between an online retailer and a high street retailer in terms of their business approach and focus. [6 marks]

3 Discuss the reasons why Amazon.com survived the dot-com crash. You should research the history of the business to provide the necessary background and support for your answer. [10 marks]

The digital revolution—information is power

One of the problems with discussing technology in any book like this, or as part of a film or TV programme, is just how quickly technology moves on, and frequently in a direction that has not been predicted. How often have you seen filmed interviews with executives who have computers in the background to show how advanced their business is? A few years down the line this technology dates both the interview and its message.

In the mid-20th century, we had films showing flying cars and jet packs, neither of which seem much closer now. However, the great advances of communications technology and the Internet were not widely predicted, yet have really become the driving force of commerce in the 21st century.

Although specific technological advances may not be easy to predict, there are some trends that are undeniable. For instance, the speed of change is accelerating.

Did you know?

Moore's Law

In 1965, Intel co-founder Gordon Moore predicted that the number of transistors on a chip would double about every two years. Moore himself admits he was simply trying to get across the idea that chip technology had a future, rather than developing a revolutionary theory. However, events proved him right.

In 1965, when Moore wrote his article, the world's most complex chip had 64 transistors. Intel's Pentium IV, introduced in 2000, contained more than 125 million transistors.

Moore's Law in practice

Almost every measure of the capabilities of digital electronic devices is linked to Moore's Law: processing speed, memory capacity, even the resolution of digital cameras.

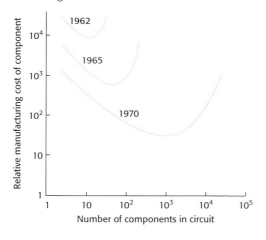

Gordon Moore's original graph, 1965

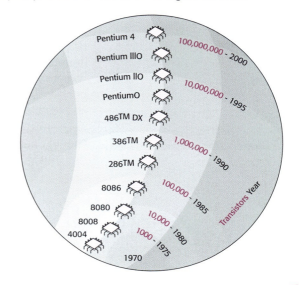

The evidence of Moore's Law is all around us. It's why today's laptop will cost half as much next year (yet be more powerful) and then be obsolete the year after that. It's why the children who grew up playing Space Invaders in game arcades now have children who grow up playing Counter-Strike across the Internet. It's why floppy disks have been replaced by USB sticks, and live television can be paused and replayed.

Source: http://gridcafe.web.cern.ch/

You can watch a dynamic demonstration of Moore's Law on the Intel website:

www.intel.com/technology/mooreslaw/index.htm on the "learn more" section.

Another significant trend is increasing access to information. It can be argued that the age of megalithic corporations dominating the world is over. There has been a revolution that has sent shock waves through the way businesses presently operate. In the past, many multinationals dominated markets by preventing access to information necessary to compete. Microsoft, for instance, developed and retained its dominant position in the software market by restricting access to its operating platform and bundling its applications, much to the anger of competition authorities in the US and worldwide. When you buy a computer with Microsoft Office, you get Microsoft's media player and Internet Explorer as well, and they cannot be deleted. These utilities provide Microsoft with a host of other revenue-earning opportunities and make it extremely difficult for rival players and Internet browsers to gain a larger market share.

The Internet and the world wide web have enabled the expansion of the global market. In its first generation, Web 1.0, the information was static—it could be controlled, manipulated, and restricted. Business websites contained "good news" stories and filtered data. Information was as it was.

Well, things are changing. Web 2.0, the "new generation" made the Internet interactive, creative, incremental, and dynamic and most importantly has increased collaboration and web-based communities among users. Web 2.0 does not refer to an update to any technical specifications, but to changes in the ways software developers and end-users use the web. This has changed the rules of the game. Perhaps the most important evolution is that the digital revolution has made the acquisition, manipulation, and transfer of information convenient and accessible to virtually everyone.

There has been an explosion of private and social sites, created by individuals, or groups of individuals, and to a great extent uncontrolled. Virtually every student reading this book will have accessed some sort of social networking site, such as Facebook or Myspace, watched videos on YouTube and Google videos and talked online with Windows Live (MSN) Messenger. Although these sites are owned by large corporations, much of the content is created by individuals and shared rapidly among friendship groups and then possibly beyond to a mass market. Information is captured and processed, stored and transmitted—indeed information has become public property, and with this ownership has come greater power to influence and inform.

It has become the age of participation. On television, reality shows dominate the networks. Online, for instance, wikis have been created where individuals combine and edit information to create massive databases. Most of us will at one time refer to, or cut and paste from, Wikipedia. Of course, there are dangers in this revolution. Without knowledge of who is creating the information we read online, we have little understanding of possible motives and bias. The information may be inaccurate and out of date. At least, however, we normally have the ability to look for opposing views from other websites.

It has been estimated that one new blog (an online journal) is created every second. The creation of the "blogosphere" has been accompanied by the explosion of "spam"—unwanted invitations to sites and information from around the world—ranging from pornography to fraudulent sites. It has been said that this blogosphere is "99% chatter and 1% matter". Nonetheless, the 1% is significant. Blogs contain all sorts of information. The content can be news, views, images, links, and videos. All of this is shared and disseminated and provides a commercial opportunity for someone.

The huge changes initiated by the world wide web and the role of the Internet have been supplemented by changes in other information and communication technologies, especially in the field of satellite technologies. These have created strategic opportunities for greater mobility in business transactions. Businesses can use GPS (global positioning systems), communicate through mobile phones and video-conferencing, outsource to call centres around the world where wage levels are lower, and access markets, customers, and financial markets around the clock. New technologies offer the potential for firms to alter the nature of their physical and human resources. Many large organizations are taking the opportunity to close down expensive headquarters in city centres and relocate to regional centres and business parks. Increasing numbers of employees are teleworking, either from home or using more local resources, such as hotels and restaurants, to conduct business using mobile technologies.

The implications of these developments are:

- increased outsourcing of key functions
- fewer full-time core staff
- changes to staffing needs
- increasing reliance on technologies and ICT support services
- more flexible working practices, for example teleworking
- 24-hour access to information
- reduction in some costs, for example rent and wages
- increases in some costs, for example technology-related purchase costs, maintenance, and training.

With these changes comes a need for a whole new approach to business strategy. The external environment is constantly changing. The days of the corporate plan charting an organization's progress for the next five years is, for the most part, redundant. Traditional methods of promotion are becoming outmoded in many fast-moving

Did you know?

Apparently your choice of social networking site indicates what social class you belong to. A US research project by a PhD student from the School of Information Sciences at UC Berkeley has reported that users of Facebook come from wealthier homes and are more likely to attend college. By contrast, MySpace users tend to get a job after finishing high school rather than continue their education. Some users now refer to the two social networking sites as MyFace and Spacebook, which has generated many parodies on YouTube.

business environments, affected by technological change. Small "niche" sellers are able to access mass markets; especially with the establishment of shopping search engines which scour the web for examples of products from portable staircases for small pets to battery operated twirling ice-cream cones.

Theory of Knowledge

Theory of Knowledge discussion

1 How do we acquire knowledge?

2 Does Wikipedia provide facts or opinions?

3 Is Wikipedia any more or less reliable than a textbook if we want to know something?

4 How can we use language, reason, perception, and emotion to test the ideas presented on a wiki site?

5 How important is it to know who is writing an article?

6 Is the combination of knowledge in a wiki a more or less reliable source for discovering the truth than a reference book written by an "expert"?

7 Discuss the power of the wiki and pressure sites by reference to sites such as those operated by Ralph Nader (www.nader.org) and the international pressure group Greenpeace (www.greenpeace.org/international).

8 Examine a conspiracy theory on the net and discuss the difficulty in proving this conspiracy right or wrong, for example the 9/11 conspiracy theories (see www.popularmechanics.com/technology/military_law/).

The phrase "the long tail" was first coined by Chris Anderson in a 2004 *Wired* magazine article to describe the niche strategy of businesses such as Amazon.com that sell a large number of unique items in relatively small quantities. The phrase later became the basis of Anderson's book (2006)[1], and led to Anderson being named by *Time* magazine as one of the world's 100 most influential people.

The book was unusual as it was an "open-source research project" on Anderson's blog at www.longtail.com. Here he shared data and ideas in progress with his readers who helped improve them and flesh out the theory. In the book, Anderson identifies the new world of niche markets and explains how in traditional retail there is an 80/20 rule (called the Pareto Principle), where 20% of products sold account for 80% of all revenue. Online, Anderson now sees the "98% rule". Here 98% of all the possible choices get chosen by someone, and the 90% of products available, only online, account for half the revenue and two thirds of the profits.

In summary, Anderson's theory is that mass culture is fading and being replaced by a series of niches. However, recent research has cast some doubt on the theory of the long tail. More than 10 million of the 13 million music tracks available for sale on the Internet in 2008 failed to find a single buyer.

---

[1] Anderson, C. 2006. *The Long Tail: Why the future of business is selling less of more.* New York. Hyperion.

Did you know?

"Cloud computing" is considered the next big thing in the world of technology. Instead of storing personal files and documents on a home computer, you store them on remote servers — known as the "cloud" — that can be accessed from any Internet-enabled computer. Software and programs, such as word-processing packages or photo-editing software, are not installed on the computer but instead are accessed online.

Microsoft, Google, Amazon and IBM are already developing cloud technology systems. For example, Google already offers a suite of Microsoft Office-style products that allows you to write letters and spreadsheets, and create presentations online, and then load these documents up to any Internet-enabled computer in the world.

Adapted from: http://www.telegraph.co.uk/digitallife23/102008

"Today, websites and online retailers offer seemingly infinite inventory, and the result is the shattering of the mainstream into a zillion different cultural shards."
Anderson, 2006

6 Business strategy

Already there is evidence of the power of the Internet having a major strategic impact on many large industries, which are finding their traditional distribution and marketing strategies threatened. For instance, the mainstream media and entertainment industry is struggling to find an effective solution to the threat of Internet piracy with the free downloading of music albums and the latest blockbuster films using illegal media sharing sites. It is quite clear that a new approach to marketing and selling is required, such as "**viral marketing**" using social networking sites to spread news about, for example, new bands, films, or DVDs.

Arctic Monkeys

The band Arctic Monkeys quietly made history when, without an album release, their debut single hit No.1 in the UK charts. Downloads and a presence on MySpace helped fuel this rapid success. The online-facilitated explosion of Arctic Monkeys into the mainstream music business came as a surprise to many but those who had seen the growing influence of community sites and the viral power of online communication might have predicted that the Internet would one day propel a band fully formed into the big time.

The UK-based band gave their songs away for free by posting them on MySpace and the name Arctic Monkeys began to spread on chat rooms across the Internet. Their fan base grew and grew and the times and dates of gigs posted online enabled the group's followers to turn up ready to sing every word to every song. After the band's demos began to sell in large quantities on eBay they were finally picked up by a major label.

Jac Holzman of Cordless Records, the first purely online record label, talking to Q magazine, identifies the speed and ease of the Internet as a reason why Arctic Monkeys' ascent was so swift: "Physical product has its place, but using the Internet is a faster way of searching for and validating talent."

And what an ascent it was. Arctic Monkeys achieved two No.1 singles with their first two releases and have their names in the record books as having the fastest selling debut album of all time. "Whatever you say I am" was released in January 2006. It clocked up sales of 360,000 and outsold the rest of the top 20 albums combined in its first week.

Other bands have developed similar business models. "In Rainbows", the seventh studio album by alternative rock group Radiohead, became available for download from their official website. The band let their fans decide what to pay for the 10 MP3 files—from nothing to £100.

Source: Adapted from www.iabuk.net

Social networking is supposed to be the next big marketing opportunity. MySpace, Facebook, and other sites have been attracting millions of new users. Advertising on social networking sites is growing fast with large corporations looking to increase their online presence. Google, for instance, has a $900 million deal with MySpace to place adverts alongside search results. MySpace has also begun posting lists of friends' favourite products on users' home pages.

However, there is already research evidence that not only is the average amount of time each user spends on social networking sites falling, but the best-known sites have some of the lowest response rates on the web. Marketers say as few as 4 in 10,000 people who see adverts on social networking sites click on them, compared with 20 in 10,000 across the web.

Clearly, any organization wanting to move its operations online will need to consider whether it has the internal capabilities to support this strategic option.

Student workpoint 6.2

Business project

The purpose of your project is to produce a report (1,000–1,500 words) on becoming an e-tailer. The project should focus on an existing small to medium-sized retailer which at the moment has no online presence. This retailer can be purely fictional or you could select a local or national retailer to examine.

The report should cover all or some of the following issues:

- HR and workforce planning
- financial implications
- marketing effects
- distribution channels
- ICT support and technology issues.

This project might form the basis of a business investigation for your business and management internal assessment.

McKinsey & Company, the US management consultancy, recently researched technology trends in the market-place and identified virtual worlds, such as Second Life, as indispensable marketing tools vital to the strategy of businesses hoping to gain the attention of younger market segments. In Web 3.0, users will live between the real world and a range of virtual worlds. McKinsey & Company believes that virtual worlds are on the point of rapid expansion and see the 3-D web as the next major wave of Internet development.

Data response exercise

Read the text below and answer the questions that follow.

Case study

Second Life

Second Life is an online, virtual (computer-generated) world that exists only on the web. Using a 3-D virtual character, subscribers lead a second life, mimicking everything from visiting a nightclub to a career in real estate. Hundreds of thousands of dollars change hands daily as residents create and sell virtual commodities, which may include designing clothes, making vehicles, or owning a casino. Second Life recorded its one millionth resident in late 2006 with one user making more than US$1 million buying, selling, and renting virtual real estate.

Major technology corporations use Second Life to market products or services to a niche audience and to target younger and technologically aware market segments. Dell, for instance, opened an "in-world island" with a virtual replica of the Dell factory and a retail store where customers order PCs to be delivered to their home. On the island, customers pay in linden, the official Second Life currency (US$1 = L$250). Customers who want to order a physical Dell computer delivered to their real home will pay in US dollars.

IBM recently purchased 12 islands in Second Life for virtual business training and simulations. Musicians, and news organizations, including the BBC and the Reuters news agency, have a presence in Second Life.

The BBC, which is frequently an early adopter, used the island to debut new bands at a virtual rock festival.

According to *Business Week*, the biggest Second Life design shops charge corporate clients between US$10,000 and US$200,000 to establish a virtual world presence.

Adapted from: http://secondlife.reuters.com and http://whatis.techtarget.com

Examination questions

1 Define the term niche market. [2 marks]

2 Explain the advantages to major corporations, like Dell and IBM, of market segmentation and consumer targeting. [8 marks]

3 Discuss how firms may adapt their marketing strategies and marketing mixes to changes in technology as illustrated by the growth of Second Life. [10 marks]

The market and competitive environments

Having completed a SWOT and PEST analysis, an organization should collect data on the markets in which it operates and information on the competition it faces. This will offer quantitative and qualitative data to support its strategic planning.

Key data about the nature of the markets in which the organization operates include:

● market size measured by the value and volume of sales revenues
● market growth measured by the percentage increase in the value and volume of sales revenue
● relative market shares of each organization operating in a market or market segment
● the changing patterns of demand in the target market and segments driven by new trends and fashions
● the perception of customers of the organization's products and those of its competition—this may be presented in the form of a perception or position map.

Organizations may choose to conduct market research themselves, but this can be very time consuming and expensive. There are many professional market research consultancies, such as A C Nielsen, Mintel, and Keynote, which offer a range of commercial reports for sale, covering hundreds of industries and products from seasonings in ethnic foods to cosmetic surgery.

These reports help businesses that buy them to gain an insight into consumers' behaviour, product innovation, and competitive marketing strategies in their markets. The reports also help them tap into new product opportunities, increase price margins, and recognize threats so they remain competitive and profitable.

Although buying full reports may be beyond the means of most students and teachers, it is possible to access executive summaries of market reports on the main websites of research consultancies. These summaries provide a basic overview of industries and trends in markets, such as the data on the consumer packaging industry in a recent A C Nielsen industry report (given below).

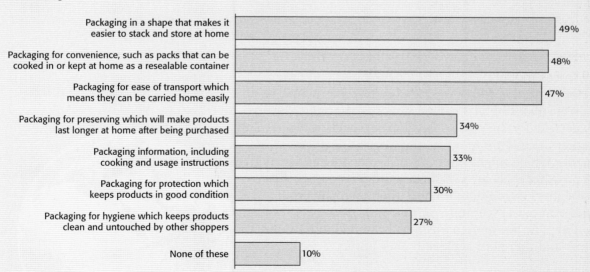

Packaging and the environment

According to a global food packaging survey conducted by The Nielsen Company, the world's leading media and consumer research company, 90% of consumers who cited recyclable bags and packaging as a key driver of store choice would be willing to give up an aspect of packaging if it meant it would help the environment.

Conducted in mid 2007, the study surveyed 26,486 Internet users in 47 markets from Europe, Asia Pacific, the Americas, the Middle East, and Africa, on the factors that influenced their choice of grocery store and their preferences in packaging. Consumers who claimed they considered a store's environmental friendliness important when choosing where to shop were then asked which aspects of packaging they'd be willing to give up if it meant it would benefit the environment.

Interestingly, environmentally-aware New Zealanders topped global rankings as the nation most prepared to give up all aspects of packaging for the sake of the environment. This may in large part be due to high levels of "eco-consciousness", including in-store reminders and recyclable bag merchandising by supermarkets, and weekly recyclable rubbish collection instituted by local authorities in most cities.

Which of these aspects of packaging would you be prepared to give up if it meant that it would benefit the environment?

Global average

Aspect	%
Packaging in a shape that makes it easier to stack and store at home	49%
Packaging for convenience, such as packs that can be cooked in or kept at home as a resealable container	48%
Packaging for ease of transport which means they can be carried home easily	47%
Packaging for preserving which will make products last longer at home after being purchased	34%
Packaging information, including cooking and usage instructions	33%
Packaging for protection which keeps products in good condition	30%
Packaging for hygiene which keeps products clean and untouched by other shoppers	27%
None of these	10%

Base: Those rated "Uses recyclable bags and packaging" as very or quite important when deciding where to do grocery shopping

Source: Nielsen Climate Change Barometer, November 2007

It is also essential for businesses to have a thorough understanding of the direct and indirect competition that they face in the market-place. By conducting a competitive market audit, businesses can identify:

● key competitors and the products and services they offer
● competitors' market shares in terms of the value and volume of sales
● the technologies employed in competitors' products and in their production and whether the competitors are planning to improve these technologies
● the financial strength of competitors established from published accounts and other market intelligence, such as media reports
● new product developments.

Some businesses will go to considerable lengths to find out sensitive market information about their rivals. Some businesses will plant employees in rivals' companies to conduct covert surveillance and some businesses have been accused of stealing secrets from their competitors.

Data response exercise
Read the text below and discuss the point that follows.

Case study

Ferrari wants technical documents back

McLaren Formula One team has suspended one of its top engineers following an investigation into allegations that the engineer had a stash of high-level technical information from rival F1 team Ferrari.

McLaren has declined to name the employee at the centre of the allegations, but Ferrari has accused its former technical manager of passing on confidential documents.

McLaren said today that it had completed its own internal investigation into the allegations and claimed that "no Ferrari intellectual property has been passed to any other members of the team or incorporated into its cars".

Source: The Register, 27 July 2007

Be a thinker

What methods can be employed by firms to learn more about competitors and their plans and operations?

Porter's five forces model
Porter developed his five forces theory of industry structure to support strategic planning in a competitive environment. Porter's theory was designed to help firms develop survival strategies in an existing market in addition to evaluating the "attractiveness" of other industries which might offer expansion opportunities. Porter's framework provides tools for investigating the five forces that determine the level of competition and, therefore, the profit opportunities that exist (see more on this on p. 190–2). The stronger each of the forces is, the more a business is limited in its ability to raise its prices and therefore achieve higher profits.

The five driving forces are:

● the bargaining power of suppliers
● the bargaining power of buyers
● the threat of new entrants
● the threat of substitute products and technologies
● the intensity of competition in the industry.

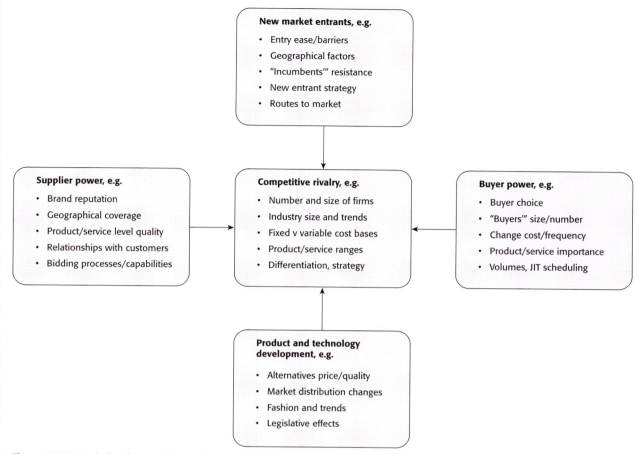

Figure 6.5 Porter's five forces of competitive position

How can this model be used strategically?

An illustration—a delicatessen (a specialist grocer)
If a business is contemplating entering a new industry, it will need to examine the factors that will influence each of the five driving forces. For instance, let's assume that you are thinking of setting up a delicatessen in your local town. You will need to consider the following issues.

● *The bargaining power of suppliers.* The suppliers of food products will have the opportunity to supply many businesses, most of which are not as specialist as yours. Large general supermarkets will stock a range of products in the grocery section, several of which would be regarded as delicatessen items. Suppliers of specialist foods may also sell to restaurants and other food outlets. So it is unlikely that your small single delicatessen will have much leverage in the food market to force suppliers to offer discounts or very competitive prices.

The only opportunities that you will have to influence suppliers' prices is on particularly specialist foods, for example truffles, buffalo mozzarella, and *foie gras*. You may be able to influence prices if the suppliers of these products are very small and locally based and there are few businesses stocking these items, or if there are several suppliers of these specialist products in the area.

Suppliers faced with pressures to reduce price from delicatessens may even take the opportunity to set up their own distribution channels, for example farm shops, or buy their own retail outlets (forwards vertical integration).

- *The bargaining power of buyers*. The buyers of products from delicatessens will be able to demand lower prices if they can play one competitor off against another. It is unlikely in the specialist food market that this will be possible, unless there are particularly large supermarkets offering a large range of grocery products or there are other delicatessens in the immediate vicinity. In many cases the specialist nature of the products should allow for premium pricing.

In addition, the buyers of specialist food products are unlikely to buy in sufficiently large volumes to be able to demand discounts, unless they are "in the trade", such as buyers for restaurants or hotels.

- *The threat of new entrants*. There are few barriers to entry to the market. Setting up your delicatessen is relatively easy—and so would be setting up a competing shop. Another retailer could open a shop in the area at a low cost and would not have to achieve high-volume sales to be successful. Capital requirements are low and it would be difficult for an existing delicatessen to retaliate by cutting prices without significantly affecting profit margins.
- *The threat of substitute products and technologies*. There are many potential substitute food products. A customer may enjoy a particular type of ham or salad item that is unusual, but can be satisfied with a mass-produced, lower-quality item from a large supermarket. Most buyers are prepared to substitute different foods if the price differential is too large. In addition, many supermarkets are now stocking high-quality, specialist foods to appeal to their high-end users. The choice may not be as great, but the convenience of buying everything they need under one roof may provide enough incentive for people to buy from the supermarket.
- *The intensity of competition in the industry*. This may well be the deciding factor when considering setting up your delicatessen. If there are already several existing retailers selling similar items in the area, it would be difficult to find a USP to justify opening your shop unless the potential market was growing significantly, or the shop was able to sell particularly unusual products to persuade customers that it was, indeed, different.

Overall, the delicatessen market is competitive and launching a new shop is strategically a risky option, unless a USP can be established. A shop just selling cheese opened recently in my local town. This is a niche operation so it is likely to have a competitive advantage in the range and quality of cheeses sold. The downsides of this type of operation are the size of the potential market, which will limit both revenue and profit opportunities, and the risk that customers will not like the cheeses stocked or will not buy in sufficient volumes to make the business viable.

Table 6.1 gives a summary of issues linked to these five forces.

Force	Strategies to minimize market threats
1 The bargaining power of suppliers	Find alternative suppliers, or backwards integration with suppliers.
2 The bargaining power of buyers	Tie buyers into contracts, make products specific to buyers' needs, or forwards integration.
3 The threat of new entrants	Create barriers to entry, such as heavy investment in capital, patented products and copyrighted ideas.
4 The threat of substitute products and technologies	Invest heavily in R&D. Control distribution channels. React aggressively to new entrants, for example with price reductions.
5 The intensity of competition in the industry	Create differentiated products with a USP. Agree to share markets or work cooperatively.

Table 6.1 Summary of strategic approaches to reduce threats

What Porter's approach does is to make businesses consider all aspects of their environment and evaluate levels of risk. Of course, five forces analysis alone cannot provide all the answers as to whether you should open a delicatessen.

Strategic analysis involves the combination of a range of information, using a number of tools in an entrepreneur's toolbox. First, you will need to conduct extensive market research and a product and benefit analysis. As a new business, your delicatessen will not have any customer or brand loyalty. You should produce a business plan, including financial and cash flow predictions, and carry out an external audit. A delicatessen sells luxury items, so price and income elasticities of demand will have a significant impact on the potential revenues and profits. Knowledge of local planning laws may also be important as this may restrict the issuing of retail licences and may limit the alteration or upgrading of existing premises.

You will also need to examine the potential internal strengths and weaknesses of the business. Do you have a vision for the business and are you committed to potential long hours of work to see your vision put into practice? Do you possess the range of skills required not only to buy, display, and market your merchandise, but to deal with the financial requirements such as cost control, cash flow analysis and producing final accounts? If not, can you afford the specialists who can provide these services?

In the long run, you will need to understand that the forces identified by Porter are dynamic and that a new business must seek out areas where it can use its strengths to take advantage of market opportunities. Entrepreneurs may be able to devise strategies that minimize some of the forces and increase the competitive advantages of the business.

Student workpoint 6.3
Business investigation

Examine the following potential business set-ups in your local area and use five forces analysis to evaluate the attractiveness of entering the industry:

1 a computer software company offering accounting support programs

2 a retail outlet offering high-end, exclusive fashion items

3 a window cleaning business

4 a taxi company

5 an organic food producer.

Strategic analysis and environmental scanning—summary

Most successful businesses are successful because they have an accurate picture of their present position in the market-place and a clear focus on their strengths and weaknesses. This process is usually structured, but will vary in nature according to the size of the organization.

An entrepreneur may be able to conduct a more informal approach to strategic analysis, often by being involved in the day-to-day operation of the business and therefore able to speak directly to staff and customers. This will provide information on areas of the business that are performing well and those that need further attention.

A larger organization will probably require a more formalized and detailed process. Senior managers may not be involved in the "sharp end" of the business, so coordination of functions will be required to centralize market intelligence. This ensures that most staff will be involved in the planning process and aware of the strategic direction of the business.

The basis of successful strategy, therefore, is recognizing that changes in the market-place and the external environment require a broader perspective.

In 1960, in a landmark article[2] Levitt argued that businesses spend too much time examining their products, rather than looking outwards at the external environment and researching their customers' needs. He was analysing the decline of the US train industry, which had failed to recognize that customers had the choice of many other transport options. As a result, they foolishly ignored the challenge of other transport, such as cars and planes, and found their industry bankrupt and in need of government subsidy.

Levitt urged senior managers to review their corporate vision; and redefine their markets in terms of a wider perspective. He exhorted organizations to define their industries broadly to take advantage of growth opportunities. Levitt wrote that customers are concerned with their needs, rather than the tools to satisfy these needs. Customers, he said, do not necessarily want to buy a drill; they just want to make a hole.

In short, Levitt describes the difference between sales and marketing. He used railroads, oil, and corner grocery industries to explain his ideas.

In the same way that the US railways had to redefine their markets in the 1950s, airlines are now faced with challenges to their business models.

"Selling focuses on the needs of the seller, marketing on the needs of the buyer."
Theodore Levitt

"The organization must learn to think of itself not as producing goods or services, but as buying customers, as doing the things that will make people want to do business with it."
Theodore Levitt, 1960

[2] Levitt, T. 1960. "Marketing myopia". *Harvard Business Review*. July–August.

Case study

High-speed trains seize short-haul market as fuel cost cripples the airlines

Only eight months after opening its doors Eurostar and its biggest shareholder, SNCF, the French state railway have gained 70 per cent of traffic on the London–Paris route. Traffic growth on Eurostar increased by 21 per cent in the first quarter, compared with the same period in 2007. Revenues are up by a quarter.

Last week Air France threw in the towel and said it was in talks with Veolia, Europe's leading private rail-freight operator, about launching high-speed train services with Air France livery. The airline industry has been crushed by the price of kerosene and deserted by passengers fed up with delays. After decades of disappointment, false dawns and virtually bankrupt Channel Tunnels, we have finally arrived at the age of the train.

Airlines are left with the awful question of whether short-haul air traffic has any future in Europe. The answer has to be a resounding "no". When did you last hear of a service business where the fuel bill represented more than a third of the operating cost, substantially higher than the cost of the staff? Oil prices have "totally changed the game", said John Armbrust, chairman of consulting firm Armbrust Aviation Group. "You begin to wonder: Where do airlines go from here? They either raise their fares or they have got to shrink to become profitable."

To make matters worse, the European Commission has secured the agreement of Parliament and Council for the inclusion of airlines in the European Union's Emissions Trading System—the electrified railways won't pay it.

Air France has watched over the past decade as SNCF's Train à Grande Vitesse (TGV) eroded its domestic business. Air services between Paris and Lyons and between Paris and Brussels have been suspended. The train is dominating traffic to Marseilles and Geneva and the new line east to Strasbourg will quickly extinguish air links. However, in 2010, Europe's high-speed rail network will be open to competing operators.

Source: *The Times*, 9 July 2008, and Reuters, 30 May 2008

Student workpoint 6.4
Business investigation

Write a short report (750–1,000 words) on IBM, discussing how the organization has had to adapt its business over the years to react to changing market conditions. Evaluate the success of IBM in adapting its business model.

A good start for your investigation would be to visit the IBM website: www.ibm.com/us/. Look at the section "About us".

6.3 Strategic choice

Strategy formulation and planning—where is the business aiming to be?

Strategic choices

- What are the processes of decision making about the direction of the business?
  — scientific and formal decision making
  — decision trees
  — cause and effect diagram (fishbone diagram—see p. 57)
  — force field analysis (see p. 84)
  — the five whys (see p. 64).
- How are markets developing? Forecasting future market changes.
- What are the future directions available to the firm? This may include rationalization, refocusing, or expansion:
  — identifying and developing core competence
  — potential growth strategies—Ansoff's matrix[3]
  — investment appraisal.
- What are competitors doing and can their offer be matched or bettered?
- Target setting and benchmarking to measure success:
  — return on investment
  — benchmarking.

Source: Adapted from the IB Diploma Programme Business and Management Guide

---

> "Cheshire Puss" said Alice, "Would you tell me, please, which way I ought to go from here?"
> "That depends a good deal on where you want to get to," said the Cat.
> "I don't much care where…" said Alice.
> "Then it doesn't matter which way you go," said the Cat.
>
> Lewis Carroll, *Alice's Adventures in Wonderland*

Most organizations, big or small, plan in some ways for the future. The extent and the nature of business planning may vary, but the object is the same. Planning examines how an organization can achieve its objectives. It is the primary management function because it forms the foundation for all the other management functions: those of organizing, commanding, coordinating, and controlling. Only when plans have been developed can managers decide how to structure the business, utilize their staff and put in place appropriate control mechanisms.

Strategic business planning can be defined as: "the managerial process of developing and maintaining a viable fit between the organization's objectives and resources and its changing market opportunities".

The extent of planning varies considerably from business to business. Small businesses often appear to survive in the short term without strategic planning. They are typically started and managed by entrepreneurs who are by definition highly motivated, but frequently lack training in business practices.

Figure 6.6 Strategic planning

---

[3] Ansoff, I. H. 1957. "Strategies for diversification". *Harvard Business Review.* September–October.

However, the failure rate of these small businesses over the medium to long term is very high. One reason is that almost all entrepreneurs use their personal funds as business capital and as a consequence want to be involved in all major decisions. Although they may have a clear vision about the direction of the business, not all communicate this well to their employees. Indeed, many are very protective of their ideas. This is not ideal as it is highly unlikely that the entrepreneur will be the only person to carry out the business plan.

If entrepreneurs prepare more formalized business plans, to which their employees can refer, it can drive the business forward. It also allows other decision makers to be focused on achieving the organization's goals, rather than simply following the entrepreneur acting on impulse. The plans will also assist in the allocation of resources, the setting of time frames for completion of projects, appointing suitable staff, and setting appropriate budgets.

The basis for strategic planning

The basis for strategic planning has to be the analysis of the strengths and weaknesses of the existing organization, so that any planned strategy develops the assets of the business and addresses its weaknesses. As examined in the context of HR on p. 107, to explain the success of the best performing companies of the time, Peters and Waterman developed their "seven S" model (1982)[4]—a model first developed by McKinsey consultancy.

The seven Ss are:

- structure
- skills
- staff
- strategy.
- systems
- style
- shared values/subordinate goals

Peters and Waterman developed the idea that in "excellent" organizations the seven Ss complement each other, so that the sum of the parts is greater than each individual element. Figure 6.7

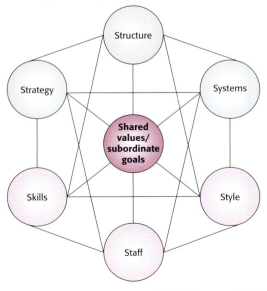

Figure 6.7 The McKinsey seven S model as developed in Peters, T. and Waterman, R. 1982. *In Search of Excellence*. New York, Harper & Row.

---

[4] Peters, T. and Waterman, R. 1982. *In Search of Excellence: Lessons from America's best-run companies*. New York, Harper & Row.

illustrates this. Each of the Ss must also be consistent with the other factors for them to reinforce one another.

The model links strategy with organizational effectiveness. The model can be used as both a checklist of where the business is at present and as a tool to assess potential conflicts when a new strategy is planned and then implemented.

In the planning process, the organization assesses each of the seven Ss and checks for consistency and suitability for the planned future strategic direction of the business.

Shared values/subordinate goals

Placing shared values at the centre of the model emphasizes that these values are central to the development of all the other elements. The organization's structure, strategy, systems, style, staff, and skills all develop from the reasons the business was created and what it stands for. These core shared values, set out in the mission and value statements of the business, drive all the other elements.

Structure

This refers to the existing organizational structure and hierarchy. It examines the way that departments communicate and interact and whether decision making is centralized or decentralized. Lines of communication are identified and measured against future requirements. The most successful organizations adapt their organizational structures to meet the needs of their customers. For instance, organizations in dynamic environments will employ matrix organization structures, which are flexible and adaptable.

Systems

This covers procedures and routine processes, both formal and informal, required to achieve the organization's strategic objectives. It includes ways in which information moves through the organization. This incorporates aspects of the business such as market research and intelligence about the competition, as well as measures focusing on the financial health of the business.

Skills

This examines the distinctive capabilities and strengths of the organization as a whole and the skills and abilities of its staff. For example, if a business is aiming to expand internationally, it will be necessary to develop those individuals with language skills and an in-depth knowledge of customs and cultures in other countries. The business must identify any skills gaps and fill these through recruitment and/or training.

Style

This is closely linked to corporate culture and asks questions about management styles and the effectiveness of leadership. For instance, how participative and approachable are the managers? Do departments and teams compete or cooperate? Are existing styles suited to the future marketing environment?

Staff

This refers to the human resources of the business—the motivation of individuals and teams, their attitude to the business and its values. This is often regarded as a "soft function" to be left to the HR department. Peters and Waterman argue that staff concerns are the concern of all senior management and those developing strategy.

Strategy

This is the actions of the organization to implement its vision and direction. Strategy is either the planned response of the organization to a changing environment or actions that anticipate changes in the environment, customers, and the market-place.

Student workpoint 6.5

Business investigation

Once information has been gathered about each of the seven Ss, the organization must identify gaps and inconsistencies between elements. Questions such as these can be asked.

- Are shared values consistent with structure, strategy, and systems? If not, what needs to change?
- How well does each element support and reinforce the others? Have we identified where changes need to be planned and implemented?

Taking the seven S model and the questions posed above, choose one or both of these organizations:

1 your school

2 a local business or a business known to you.

Evaluate the organization against each of the seven Ss and make recommendations for change where you believe there are weaknesses, gaps, or inconsistencies.

Developing the business plan

Over the last century, the process of business planning has been developed and written about in many business manuals. Senior executives and management gurus have identified the need for planning to achieve competitive advantage. Strategic business planning is beneficial because it requires:

- formal examination of the organization's position
- identification of the organization's key objectives
- managers to examine the future
- staff to work together as a team.

However, there are also disadvantages because strategic planning:

- takes up managers' time and may remove the focus from current activities
- is costly in terms of resources
- may restrict management freedom and flexibility
- may quickly become overtaken by changes in the external environment.

Indeed, some modern management theorists, although accepting the need for a planning process, doubt the value of setting plans in a fast-moving business environment that stretch too far into the future. They argue that the resources employed in this process are wasted as planning horizons have shortened and business plans can become out of date almost as they are written.

The contrast between traditional strategic planning and modern approaches is well illustrated by the work of two management theorists we have looked at in the context of HR (on p. 116 and 105): Henri Fayol and Henry Mintzberg. Naturally, their ideas about planning were for the most part determined by their times, and the ideas are a product of very different business environments. Nonetheless, these two theorists' approach to planning is fundamentally different.

Fayol concentrates on formal organization, planning and structure, whereas Mintzberg emphasizes a more creative approach to management decision making, where strategy tends to "emerge" rather than being formally developed.

Profile

Henri Fayol (1841—1925)

Fayol has been described as the father of modern management. He was a French management theorist whose ideas became influential during the 20th century. Fayol began his working life as a mining engineer for Compagnie de Commentry-Fourchambeau-Decazeville, but soon moved into management, eventually becoming the company's managing director in 1888.

As we've examined in relation to HR (see p. 116), Fayol saw a manager's job as:

● planning
● organizing
● commanding
● coordinating activities
● controlling performance.

Based largely on his management experience, Fayol (1916) developed 14 principles of management.[5] Fayol's ideas were based on efficient organization to minimize production costs. Although his ideas became a universal part of the modern management concepts, he has often been associated with Frederick Winslow Taylor and the classical scientific school of management, because like Taylor most of the activities detailed are focused on the task, rather than people.

Fayol laid down the following principles of management.

● *Specialization of labour.* Specializing encourages continuous improvement in skills and the development of improvements in methods.
● *Authority.* The right to give orders and the power to exact obedience.
● *Discipline.* No slacking or bending of rules. The worker should be respectful.
● *Unity of command.* Each employee has one and only one boss.
● *Unity of direction.* A single mind generates a single plan and all play their part in that plan.
● *Subordination of individual interests.* When at work, only work things should be pursued or thought about.
● *Remuneration.* Employees should receive fair payment for services, not what the company can get away with.
● *Centralization*: consolidation of management functions. Decisions should be made from the top.
● *Scalar chain (line of authority).* A formal chain of command should run from the top to the bottom of the organization, as in military contexts.

[5] Fayol, H. 1916. *Administration Industrielle et Generale*—English translation: Storrs, C. 1949. *General and Industrial Management by Henri Fayol.* London. Pitman and Sons Ltd.

- *Order.* All materials and personnel have a prescribed place, and they must remain there.
- *Equity.* There should be equality of treatment (but not necessarily identical treatment).
- *Personnel tenure.* There will be limited turnover of personnel, with lifetime employment offered for good workers.
- *Initiative.* Members of the organization think out a plan and do what it takes to make it happen.
- *Esprit de corps.* There should be harmony and cohesion among personnel.

Henry Mintzberg (1939–)

Henry Mintzberg was born in Montreal in 1939 and graduated in mechanical engineering from McGill University where he is now Cleghorn Professor of Management Studies. He is a prolific author on business and management with more than 140 articles and 13 books to his name. His focus was on the structure of organizations and strategic management.

Tom Peters has referred to Dr Mintzberg as "perhaps the world's premier management thinker".

In many of his books his belief in the importance of practical knowledge is readily apparent. Getting to grips with change dominates his thinking on strategy. Instead of considering organizations as pure machines, he prefers to see them as a collective of individuals. He regards corporate management not as a science but more as an art.

Mintzberg (1993) criticizes practices of strategic traditional corporate planning as mechanical and repetitive and not suited to dynamic modern environments.[6] Mintzberg shadowed senior-level managers and illustrated how directors do not spend most of their time developing and sticking to rationally designed plans. Rather the opposite. They spend the majority of their day resolving unforeseen crises sparked off by irrational elements in the world of management. Strategy often emerges over time, rather being than rationally planned.

Student workpoint 6.6

Business investigation and class discussion

To what extent do you believe there is a need for long-term formal business plans? Discuss the following organizations in your evaluation:

1 a sole trader who works from home selling software programs
2 a large IT consultancy with several multinational clients
3 a medium-sized engineering company producing railway tracks and points
4 a large media company selling documentaries to several large TV broadcasters
5 a medium-sized independent mortgage provider.

Despite the disadvantages of long-term planning identified by some management theorists, most organizations will prepare a plan of some description. To achieve this, managers will carry out these tasks.

- They define a purpose and strategic direction and prepare a brief statement involving key stakeholders on the future aims of the business.

"The real challenge in crafting strategy lies in detecting the subtle discontinuities that may undermine an organization in the future. And for that there is no technique, no program, just a sharp mind in touch with the situation. Such discontinuities are unexpected and irregular, … they can be dealt with only by minds that are attuned to existing patterns yet able to perceive important breaks in them."

Henry Mintzberg (1989)[7]

---

[6] Mintzberg, H. 1994. *The Rise and Fall of Strategic Planning*. Prentice Hall, Harlow.

[7] Mintzberg, H. 1989. *Mintzberg on Management: Inside our strange world of organizations.* Sydney. John Wiley and Sons, Australia.

- They identify existing and potential competitive advantage and outline what they believe are the organization's core competences and distinctive advantages that can be defended into the future. They ask customers why they buy from the organization and use this to identify what products and services the organization will produce, sell, and deliver.
- They identify the core customers the business will serve and target those customers and market segments with products that allow the business to be cost effective and profitable. This may mean rejecting some orders if these do not offer sufficient return on investment (ROI).
- They prepare market forecasts and examine current and future sales revenues and profits available from selected target markets to ensure the correct allocation of resources.
- They draw up budgets and use market forecasts to estimate financial resource requirements. They build in target profit margins.
- They identify measures used to judge the success of the strategy.

The resulting report will be distributed to all those involved in putting the plan into place.

Defining a purpose and strategic direction

Having a strategic focus is vital. In a fast-moving market-place, it is easy for managers to be sucked into day-to-day routine, being reactive rather than proactive. The role of senior management is to look to the future to ensure that business decisions made today contribute to the future well-being of the organization. This long-term plan will lay down actions to exploit environmental opportunities and to defend against threats in light of the analysis of the organization's strengths and weaknesses.

The process will start from the business mission and vision statements (see p. 26) and the identification of corporate objectives. The first decision a business needs to make as part of its planning process is to decide on its **strategic direction**—where the business aims to be in the future to develop and maximize its competitive advantage.

Before choosing its strategic direction, a business must consider some, or all, of:

- the products it intends to offer
- the distribution channels available
- the target market and the nature of its existing and potential customers
- the geographic area or areas to be served
- the competitors
- the resources available
- new fashions or trends
- demographic changes.

Identifying core competences and competitive advantage

A core (distinctive) competence relates to experience and skills acquired over many years that means a business does some things exceptionally well and also better than its competitors.

Hamel and Prahalad's work on core competence

The concept was developed by Hamel and Prahalad (1990).[8] They identified three conditions that defined a core competence.

- It provides cost benefits.
- It is hard for competitors to imitate.
- It can be leveraged (applied) widely to many product markets.

A core competence can take various forms, such as technical expertise and knowledge and a close relationship with customers and suppliers. It may also include innovation or a corporate culture that creates a highly motivated and efficient staff. Modern business theory suggests that activities not part of an organization's core competence should be outsourced (see p. 288).

Hamel and Prahalad used the example of Honda to illustrate the application of a core competence. They identified Honda's expertise in production of superior engines. Honda was able to exploit this core competence to develop a variety of quality products from lawn mowers and generators to motorbikes and cars.

If a core competence yields a long-term advantage to the business, it is said to be a **sustainable competitive advantage**. Competitive advantage is the means by which a business seeks to create and sustain a superior performance over its rivals.

Possible strategic approaches to create competitive advantage include:

- product or service differentiation, for example persuading consumers to believe that the product is sufficiently different or unique in some way
- pricing strategies, for example supplying goods and services at a lower price than the competitors' price, thereby increasing profits and gaining market share
- excellent marketing strategies, for example advertising campaigns
- ethical management and corporate social responsibility (CSR)—see p. 38.

If customers perceive the business as different from its competitors this may create brand and corporate loyalty and will allow for considerable marketing advantages, such as premium pricing.

"Competitive advantage is a company's ability to perform in one or more ways that competitors cannot or will not match."
Philip Kotler (1931–), professor of international marketing

Identify core customers and products

In its business plan, a business will identify those customers and market segments that would be most profitable to target. Having done this it will need to select the appropriate products and services to produce, sell, and deliver.

To achieve this, the business must be clear on how it will defend its position in the market and outperform its competitors. There are two main ways that a business can achieve an advantage over its competitors.

- *Cost leadership*. By reducing the cost of producing products and services below that of competitors, the business can charge a

---

[8] Hamel, G. and Prahalad, C. K. 1990. "The core competence of the corporation". *Harvard Business Review*. May–June.

lower price and/or earn a higher profit. This will require a focus on production efficiency.

- *Product or service differentiation.* The business makes its product or service appear different in the mind of the customer through methods other than price. This could be by producing higher-quality products or a service delivered using greater expertise. This should create brand and corporate loyalty and allow the business to charge a higher or premium price.

Having decided on the competitive strategy, the business must decide on its **competitive focus** or **competitive scope**. This describes the breadth (and size) of the target market. The business can decide to concentrate on a specific market area, market segment, or product. Again, this provides the business with two approaches.

- *A broad target*—competing in the mass market, where the potential for significant profits exists, but where competition is likely to be fierce and the business will struggle to gain market share.
- *A narrow target*—aiming at a niche market segment or a group of customers with specific characteristics. The potential profit is likely to be smaller, but the business can be a "big player" with high market share and power.

Porter's generic strategies

In 1980, Porter[9] identified his generic planning strategies (see more on this on p. 190). A generic strategy is one that can be applied to many industries from coal to computers and can be pursued by any type or size of organization, profit making or not—that is, it applies to all businesses. Porter identified three generic strategies:

- cost
- differentiation
- focus.

However, the combination of these strategies results in four possible approaches, as the focus strategy can be sub-divided into a cost or differentiation approach.

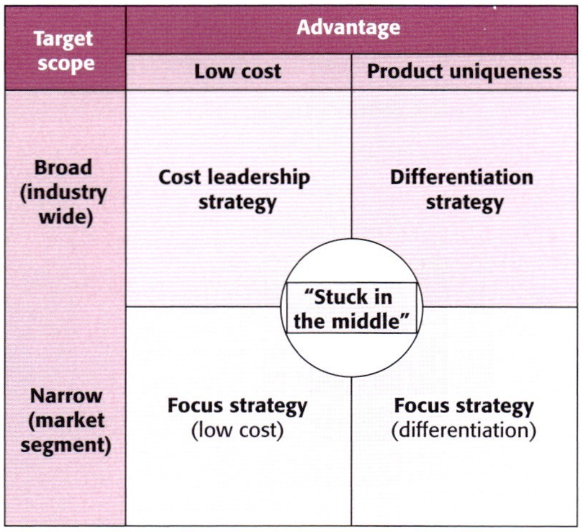

Target scope	Advantage	
	Low cost	**Product uniqueness**
Broad (industry wide)	Cost leadership strategy	Differentiation strategy
	"Stuck in the middle"	
Narrow (market segment)	Focus strategy (low cost)	Focus strategy (differentiation)

Figure 6.8 Porter's generic strategies

[9] Porter, M. E. 1980. *Competitive Strategy: Techniques for analyzing industries and competitors.* New York. Free Press.

The industry's character determines the range of effective strategies. In a commodity market, for instance, only costs matter—differentiation is impossible as there is no branding. In economic terms, this is called "perfect competition". High-fashion markets, on the other hand, are driven solely by differentiation. Price is rarely the deciding factor in a customer's purchasing decision.

Importantly, Porter emphasized the need for businesses to focus on either cost or differentiation, or risk getting "stuck in the middle", where competitors surpass them both on cost and superior product offerings. In other words, companies cannot afford to compete with everyone. If customers perceive a company as offering high-quality products such as in fashion markets, reducing price to compete with "bargain basement" businesses will cause confusion for customers, who will probably lose trust in the quality and exclusivity of the products on offer. However, this is not a view held by all strategists. Some argue that there is a viable "middle ground" between strategies.

"You've got to accentuate the positive, eliminate the negatives. Latch on to the affirmative, don't mess with Mister In-Between."

"Here comes the wave", Mercer and Arlen, 1944

Student workpoint 6.7

Business investigation and class discussion

Evaluate the decision by Mercedes to produce its A Class model and the decision by BMW to produce its 1 Series.

1 What potential dangers were there to Mercedes and BMW by producing these cheaper models?

2 How and to what extent have these dangers been avoided?

Potential growth strategies

Ansoff developed a decision-making tool that provides a range of strategic growth options for a business, each associated with different degrees of risk. Ansoff (1957)[10] identified four broad strategies that a business may adopt to respond to changes in its competitive environment (see Figure 6.9). Ansoff's approach is presented in the form of a matrix with four possible growth strategies (see more on this on p. 75).

Market \ Products	Existing	New
Existing	Market penetration	Product development
New	Market development	Diversification

Figure 6.9 Ansoff's matrix

Source: Ansoff, I. H. 1957. "Strategies for diversification." *Harvard Business Review*. September–October).

Ansoff managed to create a shorthand for all possible strategic direction.

- *Market penetration* is simply selling more of an existing product or service to existing customers. In other words, the business persuades customers to buy more of their favourites. To do this, the strategic approach is to amend the elements of the marketing mix, such as price discounts, new packaging, and better advertising of new improved versions of the product. Kellogg's, for instance, ran a remarkably effective reminder campaign for its cornflakes with the tag line: "Have you forgotten how good they taste?" The campaign was designed to drive retrial of the brand and people who had strayed to new cereals returned to the "original and best" in droves.

[10] Ansoff, I. H. 1957. "Strategies for diversification." *Harvard Business Review*. September–October).

- *Market development* is selling existing products to new markets. Several European retailers, such as Tesco and IKEA, have examined their domestic saturated markets and taken the strategic decision to expand into the relatively untapped markets of Eastern Europe, selling essentially the same range of products, though possibly in different quantities.
- *Product development* is offering existing customers a wider range of products. This could be the development of existing products or innovations in the same product areas.
- *Diversification* is a new strategic direction for the business when it develops new products and offers them to new customers in new markets.

There are different levels of risk associated with each of these strategies. If a business sticks close to its current products and markets, the risks will be lower, because the business has knowledge and experience it can bring to bear. However, risk is often associated with higher profit. Those strategies involving new products and markets carry higher risks, but offer higher potential returns.

It must also be remembered that in each box in the matrix there are different categories of commitment. For instance, market development is the selling of existing products in a new market. That new market could simply be a different region of the country, or it could involve opening a new branch in another country. Clearly, the second scenario is likely to involve a far wider range of business problems and challenges (and therefore risk) than expansion in the home country.

Examiner's note: Strategic decision making

As business and management students you are required to use formalized decision-making models as the basis for planning strategic approaches. Most of these models were discussed in detail in Chapter 1.3. The combination of tools will provide a stronger foundation for strategic planning than the use of an individual technique.

For instance, a plan to expand the business may have been determined by a force field analysis showing that the forces for change are greater than the resistors and by the use of a fishbone diagram identifying that the underlying cause of poor performance is the relatively small size of the business. Managers may then have used Ansoff's matrix to identify a growth strategy and applied a decision tree to identify the expansion option with the greatest financial return and an investment appraisal to indicate the best choice of project for the expansion.

Having decided on the project best suited for expansion, the business may use critical path analysis (see p. 291) to schedule and manage the project, allocate resources, and plan the cash flow required.

In conjunction with Ansoff's matrix, managers may use a position or perception map to identify potential target markets for growth. Figure 6.10 is an example.

Figure 6.10 shows an apparent gap in the market for a low-calorie product, which is offered at a low price. The question for the business is whether it has the strengths to take advantage of this market opportunity, or whether offering a product like this is feasible. The reason there may be a gap in the market is because it is not profitable to produce such a product.

Having planned the customers and market segments to target and any growth strategy, the business will need to select the products it intends to offer its target markets. If the business intends to offer new goods or services (through product development or diversification) it will have to examine these in relation to its existing brands, its corporate culture, and its financial position.

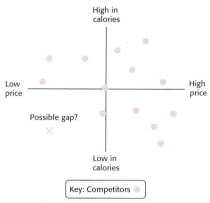

Figure 6.10 A position (or perception) map for a new food product

Product portfolio analysis

Let's return to the BCG matrix (already explored on p. 206–207 and 303). This is a useful, simple, and visual tool, which can provide the basis for a strategic analysis of the organization's product portfolio as well as considering the implications of product development for the organization's cash flow. The matrix can be used to examine products and strategic business units (SBUs).

The strategies that follow from the analysis can also be simplified. One approach provides the following four strategic options:

● sow—invest in R&D and marketing to launch the product on to the market, raise awareness and develop distribution channels
● nurture—provide continuing investment to develop market share further and to enter new markets
● harvest—use the funds generated from sales to finance other products in the portfolio and to improve company cash flows in general
● plough (divest)—remove the product from the portfolio by liquidating the product and its assets, or divest by selling the product to another business.

There are four groups of products in the BCG matrix. For each group it is possible to suggest strategic options.

1 **Question marks—sow**. Question marks (or "problem children") are products with relatively low market in high growth markets. They tend to be large cash users, because the business needs to invest in product development and marketing to raise awareness of them. A new product is regarded as a question mark when launched into a high growth market with an existing market leader. Successful question marks become stars.

If research indicates that a question mark is unlikely ever to achieve significant market share, the business should consider liquidation or divestment (disposing of the investment) of the product and rights, such as patents and licences, before the product becomes a dog. This will allow the business to recoup some of its investment.

The strategic options are:

- market penetration
- market development
- product development
- liquidation or divestment.

2 **Stars—nurture**. Stars are products that have the potential to become cash cows, but still require heavy investment to sustain their growth—so they can be significant cash users. However, as they mature and sales revenues increase, they should become profitable with positive cash flows. Stars are crucial to a business as they provide the basis for long-term growth and profitability.

The strategic options are:

- market penetration
- market development
- product development
- joint ventures and integration.

3 **Cash cows—harvest.** Cash cows have high relative market share in low growth markets. They have high sales and benefit from economies of scale. As the market matures, the need for investment reduces as customers have good knowledge and recall of the product. Cash cows are the most profitable products in the business portfolio and generate valuable cash flow.

Such products should be "milked" or "harvested", extracting the profits and using the cash flow to turn question marks into stars, and stars into cash cows. The cash can also be used to cover administrative costs, to fund R&D, to reduce debt, and to pay dividends to shareholders. As cash cows mature, profits may drop and it is possible that these products turn into dogs as new products enter the market. At this point the business should consider divestment or liquidation.

The strategic options are:

- product development
- extension strategies
- possible liquidation or divestment.

4 **Dogs—plough.** Dogs are products with low market shares in slow growth markets. They tend to be cash neutral—revenues are low, but so is market support and, therefore, costs. They are likely to have been cash cows. They may still be profitable, but probably at a low level. It is also possible that they are now making losses. Managers may retain dogs to provide breadth and balance to the company portfolio or if the item has a fashion element they may believe that future demand could be higher.

The strategic options are:

- liquidation of the product
- divestment if any other business is prepared to purchase.

Successful products will move from question mark through star to cash cow and finally to dog. Unsuccessful products never gain market share and will move straight from question mark to dog.

Limitations of the BCG matrix

Users of the BCG matrix to support strategic planning must be aware of its limitations.

- It is sometimes difficult to identify the stage a product is in.
- Market share and profitability may not be related.
- High growth rate is not the only criteria for profitability.
- The matrix ignores the role of the entire product portfolio. The availability of dogs, for instance, may support the overall image of the company as one that provides a comprehensive range of products.

In fact, businesses may prefer a balanced product portfolio for the following reasons.

- Too few question marks can lead to low growth and a lack of innovation.
- Too many question marks may affect current profitability.
- Too many stars can result in liquidity problems, as they are net cash users.
- Too many cash cows can lead to slow growth, risking lower future profitability.

The business can use the BCG matrix to:

1 examine its current product portfolio and decide on the level of investment for its products
2 develop growth strategies by adding new products while considering whether to remove any of the existing products.

Data response exercise

Look at the product portfolios for company A and company B then answer the questions that follow.

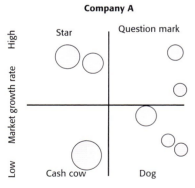

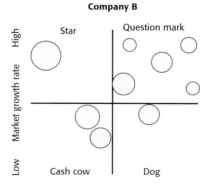

Examination questions

1 Describe the product portfolio of each company. [4 marks]
2 Analyse the relative strengths and weaknesses of each portfolio. [8 marks]
3 Examine what other information you would need to support your analysis of each portfolio. [4 marks]
4 Discuss possible strategies to improve the product portfolios of both companies. [9 marks]

Prepare market forecasts

Data gathered by environmental scanning provides the basis for forecasting future markets and customer needs and setting long-term plans, by extrapolating present trends into the future. Forecasts may be quantitative or qualitative. Quantitative techniques are most appropriate where historic data is available and when there is expected to be some consistency in environments. This forecasting can be achieved by time-series analysis or by other popular forecasting techniques such as statistical modelling, where several trends are linked to examine causal factors. Qualitative techniques such as brainstorming and scenario building are more useful when visioning futures, which are less predictable.

However, organizations must guard against the false assumption that existing patterns and trends will necessarily apply in the future. Significant change in the external environment will make forecasting almost worthless. The complexity of forecasting is the result of technological innovation, changing social and cultural values, unstable economic conditions, changing governments and unexpected events such as wars and severe weather. Forecasts are only as good as the information on which they are based. As they say in the computer industry: "Garbage in, garbage out."

Benchmarking

Having conducted audits on their markets and competition, organizations will use this information as a basis for their strategic planning. One application of market research is to undertake **best practice benchmarking** (BPB) to help the business become as good as, or better than, the best in the world in the most important aspects of their operations. Benchmarking provides "market intelligence" information for the business, allowing it to measure its quality and production against the highest standards in the industry.

Companies worldwide have found that there are very significant gains to be made from the BPB approach. The benefits organizations gain through benchmarking are:

- a better understanding of their customers and competitors
- fewer complaints and more satisfied customers
- a reduction in waste, quality problems and reworking
- a faster awareness of important innovations
- a stronger reputation in their markets
- increased profits and sales turnover.

BPB—five questions that organizations should ask

1 **What are we going to benchmark?** To discover which issues are most important for customers, the most effective way is to ask them. Benchmarks important for customer satisfaction might include:

   - consistency and quality of products
   - correct invoices and discount opportunities for early payment
   - speed of service and delivery.

2 **Who are we going to benchmark against?** One obvious method is to ask customers who they think is best at a particular activity. Another is to ask industry observers, such as journalists

and academics. Benchmarking against direct competitors is difficult as relevant data can be hard to collect—few direct competitors will cooperate. However, a business can look for comparisons with companies in totally different industries against specific activities, such as the time between customer order and delivery. Here information should be easier to get as companies will not see those carrying out the benchmarking as a direct threat.

3 How will we get the information? A great deal of the information is available in magazines and newspapers, in trade association reports and in specialist databases. Finding a benchmarking partner is possible if the information exchanged has mutual benefits.

4 How will we analyse the information?
- Quantify it, as closely as possible.
- Make sure we are comparing like with like.
- Identify key areas for improvement in the organizations involved.

5 How will we use the information?
- Set new standards for the performance and communicate these to everyone concerned, along with an explanation of why standards have been raised.
- Make a senior manager responsible for devising an action plan to reach the new standards.
- Provide the resources for employees to carry out additional research, if necessary.
- Monitor progress so that the plan really does come into effect.

Source: Section on five BPB questions adapted from: www.motorsport100.co.uk/ pdocs/benchmarking.pdf

Firms should continuously benchmark, as today's best practice rapidly becomes tomorrow's common practice.

Contingency planning

A strategic plan will be based upon certain assumptions about the firm, the market, and the external environment. When developing the strategic plan, managers should pose "What if…?" questions, for example the following.

- What if the price of oil rose faster than expected?
- What if economic growth fell unexpectedly?
- What if a new competitor entered the market?
- What if a new technology made our product out of date?

Contingency planning is the development of a fallback position to address specific threats or opportunities that may emerge and affect the strategic direction of the business.

Contingency planning makes the assumption that the unexpected event can be predicted and that there are solutions that can be implemented, but if the event is significant, such as world recession, it is unlikely that the business will be able to plan for all the likely consequences.

6 Business strategy

Strategic implementation—how is the business going to achieve its objectives?

> "I keep six honest serving-men
> (They taught me all I knew);
> Their names are What and Why and When
> And How and Where and Who."
>
> Rudyard Kipling, Just So Stories

How can the business gain competitive advantage, for example in terms of Porter's three generic strategies (see p. 332)?

- What new product should be developed and what new technologies could be applied?
- How can differentiation be achieved?
- Should the business refocus on core competence and who is best to manage the process?
  — de-mergers and divestment
  — management buyouts.
- How should the business plan for changes in the size of business operations?
  — selecting appropriate scale operations: economies and diseconomies of scale
  — workforce planning
  — developing flexible working patterns, such as homeworking and/or applying mobile technologies
  — introducing flexible organizational structures, for example Handy's shamrock of core, peripheral, and part-time staff (see p. 97)
  — flattening hierarchies
  — dynamic decision making and flexible organization structures, for example Mintzberg's models (see p. 105)
  — analysing and reviewing communication structures
  — reviewing management and leadership styles
  — developing resources: investment appraisal recruitment, training, and multiskilling new ICT.

If growth is an objective, how best can this be achieved and what safeguards should be put in place?

- What growth methods can and should be selected?
  — internal or organic growth
  — external growth: mergers and acquisitions.
- What marketing strategies can be implemented?
  — market leadership and market penetration
  — segmentation, targeting, and positioning
  — distribution chain management
  — e-commerce.
- Should the business incorporate CSR and ethical approaches?
- How can sales, manufacturing and operations be globalized?
  — offshoring of operations and job migration
  — outsourcing business activities
  — strategic alliances, joint ventures, and mergers
  — decentralization and the development of regional headquarters
  — multicultural and international cultures
  — ethical and moral considerations
  — CSR.
- How can change be effectively managed?
  — developing a change culture
  — contingency planning and crisis management.

Source: Adapted from the IB Diploma Programme Business and Management Guide

Once the mission statement, aims, and objectives have been agreed and business plans drawn up, it is the responsibility of senior managers to control the identified strategic direction of the business through appropriate programmes, budgets, and procedures.

In practice, this will mean that managers have to set time periods or planning horizons, within which planned strategic activities should be carried out and the actual results of these activities compared with desired outcomes. At this point a "strategic gap" may be acknowledged. This is where there is a difference between the desired performance levels and the forecast performance levels (see Figure 6.11).

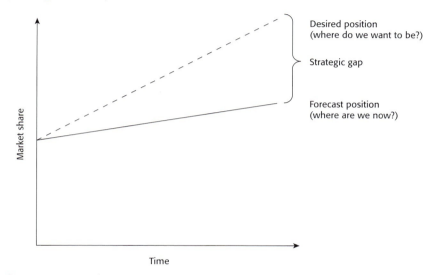

Figure 6.11 Strategic gap

Gap analysis is a very useful tool for managers. A strategic gap shows the need for a change in strategic direction and the implementation of alternative strategic approaches.

The need to change strategic direction may be triggered by a range of different events such as:

- a new managing director or CEO
- a risk to the business from a sudden and significant change in the market-place, for example a new technology or recession
- a threat of takeover by another business
- a sudden change in performance levels leading to reduced profits and revenues, or possibly losses.

Case study

US Treasury rescue for Fannie Mae and Freddie Mac

Treasury secretary looks at $15 billion cash injection for crisis-hit mortgage lenders

US Treasury secretary Hank Paulson is working on plans to inject up to $15 billion of capital into Fannie Mae and Freddie Mac to stem the crisis at America's biggest mortgage firms.

The two companies lost almost half their market value last week as rumours of a government bail-out swept the stock markets, hammering share prices around the world. Together, the two stockholder-owned, government-sponsored companies own or guarantee almost half of America's $12 trillion home-loan market and are vital to the functioning of the housing market.

Under the terms of the proposed move, the US government would receive a new class of shares in exchange for the capital, which would be hugely dilutive to shareholders.

Both banks are expected to post sizeable losses for the second quarter, and reveal plans to sell off billions of dollars' worth of assets.

Source: TimesOnline, 13 July 2008

Programmes, budgets, and procedures

Strategic implementation is the process by which strategies are put into action through the development of appropriate programmes, budgets and procedures.

Programmes include any action plans to meet the organization's mission, objectives, or goals. For example:

- the development of a marketing mix for a product or product line
- changing corporate culture and management styles
- recruitment drives and training initiatives
- automation of production processes
- outsourcing company activities
- expansion overseas
- adopting new communication technologies.

Budgets are statements of the organization's programmes in financial terms. They are controlling mechanisms in that they set financial targets for programmes in terms of costs and revenues as a measure of meeting performance targets. They also allow a business to evaluate the success of its strategy. For instance, businesses will often set a Return on Investment (ROI) as a performance measure for a project.

Procedures describe the steps required to achieve particular aspects of a programme. These tend to be more tactical in nature as they relate to smaller activities that contribute to an overall strategy. For example, they may relate to elements of the marketing mix, such as improved channels of distribution or the implementation of just-in-time (JIT) management.

Strategic programmes and action plans

Setting excellent strategic plans does not guarantee effective implementation of those plans. Many businesses repeatedly fail to motivate their employees enough to turn their plans into sustainable competitive advantage. A *Fortune* magazine study suggested that 70% of companies that fail to meet their corporate objectives do so not because of bad strategy, but because of bad execution.

"When it comes to the future, there are three kinds of people: those who let it happen, those who make it happen, and those who wonder what happened."

John M. Richardson, American University, Washington

As we have seen, to achieve corporate objectives and strategic aims, organizations must:

- communicate the desired strategic direction and corporate objectives
- use rigorous project management principles to drive the implementation of their strategy
- appoint motivated and task-driven individuals to key posts
- set clear and measurable individual targets (SMART targets) for managers and planning horizons consistent with their strategic priorities
- consistently monitor and measure progress against targets and provide feedback about performance
- develop an appropriate customer focus.

Kenichi Ohmae's 3Cs strategic model

Kenichi Ohmae is one of the world's leading business and corporate strategists. For 23 years, he was a senior partner in the international management consulting firm McKinsey & Company. He is known as "Mr Strategy" and in 1994 was voted by *The Economist* as "one of the world's top five management gurus".

Like Mintzberg, Ohmae believes that successful business strategies do not come from rigorous analysis, but from a thought process that is basically creative and intuitive rather than rational. In 1975, Ohmae outlined his "three Cs" framework.[11]

Ohmae stresses that a strategist must focus on three key factors for success:

- the customer
- the corporation
- the competition.

Only by integrating these three Cs (corporation, customer, competitors) in a strategic triangle, can a sustained competitive advantage exist.

"It helps to base your strategy on things that won't change. When I'm talking with people outside the company, there's a question that comes up very commonly: 'What's going to change in the next five to ten years?' But I very rarely get asked 'What's not going to change in the next five to ten years?' At Amazon we're always trying to figure that out, because you can really spin up flywheels around those things. All the energy you invest in them today will still be paying you dividends ten years from now.

"Whereas if you base your strategy first and foremost on more transitory things—who your competitors are, what kind of technologies are available, and so on—those things are going to change so rapidly that you're going to have to change your strategy very rapidly, too."
Jeff Bezos (1964–), president, CEO and chairman of Amazon.com

Source: "The Institutional Yes". *Harvard Business Review*. October 2007.

"There is no doubt that a corporation's foremost concern ought to be the interests of its customers rather than that of its stockholders and other parties. In the long run, the corporation that is genuinely interested in its customers is the one that will be interesting to investors."
Kenichi Ohmae

[11] Ohmae, K. 1975. *The Mind of the Strategist: The art of Japanese business*. New York. McGraw-Hill.

6 Business strategy

Customer-based strategies

Ohmae believes that customer-based strategies must be the basis of all strategy.

To achieve customer focus and differentiate the business from its competitors, the strategist should segment the market as follows.

- Segment by **objectives**—that is, differentiation is achieved in terms of customers' use of a product. Take alcohol, for example. Some customers buy alcohol purely for the pleasure of drinking it, while others see alcohol as the focus for social interactions. Others may buy alcohol, wine for example, for investment purposes. The business must recognize all these different uses, so that it can focus its efforts on its target market.
- Segment by **customer coverage**—the organization's focus is to optimize its range of market coverage based, for example, on geography or age, so that its marketing costs will be lower than the competition's.

To maintain competitive advantage, it is necessary for businesses to research their target market regularly to review customers' needs and wants.

Corporate-based strategies

This approach aims to maximize the corporation's strengths relative to the competition in the functional areas that are critical to success in the industry. If the business gains a decisive edge in one key function, it will eventually be able to pull ahead of the competition in other functions. For example, a business is able to improve its cost effectiveness by employing these three basic methods.

- It can reduce basic costs much more effectively than the competition.
- It can be more selective in accepting orders. Sometimes organizations should reject orders and potential customers if they will contribute little revenue in relation to the operational costs.
- It can share key functions with other businesses, especially when these are extremely expensive. For instance, car manufacturers often share R&D costs.

Competitor-based strategies

Competitor-based strategies, according to Kenichi Ohmae, can be constructed by looking at possible sources of differentiation in functions ranging from purchasing, design, and engineering to sales, and servicing. Differentiation can be achieved by:

- promoting heavily to create a powerful brand image and brand loyalty
- lowering costs and price to win market share
- offering variable dealer incentives, guaranteeing the dealer a larger percentage of each extra unit sold.

Increasing environmental uncertainty means that businesses must develop strategic flexibility where they have the ability to shift from one dominant strategy to another.

"If you're competitor focused, you tend to slack off when your benchmarks say that you're the best. But if you focus on customers, you keep improving. So there are a lot of advantages."
Jeff Bezos, president, CEO and chairman of Amazon.

Did you know?

The problem of obesity is increasing in most developed countries. Some clothing companies have dealt with this issue by:

- increasing standard sizes so customers believe they still fit their regular size
- incorporating "active waists" (elasticated waists) in trousers and skirts
- incorporating inserts that allow clothes still to fit after someone has put on weight, so allowing people to avoid the issue of their weight gain.

Even if a strategic change is relatively minor, it can have significant implications for the sales and the overall success of the business. It helps create total customer satisfaction.

Porter proposed a three-stage analysis to determine and execute a competitive strategy:

1 Analyse and choose the industry in which to compete (five forces—see p. 190).
2 Analyse and choose the organization's competitive strategy (generic strategies—see p. 332).
3 Implement the strategy by managing the firm's activities (value chain analysis—see below).

We have already examined Porter's five forces and generic strategies in some detail. To develop these into an executable strategy, we now consider the final element of Porter's three-stage approach, value chain analysis.

Porter's value chain analysis

Porter first described the value chain in 1985.[12] The value chain consists of a series of activities that create and build value, contributing to the total value delivered by an organization.

Products pass through all activities of the chain in order and at each activity the product gains some value. This is easy to see in manufacturing, where the manufacturer "adds value" by taking a raw material of little use to the end user (for example, wood pulp) and converting it into something that people are prepared to pay for (paper).

Porter recommended that the activities of a business should be grouped under two headings.

Primary activities are activities directly concerned with creating and delivering a product, such as operations management, logistics (warehousing, transport, and stock control), and marketing and sales.

Any or all of these primary activities may be vital in developing a competitive advantage. For example, logistics activities are critical for a provider of distribution services.

Support activities are activities that support the primary activities by increasing the efficiency of the organization, such as HR management.

Value chain analysis seeks to identify which activities are best undertaken by a business and which are best *outsourced* to specialist organizations. The choice of activities to outsource depends on what strategy the business is pursuing.

If the business intends to build competitive advantage through differentiation based on offering higher quality, it will have to perform its value chain activities better than its competitors. By contrast, a strategy based on cost leadership will require a reduction in the costs associated with the value chain activities, or a reduction in the total amount of resources used. This may lead to outsourcing of non-core functions.

Value chain analysis is a three-step process:

● *Activity analysis*. Identify the activities the business undertakes to deliver the product or service.

---

[12] Porter, M. E. 1985. *Competitive Advantage: Creating and sustaining superior performance*. New York. Free Press.

- *Value analysis*. For each activity, assess the potential for adding value via cost advantage or differentiation, or identify current activities where a business appears to be at a competitive disadvantage.
- *Evaluation and planning*. Develop strategies built around focusing on activities where competitive advantage can be sustained.

Strategy and organizational change

Changes in strategy may require organizations to examine their structure and the size of the business and its operations.

Strategic change may require any of the following.

- *Downsizing*. This involves the reduction in size of the business in terms of the number of employees or the layers of management and may include the closure of divisions, factories, subsidiaries, and so on. The intention is to make the business more efficient and cost effective in its operations and may be forced by changes in economic conditions or by a more competitive market.
- *Re-engineering*. This is a radical approach where all existing structures are re-examined and a totally new structure developed. This approach was first proposed by Hammer and Champy (1993).[13] The authors promoted the idea that sometimes redesign and reorganization of a business is necessary to lower costs and increase quality. They believe that the design of workflow in most organizations is based on assumptions about technology, people, and organizational goals that are no longer valid.
- *Growth*. Organizational growth is one of the main objectives of many businesses.

Growth strategies

Why do businesses consider growth strategies? The advantages of growth for stakeholders include:

- increased profits and shareholder value
- higher dividends for shareholders
- capital gains from rising share prices
- profits to finance future business expansion
- increasing market share and market power
- monopoly power providing the opportunity for premium pricing
- economies of scale
- lower average cost and higher profit margins
- greater status for owners and managers.

Growth can be of two basic types. One is **internal** or natural (organic) growth—when the organization increases naturally in size through:

- increased demand and sales revenue
- expanding range (scope) of products
- selling products in new locations
- investment in capital and labour inputs.

---

[13] Hammer and Champy. 1993. *Reengineering the Corporation: A manifesto for business revolution*. New York. Harper Collins.

The other type of growth is **external** growth. This is an instantaneous growth through the joining or integration of two or more businesses. This can be achieved through:

- a merger, where two organizations combine to become one new organization
- a takeover, where one organization acquires another and makes it part of its existing business by buying over 51% of its shares. The takeover is often unwanted and resisted and said to be "unfriendly".

Similar advantages to mergers and takeovers can be achieved by working together with another organization for a single project or a fixed period, by operating a joint venture. This was the case when Swatch and Mercedes produced the Smart car.

Integration can be of different types, as shown in Figure 6.12.

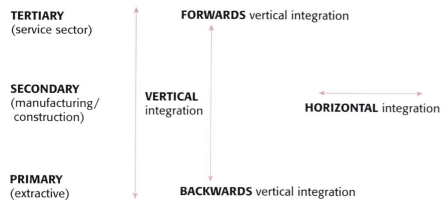

Figure 6.12 Types of integration

Vertical integration describes the joining of firms in different levels of the production chain, for example a brewery taking over a bar (forwards vertical integration) or a supermarket taking over a food manufacturer (backwards vertical integration). **Horizontal** integration describes two organizations joining in the same level of production, for example Ford and Mazda.

If an organization owns all the operations in its distribution channel it is said to be **totally vertically integrated**. For example, BP owns oil rigs, oil tankers and pipes, refineries, and petrol stations.

When a business acquires different businesses in other industries and levels, the resulting organization is called a **conglomerate**. If the business has branches or factories in different countries, it is then referred to as a **multinational company**.

Dangerous liaisons: mergers and acquisitions

HayGroup

More than 90% of corporate mergers and acquisitions [M&As] fall short of their objectives, as companies struggle to combine corporate cultures and structures, according to the results of a major study carried out in 2007 by global management consultancy Hay Group.

The study of senior business leaders, with M&A experience, revealed that just 9% of mergers are considered "completely successful" in achieving their objectives. Hay Group studied over 200 European M&As during 2004–07. The report makes worrying reading in the light of the frenetic acquisitions boom of 2006, when deals topped an eye-popping €1.35 trillion.

More than half of business leaders believe that neglecting non-financial assets such as business culture increases the danger of making a wrong acquisition. The report author David Derain, European M&A Director at Hay Group said,

"The enormous amounts invested in M&A are not delivering their promised value. Business leaders must recognise that the value of today's companies is primarily in their intangible assets—the strategic, people, and cultural factors that don't show up on a balance sheet. A strategic focus on aligning the intangible as well as tangible assets of companies is critical to the success of any merger or acquisition. Business culture represents a class of assets which must be protected and properly aligned if a merger is to succeed."

A little over a quarter of organizations questioned analysed the cultural compatibility of the organizations to be merged. Crucially, two thirds also failed to prioritize a leadership capability review. According to executives, 78% of acquired company employees opposed the mergers, 50% of them actively.

In addition, well over a third of business leaders expressed dissatisfaction with the post-merger climate, with one fifth describing the early months as "culture shock" and a further 16% going so far as to label them 'trench warfare'.

Source: www.haygroup.com, 26 March 2007

Alternatively, a business may reduce the size of its operations. This may be in response to poor market conditions, recession, reduced demand, or increased competition. This will usually involve the selling of productive assets or whole subsidiaries, and/or the retrenchment of staff through voluntary or compulsory redundancy. The purpose is to reduce the costs of the business so that it can compete more effectively.

If an integrated organization decides to split the business up or sell off some of its businesses, this is referred to as a **de-merger** or **de-integration**. The purpose of this is to concentrate on competitive strengths or core competences, or a sign that the original merger was unsuccessful.

Case study

AOL-Time Warner

In 2001, the merger of AOL-Time Warner was hailed as a brilliant vision of the future; a company with the ability to deliver all manner of entertainment to the world over the world wide web. Everything from *Time* magazine to popular TV series would be delivered to people's desks, their homes and their hand-held computers. It was a $125 billion deal bonding the magic of Hollywood films, the TV news of CNN and the all-conquering technology of the Internet as supplied by AOL. The merger bought together three billionaire entrepreneurs, Ted Turner of CNN, Steve Case of AOL, and the movie maker Gerald Levin.

Two years later, the company formed from the world's biggest, brightest, and most revolutionary business merger reported losses of an astonishing $110 billion, a sum equivalent to the total wealth of a medium-sized country

such as Ireland. Ted Turner was expelled from the Board of Directors. In fact, 75% of AOL-Time Warner's sales still came from the traditional businesses of publishing, film making and cable subscriptions. Overvalued Internet shares, including AOL, crashed dramatically worldwide. More damaging was that revenues from the media parts of the new conglomerate were undermined by pirating (illegal downloading) of films and music using Internet sites, often provided by AOL!

Mega-mergers almost never fulfill their promise. Research shows that, more often than not, they destroy the value which comes with more focused management. By bringing together three extraordinarily different corporate cultures, the creativity was certain to result in a clash of empires and egos. AOL has admitted it overstated its sales in its accounts and is now under federal investigation. AOL-Time Warner will be remembered as a star that burned itself out in record time.

Jeff Bewkes, the new boss of Time Warner appointed in 2002, had plans to break up the company and was then widely expected to reshape Time Warner into a much smaller company by selling or spinning off some of its

6 Business strategy

businesses such as AOL, possibly to Microsoft or Yahoo. In 2003 AOL was still a problem. Most of its revenues came from its Internet access business, which was in decline.

Source: Adapted from: "End of the empire of mighty egos." *Daily Mail*, January, 2003, and *The Economist*, November 2007

Examination questions

Refer to the AOL-Time Warner case study and answer these questions.

1 Define corporate culture. [4 marks]

2 Explain the problems that AOL-Time Warner may have faced in merging two different corporate cultures. [4 marks]

3 With reference to AOL-Time Warner, analyse the advantages and disadvantages of organizational growth through mergers and acquisitions. [6 marks]

4 Analyse the reasons why Bewkes planned to break up the company. [6 marks]

Global growth and global strategy

In today's global economy the time taken to move around the world has significantly reduced and instant communication has been made possible through satellite technologies and the Internet. There are few industries untouched by global competitive forces. Businesses recognizing the realities of the global market-place have been forced to develop new strategic approaches to how they conduct their business.

Companies such as Sony and Unilever have developed global distribution and marketing networks, based on 'powerbrands', market leading brands that are recognizable in nearly every country in the world.

"Fundamentally, globalization is the closer integration of countries and peoples of the world which has been brought about by the enormous reductions of costs of transport and communications and the breaking down of artificial barriers to the flow of goods, services, capital, knowledge, and to a lesser extent, people across borders."

Joseph Stiglitz (1943–), former chief economist at the World Bank

Case study

Global brand identity

It's no accident that most of the companies with the biggest increases in brand value operate as single brands everywhere in the world. Global marketing used to mean crafting a new name and identity for each local market. The No. 1 laundry detergent in the US, Tide, is called Ariel in Europe, for example. The goal today for many, though, is to create consistency and impact, both of which are a lot easier to manage with a single worldwide identity. It's also a more efficient approach, since the same strategy can be used everywhere. An eBay shopper in Paris, France, sees the same screen as someone logging in from Paris, Texas. Only the language is different.

Global banks HSBC, which posted a 20% increase in brand value and UBS, up 16%, use the same advertising pitches around the world. "Given how hard the consumer is to reach today, a strong and unified brand message is increasingly becoming the only way to break through," says Jan Lindemann, Interbrand's managing director, who directed the Top 100 Brands ranking. Possibly no brand has done a better job of mining the potential of these new brand-building principles than Korean consumer electronics manufacturer Samsung Electronics Co. Since 2002 Samsung has posted the biggest gain in value of any Global 100 brand. Even sweeter, in 2004 Samsung surpassed Sony, a far more entrenched rival that once owned the electronics category, in overall brand value.

Now LG Electronics Inc. has followed its rival's playbook and has sought to elevate its product under a single brand.

Many young brands that scored big gains in brand value, like Google, Yahoo!, and eBay, depend on their own interactive websites to shout about their brands.

Source: Adapted from BusinessWeek.com

Key features of a global strategy

In this section we'll pick up some of the issues already outlined in relation to marketing.

Since every organization's strategy, market, and competitive advantage is unique, it is impossible to define one single, perfect, organizational structure for an international business. However, there are key aspects to be considered when developing a global strategy.

Businesses need to "think global, act local". Many multinationals try to develop a global marketing mix that recognizes and retains regional and national differences.

Did you know?

According to the *Malaysian Star*, "Worldwide consumer research has found that while people appreciated the value of international organizations and services, they questioned the prevailing 'one size fits all' global model."

Consumers want to be treated as individuals and to feel that the companies care about them, recognize their needs and understand what makes their community unique. This was one key finding from research partly completed in Malaysia, which led to the HSBC's brand launch as "The world's local bank".

The old saying "Think global, act local" may not be an earth-shattering concept for some, but it is a reality that has been ignored in the rush in Asia for global brands. The power of the global brand is beyond question, but research has shown an increasing disaffection for "things global", in various manifestations.

Source: Adapted from www.asiamarketresearch.com

- Businesses developing a global strategy need to identify the elements of the product that can be standardized across markets, and those which need to be customized. A globally standardized product can be produced at a low cost, but may end up pleasing few customers. On the other hand, customized products targeted at different markets across the world may be too expensive.
- Concentrating on a narrower range of universal brands and products is inviting as the business can benefit from economies of large-scale production, marketing, and distribution, but it is important for businesses to recognize that customer preferences vary across countries.
- As mentioned in earlier chapters, businesses in a global market must be aware of religious and cultural issues: businesses should employ local experts to ensure that products and promotions do not violate any cultural norms.

"When it comes to product strategy, managing in a borderless economy doesn't mean managing by averages. It doesn't mean that all tastes run together into one amorphous mass of universal appeal. And it doesn't mean that the appeal of operating globally removes the obligation to localize products. The lure of a universal product is a false allure."

Kenichi Ohmae (1990)[14]

[14] Ohmae, K. 1990. *The Borderless World*. New York. Harper Collins.

6 Business strategy

Entering overseas markets

Businesses aiming to grow through international expansion can enter markets by a variety of routes. These include:

- exporting—the business makes the products at home and then sends them to the country of consumption
- franchising—the business sells the right to trade under its name and logo
- licensing—almost the same as franchising but in this case a business buys the right to produce your goods
- joint venture—two or more companies join together to fulfill a particular contract
- direct investment—a business sets up the means of producing and distributing products in an overseas market
- mergers and takeovers—a business buys another that is operating in the country in which the business wants to sell its products.

Problems of marketing overseas

- *Exporting*. There are potential operating issues associated with the choice of expansion routes. There is a lack of control over the marketing of the product, especially if sales are via an agent. To counter this some companies set up fully-owned subsidiaries.
- *Franchising*. The franchisee keeps some of the profits. The franchisor is also dependent on the franchisee to maintain the quality and reputation of the brand, though ultimately most franchise agreements would allow for removal of the franchise. This may be too late to prevent damage to the brand's reputation.
- *Licensing*. Although the goods are actually produced abroad, which saves costs, the quality control is not directly the responsibility of the original company.
- *Joint ventures*. The risks are shared by those participating in the venture but conflicts can arise and the venture may disintegrate.
- *Direct investment*. This appears to have few problems associated with it, as long as the initial investment can be afforded.
- *Mergers and takeovers*. The joined businesses may suffer from "culture shock" and internal rivalry.

Ethical global strategies and corporate social responsibility (CSR)

As recently as a decade ago, many companies viewed business ethics only in terms of administrative compliance with legal standards. Today the situation is different. Attention to business ethics is on the rise across the world and organizations realize that, in order to succeed, they must earn the respect and confidence of their customers. Being seen as ethical by taking responsibility for the impact of its activities on stakeholders and the environment, and implementing strategic CSR programmes, can provide the business with competitive advantage when expanding overseas.

Potential business benefits of ethics and social responsibility

- *HR management*. A CSR programme can help recruitment and retention. It can also improve motivation of employees, particularly when they become involved with local communities through fundraising activities or community volunteering.

- *Risk management*. Managing risk is a core element of corporate strategy. Reputations that take decades to build up can be ruined in hours through incidents such as corruption scandals or environmental accidents, which draw unwanted attention from courts, governments, and media. Building a genuine culture of "doing the right thing" can offset these risks.

- *Brand differentiation*. In crowded global market-places, CSR can play a role in building customer loyalty based on distinctive ethical values and a reputation for integrity and best practice.

- *Licence to operate*. Firms are keen to avoid interference in their business through taxation or regulations. By taking voluntary steps, they can persuade governments and the wider public that they are taking issues such as health and safety, diversity, or the environment seriously, and so avoid intervention. Those operating overseas can make sure they stay welcome by being good corporate citizens.

Read more about ethics and CSR on p. 34–40.

Case study

The IKEA Group participates in a wide range of activities internationally, nationally, and locally.

An organization called the IKEA Social Initiative handles social involvement on a global level. We work together with UNICEF and Save the Children to fight for children's rights to a healthy and secure childhood with access to quality education. Our projects take a holistic approach: improving the health of women and children, creating access to a quality education, and empowering women to create a better future for themselves and their communities.

Regarding environmental involvement, the IKEA Group works with WWF, the global conservation organization, on projects that support responsible forestry, better cotton management, and to reduce our impact on climate change.

Improving children's rights in India

The IKEA Social Initiative supports a project, run by UNICEF, promoting child rights in the northern Indian state of Uttar Pradesh, from where IKEA sources many of its carpets. The aim is to prevent and eliminate child labour in the carpet belt by addressing root causes such as debt, poverty, lack of access to education, disability and ill health.

Source: www.ikea.com/gb/en/

Discuss and analyse the value of IKEA operating a CSR programme to **four** of its stakeholder groups.

Evaluation and control—how does a business know its strategy is successful?

All strategic decision-making processes require an important final stage—that of evaluation and control. Evaluation is deciding on how well the planned process has gone. Control is required when things are not going to plan. In these circumstances, managers must take corrective action before the plan fails.

All organizations need objective measures to monitor performance by comparing actual performance with planned or desired performance. Managers use feedback from these measures to take corrective action where necessary to address any identified problems. At this stage, we can use some more of the business tools identified in this book. For example, we can employ variance analysis, performance ratios, and financial accounts as measures of financial performance. These financial measures provide feedback to stakeholders, such as managers, employees, and shareholders and provide a learning process for the business. Other measures that can be used to measure performance include:

- productivity, for example sales per employee, sales per square foot
- staff turnover and absence
- market share and market growth
- quality standards
- customer satisfaction
- environmental impact.

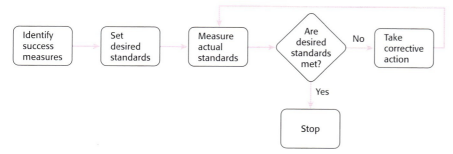

Figure 6.13 The evaluation and control process

Identify success measures

Determining which objectives are most important in evaluating strategic success can be difficult. The evaluation of strategy can be based on both quantitative and qualitative measures. Managers must identify the measures that are most significant to the operations of that particular business and the measures usually employed in the industry. The criteria will be influenced by the size of the business, the strategy being pursued, and the management philosophy.

Measures may be internal and external. The organization should not just look internally, but must relate measures of success to what competitors are doing. After all, if competitors change their strategies, this can have a significant impact on the relevance of the measures applied to the organization. Whatever measures are selected they must be possible to measure in a reasonably objective and consistent manner.

Set desired standards

Setting desired standards of performance can be difficult if the venture undertaken is new or unusual. In a dynamic environment, key internal and external factors can change quickly and dramatically, so managers must keep their measures under constant review. Improvements in competitors' performance may push up the bar of success.

Performance standards are normally set for all stages of the production process, not simply for the final output. It is common practice to allow an acceptable tolerance range for performance; otherwise management would be investigating small and relatively unimportant variations in performance the whole time.

Measure actual standards

Measurement of performance will be made at times that fit with other reporting periods. Clearly all firms will report annually, but measurement may occur at other times to assist with management control and to coincide with management reviews and appraisal.

Are desired standards met?

Is performance within tolerance? If it is, measurement will stop. This is often called management by exception. Action is only taken if there is an identified problem.

Take corrective action

If actual results are not within tolerance, managers will act to identify the problem and take some corrective action. To begin with, they will have to establish an underlying cause and then establish whether the original standards set are appropriate. If they are, managers will have to make changes to bring performance back within tolerance. These changes can include:

- altering the organization's structure
- replacing individuals in key positions
- reviewing and revising the mission statement
- selling underperforming assets
- offering performance-related pay and other incentives
- altering product and service ranges
- re-evaluating the strategic direction.

Measuring performance

Without objective measures of performance, it would be almost impossible to judge the success of a business strategy. The business has to identify key areas of measurement. These will probably relate to:

- the value of the organization's outputs
- the way it achieved its outputs
- the resources employed.

The measurement of the organization's outputs is normally quantifiable and relate to aspects of the business which can be measured according to standardized criteria. For example, the key measure of success used by most organizations is **ROI** (return on investment). In general terms, this is the income that an investment provides in a year relative to the amount of money invested. ROI measures the profit or loss of a business by dividing the net income by its total assets. This is a crucial measure because it is influenced by everything that happens in a business, from resource management to selling effectiveness. Other profitability, liquidity, activity, and stakeholder ratios will provide alternative objective measures of performance (see p. 174–9).

The ways in which a business achieves its results are not always so easy to measure. However, businesses will seek to judge their environmental impacts, how employees perform their jobs and the quality of the business operations. Organizations may use customer satisfaction surveys to judge how employees sell products and services and apply internationally accepted standards such as ISO 9000 to measure quality. An environmental impact audit will examine aspects such as pollution and waste.

Resource measures are often used in the service sector when the value of outputs is difficult to quantify. In a hospital, for instance, the organization can set measures related to the employment of doctors and nurses with appropriate skills and knowledge. Benchmarking these against other similar hospitals can provide a more objective measure.

The balanced scorecard

The balanced scorecard is an important tool used to evaluate strategy by many of the world's largest companies. It was introduced by Kaplan and Norton (1996).[15] The balanced scorecard allows businesses to measure their effectiveness in four areas.

- Financial performance—how well is the business maximizing shareholder value?
- Customers—how satisfied are the organization's customers?
- Technology and innovation—how well is the business improving and creating value in terms of technology, innovation, quality, and operational efficiency?
- Core competence—how is the business maintaining and improving its competitive advantage?

The business then identifies and quantifies several goals in each of the areas to use as measures of performance and allocates responsibility for the target to specific managers. For instance, it could measure average costs for efficiency and market share for customer satisfaction. The selected measures are regarded as key performance measures for the achievement of the chosen strategic option.

Some businesses may identify other objectives to be included on the scorecard, such as performance in the areas of business ethics or CSR.

---

[15] See for example Kaplan, R. S. and Norton, D. P. 1996. *Using the Balanced Scorecard as a Strategic Management System*. Harvard Business School Press.

HL

Data response exercise

Read the text below and answer the questions that follow it.

Case study

VW and Skoda: An Eastern European success

Registered Trademark of ŠKODA AUTO a.s.

The Skoda story is one which brings together many of the strategic issues discussed in the strategy chapter and in previous topics. Founded in 1895 in Czechoslovakia to manufacture motorbikes, Skoda began to manufacture cars ten years later, but remained only a minnow in the European car industry. Its downward slide began soon after the war ended, when the company came under state control and produced some of the worst models of its time.

However, Skoda retained a monopoly in car manufacturing in Czechoslovakia until the Soviet Bloc crumbled in the "Velvet Revolution" of 1989. Now, Skoda began to operate in a free market environment. Regarded as "cheap and cheerful", there was a steady stream of exports destined for bargain hunters in Europe, who were prepared to pay money for a set of wheels, no matter how bad they were. However, during this period Skoda developed a terrible reputation that, even today, hinders the company's progress.

Despite everything that was wrong with Skoda, the Volkswagen Group, seeing a potential for growth, acquired 30% stake of the business in April 1991 and, with it, total management control. Volkswagen decided not to scrap the Skoda brand despite its poor image in some European countries. The Skoda brand still commanded respect in Eastern Europe.

Skoda began operating as Volkswagen's fourth brand, after VW, Audi, and Seat. By 1993, more than half of all Skoda models sold in the European Community were going to Germany, where they underpriced Volkswagen models by 20%. Another important market was the United Kingdom, which imported about 10,000 of the vehicles a year.

In 1995, Volkswagen increased its shareholding further to 70%, with investment now totalling more than $1.5 billion in the company. Market research confirmed high brand awareness in Europe, even though it was often for the wrong reasons. Volkswagen's association with Skoda provided greater quality assurance, although it was evident that the company had a huge task on its hands to change customer perceptions in several countries. In the UK, for instance, after years of poor quality models, the brand was the subject of ridicule and a whole series of jokes including:

Question: How do you double the value of a Skoda?

Answer: Fill it up with petrol.

Question: Why does a Skoda have a heated rear windscreen?

Answer: To keep your hands warm when you push it.

Skoda spent millions of pounds on advertising in the UK in an effort to persuade potential customers that the brand was now desirable. To do this the reality of the product had to fit. Volkswagen recognized the need to streamline Skoda's production process and improve its efficiency and quality control. It invested heavily in Skoda's manufacturing base, creating some of the most advanced car assembly factories in the world and introducing total quality management across all business functions.

Skoda has three manufacturing plants in the Czech Republic and others in Poland, Bosnia, Ukraine, and India. The factory in Mlada Boleslav is the jewel in the crown and assembles the Octavia and Fabia models as well as components for other Volkswagen brands. It is described as a "fractal factory", with work carried out by small teams working together. Individuals concentrate on the overall task rather than on the single parts and pre-assembled components feed into the central "spine" from the sides likes "ribs". Uniquely in Europe, four suppliers, including Siemens, have production facilities actually within the factory. All Skoda's other suppliers are linked to the production control system on a just-in-time (JIT) basis.

The 1998, the Octavia model was built on the Volkswagen group platform in order to achieve maximum economies of scale. Like other auto manufacturers, Volkswagen used existing automobile platforms, which cost billions of dollars to develop, as the bases for multiple different brand and model combinations.

For example, the Octavia shares much of the same platform as versions of the Audi A3 and the VW Golf.

Skoda's worldwide sales grew substantially in the late 1990s, most notably in central Europe, such as Slovakia, and Poland. The Czech Republic itself remained a significant market. Skoda is now one of the fastest-growing car brands in the European motor industry, especially since the Czech Republic joined the EU.

However, the costs of the improved manufacturing quality and R&D has pushed up Skoda prices. Skoda's task is to convince consumers that this higher price is justified. This is a slow task, but has been helped by a series of accolades in customer satisfaction surveys, which rate Skoda models very highly. Nonetheless, there are still potential customers, who would be prepared to buy an Audi or a Volkswagen, but who will steadfastly refuse to buy a Skoda. This is a situation that Volkswagen will have to continue to address.

Skoda revival

Has Volkswagen gone too far? By borrowing heavily from its upper-echelon products, it may have diluted the cache of Audi and Volkswagen. Frugal European automotive consumers realize that a Seat or Skoda is almost identical to its VW sibling at several thousand euros less. Cannibalization of brand identities is a huge risk to planners looking to reduce complexities but maintain a brand's character. To some extent this strategy is deliberate. It allows VW to segment the market, position different "marques" or brands within it and target customers with appropriate marketing messages.

There is a distinct "price pyramid" operated by Volkswagen, as shown in the Volkswagen perception map below. At the bottom of the pyramid is Skoda, with the lowest average prices and at the top of the pyramid are Bentley and Lamborghini. At times, however, price pyramids can be victims of their own success. Skoda, once the laughing

stock of the car trade has become something of a cult brand. Its styling and engineering are right up to date and it shares many of the parts of its more expensive siblings.

As a result, Volkswagen's pyramid is starting to look rather muddled with brands overlapping. Skoda has encroached on the Volkswagen car and price band, and may begin to cannibalize sales. Skoda's profit has risen significantly. Volkswagen has denied rumours that it intends to sell Seat, but rumours persists and Volkswagen's strategic direction may change if it is taken over by its smaller rival Porsche.

It appears that Volkswagen's strategy of cutting production costs and improving productivity is working. In 2008, while other major car manufacturers, such as General Motors and Ford, announced declining sales and in several cases losses, Volkswagen announced profits well above analysts' expectations, attributed to successful new model, leaner production processes and disciplined cost management.

Volkswagen is moving into new market areas and expanding its product portfolio. The company is achieving record global sales on strong demand in India, Russia and China, where it delivered nearly 3.3 million vehicles in 2008.

Volkswagen said its hallmark VW brand delivered 1.9 million vehicles in the first six months of 2008, nearly a 6% increase. Audi delivered 516,000 vehicles, a 1.4% increase; while Skoda delivered 367,000 vehicles, an 18% increase. Seat sold 206,000 vehicles—a decline of 7.5%.

Tougher trading conditions and rising raw material costs are now affecting the global car market, and analysts fear that the impact of weaker European and US markets will hit car makers badly in 2009 and 2010. The company is considering price increases and the use of lighter materials such as aluminium and plastics in production.

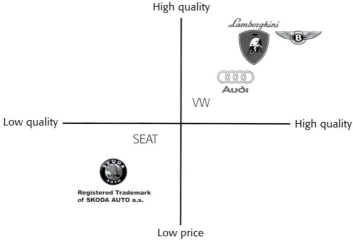

VW's product mix placed according to customer perception

Examination questions

1 a Identify two advantages and two disadvantages of Skoda operating in the private sector as opposed to being under state control. [4 marks]

b Explain the impact on Skoda of the Czech Republic joining the EU. [8 marks]

c Analyse mergers and takeovers as a method of achieving Volkswagen's growth objectives. [8 marks]

d Evaluate Volkswagen's strategic approach to marketing and selling its cars as several different brands, rather than using Volkswagen as a family brand. [10 marks]

2 a Describe two appropriate above-the-line' and two below-the-line promotional activities (see p. 219 for definitions) that Skoda can employ as part of its marketing. [4 marks]

b Explain how Volkswagen can use primary and secondary research to investigate and improve the image of the Skoda brand. [8 marks]

c Using Porter's five forces, analyse Skoda's competitive position in the European car market. [8 marks]

d Prepare a SWOT analysis and use this, along with other information from the case study, to evaluate Skoda's present market position. [10 marks]

3 a Identify two fixed costs and two variable costs in the Skoda factory. [4 marks]

b Explain how Volkswagen can use position maps to support its marketing strategy. [8 marks]

c Analyse the advantages and disadvantages to Volkswagon of introducing JIT management in its Skoda factories. [8 marks]

d Evaluate the opportunities and threats posed for Volkswagen by increasing its marketing presence in emerging markets, such as China and India. [10 marks]

Extension activities

Choose one of the following car manufacturers:

● General Motors
● Tata Motors
● Shanghai Automotive Industry Corporation (SAIC).

Investigate the manufacturer you have chosen, using relevant secondary sources, and produce a strategic plan to include where possible:

● the organization's mission and/or vision statement
● a SWOT, PEST, and five forces analysis
● a description of any existing or potential competitive advantage
● market forecasts
● proposals for significant operational and marketing changes for a two- to three-year planning horizon.

Include relevant marketing and financial data, and employ business techniques such as product portfolio analysis and Ansoff's matrix.

Data response exercise

Read the text on the next page and answer the questions that follow.

Case study

Boeing and Airbus—the strategic challenge

The aircraft manufacturing industry is dominated by two huge corporations, Airbus Industrie and the Boeing Company.

Boeing was incorporated in Seattle in 1916 by William E. Boeing, later transferring its headquarters to Chicago. Airbus, a subsidiary of EADS, a European aerospace organization, is based in Toulouse, France. It was formed in 1970 as a consortium of France's Aerospatiale and Deutsche Airbus, a grouping of leading German aircraft manufacturing firms. British Aerospace joined Airbus Industrie in 1979.

The airline manufacturing industry, valued by Airbus at $1.9 trillion, is now a duopoly with very high barriers to entry. In 2003, Airbus overtook Boeing to become the world's best-selling aircraft maker, but the recent success of Boeing's new aircraft means that the two rivals' market shares are closer to 50:50. Boeing and Airbus both state that profits matter more than individual market share. They also share an optimistic overview of the market, predicting 800 new aircraft deliveries a year for the next 20 years. The two competitors continue to sell head to head in every market segment.

Marketing strategy

Producing competitive advantage in the market-place relies on establishing a USP. For four decades Boeing

has ensured its control of the long-haul market through production of its B747 Jumbo Jet. Airbus is now challenging this with its Airbus A380 superjumbo which is the biggest airliner in production, capable of carrying from 550 to 800 passengers according to its configuration. With two full-length decks and a range of possible of amenities such as sleeper cabins, cocktail lounges, casinos, and a gym, it is targeting passengers currently flying the B747.

Despite the design innovations of the A380, its production is based on an existing model of air travel: the so-called "hub and spoke". This strategic approach assumes that airlines will continue to fly smaller planes on shorter routes (spokes) into a few large hubs, then onward to the next hub on larger aircraft. Airbus sees a very large 20-year market for wide-body aircraft, amounting to 1,250 passenger aircraft.

Ironically, Boeing, founder of the giant air cruiser, has decided on a future strategy employing a distinctively different and smaller product range. Rather than seek economies through scale, the strategy being pursued by Airbus, Boeing has a fundamentally different vision or the future global market. It forecasts that airlines will need barely more than 300 passenger aircraft larger than the B747 and around 400 aircraft in the B747 market, believing research that shows customers prefer more point-to-point flights, flown more frequently, on smaller airplanes. In essence, the two firms have a diametrically opposite vision of the future.

Marty Bentrott, vice president of sales and marketing for the B787 stated that Boeing's "strategy has been to design and build an airplane that will take passengers where they want to go, when they want to go, without intermediate stops; do it efficiently while providing the utmost comfort to passengers; and make it simple and cost-effective for airlines to operate". Based on the B787 Dreamliner, its first completely new aircraft since 1995, Boeing's goal is to deliver economy through technological innovation, fuel-efficient twin engines and a body produced from

lightweight composite materials and a focus on passenger comfort. Boeing is attempting to gain competitive advantage through design, looking at the strategic challenge of returning some of the magic to flying.

Over a decade, Boeing engineers have used qualitative as well as quantitative research methods to explore the psychology of airline passengers, involving thousands of participants in simulations, surveys, and focus groups. They teamed up with universities to simulate aircraft cabins and experimented in areas such as cabin pressure, humidity, light, and air filtration. In addition, Boeing designers looked at the psychological impact of the cabin, including ways they could design the interior to make it appear more spacious and better lit. In the final design of the new B787 Dreamliner, Boeing designers decided on an architecturally imposing entry to the aircraft with the aim of making passengers feel better about boarding.

It appears that Boeing may be following the correct strategy with much large orders for the Dreamliner, almost double of that of the A380. Even before its initial rollout from Boeing's Everett factory in July 2007, the B787 Dreamliner was already the most successful new commercial airplane in the company's history.

However, despite a focus on different market segments, both airlines have hedged their bets by producing aircraft that directly challenge their rivals. The new, larger Boeing's 747-8 carries 450 passengers and Airbus is challenging the B787 with its own mid-size aircraft, the A350.

Production and operations management

With aircraft being comprised of thousands of components, the airline manufacturing industry has always been global, but the trend to greater outsourcing is increasing. Airbus may be associated with the EU and Boeing with the US, but when it comes to the development and manufacturing of aircraft, the approach of both organizations is fundamentally global. Indeed, with soaring component costs, no company could accept the risk and cost of developing and creating everything involved in a new commercial aircraft in-house. However, despite these commercial realities, Boeing and Airbus do have contrasting approaches to manufacture. Some of these differences are historical and cultural and some arise from fundamentally different views on product design.

Boeing's product ranges are different in configuration, technology, and manufacture. The B737, B777, and B747, for instance, have no common parts and major components are mostly made in different locations, often by different companies. Airbus, by contrast, is more focused on economies of scale, cost control, and integrated manufacture. Outsourcing will only happen in areas not considered to be a "core competence" of the

company itself. It has eight "centres of excellence", which are benchmarked against highest industry standards. However, Airbus also states that any failure to fulfill industry-leading quality in these centres of excellence may also lead to work being subcontracted in the future.

The external environment

Both Boeing and Airbus have faced major manufacturing delays and economic barriers. The Airbus A380 suffered hefty delays before it finally entered service in October 2008. Its superjumbo cost Airbus an estimated $6.8 billion in late delivery penalties and lost sales. Boeing too has suffered delays. It originally scheduled in the first commercial flight of the B747 Dreamliner, for May 2008, but this schedule slipped to early 2009. Boeing blamed delays on assembly issues and continuing problems with suppliers. As a result of failure to fulfill contracts with customers such as Nippon Airlines, Boeing faced large claims for compensation from their customers.

Other external factors influence the long-term success in the battle between Airbus and Boeing. Appreciation in the euro against the dollar negatively affects Airbus's profits. Airbus's costs are largely in euros, but like oil, its planes are priced in US dollars. Every 10% rise in the euro against the dollar, costs Airbus more than $1 billion in operating profits. In contrast, US-based Boeing's costs are all in dollars, giving Airbus's arch-rival a crucial advantage in an already highly competitive industry and threatening the very existence of Airbus. Indeed, in 2007, Airbus made pre-tax losses of $572 million.

In reaction to a negative external environment, EADS, Airbus's parent company, is determined to eventually shift production of Airbus planes out of Europe into dollar-denominated areas such as China, and possibly the US, Japan, and Russia. It intends to open a manufacturing plant in China to manufacture A320 single-aisle jets and has suggested it will build more than half of each new plane, including the A350 long-haul jet, overseas. Airbus hopes joint ventures in China will help it sell more planes to Chinese airlines, a huge growth market.

The massive investment required to develop large aircraft has allowed Boeing and Airbus to dominate the market, but now they face challenges. China, a booming market for Airbus and Boeing, could soon emerge as a medium-term competitor. The newly created China Commercial Aircraft Co. Ltd. has a goal to develop a 150-plus-seat airliner by about 2020 at a project cost of 50 billion-60 billion yuan ($7.1–8.6 billion). In Canada, the engineering group Bombadier is to build a new passenger jet, the C-Series. Lufthansa, the German airline, has already placed orders for 30 aircraft worth $1.4 billion.

Finance

Analysts now estimate that more than $100 billion of aircraft orders could be cancelled or postponed in the next couple of years as high fuel prices and the recession drives airlines into losses or bankruptcy. This represents as much as 20–30% of the order backlog held by Boeing and Airbus.

The development of the new plane will cost Airbus some €10 billion and delays to the production of the company's

A380 super-jumbo will knock €4.8 billion off profits at EADS. The company says it will pay for the new plane's initial development out of cash flow and cost savings from its Power 8 restructuring scheme, which is intended to save €2.1 billion in costs, but will eliminate 10,000 jobs.

Most of the spending on the A350 will be required between 2010 and 2013, when the first planes are due to be delivered.

Examination questions

1 **a** Define these terms:

   duopoly [2 marks]

   competitive advantage. [2 marks]

   b Explain the effect on Airbus of fluctuations in the exchange rate between the euro and the US dollar. [8 marks]

   c Using Ansoff's matrix, classify and analyse the growth strategies proposed by Airbus in the medium to long term. [8 marks]

   d Discuss the proposal by Airbus to shift its production of planes from Europe to the Far East. [10 marks]

2 **a** Define these terms:

   joint venture [2 marks]

   focus groups. [2 marks]

   b Compare and contrast the strategies being employed by Boeing and Airbus on their future models of air travel. [8 marks]

   c Analyse the impact that external opportunities and threats have had on the business objectives and strategy of Boeing. [8 marks]

   d Prepare a PEST analysis and use this, along with other information from the case study, to evaluate Airbus's present market position. [10 marks]

3 **a** Define these terms:

   outsourcing [2 marks]

   competitive advantage. [2 marks]

   b Compare and contrast the manufacturing strategies of Boeing and Airbus. [8 marks]

   c Analyse how it is possible for Boeing and Airbus both to carry out extensive market research, yet reach totally different conclusions about the customer preferences for air travel. [8 marks]

   d Using information in the case study prepare a PEST analysis and evaluate the impact of external factors on the future strategy of Airbus. [10 marks]

4 **a** Distinguish between qualitative and quantitative market research. [4 marks]

   b Explain the reasons for Boeing's strategy of outsourcing production of many of its components and Airbus' decision to produce in-house. [8 marks]

   c Examine the proposal by Airbus to form joint ventures in China as part of its expansion strategy in the region. [8 marks]

   d Prepare a SWOT analysis for Airbus and evaluate its present strategic position. [10 marks]

Extension activities

You are the on the Board of Directors of China Commercial Aircraft Co. Ltd. Prepare for your first strategic planning meeting to consider entering the aircraft manufacturing industry.

Before the meeting:

1 use secondary research to:
   a find out information about the current global airline industry
   b examine forecasts for the airline market over the coming five years
   c collect the latest information available on Boeing and Airbus and, if possible, construct a product portfolio for both companies
2 prepare a five forces analysis of the aircraft manufacturing market.

Hold a meeting and identify and examine key strategic issues involved. Produce a summary report of the major issues you have investigated.

Note: Examine functional issues such as workforce planning, marketing plans, R&D, and financial requirements.

Internal assessment is an integral and compulsory element of the business and management programme for both HL and SL students and accounts for 25% of the final mark. It enables you to demonstrate the application of your business skills and knowledge to a range of practical business situations.

Students complete a research project at HL and a written commentary at SL. Before attempting either, it is important to meet with teachers and look at the IB Diploma Programme Business and Management Guide:

- requirements of the HL research project: p. 49–52
- requirements of the HL research project: p. 52–54
- HL assessment criteria: p. 55–61
- SL assessment criteria: p. 62–68.

It is vital that the assessment criteria are referred to at all times—after all, this is what you will be marked against. It is good practice having finished your internal assessment to mark your project or commentary using the assessment criteria and ask yourself: "Have I met the requirements for the higher levels of each criterion?"

HL research project

The project is written as a business report and addresses an issue facing an organization or analyses a decision to be made by an organization. The maximum length is 2,000 words and it is important that you stay within this limit or you will be penalized, as a maximum of 1 mark can be awarded for criterion E. (The criteria are listed on p. 365). It is recommended that 30 hours of class time at HL should be allocated to your research project.

You must select a real organization, not a fictional one. So, for instance, it would not be appropriate to develop a business plan for a commercial venture that you would like to set up. The issue or decision under investigation must also be real. The expectation is that you should gather primary research from the organization, not simply download information about a business from the Internet. So it is essential that you have access to individuals in the organization and also to gather data. This could be from business records, interviews with managers, or surveys of staff.

The style and format of the report should be in the form of a useful working document for management. It is crucial, therefore, to phrase the title of your project as:

1 a question requiring an answer or answers
2 a question that looks forward in time.

The worst mistake that students make is to produce a descriptive report about what a business has done in the past, which does not invite analysis or evaluation, and cannot lead to supported recommendations. A title such as "How did Shell cope with the bad publicity following the Brent Spar disaster?" may be a question, but it is a backward-looking investigation and the project will be of little help to a manager. Similarly, it is common for students to produce projects such as "An analysis of the marketing of XYZ Ltd." In reality there is no analysis—the project is purely descriptive.

Here are three titles used in previous examination sessions with the name of the companies replaced with "X".

● What is the marketing mix of X hotel?
● Why didn't X Airways derive economies of scale and increase its market share through its merger with Air X?
● An in-depth analysis of the economic success of the X.

In most circumstances it is very easy to change a title to make it appropriate. For example, instead of: "What is the marketing mix of X hotel?" the student could have asked: "How can X hotel improve its marketing mix to increase room occupancy?"

The second question covers much of the same ground, but demands analysis, evaluation, and the making of recommendations by looking forward, rather than merely describing. But even though the title is better phrased, it may be even better to select one or two elements of the marketing mix, rather than all components—especially for a larger business. After all, you only have 2,000 words—and not all elements of the mix may need improving.

Summary advice on the preparation of research questions
● If possible keep research questions short.
● Look forwards, not backwards.
● Demand conclusions **and** recommendations.
● Create a focus rather than a general approach—think about what part of the syllabus is covered.

Here are examples of titles for HL projects.

● Should ABC recruit a new CEO?
● Should ABC merge with XYZ?
● Should Jaguar produce a new model to compete with the Mercedes A Class?
● Should ABC become a public limited company?
● Should ABC use franchising to expand its business?
● How can ABC change its distribution channel to improve its profit levels?
● How can ABC improve its liquidity position?
● What community projects could ABC introduce to help integrate it into the local community?

HL students need to develop two pieces of work for the project:

● a research proposal and action plan
● a written report.

Discussion
Why are the three titles inappropriate?

Exercise
Take the two remaining inappropriate titles given above and change them to make them more effective.

Exercise
Suggest **four** of your own titles for an HL project.

HL assessment criteria

These are assessed against criteria laid out in the IB Diploma Programme Business and Management Guide.

A Research proposal and action plan
B Use of theoretical concepts, sources, and data (written report)
C Analysis and evaluation (written report)
D Conclusions and recommendations (written report)
E Value to management (written report)

Criterion A: Research proposal and action plan

The research proposal and action plan are designed to be the primary planning documents, giving direction to the research project. They should, therefore, be prepared **before** the written report, not completed afterwards, describing what was done. As this work is a planning document, it may be necessary to review and modify aspects as the project progresses.

The required format for the research proposal and action plan is:

- research question
- theoretical framework
- methodology
- anticipated difficulties
- action plan.

To meet the requirements, it is essential to cover all of these elements to ensure that the "research proposal and action plan are appropriate, clear, and focused". The theoretical base and methodology must be identified and explained and any possible difficulties anticipated, for example confidential issues, access to records and staff, and suggestions to overcome these. If it's not possible to overcome difficulties, a new project should be selected.

Too many projects are practical, but do not apply business theory effectively. All projects should include theory and business tools learned in the classroom, which are then applied to the business problem or issue. After all, what is the point of a business project that doesn't do this?

The action plan should include details of people to be interviewed, surveys and questionnaires to be conducted, and other necessary actions such as writing the report. All of these activities should have dates attached. Some students use a presentation similar to a Gantt chart to represent timings and progress and, although **not** a requirement, this technique can be very effective.

Criterion B: Use of theoretical concepts, sources, and data

The use of business theories, sources, and data is what distinguishes a business and management report from a report in another subject. Before starting your project, identify what business theory could be used to analyse and evaluate your subject.

For the highest level, you must show you understand the business theories used and apply them effectively. The project should include appropriate data gathered from primary and secondary research, which is used to support the theory. For instance, if you are using a

> "Moderators commented that too many projects focused on marketing and motivation with too broad a coverage. These would have been more effective if specific aspects of the marketing mix had been selected or measurable aspects of motivation were examined, such as labour turnover or absenteeism."
> Examiner's report, May 2008

> "Marks were lost where reports had a weak theoretical framework and methodology. Clearer objectives for the research would have provided candidates with a better focus, as well as encouraging specific recommendations. Anticipated difficulties of the research were often not addressed or mentioned very briefly in the research proposal. In most cases this limited marks to the lower two levels. The better projects not only identified potential research problems, but also suggested some sensible solutions. The weaker projects anticipated difficulties that could easily have been overcome by a thoughtful methodology and careful planning."
> Examiner's report, May 2008

SWOT analysis, each segment should have data that is evidenced and sourced. Also, the entries should be accurate. So if you put internal, controllable elements into the opportunities section, such as "open a second shop", you will be penalized for a lack of understanding of SWOT analysis.

Criterion C: Analysis and evaluation

This is where a descriptive or backward-looking research title really causes problems. The criterion requires "appropriate analysis and evaluation, a sound integration of ideas and issues in a coherent structure, and consistent evidence of critical, reflective thinking."

To make analysis appropriate, you will need to analyse the data collected using tables, graphs and/or business tools, such as ratio analysis or break even. To evaluate, you will need to make judgments about the data or information collected and reach conclusions:

- What does the data show?
- Are the results significant?
- How should management use the information?

The structure of the report is clearly important, and you will need to challenge some of the data collected. For instance:

- Can you believe all the information on a company website or in company publications?
- Do other sources of information challenge what the managing director said in the interview you had with him?
- Why do the opinions of employees differ from those of managers?

Criterion D: Conclusions and recommendations

- If your research title is descriptive or backward looking, you will also lose marks on this criterion—how can you make recommendations when you have not asked a question requiring them?

To score highly here "the conclusions and recommendations must be consistent with the evidence presented in the main body of the report and with the research question." So this is not the time to introduce new ideas. It is very common for students to come up with ideas that may be sensible but have not been investigated in the main body of the report. At this point, they become statements of opinion or mere generalized assertions.

It is also sensible to think about the financial costs of your proposals and whether they are appropriate for the business you are investigating. For instance, a business with liquidity problems is hardly likely to be able to spend significant funds on additional marketing.

It may be sensible, having produced your conclusions and recommendations, to return to the research question and ask whether you have answered it. Alternatively, you may feel that the research question needs modifying.

"Some assignments relied on primary sources alone, usually a questionnaire, but did not really introduce any business theory to support the analysis. Neither of these limited approaches allowed candidates to access higher mark levels.

Those who used a good balance of primary and secondary research produced better quality research projects. However, there was an over-reliance on the questionnaire or a single interview of someone in senior position, as the sole base for primary research."
Examiner's report, May 2008

"Reports based on marketing and motivation often ignored the financial implications of what was being recommended. In fact, in some cases, the recommendations were simply not feasible for the organizations under investigation."
Examiner's report, May 2008

It is also a **requirement** of this criterion to "propose future action to address limitations of the research". This is not an evaluation of what you have done, although this may be valuable, but suggestions as to future action by the business to answer questions you have been unable to address.

Criterion E: Value to management

To score well on this criterion, your report should be "of practical value to management". To suggest the obvious, or to make very general, unsupported recommendations, can hardly be of practical use. Again, a well-focused research question should make the report of value.

This criterion also rewards presentation, bibliography, and referencing.

The required format for the research project is:

- title page
- acknowledgments
- contents page
- executive summary (abstract)
- introduction
- research question
- procedure or method
- main results and findings
- analysis and discussion
- conclusions and recommendations
- bibliography and references
- appendices.

The 2,000 word limit does not include supplementary information such as the title page, executive summary, diagrams, figures, tables of data, references, and appendices, but you must not try to avoid the word limit by putting text into boxes, or pushing relevant information into the appendices. The HL report requires precision.

The executive summary (abstract) must be included and not exceed 200 words (like the abstract in the extended essay). It is good practice to include the research question, the scope of research (methodology), and the conclusions and recommendations.

When figures and data are presented or business theories explained you should, wherever possible, source the information through footnotes and include the website, book, or journal in your bibliography. The bibliography is often the "big giveaway" of a poorly researched project. It is not appropriate just to put down the name of a book —especially your class textbook (even this one!), unless you indicate the relevant page numbers. Similarly, you should be specific about the websites accessed and the dates you accessed them.

Appendices should be included, but only when they are referred to in the main body of the report. Do not simply include wads of information, such as accounts, to pad out your project.

SL commentary

The written commentary is based on three to five supporting documents about a real issue or problem facing a particular organization. The maximum length is 2,000 words and it is important that you stay within this limit or you will be penalized under criterion E, losing three potential marks. It is recommended that 15 hours of your class time should be allocated to the written commentary.

Although it is mandatory to include three to five sources as supporting documents, this does not mean that your investigation must be limited to these documents. Any sources you consulted but did not choose as supporting documents should be referenced in the body of the commentary and included in your bibliography.

While the problem or issue you choose should be focused on a specific organization, it may affect a number of organizations or the industry as a whole. You must select a real and contemporary issue or problem, not a fictional one, facing a single business organization, and you must be aware of the following points.

- The title of the written commentary must be phrased in the form of a question.
- The commentary can be based on primary and/or secondary sources.
- The commentary requires analysis and evaluation of the issue or problem, and you must form judgments, and incorporate them into the commentary in light of the question posed in the title.
- The maximum number of words for the written commentary is 1,500.

It is clear, therefore, that primary research is not excluded, so the trusted questionnaire is still a possibility!

Although there is no mandatory format for the written commentary, a suggested format is given below and this should be followed unless there are good reasons not to:

- title (in the form of a question)
- introduction (including a description of methodology)
- findings (based on the supporting documents)
- analysis of the findings
- conclusion or conclusions
- bibliography and references
- appendices: supporting documents.

How do you select a topic for the written commentary?

It is important that, with your teacher's guidance, you choose an issue that:

- engages your interest
- is realistic in terms of resources
- meets the criteria for assessment.

The title question must be clear and focused, allowing the topic to be adequately investigated within the 1,500 word limit.

The following are examples of suitable questions suggested in the programme guide.

- Is including a line for male customers a profitable decision for company X?
- Is an increase in wages an effective way to increase productivity and motivation in company Y?
- Is company Z's decision to increase productive capacity by building a new plant a sound financial decision?
- Can company X, an independent food retailer, survive?

How do you select your supporting documents and what can be included?

Your supporting documents must be of a contemporary nature and written a maximum of two years before the submission of the written commentary.

The commentary can be based on secondary sources and/or primary data.

Examples of **secondary sources** might include:

- market research surveys
- articles from the local, national or international press
- financial reports
- business accounts
- business plans
- mission statements
- web-based surveys
- extracts from company websites
- government and other statistics
- academic publications.

Examples of **primary data** might include:

- responses to questionnaires (you must include a blank copy of the questionnaire and a tally or summary of your results)
- transcripts of interviews and discussions with focus groups
- results of surveys you have conducted.

It is strongly recommended that your supporting documents present a range of ideas and views that provide balance and objectivity.

Your commentary is assessed against criteria laid out in the programme guide.

SL assessment criteria

A Supporting documents
B Choice and application of business tools, techniques, and theory
C Use, analysis, and synthesis of data
D Conclusions
E Evaluation and critical thinking
F Presentation

Criterion A: Supporting documents

If fewer than three supporting documents are presented, a maximum of three marks can be awarded. The documents should, of course, be relevant and have enough depth and breadth to support your analysis. In addition, you should ensure that you attempt to cover a range of opinions. It would be unwise to use documents produced solely by the organization you are examining as they are likely to be biased.

Criterion B: Choice and application of business tools, techniques, and theory

This is a business studies commentary, so it is anticipated that you select and apply a range of business theories and tools to analyse and evaluate a business issue or problem. This criterion expects the application to be skilfully applied, which suggests that you should be able to explain why you have selected a particular tool or theory and its relevance to the situation investigated.

Criterion C: Use, analysis, and synthesis of data

The selection of the supporting documents is one important aspect of the commentary, but equally important is the appropriate selection of data from these documents to support appropriate and detailed analysis. The different supporting documents should be analysed in such a manner that their relevance to the question is clearly established, and also you should show how the supporting documents relate to each other.

When looking for your documents, you need to be looking for those with "hard data" which can be extracted and manipulated using, as far as possible, business tools and techniques.

It is also a requirement of the top level of this criterion that your ideas are synthesized and integrated with the theory selected. Try not to repeat yourself, and look for natural ways to progress your ideas, analysis, and evaluation in a structured format.

Criterion D: Conclusions

Your conclusions must be consistent with the evidence you have presented throughout the commentary and must answer the commentary question based on your analysis of the supporting documents. You should not present new ideas in your conclusions that have not been addressed before, or are not from your supporting documents.

It is good practice to identify aspects of the commentary question that have not been fully answered in the commentary or that might need further analysis or investigation.

Criterion E: Evaluation and critical thinking

Your judgments are important, but you must avoid making generalized assertions. There must be evidence for your evaluation, and your judgments should be substantiated.

Critical and reflective thinking is expected throughout the commentary. You should look objectively at your supporting documents and, where necessary, challenge or doubt some of the findings. You could also suggest other evidence that may be required or future investigation that would provide a better understanding of the situation.

Criterion F: Presentation

The commentary must not exceed 1,500 words. The moderator will be looking for a commentary that is well organized and structured, with consistent use of appropriate business terminology. Sources must be appropriately referenced and an appropriate bibliography should be provided.

8 Extended essay

What is the extended essay in business and management?

The extended essay gives you the opportunity to carry out in-depth research in an area of personal interest relating to business and management. It allows you to develop research skills by reviewing business theory, concepts, and principles, and critically analysing how these have been put into practice. Your work on the extended essay requires the application of business theory, tools, and techniques to produce a coherent and structured analytical essay that effectively addresses your research question.

How does it fit into my IB package?

All extended essays are externally assessed by examiners and are marked on a scale from 0 to 36 and then placed in the following bands.*

Grade	Descriptor	Marks
A	Excellent	36–31
B	Good	30–26
C	Satisfactory	25–18
D	Mediocre	17–11
E	Elementary	10–00

The extended essay contributes to the overall diploma score as shown in the chart on the next page. A maximum of three points are awarded according to a student's combined performance in the extended essay and theory of knowledge. Your performance in these two areas will determine how many points you will be awarded.

Why should I take my extended essay seriously?

The extended essay gives you an opportunity to demonstrate to a university that you have developed your research skills and made an in-depth enquiry. This will help you stand out from other students in the application process. It goes without saying that the knowledge and skills you acquire on the way will also help you in the final examinations and in other coursework—including coursework you do at university.

*The extended essay grade boundaries are being reviewed.

The EE/TOK matrix as of 2010

		Theory of knowledge				
		Excellent A	Good B	Satisfactory C	Mediocre D	Elementary E
Extended essay	Excellent A	+ 3	+ 3	+ 2	+ 2	+ 1
	Good B	+ 3	+ 2	+ 1	+ 1	F*
	Satisfactory C	+ 2	+ 1	+ 1	0	F*
	Mediocre D	+ 2	+ 1	0	0	F*
	Elementary E	+ 1 F*	F*	F*	F*	F

F*: 28 points are required to be eligible for the diploma if you achieve an E in your extended essay or ToK. An A grade in one of the components earns an extra point even if the other grade is an E . An E grade in both components represents automatic failure.

What makes a good extended essay in business and management?

The best extended essays in business and management tend to ask a forward-looking question. The essay will include primary and secondary data, and will apply a number of business concepts. These essays tend to reach firm conclusions and fit in well with the assessment criteria.

Here are some examples of forward-looking questions.

- Should company X invest in new machinery?
- Should company X change its method of distribution?
- Should company X introduce performance-related pay to improve motivation?
- Should company X introduce JIT stock control?

How do I get the most marks?

The best way to get the most marks is to follow the assessment criteria very closely. However, having said that, it is absolutely vital that you have a forward-looking question since that tends to fit in best with the criteria. The most common trap students fall into is that they get bogged down in the detail of the essay. The subsequent tunnel vision means that they lose lots of marks on really simple matters, such as including the right things in the abstract, having a detailed contents page, including footnotes, and so on.

From the outset make sure that you have these elements.

- A cover page—with the question, name of your school, your name and candidate number, subject, year, and month of assessment.
- An abstract—with the question, how you approached it, and the conclusions that you reached. It really is that simple. So keep it simple and to the point.

- A contents page—this acts as a road map that shows the journey you covered.
- An introduction—this should explain why you are interested in the question, and why the answer is significant to you and society. In other words, the introduction places the question in an academic context. If you get this bit right, you will have the attention of the examiner. You will be off to a good start.
- Main body—this is likely to explain appropriate theory and then apply it to the primary and secondary data you have gathered.
- Conclusions—based on your investigation, this states what you have concluded. What action should the organization take?
- Evaluation—how reliable are your conclusions? How reliable is the data you used? What further information would you like—and why? What factors have had the biggest impact on your recommendations?
- Bibliography—the books, websites and other sources you've used should be listed using an appropriate referencing system.
- Appendices—samples of questionnaires used for gathering primary data should be placed here as should, for example, extracts from company accounts.

As the essay is getting nearer completion you should then check that you are satisfying the following criteria.

Assessment criteria

Criterion A: Research question

Achievement level	Descriptor
0	The research question is not stated in the introduction or does not lend itself to a systematic investigation in an extended essay in the subject in which it is registered.
1	The research question is stated in the introduction but is not clearly expressed or is too broad in scope to be treated effectively within the word limit.
2	The research question is clearly stated in the introduction and sharply focused, making effective treatment possible within the word limit.

Criterion B: Introduction
This criterion assesses the extent to which the introduction:

- makes clear how the research question relates to existing knowledge
- explains how the topic chosen is significant and worthy of investigation.

Achievement level	Descriptor
0	Little or no attempt is made to set the research question into context. There is little or no attempt to explain the significance of the topic.
1	Some attempt is made to set the research question into context. There is some attempt to explain the significance of the topic and why it is worthy of investigation.
2	The context of the research question is clearly demonstrated. The introduction clearly explains the significance of the topic and why it is worthy of investigation.

Criterion C: Investigation

This criterion assesses the extent to which the investigation is planned and an appropriate range of sources has been consulted, or data has been gathered, that is relevant to the research question.

Achievement level	Descriptor
0	There is little or no evidence that sources have been consulted or data gathered, and little or no evidence of planning in the investigation.
1	A range of inappropriate sources has been consulted, or inappropriate data has been gathered, and there is little evidence that the investigation has been planned.
2	A limited range of appropriate sources has been consulted, or data has been gathered, and some relevant material has been selected. There is evidence of some planning in the investigation.
3	A sufficient range of appropriate sources has been consulted, or data has been gathered, and relevant material has been selected. The investigation has been satisfactorily planned.
4	An imaginative range of appropriate sources has been consulted, or data has been gathered, and relevant material has been carefully selected. The investigation has been well planned.

Criterion D: Knowledge and understanding of the topic studied

To get high marks here you need to explain why the topic is worthy of investigation (thus giving it an academic context) and demonstrate that you know what you are writing about. You do this by making appropriate application of business concepts to the primary and secondary data you have gathered.

Achievement level	Descriptor
0	The essay demonstrates no real knowledge or understanding of the topic studied.
1	The essay demonstrates some knowledge but little understanding of the topic studied. The essay shows little awareness of an academic context for the investigation.
2	The essay demonstrates adequate knowledge and some understanding of the topic studied. The essay shows some awareness of an academic context for the investigation.
3	The essay demonstrates a good knowledge and understanding of the topic studied. Where appropriate, the essay successfully outlines an academic context for the investigation.
4	The essay demonstrates a very good knowledge and understanding of the topic studied. Where appropriate, the essay clearly and precisely locates the investigation in an academic context.

Criterion E: Reasoned argument

This criterion assesses the extent to which the essay uses the material collected to present ideas in a logical and coherent manner, and develops a reasoned argument in relation to the research question. If you have a logically sequenced contents page then you should score highly here—assuming that you then stick to it in the essay itself.

Achievement level	Descriptor
0	There is no attempt to develop a reasoned argument in relation to the research question.
1	There is a limited or superficial attempt to present ideas in a logical and coherent manner, and to develop a reasoned argument in relation to the research question.
2	There is some attempt to present ideas in a logical and coherent manner, and to develop a reasoned argument in relation to the research question, but this is only partially successful.
3	Ideas are presented in a logical and coherent manner, and a reasoned argument is developed in relation to the research question, but with some weaknesses.
4	Ideas are presented clearly and in a logical and coherent manner. The essay succeeds in developing a reasoned and convincing argument in relation to the research question.

Criterion F: Application of analytical and evaluative skills appropriate to the subject

To get marks here you need to apply appropriate techniques and make sure that you support ideas with reasons and examples. You also need to explain which factors have most significance (and why). You need to consider your answer or answers from different perspectives and the context of the organization you are studying.

Achievement level	Descriptor
0	The essay shows no application of appropriate analytical and evaluative skills.
1	The essay shows little application of appropriate analytical and evaluative skills.
2	The essay shows some application of appropriate analytical and evaluative skills, which may be only partially effective.
3	The essay shows sound application of appropriate analytical and evaluative skills.
4	The essay shows effective and sophisticated application of appropriate analytical and evaluative skills.

Criterion G: Use of language appropriate to the subject

Achievement level	Descriptor
0	The language used is inaccurate and unclear. There is no effective use of terminology appropriate to the subject.
1	The language used sometimes communicates clearly but does not do so consistently. The use of terminology appropriate to the subject is only partly accurate.
2	The language used for the most part communicates clearly. The use of terminology appropriate to the subject is usually accurate.
3	The language used communicates clearly. The use of terminology appropriate to the subject is accurate, although there may be occasional lapses.
4	The language used communicates clearly and precisely. Terminology appropriate to the subject is used accurately, with skill and understanding.

Criterion H: Conclusions

These should directly address the research question and be consistent with the previous analysis.

Achievement level	Descriptor
0	Little or no attempt is made to provide a conclusion that is relevant to the research question.
1	A conclusion is attempted that is relevant to the research question but may not be entirely consistent with the evidence presented in the essay.
2	An effective conclusion is clearly stated; it is relevant to the research question and consistent with the evidence presented in the essay. It should include unresolved questions where appropriate to the subject concerned.

Criterion I: Formal presentation

The layout, organization, appearance, and formal elements of the essay consistently follow a standard format. It is really easy to gain (and lose!) marks here—so make sure you check that you have:

- title page
- table of contents
- page numbers
- illustrative material
- quotations

- documentation (including references, citations, and bibliography)
- appendices (if used).

Achievement level	Descriptor
0	The formal presentation is unacceptable, or the essay exceeds 4,000 words.
1	The formal presentation is poor.
2	The formal presentation is satisfactory.
3	The formal presentation is good.
4	The formal presentation is excellent.

Criterion J: Abstract

The requirements for the abstract are for it to state clearly the research question that was investigated, how the investigation was undertaken, and the conclusions of the essay. It really is that simple!

Achievement level	Descriptor
0	The abstract exceeds 300 words or one or more of the required elements of an abstract (listed on p. 373) is missing.
1	The abstract contains the elements listed (on p. 373) but they are not all clearly stated.
2	The abstract clearly states all the elements listed (on p. 373).

Criterion K: Holistic judgment

To score highly here you need to demonstrate:

- intellectual initiative
- depth of understanding
- insight.

Achievement level	Descriptor
0	The essay shows no evidence of such qualities.
1	The essay shows little evidence of such qualities.
2	The essay shows some evidence of such qualities.
3	The essay shows clear evidence of such qualities.
4	The essay shows considerable evidence of such qualities.

Having completed your essay you may then undertake a vive voce.

The vive voce

This is a short interview between you and the supervisor, and is a recommended conclusion to the extended essay process. It helps you demonstrate what you have learned and gain extra marks. The viva voce should last between 10 and 15 minutes.

The following are examples of questions that can be asked.

- *"I am not clear what you mean on page XX. Could you explain a little more about what this tells us?"*
- *"On page XX you cite Z. I couldn't find this reference* (for example a website). *Could you tell me more about it?"*
- *"What have been the high and low points of the research and writing processes?"*

- *"What were the most interesting aspects of the process? Did you discover anything that surprised you?"*
- *"What have you learned through writing this essay? Is there any advice you would want to pass on to someone just starting out on an extended essay?"*
- *"Is there anything else that you would particularly like me to mention in my report?"*

Conclusion

The extended essay is a great opportunity for you to show off what you can do in business and management. View it as such, make sure that you fit in with the assessment criteria, and you are more likely to get the most out of it. Good luck!

9 External assessment

The business and management examination is assessed in three parts.

	HL	Weight	SL	Weight
External assessment	Paper 1—Seen case study	40%	Paper 1—Seen case study	35%
	Paper 2—Data response	35%	Paper 2—Data response	40%
Internal assessment	Business project	25%	Written assignment	25%

As the table above shows, there are two external examinations for business and management at both HL and SL.

The structure of the HL exams is set out here:

Examination	Context	Time	Marks	Content
Paper 1	Case study	$2\frac{1}{4}$ hrs	80	**Section A**—Two out of three structured questions (30 marks) **Section B**—One compulsory evaluation question (20 marks) **Note: Section B uses unseen material based on the case study.** **Section C**—One compulsory strategy question. (30 marks) **Note: Section C uses unseen material based on the case study.**
Paper 2	Data response	$2\frac{1}{4}$ hrs	75	**Section A**—One out of two structured (numerical) questions (25 marks) **Section B**—Two out of three structured questions (50 marks)

And the SL is set out below:

Examination	Context	Time	Marks	Content
Paper 1	Case study	$1\frac{1}{4}$ hrs	50	**Section A**—Two out of three structured questions (30 marks) **Section B**—One compulsory evaluation question (20 marks) **Note: Section B uses unseen material based on the case study.**
Paper 2	Data response	$1\frac{3}{4}$ hrs	60	**Section A**—One out of two structured (numerical) questions (20 marks) **Section B**—Two out of three structured questions (40 marks)

Differences between the HL and SL examinations

Paper 1
The HL students have an extra section C which tallies with the extra topic (6—Business strategy) that the HL students must do as part of their syllabus.

Timings/mark allocations
The SL students will find that they have proportionately less time to answer the questions compared to HL students. For example, see the table below, which just shows the time allowed divided by the marks available, to get minutes per mark.

Examination	HL	SL
Paper 1	1.69	1.5
Paper 2	1.8	1.75

Weighting

For HL, paper 1 has the higher weighting; for SL the opposite, paper 2, is more important both in terms of marks allocated and the proportion of the final mark it carries.

Similarities

The similarities between the examinations are more striking than the differences.

Marking

The examination is marked holistically—all examinations are marked in bands. You must realize that it is **not** the number of points students make that get the marks, it is how they answer the question. You should look at the command terms (found in the IB syllabus guide) and pay attention to what the IB wants you to do. The tables below and on the next page show our understanding of the IB command terms and their place in the levels of response that the IB is expecting.

	Command term	What does this mean?	Key phrase/action
Level 1 **Knowledge** **1–2 marks**	Define	Give a clear and precise meaning	Precise definition in own words
	Identify	Recognize key features	Bullet or list important points
	Complete	Finish off	Fill in the gaps
	Outline	Summarize key points	"To summarize briefly…"
	Describe	Give an account	Tell a simple story
	Classify	Arrange in order	Put in the correct place

	Command term	What does this mean?	Key phrase/action
Level 2 **Understanding** **3–4 marks**	Compare	Show similarities between	"The similarities are…"
	Contrast	Show differences between	"The differences are…"
	Distinguish	Show differences between	"The differences are…"
	Prepare	Write up a set of data	Turn data into the correct format
	Construct	Make or draw up	Turn data into the correct format
	Calculate	Work out necessary figures	Show your working and use the formula
	Explain	Describe with reasons	"The reason for this is…"
	Comment	Give an explanation of	"The reason for this is…"

Level 3	Command term	What does this mean?	Key phrase/action
Application	Apply	Use a theory or concept	"Using the theory we can see that…"
	Examine	Inspect closely	"Looking at the situation carefully we can see that…"
5–7 marks	Analyse	Divide and break down	"The reasons for the situation are many and can be broken down into…"
	Interpret	Explain reasons why	"The reasons for the situation are many and can be explained by…"
	Formulate	Develop a considered plan	"After careful consideration I have come up with a plan…"

Level 4	Command term	What does this mean?	Key phrase/action
Opinion	To what extent	Decide whether it is because or not	"To some extent (or not) it may be the case that…"
	Evaluate	Make a reasoned decision	"After considering both sides, in my opinion it would be…"
8–10 marks	Discuss	Investigate by reasoned argument	"After considering both sides, in my opinion it would be…"
	Justify	Prove by reasoning	"In my opinion the company should take this action because…."
	Advise	Suggest a course of action	"After considering both points of view I would recommend that…"
	Recommend	Suggest a course of action	"After considering both points of view I would recommend that…"

Structure

The IB rewards students who structure their answers correctly. The two common opposite extremes are given below.

Bullet format

Bullets:
- are
- often
- just
- lists
- that
- don't
- explain
- anything.

From the tables above you will see that if you just use simple bullets or lists that do not explain your point you will only score within the level 1 band of marks. A simple descriptive sentence also only scores within this band.

Stream of consciousness

This is an example of stream of consciousness writing:

"……yes because he never did a thing like that before as ask to get his breakfast in bed with a couple of eggs since the City Arms hotel when he used to be pretending to be laid up with a sick voice doing his highness to make himself interesting for that old faggot Mrs Riordan that he thought he had a great leg of and she never left us a farthing all for masses for herself and her soul greatest miser ever was actually afraid to lay out 4d for her methylated spirit telling me all her ailments she had too much old chat in her about politics and earthquakes and the end of the world let us have a bit of fun first God help the world if all the women were her sort down on bathingsuits and lownecks of course nobody wanted her to wear them I suppose she was pious because no man would look at her twice I hope Ill never be like her but she was a welleducated woman certainly and her gabby talk about Mr Riordan here and Mr Riordan there I suppose he was glad to get shut of her and her dog smelling still I like that in him polite to old women like that and waiters and beggars too hes not proud out of nothing but not always if ever he got anything really serious the matter with him its much better for them to go into a hospital where everything is clean…"

The extract is from the final chapter of James Joyce's *Ulysses* (1922) and in full is over 20 pages long without any punctuation at all! It is a beautiful passage but James Joyce was a poet and we can follow the cadence of Nora Bloom's meandering mind by paying attention to the flow of the language. Sadly, writing like this is a skill too many IB students don't possess and therefore what happens is that most IB students who write like this will:

- repeat themselves
- get confused
- make digressions

and in doing so waste **time, effort, and marks**.

The trick is to write somewhere between these extremes and use structured paragraphs for your answers. Each new point deserves a new paragraph and every new paragraph builds on the one before it. There should also be **balance**. Especially if the command term is a level 3 or 4 you should always be thinking of both points of view.

Evaluation

All examination papers will have questions that expect you to use your skills to evaluate a course of action. Look for the level 4 command terms. If you see these then you know that you must have a separate concluding paragraph that gives an opinion. And. no, writing "as we can see there are more advantages than disadvantages…" is not a substantial evaluation.

A substantial evaluation should take at least one of the points shown in the figure into consideration.

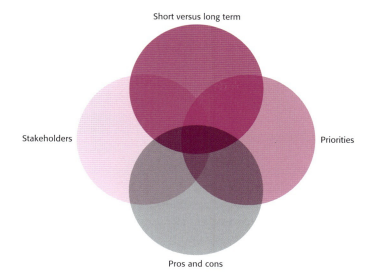

Short versus long term

Stakeholders

Priorities

Pros and cons

10 Top examination tips
1 Don't do a preamble—just answer the question.
2 Don't use bullets—unless for level 1 answers.
3 Do structure your answer.
4 Do show working out.
5 Do use a watch—keep an eye on the time.
6 Do plan your answers.
7 Do use a ruler and make your diagrams big and neat.
8 Do know the difference between "describe" and "explain".
9 Do use balance—always think of both sides to a point of view.
10 Do look out for level 4 questions—make sure you evaluate.

Sample examination question

This sample shows either an HL or SL paper 2 based on the 2008 case study—Organix). Terry, from the restaurant Organix, has asked accountants Seagers to produce a set of accounts to show the impact of the decline in restaurant bookings. Based on the assumption that the restaurant is open 5 days a week for 50 weeks of the year, Seagers has calculated the following figures.

	US$
Fixed costs	600,000 per annum
Variable costs for a typical meal	10
Average bill for a typical meal	40

Table 1 Restaurant costs/revenues

The fixed costs per annum: US$		The variable costs: US$	
Drawings	250, 000	Direct labour	4 per meal
Interest on the mortgage per annum	140, 000	Electricity	3 per meal
Oliver's salary	70, 000	Ingredients	3 per meal
Depreciation on equipment	90, 000		
Tax (on the land)	50, 000		

Table 2 Breakdown of the costs

Capacity	Lunch	Evening
Maximum	60 meals	80 meals
Bookings (2006)	55%	83%
Bookings (2007)	42%	61%

Table 3 Seating capacity per day

a) i) Use the data in **Table 1** to calculate the contribution per meal. [*1 mark*]
    ii) What is the break even quantity of meals? [*2 marks*]
b) Use **Table 3** to identify the profit/loss made by Organix in 2006 and 2007 if the bookings recorded in those years were accurate for the whole year. [*4 marks*]
c) Assuming sales were based on the bookings for 2006 and 2007, use **Table 2** to prepare profit & loss accounts for the Organix restaurant for the years 2006 and 2007. [*4 marks*]
d) Seagers has also highlighted a further set of restraining factors which might have an impact on the restaurant:

  • increased returns of poor quality food
  • increased staff dissatisfaction with falling real wages
  • conflict between Oliver and Terry
  • changing external environment—rising fuel prices and falling real incomes of potential customers.

  Using these points and any other information from the case study evaluate the possibility for Organix to turn around the fall in bookings. [*9 marks*]

Mark scheme

a) i) Use the data in **Table 1** to calculate the contribution per meal. [*1 mark*]
$$\$40 - \$30 = \$10 \text{ per meal}$$
  • Incorrect answer showing a lack of knowledge. [*0*]
  • Correct showing knowledge. [*1*]

   ii) What is the break even quantity of meals? [*2 marks*]
$$\frac{FC}{\text{contribution}} = \frac{600,000}{30} = 20,000 \text{ meals}$$
  • Incorrect answer showing a lack of knowledge and understanding. [*0*]
  • Vague answer showing limited knowledge and understanding. [*1*]
  • Correct answer showing adequate knowledge and understanding. [*2*]

b) Use **Table 3** to identify the profit/loss made by Organix in 2006 and 2007 if the bookings recorded in those years were accurate for the whole year. [*4 marks*]
$$2006 = \text{Lunch bookings } (55 \times 0.6) = 33 \text{ meals per day}$$
$$\text{Evening bookings } (83 \times 0.8) = \frac{66.4 \text{ meals per day}}{99.4 \text{ meals per day}}$$
$$50 \times 5 = 250 \text{ days operation}$$
$$250 \times 99.4 = 24,850 \text{ meals per annum}$$
$$24,850 \times 30 \text{ (contribution)} - 600,000 = \textbf{\$145,500 profit}$$

$$2007 = \text{Lunch bookings } (42 \times 0.6) = 25.2 \text{ meals per day}$$
$$\text{Evening bookings } (61 \times 0.8) = \frac{48.8 \text{ meals per day}}{74 \text{ meals per day}}$$
$$50 \times 5 = 250 \text{ days operation}$$
$$250 \times 74 = 18,500 \text{ meals per annum}$$
$$18,500 \times 30 \text{ (contribution)} - 600,000 = \textbf{\$45,500 loss}$$

Note: There are no follow-through marks; for example if the same mistake is made in both cases the student is not penalized twice.

Two marks are awarded for correct identification of each year's profit & loss.

- Incorrect answer showing a lack of knowledge and understanding. [0]
- Vague answer showing limited knowledge and understanding. [1–2]
- Clear answer showing good knowledge and understanding. For 4 marks all calculations are accurate and full working out is shown. [3–4]

c) Assuming sales were based on the bookings for 2006 and 2007, use Table 2 to prepare profit & loss accounts for the Organix restaurant for the years 2006 and 2007. *[4 marks]*

	(US$) 2006	(US$) 2007
Turnover	994,000	740,000
Cost of sales	248,500	185,000
Gross profit	745,500	555,000
Depreciation	90,000	90,000
Oliver's salary	70,000	70,000
Net profit	585,500	395,000
Interest	140,000	140,000
Profit before tax	445,500	255,000
Tax	50,000	50,000
Profit after tax	395,500	205,000
Drawings	250,000	250,000
Retained profit	145,500	(45,000)

Note: There are no follow-through marks; for example if the same mistake is made in both cases the student is not penalized twice.

Two marks are awarded for correct construct of each year's profit & loss.

- Incorrect answer showing a lack of knowledge and understanding. [0]
- Vague answer showing limited knowledge and understanding. [1–2]
- Clear answer showing good knowledge and understanding. For 4 marks the correct format and headings have been used. [3–4]

d) Seagers has also highlighted a further set of restraining factors which might have an impact on the restaurant:

- increased returns of poor quality food
- increased staff dissatisfaction with falling real wages
- conflict between Oliver and Terry
- changing external environment—rising fuel prices and falling real incomes of potential customers.

Using these points and any other information from the case study, evaluate the possibility for Organix to turn around the fall in bookings. *[9 marks]*

The answer could be argued either way. In the context of the case study, it may be possible to turn round the fortunes of the restaurant but there will need to be a concerted effort on the part of all involved and the issues highlighted will need to be addressed. Good answers will offer considered solutions to these problems.

Students may wish to use tools for managing change. For example force field analysis or "the iceberg" model for change can be used. Students should not be penalized for not using a particular model but using one may help organize their answer.

As long as the student offers reasoned argument, he or she can achieve the higher levels. However, general optimism—or pessimism—will put the student in the lower to middle levels. A substantiated judgment is to be expected to achieve the top level.

- Incorrect answer showing a lack of knowledge and understanding and fails to apply the concepts to the specific question. [0]
- Vague answer showing limited knowledge and understanding and applies the concepts generally to the specific question and lacks an opinion. [1–2]
- Clear answer showing reasonable knowledge and understanding but fails to apply the concepts to the case and lacks an opinion. [3–4]
- Clear answer showing excellent knowledge and understanding and applies the concepts generally to the case and there is an unsubstantiated opinion. [5–6]
- Clear answer showing excellent knowledge and understanding and applies the concepts well to the specific question and there is a clear and substantiated opinion. [7–9]

10 Further reading

Adcock, D. *et al. 2004. Marketing: Principles and practice*. 4th edition. London, Pitman Publishing.

Ansoff, I. 1989. *Corporate Strategy*. Harmondsworth, Penguin.

Argyris, C. 1963. *Organization and Innovation*. New Haven, CT, Yale University Press.

Armstrong, M. 2006. *A Handbook of Human Resource Management,* 10th edition, London, Kogan Page.

Armstrong, M and Baron, A. 2008. *Strategic Human Resource Management: A guide to action*. London, Kogan Page.

Arnold. G. 2005. *Corporate Financial Management*. 3rd edition. Harlow, *Financial Times*/Prentice Hall.

Cameron, E. and Green, M. 2004. *Making Sense of Change Management: A complete guide to the models, tools and techniques of organizational change*. London, Kogan Page.

Cook, S. et al. 2004. *Change Management Excellence*. London, Kogan Page.

Doole, I. and Lowe, R. 2008. *International Marketing Strategy: Analysis, development and implementation*. 5th edition. London, Cengage Learning.

Drucker, P. F. 2008. *Management*. Revised edition. New York, HarperCollins.

Drucker, P. F. (ed.) 1969. *Preparing Tomorrow's Business Leaders Today*. Englewood Cliffs, NJ, Prentice Hall.

Drucker, P. F. 2001. *Management Challenges for the 21st Century*. New York, HarperCollins

Fayol, H. 1967. *General and Industrial Management*. London, Pitman Press.

Foss, B. and Stone, S. 2001. *Successful Customer Relationship Management*. London, Kogan Page.

Gini, A. and Marcoux, A. M. *Case Studies in Business Ethics*. 6th edition. Upper Saddle River, NJ, Prentice Hall.

Hamel, G. 2000. *Leading the Future*. Boston, MA, Harvard Business School Press.

Hamel, G. 2007. *The Future of Management*. Boston, MA, Harvard Business School Press.

Hamel, G. and Pralahad, C.K. 1996. *Competing for the Future*. Boston, MA, Harvard Business School Press.

Hart, M. A. (ed) 1995. *The Practice of Advertising*. 4th revised edition. Oxford, Butterworth-Heinemann.

Henslowe, P. 2003. *Public Relations: A practical guide to the basics*. London, Kogan Page

Hertzberg, F. 1968. *Work and the Nature of Man*. London, Staples Press.

Hoyk, R. and Hersey, P. 2008. *The Ethical Executive*. London, Kogan Page.

Johnson, G. and Scholes, K. 2005. *Exploring Corporate Strategy: Text and cases*. 7th edition. Harlow, Pearson Education.

Joyce, P. and Woods, A. 2001. *Introduction to Strategic Management: A fresh approach to developing skills, knowledge and creativity*. London, Kogan Page.

Kaplan, R. and Norton, D. 2008. *The Execution Premium: Linking strategy to operations for competitive advantage*. Boston, MA, Harvard Business School Press.

Kotler, P. 1994. *Marketing Management: Analysis, planning, implementation and control*. Englewood Cliffs, NJ, Prentice Hall.

Kotler, P. and Armstrong, G. 2006. *Marketing: An introduction*. 8th edition. Upper Saddle River, NJ, Prentice Hall

Kotler, P. and Lee, N. 2005. *Corporate Social Responsibility: Doing the most good for your company and your cause*. New York, John Wiley.

Kotter, J. P. 1996. *Leading Change*. Boston, MA. Harvard Business School Press.

Kotter, J. 2002. *The Heart of Change: Real-life stories of how people change organizations*. Boston, MA. Harvard Business School Press.

Lehu, J-M. 2006. *Brand Rejuvenation*. London. Kogan Page.

Likert, R. 1967. *The Human Organization*. New York. McGraw Hill.

Lipton, M. 2002. *Guiding Growth: How vision keeps companies on course*. Boston, MA, Harvard Business Publishing.

McClelland, D. 1976. *The Achievement Motive*. 2nd ed. New York, John Wiley

McDonald, M. H. B. 2007. *Marketing Plans: How to prepare them, how to use them*. 6th edition. Oxford, Butterworth Heinemann.

McGregor, D. 1960. *The Human Side of Enterprise*. New York, McGraw Hill.

McLaney, E. J. 2006. *Business Finance: Theory and practice*. 7th edition. Harlow, Pearson Education.

Mali, P. 1972. *Management by Objectives*. New York, John Wiley.

Mayo, E. 1946. *The Social Problems of Industrial Civilization*. London, Routledge and Kegan Paul.

Mercer, D. 1996. *Marketing*. Oxford, Blackwell.

Mullins, L. J. 2007. *Management and Organizational Behaviour*. 8th edition. Harlow, Prentice Hall/*Financial Times*.

Ohmae, K. 1991. *The Mind of the Strategist: The art of Japanese business*. London, McGraw-Hill

Ohmae, K. 2005. *The Next Global Stage: The challenges and opportunities in our borderless world*. New York, Pearson Education.

Peelen, E. 2005. *Customer Relationship Management*. Harlow, Pearson Education.

Porter, M. E. 2008. *On Competition*. Boston, MA, Harvard Business Publishing.

Taylor, F. W. 1912. *Scientific Management*. New York, Harpers.

Peters, T. 2006. *Leadership: Inspire, liberate, achieve ("Essentials" series)*. New York, Dorling Kindersley.

Peters, T. 1987. *Thriving on Chaos: Handbook for a marketing revolution*. New York, Harper & Row.

Prahalad, C. K. and Doz, Y. L. 1987. *The Multinational Mission: Balancing local demands and global vision*. New York, Free Press.

Schein, E. 1985. *Organizational Culture and Leadership*. San Francisco. Jossey Publishing.

Shafritz, J. and Steven, J (eds). 2001. *Classics of Organization Theory*. Fort Worth, Harcourt Publishers.

Waterman, R. 1994. *The Frontiers of Excellence: The journey towards success in the twenty-first century*. New York, Allen & Unwin

Glossary

Owing to the dynamic and international nature of business and management the intention of this glossary is to provide clear, working definitions relevant to the IB Diploma Programme business and management course. The glossary is not exhaustive, nor are the terms necessarily universal, but the glossary aims to reduce ambiguity in the teaching and assessment of the business and management course.

absorption costing See costing, absorption.

AC (average-cost) valuation A method of stock valuation which involves recalculating the average cost of stock every time a new delivery arrives. Each unit is assumed to have been purchased at the average price of all components.

activity-based costing See costing, activity-based.

advertising elasticity of demand Represents the change in sales resulting from each monetary unit (e.g. each euro or dollar) that is spent on advertising.

appraisal An assessment, usually conducted annually, of the effectiveness and performance of an individual employee against predetermined objectives. This may lead to the identification of training needs and/or reward through pay increases, bonuses or promotion and the setting of objectives for the following year.

appropriation account Shows the various ways the company's net profit each year has been allocated, e.g. interest, dividends, tax and into retained profits

ARR (accounting rate of return) The average return from an investment project expressed as a percentage of the cost of the project.

benchmarking (Best Practice Benchmarking) Measuring an organization's performance by comparing the cost, time or quality of what it does against that of its best performing competitors; determining how competitors achieve their performance levels and then using this information as a basis for setting and implementing targets and strategies to improve performance.

break even analysis A calculation of costs compared to revenue. The point at which the total revenue is equal to costs is known as the break even point.

bureaucracy A system in which people are expected to follow precisely defined, and normally, recorded rules and procedures, rather than to use personal judgement. Paperwork and forms are common which slows decision-making.

business ethics See ethical/ethics.

business plan The document, which sets out how an organization will meet its corporate objectives, detailing marketing objectives, production costs and financial requirements.

capital Capital is one of the four factors of production, which describes man-made resources e.g. machines, factories, offices, used in the production of other goods and services.

centralization The process of concentrating decision-making power, and authority, in the hands of a few persons in the head office of an organization. This often involves the gathering together, at a corporate headquarters, of specialist functions such as finance, personnel and information technology.

chain of command The line of authority and responsibility, along which orders are passed in a formal organization. Orders are passed downwards though a vertical organizational structure, to ensure the co-ordination of functions.

charity Not-for-profit organization. Registration as a charity may give tax and legal advantages. (Traditionally, charities were established to promote good causes.)

collective bargaining The process by which management and employees have representatives, who negotiate on the terms and conditions of employment. Employees are normally represented by trade unions, which promote their members' interests.

company/corporation An organization established for a specific purpose and registered according to the provisions of domestic legislation. Once registered, a company is a separate legal entity.

conglomerate An organization which results from a merger and/or takeover of firms which are involved in a diverse range of activities.

contingency planning The development of a management plan that uses predetermined strategies to deal with a crisis that might occur.

contingency theory A theory based on the notion that the best way of structuring or leading an organization depends on a variety of interrelated factors.

contribution Sales revenue less variable costs produces contribution. This figure 'contributes' towards paying the fixed costs and providing the net profit for the business.

cooperative A business organization run and owned jointly by the members, who have equal voting rights.

corporate culture The attitudes, experiences, beliefs and values of an organization, or company, that guides decision-making.

corporate image The way a corporation is perceived by its stakeholders – its customers, employees and the general public. It is a generally accepted image of what a company "stands for". Corporate image may be created, or adjusted, through marketing, public relations and other forms of promotion.

corporate social responsibility (CSR) An organization's duties to its internal and external stakeholder groups, acting as a good corporate citizen. CSR means going beyond legal duties.

corporation See company/corporation.

cost and profit centres A firm's activities can be sub-divided into units or centres. If only costs can be allocated it is known as a cost centre; if revenue and costs can be identified it is a profit centre.

cost centre A part of an organization which can be held responsible for the generation of costs.

costing The process of giving a money value to all the activities involved in making and supplying a good or service to the customer. The method of costing is selected according to the business activity involved.

costing, absorption A method of costing to recover all costs, direct and indirect. Indirect costs or overheads are apportioned in a predetermined manner.

costing, activity-based The total cost to an organization of a particular output. The cost is assessed by considering all the resources used to produce the output and assigning all resource costs to the output.

costing, full A method of costing to recover all costs, direct and indirect. Indirect costs are apportioned by a single arbitrary ratio.

costing, marginal A method of costing which assigns variable costs of producing a unit, but does not allocate fixed costs.

costing, standard A method of costing giving the estimated cost of a product. It is prepared in advance of production given reasonably efficient working.

crisis management The response of an organization to an unexpected and unpredictable event that threatens its survival.

cultural export The export of ideas and values from one country to another.

DCF (discounted cash flow) The discounting of expected future cash flows to take into account the time value of money.

decentralization A situation where major responsibilities, and the power to make decisions, is delegated to branches or subsidiaries.

delegation The assignment to others, normally lower down (a subordinate) in the organizational hierarchy, of the authority for particular functions, tasks, and decisions.

demographic change Changes in the size, structure and distribution of populations over time and place.

dependency ratio The portion of a country's population not in employment (including the unemployed, those who have retired and children) relative to the total population in employment (Working Population). Those, not in employment, depend on those who have a job.

diseconomies of scale The rise in average or unit costs as an organization grows in size (internal), or as the industry in which an organization operates grows, and/or concentrates in a geographical area (external)

dismissal The termination of employment because of unsatisfactory work performance or breach of contract.

e-commerce Business conducted on the Internet.

economic growth The increase in the amount of the goods and services produced by an economy over time, usually measured as the percentage increase in real gross domestic product.

economic order quantity (EOQ) Refers to the optimal order size that will result in the lowest total of order and carrying costs for an item of stock, given its: expected usage; carrying costs and ordering cost.

economies of scale The reduction in average or unit costs as an organization grows in size (internal), or as the industry in which an organization operates grows, and/ or concentrates in a geographical area (external).

employee share ownership scheme A scheme which gives shares to employees, the aim being to motivate them to contribute to the success of the company.

empowerment Providing the means by which individual employees can exercise control over their working arrangements.

entrepreneur Individuals, who organise the other factors of production and who show enterprise and initiative, in order to make a profit. A risk-taker and decision- maker normally associated with new business set-ups.

ethical/ethics (business ethics) A code of behaviour which is acceptable for a person or organization to follow in a given society.

exchange rate The price of one currency in terms of another.

federal organization Where the central management have a co-ordinating function: providing vision, motivation and inspiration for the entire organization.

FIFO (first in, first out) A method of stock valuation which involves issuing stock in the order in which it is delivered so that remaining stock is valued closer to its replacement cost.

formal communications Communication processed through the official formal organizational structure, approved by the senior management.

formal organization The official structures of command and control that exist in an organization. Authority is specified by clearly laid out rules and regulations.

franchise An agreement where a business (franchiser) sells rights to other businesses (franchisees) allowing them to sell products and/or use the company name in return for a fixed fee and/or percentage of the turnover.

full costing See costing, full.

gantt chart A method of scheduling which uses a horizontal bar or line chart showing the activities needed to complete a project in the right order and at the right time.

goodwill It reflects the fact that a business has some "intrinsic value" beyond its physical assets, such as the value of its brand or customer list. It explains why people may pay more than the net assets for acquiring a firm.

holding company A joint stock company which controls another company or companies.

inflation A persistent increase in the average price level over time.

informal communications Communication processed through unofficial communication channels, unauthorised by the senior management. The ideas communicated may run counter to the official views expressed by the organization.

informal organization The unofficial organization of personal and social relations, that develops within informal groups. There are no specified rules and regulations for these relationships. This informal organization can run counter to the official organizational structure and its authority.

intangible assets The assets of a firm which can not be easily valued or physically identified. A brand name, client list, or copyright and patents are examples.

IRR (internal rate of return) The discount rate which equates the cost of an investment with the present value of expected inflows.

JIC (just in case) An approach to stock management which recognizes the need for a minimum reserve stock just in case there are supply or demand fluctuations.

JIT (just in time) A method of stock management which ensures that stock is delivered to the next stage or customer at the exact time it is needed.

job enlargement Increasing the range of tasks and duties an employee needs to perform.

job enrichment Providing employees with greater opportunities to use their existing skills and abilities. This could involve job rotation or working in different groups or environments.

joint venture/strategic alliance Two or more organizations which set up one or more business projects that will be operated jointly, so avoiding the need for a complete merger but allowing the organizations to benefit from joining forces.

lay-off See redundancy/lay-off.

lead time The time between the order and delivery of goods and/or services.

levels of hierarchy The number of authority or management layers in an organization.

LIFO (last in, first out) A method of stock valuation which involves issuing more recent deliveries first so that closing stock is valued at the older and possibly lower purchase price.

limited liability On a liquidation of a limited company, shareholder debts are limited to the amount invested in the business – i.e. the value of their shares.

liquidity Cash that is within the business. The ability of the firm to generate cash quickly.

make-or-buy A situation where an organization may decide between manufacturing a product or buying in from an outside supplier.

management The organizational process that includes strategic planning, setting objectives, managing resources, deploying the human and financial assets needed to achieve objectives, and measuring results.

marginal costing See costing, marginal.

matrix organization The combination of different patterns of organization, e.g. functional and geographic, that cut across normal departmental boundaries. In a matrix organization, individual employees may belong to two or more groups, with more than one boss.

merger The 'agreed' combination of two, or more, companies to achieve greater efficiencies of scale and productivity. This is accomplished through the elimination of duplicated plant, equipment, and staff, and the reallocation of capital assets to increase sales and profits in the enlarged company.

mission statement A concise description of what a company currently does. It defines the main purpose of an organization and the reason for its existence.

mission statement A philosophy, vision or set of principles which steers the direction and behaviour of an organization.

motivation The internal (intrinsic) and external (extrinsic) forces and influences, that drive an individual to achieving certain goals.

net current assets See working capital/net current assets.

NGO (non-governmental organization) A private sector, not-for-profit organization, formed with the objective of achieving public benefit.

non-profit organization (not-for-profit) An organization whose primary objectives do not include profit. Examples include government organizations and charities.

NPV (net present value) The sum of the discounted cash flow minus the cash flow.

offshoring The relocation of some of a company's production, services or jobs overseas in order to reduce costs.

operational objective A specific goal set to guide day-to-day operations. It should be compatible with a strategic objective and the mission statement of the organization.

outsourcing Outsourcing is subcontracting a process, such as product design or manufacturing, to a third-party company. This enables an organization to cut costs and to focus on its core activities.

overtrading When a firm is expanding quickly and is struggling to fund its working capital needs it is in danger of over trading and running out of cash.

partnership A business owned and controlled by two or more people who subscribe capital and share decision-making.

payback period A method of measuring the cash flow associated with a project to assess how long it will take for a project to generate sufficient cash to recover in full its original investment.

PEST/STEP Political, economic, social and technological analysis.

PEST/STEP/STEEPLE/PESTEL analysis A useful way of classifying and assessing the impact of the external environment on an organization's future activities.

physical evidence The tangible aspects of a service, for example, the clean tables in a restaurant.

porter's five forces The model which suggests that the profit potential for companies is influenced by the interaction of five competitive forces: rivalry in the market place; the threat of substitutes; buyer power; supplier power; and barriers to entry into the market for new players.

portfolio working Portfolio working involves earning an income from a variety of sources, combining self-employment with, for example, short-term contracts or part-time, temporary or project work. For example, working on freelance contracts or as a part-time employee for several organizations, and perhaps, running a business. It is popular with those who have specific skills that are in demand by different organizations.

position map A diagram which illustrates the position of products in relation to each other and against variables such as price, quality, and target market.

primary sector The first stage of production. Business activities involving the extraction of raw materials and includes farming, fishing, forestry and mining.

private sector Any organizations owned, controlled and managed by private individuals, usually with the objective of making profit.

product portfolio analysis A product portfolio records all the products held by a firm and is used to identify and analyse its strengths, weaknesses and future potential. An example of a product portfolio analysis is the Boston (Consultancy Group) Matrix.

profit centre A section of an organization for which both costs and revenues can be, and are, calculated for profit contribution. The profit centre is responsible for a percentage of the overall profitability of the organization.

proprietor See sole trader/proprietor.

public sector Organizations owned, controlled and managed by national or local government bodies.

public-private partnerships (PPP) Collaboration between public bodies and private companies. A government service or private business venture, which is funded and operated through a partnership of government and one or more private sector companies.

recruitment The process of sourcing, screening, and selecting people for a job or vacancy within an organization.

redundancy/lay-off The termination of employment where an employee is asked to leave through no fault of his or her own. In some countries lay-off means only a temporary suspension of the contract of employment.

regional economic group/bloc An organization of countries which have formed economic alliances for mutual benefit.

salary A payment made to an employee for his or her labour. Salary is usually expressed as an annual sum and paid to the employee each month.

secondary sector Business activities involving manufacturing and construction. The economic sector which creates a finished or useable product.

shareholders funds Long term funds that ultimately belong to the shareholders and which include: retained profits and share capital.

snowballing A method which involves starting the process with one individual or group and then using these contacts to develop more contacts to increase the sample.

sole trader/proprietor A business owned by one person who provides all capital, other than loan capital, has complete control over decisions and unlimited liability.

span of control The number of subordinates reporting, and directly responsible, to a single manager. There will be a 'wide' span, where a manager has many direct subordinates, and 'narrow' span where there are few.

stakeholder A person, group or organization with a vested interest in the performance, behaviour or conduct of an organization.

stakeholders Any individual or group who have an interest, usually financial, in the activities of an organization. Stakeholders can be internal or external.

standard costing See costing, standard.

STEP/PEST Social, technological, economic and political analysis.

stock valuation, average-cost (AC) See AC (average-cost).

stock valuation; first in, first out (FIFO) See FIFO (first in, first out).

stock valuation; last in, first out (LIFO) See LIFO (last in, first out).

strategic alliance See joint venture/strategic alliance.

strategic management The process of specifying an organization's objectives, developing policies and plans to achieve these objectives, and allocating resources so as to implement the plans. It is the highest level of managerial activity.

strategic objective A goal which determines the policy of an organization and sets the performance standard against which the success of the whole organization is measured.

strategic objectives The long-term and significant goals which determine the policy a business and which set the performance standards against which the success of the whole organization is measured.

strategy A long-term plan of action designed to achieve a particular goal or objective. The plan includes the financial, production and human resources required.

subordinate An employee, lower in rank or importance, who is responsible to a particular manager.

SWOT Strengths, weaknesses, opportunities and threats. A framework for identifying the internal strengths (S) and weaknesses (W) of an organization, and the external opportunities (O) open to it, and the threats (T) it faces, which can be used to formulated the organization's business strategy.

tactical objectives Short-term, day-to-day objectives, requiring few resources and with limited significance and consequences.

tertiary sector Business activities which provide services to businesses and individuals. Often referred to as the 'service sector'.

unique selling point (USP) The features of a product or service, which distinguishes or differentiates a business from the competition or what a business chooses to highlight to distinguish itself from the competition.

unlimited liability When the debts of a sole proprietorship or partnership are greater than its resources, the owners of the business are personally liable for all debts of the business. Personal assets may be sold to pay for the debts of the business.

viral marketing A campaign that uses word-of-mouth or "tell a friend" mechanisms.

vision statement A description of the desired future position of an organization. It defines the organization's purpose in terms of its values and core beliefs.

wage The money paid to a worker for his or her labour, usually on a weekly basis. The wage rate may be time (hourly) or piece rate.

workforce planning Workforce planning begins with an examination of the current workforce of an organization. It then involves a forecast of future human resource needs and identification and development of the knowledge, skills and experience required to ensure future success in meeting the organization's objectives. This may require recruitment and training.

working capital/net current assets Accounting terms meaning the current assets of an organization minus current liabilities. The monies or liquid assets used to fund day-to-day operations.

Index